THE LOUD & LOUSY STORY OF
GAYE BYKERS ON ACID AND CRAZYHEAD

By Rich Deakin

HEADPRESS

Author Dedication

For my very own Baby Turpentine — Trudi Woodhouse xxx
✮ ✮ ✮
In memory of Steve 'Speed Machine' Redman (1960–2021)
and Gaye Bykers On Acid and Crazyhead roadies,
Keith Penny and Michael 'Spike' Hall

A HEADPRESS BOOK
First published by Headpress in 2021, Oxford, United Kingdom
< headoffice@headpress.com >

GREBO!
The Loud & Lousy Story of Gaye Bykers On Acid and Crazyhead

Text copyright © RICH DEAKIN
This volume copyright © HEADPRESS 2021
Cover design and book layout: MARK CRITCHELL < mark.critchell@googlemail.com >
The Publisher thanks Kevin Jones, Jennifer Wallis and Gareth Wilson

10 9 8 7 6 5 4 3 2 1

A CIP catalogue record for this book is available from the British Library

ISBN 978-1-909394-79-7   *paperback*
ISBN 978-1-909394-80-3   *ebook*
ISBN NO-ISBN   *hardback colour edition*

HEADPRESS. POP AND UNPOP CULTURE

Exclusive NO-ISBN special edition hardbacks and other items
of interest are available at **HEADPRESS.COM**

CONTENTS

CONTENTS

Photo courtesy of Ian Anderson

ANDERSON

RICH DEAKIN, AUTHOR OF THIS LABOUR OF LOVE, ONE HE has been slaving over for years, has asked me to write a foreword. I tried to pass the buck to Reverb, but it's me for it! If you're reading this then I guess you are a fan of the bands (or a music lover) and I hope you enjoy the book. Never thought all those years ago — back when I was a "guitarist" in prototype Gaye Bykers On Acid, then called Petal Frenzy, for five minutes (don't think I ever rehearsed with 'em — couldn't play, just feedback, so understandably was sacked), then later Crazyhead in 1986 — would a book be written about those times and scenes or that I'd be asked to write a foreword for it!

Searching the 'net on how to write a foreword...

I understand you are supposed to 'big up' the author. Well, Rich writes for *Vive Le Rock!* and *Shindig!* magazines and has written a previous book about the Pink Fairies— well worth a read. The 'net says "keep it light and fluffy", whatever the fuck that means.

Next bit: "Why should people read this book?"

Be specific.

Two groups of freaks from sunny Leicester, home of Daniel Lambert, England's fattest man, the Elephant Man, the bones of Richard the Third, etc, playing unashamed rock'n'roll garage rock.

Name drop.

Ok, well ta to the road crew, sadly some dead: Keith Penny (Bykers, Crazyhead), Spike (Crazyhead), Adie Johnson (Crazyhead), Big Nige Coles (Bykers) and Larry Revhead (Bykers, Janitors); plus dozens still happily alive: Sparky (still waiting for that tenner back), Tony Brookes, Scotty, Hedge, John Atkins, Ian Redhead, Barry Grogan, that dude from the Whizz Sisters and many more! Space Bastards! The two bands' spiritual mentors: Muffin, Baz the Postman, Bomber, Maurice of The Bomb Party, etc.

More names?

I'm supposed to summarise.

I'm singer of Crazyhead, btw, I contributed lots of lies, exaggerations and misquotes to this book whilst high on a ridiculous amount of prescription drugs a few years back. Both bands have been playing again: Gaye Bykers On Acid doing a couple of tours, and Crazyhead playing bits and bobs. Big thanks to the Holbys at Mute Elephant and other promoters.

That's about it…

Oh yes, ta to The Bomb Party for showing the way! Oh, and thanks to the BEMS too — that's Bug Eyed Monsters to you — for following both bands around the country years ago, and some of them more recently. Cheers also to those great, true and loving people of the alternative Leicester scene over the years, and, of course, the world!

Back to red wine and change the cat litter… It's Friday night, 'nuff said!

Anderson
Brighton, February 2020

Photo courtesy of Michael Chesick

MARY BYKER

WHEN RICH MOOTED WRITING A BOOK ABOUT THE Leicester scene of the late 1980s which spawned the Bykers and Crazyhead my initial thoughts were that he was mad! I soon realised he was passionate about the project and didn't hesitate to get involved in helping to bring his idea to life. A major issue was trying to remember everything. The past remains a very hazy place given our lifestyles and what we all lived through — at least a book would help fill in the gaps and jog the frazzled memory cells.

Without doubt both bands — Gaye Bykers On Acid and Crazyhead — were inexorably linked and probably wouldn't have existed without each other. Who knew what we were going to unleash when we started deejaying together at The Chateau. The moderate success that we both achieved would not have been possible without two other bands who inspired and helped us on our respective journeys. So, I'd like to use this foreword to give credit where it's due and big up the fantastic Bomb Party and the Janitors…

Looking back at my time with the Bykers it seems hard to believe the trajectory of the band and what we accomplished in such a short period of time, from playing at the Princess Charlotte in Leicester and the initial press attention to playing festivals like Glastonbury and Roskilde to supporting The Ramones in Europe and playing the Hammersmith Odeon with Motörhead and playing at the John Anson Ford Theatre in Los Angeles and the Felt Forum in New York. Our hubris knew no bounds. We even dared to make a movie! The Bykers star burnt brightly but also faded away pretty quickly, too, from flavour of the month media darlings to a bitter aftertaste.

For a bunch of slacker degenerates, we had a strong work ethic, which, with a little luck, accounted for our overnight success. But the problem, when everything seems idyllic on the surface, is that there is always a darker side to the story. The mental and physical stress of young adult men living in such close proximity for prolonged periods, while self-medicating with different chemical cocktails, comes close to explaining why we called it a day. Basically, it stopped being fun.

Early on, Rich asked whether we would ever play together again. I was quite adamant and said no. Life for me is about moving forward and I didn't want to go back to re-live the past. It is therefore ironic that when asked to do Indie Daze back in 2016, I decided to contact the boys. Despite geographical distance, we agreed to give it a go. Rehearsals went well and, like the old cliché, it was as if we'd never been apart. Most importantly the sense of humour was still there, the fun factor was back.

Our first reunion gig at the Doghouse in Nottingham was emotional and overwhelming, particularly when the crowd started to sing along with the set. That was justification enough for having reformed and that people may be interested to read about what happened all those years ago. The bottom line: What we did in the heady days of our youth still resonated with the people that really matter… The fans.

I hope this book gives some insight into our mad moment in the sun, which we were lucky enough to share with our brothers in Crazyhead. A huge thank you to Rich for all the time and effort he's put into rebuilding everybody's memory bank. Enjoy!

Mary Byker
Brighton, February 2020

James Brown, Sounds journalist and 'grebo' champion. Limelight Club, London, 17th May 1987.

"GREBO!"

ENOUGH TO SEND A SHUDDER DOWN MANY SPINES! THE term has long been used to describe a particular breed of rock music fan or bikers, often in a derogatory way. Journalist James Brown applied it to Pop Will Eat Itself in an article in April 1987 and, by association, the rash of new bands emerging at that time, who favoured long hair, sometimes dreadlocks, and a hybrid of scruffy, occasionally spray-painted leather and denim clothes. Thus, a new musical movement was born. Informed by an eclectic range of influences — such as punk, thrash, heavy metal, psychedelia and industrial music — some of these bands, as they evolved, began to incorporate sampling and amalgamated hip hop beats.

British provincial towns and cities often boast notable music scenes. Liverpool and Manchester are probably foremost in many people's minds, given the Merseybeat boom of the early 1960s and Madchester in the early 1990s. But there were others. Coventry and Bristol had their moments, with The Specials

Photo courtesy of Per-Åke Warn.

Clint Mansell and Graham Crabb of Pop Will Eat Itself at Draupner, Gothenburg, Sweden, 13th February 1988.

and Massive Attack spearheading the 2-Tone and trip-hop movements. The West Midlands once had a reputation for producing heavy rock and metal bands, boasting the likes of Black Sabbath, Judas Priest, and half of Led Zeppelin. Likewise, 'grebo' was a largely provincial phenomenon. Pop Will Eat Itself came from the Black Country town of Stourbridge, while the focus of 'grebo' activity for the most part was the Midlands. Leicester, in the East Midlands, is often associated with 1970s rock and roll revivalists Showaddywaddy, hoary old crooner Engelbert Humperdinck, prog rockers Family, and, more recently, premiership rockers

Used with the permission of Abbey Park Festival Archive.

Sarah Corina, Bomb Party, Abbey Park Festival, Leicester, 1986. Photo by Jenny Carruthers.

The Janitors circa 1985.

Photo courtesy of Jack Daniels; jackdaniels@me.com

Kasabian. Somewhere amongst this disparate line-up was a thriving alternative music, with Diesel Park West, The Janitors, and The Bomb Party at its forefront. More crucially, and more prominent, were the bands Gaye Bykers On Acid and Crazyhead.

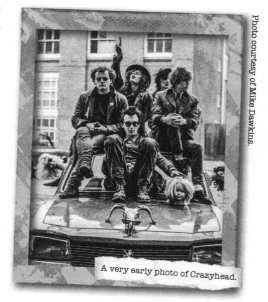

Photo courtesy of Mike Dawkins.

Initially both Gaye Bykers On Acid and Crazyhead were considered 'grebo', and for a short time during 1987 and 1988 it seemed that the world might have been theirs for the taking. Unfortunately, the Bykers fizzled out without fanfare at the end of 1990, when the time-honoured factors of musical differences, tour fatigue, and drink and drugs took their toll. The original line-up of Crazyhead also ruptured

A very early photo of Crazyhead.

Gaye Bykers On Acid, Timebox at the Bull & Gate, Kentish Town, London, 1986.

around the same time, when bassist, Porkbeast, left the band.

There were other factors that contributed to the demise of both bands, not least the relationship with the music press. It must have suited the Bykers and Crazyhead to notch up plenty of positive column inches and appear regularly as cover stars in the press; these colourful young upstarts proved to be good copy for a while. But what had once been a symbiotic relationship eventually soured, and the bands would fall prey to the fickle tradition of 'build 'em up and knock 'em down'. By the end of 1987, 'grebo' had become a byword for 'novelty' or 'comedy' in certain quarters of the music press.

The term 'grebo' still carries the stigma of the music press backlash, and the scene, such as it was, is now all but forgotten or ignored. This book aims to put that to rights, courtesy of many first-hand accounts from some of the bands and artists involved in the scene at the time. Sit back, strap yourself in, and prepare to experience the crazy and frequently chaotic highs and lows of a turbulent rocket ship ride that was the world of Gaye Bykers On Acid and Crazyhead. From the fag end of the 1980s and the dawn of the 1990s, through the subsequent years, culminating in their recent reunions, this is 'grebo' — their complete loud and lousy story! ☠

CHAPTER ONE

SOUTH WIGSTON — SWAMP DELTA

WITHOUT TOO MUCH STRETCH OF THE IMAGINATION, THE roots of Gaye Bykers On Acid and Crazyhead can be traced to a club night in Leicester, at which various future members of both bands took turns to spin discs by their favourite artists. The name of the club, The Great Red Shark, was based at several venues throughout Leicester, before members of the collective left to concentrate on forming their own bands. Acquaintanceships and friendships went back even further, to when they were teenage punks, and in some cases back to schooldays, with the district of Wigston, some five miles south of Leicester, proving to be a locus in the genesis of the two bands. It was from this "cultural wasteland", as Crazyhead drummer Rob 'Vom' Morris has since described Wigston and its environs, that these bands — later, and sometimes begrudgingly, described as "grebos" — were conceived.

Kevin Bayliss (he would later take the stage name Kev Reverb) was born on 8th February 1959 in Gosport, Hampshire, but having a father in the armed forces meant that much of his childhood was spent in Germany or Hong Kong. When he was 10 the family moved to Syston in Leicestershire, before settling in Blaby, a village five miles outside Leicester, when he was 13. There wasn't a great deal to do in Blaby, and because of a lack of firm roots, Bayliss considered himself "a bit of a loner, as I didn't really fit into social groups easily, because I didn't have the history the other kids who'd grown up together had." He had an interest in music though, and his first singles were Rock And Roll Parts 1 & 2 by Gary Glitter and Blockbuster by The Sweet. The first album he bought was by Cockney Rebel. Cockney Rebel also happened to be the first band he saw live.

During the mid-1970s, prog rock was rife. Reverb says "everyone was into Genesis, Floyd and Zep etc. I borrowed LPs from people but didn't get into it really, though one friend was a Bowie freak and I liked that, and still do". Sensing a change, Reverb discovered a new band that were the opposite to nearly all the prog dinosaurs. "My cousin told me about a band he liked who had just put out their first album called Dr Feelgood. I bought [their album] *Down By The Jetty*, played it nonstop, and got to see them at the De Montfort Hall — twice with

Photo courtesy of Kev 'Reverb' Bayliss.

The Clash, Leicester De Montfort Hall, May 1977. Reverb in audience (wearing glasses).

Wilko! They were nothing like any bands I'd seen before, no nonsense in ya face rock and roll. Loved it! Wilko was God, I tried to play guitar like him without a plectrum, but only succeeded in removing the skin from the fingers of my right hand."

It was about this time that Bayliss started at a new progressive community school called Countesthorpe College (the same school that members of more recent Leicester rock band, Kasabian, also attended). It would prove to be a very significant factor in shaping his musical development. "It had only been open a year when I went there. It was a bit anarchic and I struggled for a while but began to get into it when I was about 16 or 17. The teacher who ran the music department was Malc Nicholls. He was a really interesting guy. Although his musical background was very different from the stuff I was into he was really supportive. Countesthorpe was a great environment for students who wanted to be creative, especially musically."

If Malc Nicholls was an inspiration to Reverb, it was the emergence of a new musical phenomenon that would really fire his musical imagination. "I bought an import copy of The Ramones' first album — which had the same effect on me as Dr Feelgood had done. I loved the first four Pistols singles, but really The Clash were probably my favourite band, and Joe Strummer my new hero". Seeing

Photo courtesy of Kev 'Reverb' Bayliss.

(L-R) Ian "the hippie" King, Ronnie Slicker, Vom, Reverb.

The Clash at Leicester De Montfort Hall on The White Riot Tour in May 1977 proved a defining moment.

Like so many teenagers across the country, Reverb was galvanised into action by the clarion call of punk and, having picked up a guitar, it wasn't long before he formed a band with a few other schoolmates. They called themselves Ronnie Slicker and The Banditz. Says Reverb, "R. Slicker — arse licker — do you get it? I think the name was a nod towards Eddie and the Hot Rods, who released one of the first punk records I could get hold of. We were reading about 'punk rock' in the music press, but it wasn't that easy to hear it initially and it was a while before we got to see any of the bands we were interested in. As a result, our music was created in a kind of isolation and our own version of punk. The singer, Ronnie, was, and is, a larger-than-life figure who would wear dinner jackets onstage."

The Banditz mainly played around Countesthorpe, including the school itself, and performed a handful of gigs in Leicester. The band underwent several personnel changes, and Reverb recalls how he first met future Crazyhead drummer Rob 'Vom' Morris, "We had just got rid of our psycho drummer when I met this 14-year-old Banditz fan, at a Boomtown Rats gig, called Rob [Morris] who was keen on playing for us."

Born on 1st July 1964 at Leicester's General Hospital, Rob Morris grew up

Vom and Reverb on stage with Ronnie Slicker & The Banditz.

on Eyres Monsell council estate a few miles south of Leicester. He lived there until he was 11, at which point the family moved to South Wigston, and he attended local comprehensive Guthlaxton College. There wasn't much to do, except, says Rob, "hang around the chip shops", or "play about on the industrial estate near my home… it was a bit rough and ready, but OK on the whole."

Of his earliest musical endeavours, Morris recalls that at age eight he gave up trying to play "a keyboard/harmonium thing" due to a lack of encouragement and instruction. The drums beckoned. "I had always bashed around on pots and pans as a kid, but never really thought being a drummer would be a viable option, simply because drumkits cost too much money and they took up too much room." Rob liked The Beatles and Stones, and, as with Reverb, eschewed prog rock in favour of more glam-oriented acts like David Bowie and T.Rex. He did have a soft spot for Led Zeppelin though. "I always loved the sound of the drums, especially played by somebody like John Bonham. But he was from another planet, Planet Rock Star Drummer to be precise! Kids like me could never be on that planet."

Despite his age — still a few months shy of 13 — Rob attended the same gig that proved so influential on Reverb: The Clash at Leicester De Montfort Hall. The reaction was much the same. Says Morris, "It totally blew me away and changed my life forever." Rob had an elder brother, Dave, who shared a passion for music, particularly punk, and acted as his chaperone for gigs. This gave Rob access to the latest punk releases, which his working brother could more readily afford.

More importantly perhaps, seeing The Clash made Rob realise it wasn't necessary to be from 'Planet Rock Star Drummer' and that he could bash the skins himself. "When I saw Topper Headon playing for The Clash that night in 1977 at De Montfort Hall, I realised it was possible for a small skinny kid like me from South Wigston to play the drums, to get a band together. I got given a snare drum,

old and battered, from some kid when I was 12-years-old. His mum worked at the Premier Drum company, the biggest employer in Wigston at that time."

Rob "managed to gather a cymbal here, a floor tom there", whilst he mithered his parents for a proper kit of his own. Finally they relented and bought him a drumkit for Christmas. The logical progression was to form a band, which Rob did with his brother Dave, who had acquired a guitar — a Les Paul copy — out of one of their mother's mail order catalogues. Unfortunately, there wasn't anyone in Wigston who could give Dave basic tuition and he tired of the guitar rather quickly. Rob went on to form a punk band called The Urban Rejects with a couple of mates from school. He admits, "it was pretty crap to be honest, but it was good just to play in a band."

It was while at school that Rob met two future members of Crazyhead. "Myself, Porky and Anderson all attended Guthlaxton College in Wigston — it was a shit school back then. They were a couple of years older than me, I got talking to Ian [Anderson] first because we shared an interest in punk rock, and there wasn't too much interest in that in Wigston in 1978!"

Soon after, Rob met Kev Reverb at the Boomtown Rats gig in Leicester and offered to play drums for his band, Ronnie Slicker and The Banditz. He recalls that he had seen The Banditz "at some school concert thing at the Phoenix Theatre a couple of months earlier." He adds:

"Kev went to this super hip school called Countesthorpe College where teachers were called by their first names, smoking was allowed, and kids were left to their own devices pretty much. This school had all these students who had formed these horrible proggy type bands, and The Banditz were on this bill with them at the Phoenix. I thought they were great, a punky type thing that didn't take itself too seriously. They also had a charismatic singer, called Ronnie Slicker, he was hilarious. Anyway, Kev tells me the band has fallen out with the drummer and they have split up. I quickly informed him that I was this great drummer who would jump at the chance of trying out for The Banditz. So, we got together, and I got the job. I was 14 at the time. Kev and Ronnie were 19 and 20 respectively. It seemed a big age gap then."

It was also about this time that Rob adopted the punk name Rob Vomit, often abbreviated to "Vom".

Ian Anderson, Crazyhead's lead singer, elaborates. "Reverb and Vom had a strange twisted punk cabaret covers band in the late seventies and early eighties, called Ronnie Slicker and The Banditz. They also had some Reverb originals, all following the trademark [Charles] Bukowski style of perverted sex, twisted hypocrisy, and the sickness of everyday life — a theme [Reverb] would continue

Ian Anderson at Reverb's flat, 1979.

in Crazyhead, with a bit of my rambling poetry thrown in and formed into tight garage rock by Reverb and the boys."

Ian Anderson was born in Camberwell, London, on 2nd August 1963, and lived in Peckham. His parents had met as art school students, but after they split Ian moved with his mother to Keythorpe Street, Highfields, in Leicester. By the time Ian was 10 they had moved again, to Wigston, and, with Rob Morris and another eventual member of Crazyhead, Alex Peach AKA Porkbeast, also attended Guthlaxton College. Says Ian: "I knew Porkbeast and Vom a bit from school. Porky was the year above me, Rob Vom a year or two below. Porky looked about 25 when he was 15, so went to loads of punk gigs, was brimming with confidence, and wrote for the *Terminally Blitzed* punk fanzine. I got to know Reverb a little later. He was this weird, seedy, sick, slightly older guy — strangely charismatic in a [Oliver Twist] Faginesque manner. He ran a small indie label and a fanzine with some other guys and lived in this dirty squalid bedsit above a hairdresser with Harry Hormone — a local punk legend. Very *Withnail and I*. Despite the filth, Reverb had real leather trousers and a two-tone tonic suit. They both worshipped the New York Dolls and Johnny Thunders' Heartbreakers. I saw Reverb and Vom's band, The Banditz, a few times, fronted by Ronnie, a burly, black-suited bearded doorman lookalike. They were very sad, very weird, and very David Lynch!"

It was at Guthlaxton and Countesthorpe colleges that the relationships between future members of Crazyhead and the Bykers become more clearly defined. Gaye Bykers On Acid bassist, Ian Reynolds, later Robber Byker, lived next door to Ian Anderson in Wigston. Anderson recalls that, "We disliked each other. He was a little shit and as a 10-year-old would dress like a soldier, with his mates, Greg Semple, and a few other little shits as his shock troops. One of their escapades included breaking into my stepdad's greenhouse and shitting in it!" They later became buddies, and both got into punk. "Robber had an amazing record collection, swelled by records given to him by his elder brother, an ex-DJ at the Il Rondo, no less."

Il Rondo was a club in Leicester that hosted many 1960s R&B acts over the years, including The Yardbirds, Animals, and the Graham Bond Organisation, as well as visiting American blues legends such as Howlin' Wolf and John Lee Hooker.

Ian Anderson elaborates on the early days. "As a punk, Robber made his own Seditionaries style bondage wear. He made me a cheesecloth one for free — kind chap! And another mate did the Killing Joke Wardance sleeve for me on it."

Robber was born Ian Michael Reynolds in Wigston on 26th January 1965. He attended Glenmere Primary School and then Guthlaxton College. The first instrument he played was piano, but only so far as Grade 1. He says now, "I started listening to punk music and thought 'I wanna do that!'" Robber's brother exposed him to music from an early age. "He had all the rock stuff, all the Deep Purple and Yes stuff, he used to play all that. But he also had some of the punk stuff, so I used to nick his Sex Pistols records and have a listen to them. It was mainly the punk stuff I was into."

Athough his interest in punk was partly down to his older brother, Robber always had something of a rebellious streak, perhaps due in part to his somewhat confused political background. His father was involved in local politics, starting out as Labour councillor, and then changing allegiances to the Liberal Party, for whom he served as Mayor of Oadby and Wigston in 1969, before becoming an Independent, and finally a Conservative

Teenage punk Robber Byker AKA Ian Reynolds.

Photo courtesy of Wayne 'Spike' Large.

Leicester punks with little old ladies. Castle Gardens, Leicester, circa 1979. Ian Anderson (2nd right), Ian Reynolds AKA Robber Byker (far right).

Photo courtesy of Wayne 'Spike' Large.

councillor. The music press would never tire of the latter point, holding it against Robber when the Bykers were breaking through.

At age 11 Robber embraced punk wholeheartedly — like so many other disaffected and disenchanted teenagers and adolescents at that time. He not only loved the music, but he also looked the part, and began to dress in full punk regalia, pushing the boundaries of parental and school authority to their limits as the first person at Guthlaxton College — and, according to Ian Anderson, probably the first person in Leicester — to sport a mohawk style haircut. It didn't go down well with the school superiors. Coupled with his deteriorating behaviour, his look helped to get him expelled from Guthlaxton College in the winter of 1979. Robber ended up at the progressive community college in Countesthorpe, but not before he was paid a visit, at the request of his apoplectic parents, from a social worker and Father Green, the "local exorcist priest", as Robber now puts it. By this time Robber had ditched piano in favour of the guitar. "I bought myself a really, really bad bow and arrow guitar and I used to play about on that when I was at secondary school," he recalls. "I think it was a Kay guitar or something like that."

Like Reverb a few years earlier, Robber was inspired by Malc Nicholls, the music teacher at Countesthorpe. "There was a teacher there who used to play in a band. He said, 'Are you into music?' and I said, 'Yeah, I'm into playing guitar', so he said, 'Do you want to have a go at playing bass?' So I did and got into it that way — jamming with me form teacher!"

Of Reverb, Robber says, "I remember him. His band Ronnie Slicker and The Banditz used to come and play the punk nights [at the school in Countesthorpe]. He got me into quite a few things, musically and stuff."

It wasn't long before Robber formed his own punk band, Fury of Guns, as well as playing, he admits, "in a couple of other bands that didn't really do much."

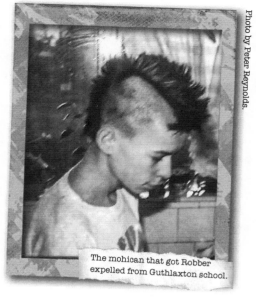

Photo by Peter Reynolds.

The mohican that got Robber expelled from Guthlaxton school.

Then came Cardinal Phink and Ha Fatto, a couple of reggae inspired anarcho punk bands. These too were short-lived affairs, performing only a handful of gigs before Robber called it a day and briefly moved up to Sheffield. Here he became involved in the squatting scene, before going to pick grapes in the south of France with Ian Anderson, early in the summer of 1983.

ENTER THE PORKBEAST

Although they had been at Guthlaxton school together, it wasn't until one of the Countesthorpe College punk nights, 'The Rude Boys' Ball' in late 1978, that Rob Morris met Alex Peach. Alex was supporting Ronnie Slicker and The Banditz in a punk band called The Stazers. Alex, future bassist of Crazyhead and better known as Porkbeast, intimates that despite an average age of only 16, The Stazers had a large Hell's Angels' following. Vom thinks they were more likely The Ratae, another Leicester biker gang, as opposed to Hell's Angels. "It's outlaw country in Leicester, so I don't think they were affiliated Hell's Angels as such," says Vom. "You still wouldn't want to ask them for a fight though!" Whatever their name or faction, the biker gang turned up late to the Rude Boys' Ball, by which point they

Photo courtesy of Alex 'Porkbeast' Peach

Alex 'Porkbeast' Peach, school photo 1977, "Porky looked about 25 when he was 15, so went to loads of punk gigs, was brimming with confidence."

had missed The Stazers and Ronnie Slicker and The Banditz were now playing. Much to the consternation of the school authorities, the late arrivals began to chant for The Stazers. (For all their liberal progressiveness, the school didn't quite know how to deal with a gang of unruly bikers.) Reverb was known for being a bit tasty when the occasion warranted, but he nearly bit off more than he could chew when, according to Porkbeast, "in one of his typical reckless moments, Reverb asked them if they wanted a fight." Vom corroborates the story. "Kev said over the mic 'Oi, do you wanna fight' and this voice went 'yeah', and then Kev thought 'Oh shit!' and just announced the next song." Luckily for Reverb, and the rest of Ronnie Slicker and The Banditz, the situation was diffused without incident.

Alex Peach AKA Porkbeast was born in Leicester on April Fool's Day 1962. He grew up in South Wigston, where he attended Guthlaxton College. Porkbeast was aware of music and bands from an early age, having regularly visited the South Wigston Working Men's Club with his parents at weekends — or, as he puts it, "since being able to be quiet enough during the bingo". Later, he washed bottles at the club for cash. Porkbeast recalls that comedian and actor Bill Maynard, famous as the bumbling oaf in 1970s sitcom, *Oh No, It's Selwyn Froggitt*, and lovable rogue Claude Greengrass in Sunday evening staple, *Heartbeat*, "lived at the bottom of our garden. Well, in the house nearby." The club featured bands and entertainers of a high quality because of Maynard, reckons Porkbeast. Maynard's agent "also booked the talent, so we got cabaret stars like The Swinging Blue Jeans and Charlie Williams. I was taking all this for granted at an early age through to adolescence."

An interest and talent for music stems back to junior school. It was while at Parklands that Porkbeast was recruited into the choir at St Thomas the Apostle's

Church, South Wigston. "The choir is still going," says Porkbeast, "and is one of the very few parish all-boys choirs in Britain, outside of the public schools." The choirmaster proved to be an early musical role model. "He taught me loads. It's where I learned to love melody, Bach and singing. It's perhaps over-egging it to say he was a massive influence, but it was my first musical performance and experience and training, although I don't remember much except the breathing exercises. The Working Men's Club was more of an influence in retrospect. I wanted to be up there!"

Growing up he listened to a lot of 1960s ska and reggae, and cites The Upsetters as a favourite, although is quick to add, "I was never a skinhead or suedehead." For Porkbeast, as with Reverb and Vom, it was The Clash that made the biggest impression and changed his musical outlook. He recalls that his "first ever proper" gig was De Montfort Hall in 1977 — a bill with The Clash, Buzzcocks, The Subway Sect, and The Slits. "I had long hair, a cheesecloth shirt and patchwork flares. Not after! There was nobody there except all these weird looking freaks in leather jackets and plastic wraparound shades — fantastic. Changed my life." More punk gigs followed. At a Damned and Dead Boys gig later that year, Porkbeast narrowly escaped "being razored by some mental Brummie punks. My mate still has the scar on his face."

Porkbeast was as much interested in politics as he was music, perhaps not surprising given his family background. His maternal grandfather was in the Irish Republican Army (IRA) and helped to smuggle Éamon de Valera, one of the leaders in the 1916 Easter Uprising, into Derry. Porkbeast describes his mother as "a working-class street fighter moulded by her dirt-poor apartheid childhood in Derry. She grew up in the squatted Springtown Camp in Derry, where Catholics, denied jobs and housing, took over the camp to live." Porkbeast's paternal grandfather was radicalised by his experiences in Ireland and India,

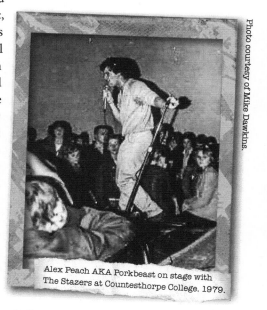

Photo courtesy of Mike Dawkins.

Alex Peach AKA Porkbeast on stage with The Stazers at Countesthorpe College. 1979.

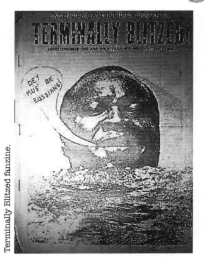

Terminally Blitzed fanzine.

where he served in the British army. The lineage on this side of the family were left-wingers, including Porkbeast's father who was an anarcho-syndicalist. Porkbeast recalls posting leaflets for his father's election campaigns in South Wigston, almost as soon as he was physically able, and at age 15 realised he was a Trotskyite. Today he is at pains to point out this in no longer the case. "I despise Trotskyism as it is run in the UK now, as they are staffed by toffs just like everything else. I'm a libertarian anarchist."

Back to Porkbeast's formative years. It wasn't long before he became a fully paid-up card-carrying member of the Militant Tendency-run Labour Party Young Socialists. Here Porkbeast honed his graffiti skills. "I once sat as student rep at a Wigston Labour Party meeting held at Guthlaxton," he recalls, "where I had to assure the council committee that the six-foot high 'SMASH THE N.F., JOIN THE LPYS' spray-canned all over the six form was nothing to do with us. I was 16."

A National Front march through Leicester city centre was a somewhat inflammatory act given the city's high immigrant population. Porkbeast remembers the large police presence afforded the march, and how he "and many others bricked [the march]. A full-scale riot broke out with mass vandalism and cars overturned and set alight. I got told off by a feminist comrade for being a sexist for calling a pig a 'fucking tit head.'"

Music and politics went hand in hand as far as the young Porkbeast was concerned. During his summer holidays, he attended the Derby Miners' Holiday Camp, where the Socialist Workers Party (SWP) held their conferences. "There was always a great party/band scene around left-wing politics. After Eric Clapton said he agreed with Enoch Powell, Rock Against Racism — which was SWP run — became a big influence on my political and musical interests. I went to all the big London concerts, and many more."

With punk such a politicised subculture anyway, Porkbeast immersed himself in both the literature and music. "It was the student-scene that made Leicester exceptional," he says, "the poly, uni, and various student nursing colleges." But it

had a downside, too, albeit one that, in this instance, led to *Terminally Blitzed*, a Leicester punk fanzine that ran for a few months in 1977 and 1978. "I remember being refused entry to a punk gig at Leicester poly because it was NUS only," says Porkbeast. "It was the piss-taking condemnation of middle-class students refusing to let us in to hear our own music that I wrote about that got me a regular spot in *Terminally Blitzed*."

Having pestered his mother for years, at age 16 he finally got his first instrument ("an old classical guitar"). From this came The Stazers, who found themselves supporting Ronnie Slicker and The Banditz at the eventful Rude Boys' Ball.

Porkbeast lived on the same council estate adjacent to Mere Road in Wigston as Robber and Ian Anderson. Anderson recalls Porkbeast's "bright red drainpipes — very shocking for Wigston at the time!" They became gig buddies. "Porkbeast took me to see a few local Leicester punk and new wave acts in '77 or early '78. I saw the Dead Fly Syndrome, who stood with their backs to the audience, The Foamettes, and the Sincere Americans. The latter featured a really cool, older punk, Leszek [Rataj], on bass, later to join the wonderful Bomb Party. All exciting stuff to a 14-year-old who had never been to a 'big' gig! I went to my first 'big' punk gig in January 1978: a punk rock all-dayer with The Adverts, Electric Chairs, Staa Marx, The Surburban Studs — with their classic I Hate School single — and The Depressions. Along with local acts I'd seen, it changed my entire life."

During the school holidays in the summer of 1979, Ian Anderson drifted into a part-time cleaning job in his local Woolworths, before half-heartedly returning to school to start sixth form. He was booted out after a fortnight, and school was finally out. "They gave me hassle because I'd dyed my hair bright orange à la Johnny Rotten, and I was lazy, to be truthful," says Anderson. "Maybe I should have stayed and gone to uni, but then I worked at the Thompson Toys warehouse for a month or two, and then went on the dole. It was easy in the seventies!"

Moving to the Highfields area of Leicester, Ian spent the next few years alternating between the dole and a number of jobs, including care assistant and a catering assistant at Leicester University Halls of Residence in Oadby. By now, he had moved into a house with Paul Brown — a Ha Fatto bandmate of Robber's — on Walnut Street, within spitting distance of the Leicester City football ground. Soon enough Robber joined them. Ian remembers Robber moving in "when he wasn't squatting in Sheffield on the anarchist punk scene there. He got fairly hardcore while I ponced about crimping my hair!"

Perhaps more significantly, it was while at Walnut Street they met a hyperactive individual through a mutual love of gigging and clubbing. This livewire individual was sometimes known as Mary, an unusual name for a young man.

"Mary was out on the clubbing and pubbing scene," says Robber. "I kind of met him down the Princess Charlotte pub, and he came and introduced himself. I think he was off his head at the time."

Ian has a similar recollection. "I was down the Princess Charlotte going for a slash in the bogs. I had long black spiky hair, round blue lens shades and a big old raincoat. There was this smaller, younger guy in the next urinal to me gurning and chewing gum manically. He had a blond flat top, leather jacket, Levi's jeans, and pointed creepers. He turned to look me in the eye and said, 'Is your dick small? Mine is!' After a few seconds' awkward silence he proceeded to become my new best friend — this crazy nonstop talking loony, looking like someone out of Bros — but more rockabilly, and whizzing his tits off!"

A BOY CALLED MARY

Photo courtesy of Mary Byker.

Mary Byker developed a lifelong passion for cycling as a child.

Mary Byker was born Ian Garfield Hoxley in the small village of Sprowston, outside Norwich, on 20th December 1963. His father was a sports reporter/journalist in Norwich for local newspaper, the *Eastern Daily Press*. The family moved around East Anglia a fair bit, moving to Kibworth, a few miles outside Leicester, when Mary was 10-years-old. After attending Kibworth Primary School, he went to Kibworth High School, finishing his formative education at the Robert Smyth School in the larger neighbouring town of Market Harborough. The young Mary was a keen cyclist and took part in races, even participating in

A young Mary Byker, AKA Ian Hoxley with brother Andrew at London Zoo circa 1969.

events in the United States whilst on holiday with his family.

Mary left school at 16 and got a job as a printing apprentice at the Artisan Press, in a village called Anstey, northwest of Leicester. Artisan printed holiday brochures and the pornographic magazine *Mayfair*. For the first year of his apprenticeship, he attended the Leicester School of Printing, which was part of Leicester Polytechnic. "It was a bit of a doss," says Mary of this period. "That year at college we didn't really do anything. We spent most of our time at the bar, did our lessons, copied a lot of the work from all the apprentices older than us. I wasn't really at work, but I was getting paid, so I wasn't like a normal student. It was actually like being employed, so I had money — it was quite fun!"

Mary enjoyed the printing aspect of the job. "I was doing graphic reproduction. It was quite a skill. But, you know, technology kind of took over and they didn't really need any more apprentices, and I was like the last of the last. It was also the end of the strong print union. Unions had an abnormally large amount of power before the likes of [media mogul Rupert] Murdoch, because if they stopped no one would get any news. That was the power they wielded, and that's why I was on such good money; I was on stupid money as an apprentice. I was earning literally twice as much as an engineering apprentice at that time."

Sheepishly, Ian Anderson admits that he took advantage of Mary's relative

Mary Byker with friends and colleagues from Southfields Printing College. Dokta Tinkle AKA Ken Bailey 2nd from left middle-row, Mary Byker 3rd from left middle-row.

wealth and generosity. "Mary would buy my drinks all night, pay for me to get in clubs that we couldn't blag our way in, buy me drugs etc. He is a generous guy by nature, but being on the dole, I exploited him as much as I could. It got to the stage that Julie Brown [a mutual mate] had to have words with him, as he was spending half his wages on me! I hadn't even thought about it 'til Julie spoke to me. She virtually begged me to blag less off him because he was spending all his cash!"

It's about this time he started being called Mary. It was later circulated in the music press that he got the name having appeared in a washing-up liquid advert as a child. But Mary dismisses the Fairy liquid story as a fairy story. Another more credible story was his penchant for t-shirts emblazoned with slogans, such as 'Maryland Bike Race' and 'Maryland Marathon'. In truth the name stems from a printing college outing to London. "I think somebody had gone to Soho and bought some porn mags, and everyone decided I looked like [British model and porn actress] Mary Millington. It was Ken Bailey, one of the Leicester punks, who called me Mary."

(It wasn't just Ian Hoxley who went under a female moniker. For a short while, Robber was Bridget and Anderson was Sue. This being an attempt to avoid confusion between bandmates whose real names were Ian.)

CHAPTER ONE

Ian Hoxley AKA Mary Byker. Circa 1981/2.

Photo courtesy of Paul Watts.

At polytechnic, Mary became immersed in the punk scene. "I'd always liked music, and I'd had a few different phases. But it was really when I went to Leicester and started spiking my hair and hanging out with the punk crowd that I began to feel more at home." Mary's earlier musical memories were of the Beach Boys and Rolling Stones, as his mother had always been a fan. But as he entered his teens his tastes were shaped by other musical influences, including Led Zeppelin and Black Sabbath, thanks to an older brother into heavy metal. But his tastes weren't defined by his brother's metal heroes. "I even had times of buying disco 12s," he says. "I was into all sorts of stuff really." Come the early 1980s, Mary had turned onto Captain Beefheart and his taste in music became more eclectic. There was a crowd of youths into Northern Soul who hung around in Market Harborough, and Mary had a brief flirtation with that too, but admits, "I never really fitted in with any of them, and it was only when I went to Leicester that I kind of realised what I was really into, which I suppose was more post-punk, you know, Echo and the Bunnymen, and that kind of stuff…"

As an apprentice at the Leicester School of Printing, Mary met likeminded individuals who were, or had been, punks and now followed a variety of the alternative subgenres into which punk had splintered. Some of these individuals would turn into members of Gaye Bykers On Acid and Crazyhead. Mary recalls the day his apprenticeship ended, and he left the prospect of a job in printing. "They got me in the office and said, 'You don't really want to be here, do you?' and I said 'No!', so they said, 'Alright then, goodbye!'"

GOING SOUTH TO ST TROPEZ

Robber and Ian headed to sunnier climes, making a sojourn to the south of France for the summer. It turned into quite an adventure. They were accompanied on the trip to Port Grimaud, a holiday destination west of Saint-Tropez, by three other Leicester punks. Their intention was to sell ice-cream on the beach. Ian picks up the story. "We all dropped two tabs of acid on the two-day coach journey. I had a beatbox blasting out mix tapes of old 1970s punk, as well as fifties, sixties and seventies stuff from the library, thus torturing the other poor passengers — there were no personal stereos then and I was selfish and off my head tripping! We came down [off the acid trip] in Marseilles train station, which had a very rough and dodgy reputation. We stood out like a sore thumb as we all had new mohawk haircuts, including my bright postbox red crazy colour hair that was making my entire face red as it sweated down my face! No wonder I had a bad comedown."

The wait for the ongoing train from Marseilles to Port Grimaud was tense. "We kept expecting to get mugged or robbed." Finally, without incident, they got the train and started on the booze "to get rid of the fear". This was the final leg of the journey and the amazing French countryside flashed by. On arriving in Port Grimaud they weren't exactly made to feel welcome; locals still remembered that a group of hardcore English punks with mohicans had stabbed a French man there the previous summer. Nevertheless they got down to the business of selling drinks and ice-cream on the beach. Being early season it wasn't easy, and wages were paltry. They were thrown off a couple of campsites, before finally setting up their own camp on a patch of land near a gravel pit, sheltered from prying eyes by trees. Word soon got around among other ex-pat Brit beach workers, and their ranks swelled to around 15. Anderson remembers, "We'd 'found' a small twist-and-go motorbike unlocked close to the beach, which we took back to the campsite. Everyone shared it to take a trip, with bog roll and spade, for a dump in the gravel pit."

It wasn't all work and no play and there was a fair share of sexual encounters, one being particularly memorable for Anderson. "One night Robber and I met

Photo courtesy of Guy Milne.

Greg Semple (L) and Ian Reynolds AKA Robber Byker, 1983.

two French girls. We went back to their site, meeting their friend, a rival beach seller boss, who had a Sten machine gun hanging from the entrance of his tent! He offered us wine and work. We gladly shared the wine! Later I took my girl back to the Brit campsite by the gravel pit. We had a drunken shag, her howling 'oui oui', loudly for some time. I was a young man then! I found out later she was a local coke dealer, and when the high season kicked off my mates made loads of cash!" After a couple of weeks, the gendarme, consisting of around 20 officers, moved in on the makeshift campsite. Anderson recalls that Robber's manic cackling added to the unreal if rude awakening. He found it difficult to take the French police seriously, with their "huge 1970s flares flapping in the light French breeze."

With the intention of working until he had the money for another campsite, Anderson fell into old habits and soon squandered his meagre wages on cheese, baguettes and cheap plonk (often getting blind drunk with a group of Scottish punks he had fallen in with). He rather apologetically admits that Robber and the others worked hard "subsidising their useless mate — i.e. me!"

Some incidents weren't quite so much fun, and some were downright disturbing. Anderson was witness to "a mass beach riot when campsite security guards attacked the African 'lookie lookie' guys, selling cheap African

Greg Semple and Nikki David. Early 1980s.

fake carvings, with CS gas and batons. This went on in full view of distressed holidaymakers." There was also an incident when a speedboat lost control and swimmers wandered out of the sea with huge slashes from the propeller, "like something from a [George] Romero zombie movie." There was a run-in with some cockney gangster types with guns and dogs over a stolen car. There was a time when Robber was threatened with a huge fishing hook for selling ice-cream on a private beach. Eventually, Anderson decided enough was enough and hitched back to England. Robber stayed the whole summer, grape-picking, before he too hitched his way back, albeit via Amsterdam, where he became involved with the local squatting scene, arriving in England five months later.

ACID DAYS

In 1984, Ian Anderson was forced into a Tory job creation scheme, building country footpaths for Leicester City Council. He describes it thus: "The work gang I was with included a Rasta guy, a Hell's Angel, various stoners, and the lodger of one of my punky mates, Andy Moss, who was made site boss as he worked hard. I, on the other hand, was always lazy and hungover. After a while, the rest of the work gang would let me kip in the van for the first couple of hours, as long as I made the tea and took their good-natured jibes. I dug a lot of holes when not asleep — I think I was waiting for my rock star job to fall into my lap without making any effort whatsoever!"

Soon after, Ian moved into a terraced house on Stafford Street with a guy called Greg Semple, and his friends, Q Ball AKA Andy Kew and Justine. Semple had been one of Robber's "shock troop" schoolfriends who'd carried out turd attacks on his stepdad's greenhouse years earlier. In spite of these escapades, Semple doesn't recall much animosity as Anderson had put aside adolescent differences and they now gravitated towards the same circles. The few years between them didn't seem so wide as they grew older. Greg remembers how Anderson and Robber provided him with his first trip. "I was anti-drugs before then, and remember giving Robber grief when he first dabbled," says Greg. "It was hearing the after-trip chats between them that intrigued me so much I had to try it and discover 'Wonderland'!" Greg estimates this would be around 1983 as Anderson, nicknamed 'Angry' or 'Mad Dog' at this time, shared a house on Walnut Street with Robber and Paul Brown from Ha Fatto.

A year later, ensconced in Stafford Street, they were scoring acid together from peace convoy travellers to sell on. With nearly 100 vehicles, the travellers were parked on an old railway embankment in Shepshed. Greg remembers with clarity, "We weren't the wisest of dealers, selling trips at £2.50 to anyone at the Helsinki or Centre Bar. Then we had this mad, mad party, inviting our customers. I had to make a choice that night as I'd finally got the attention from a girl I'd fancied, Candy. The choice was girl or trip. It was trip."

Greg continues his recollections of the party. "It was mad, mad, mad... the music was through a 100-watt guitar amp blasting a selection from Q Ball's collection — Joy Division, Cabaret Voltaire, Gang of Four, early Sisters Of Mercy, Spear Of Destiny, Bauhaus, and so on." As the acid grew stronger and the trip took hold, Greg found refuge in a quiet bedroom. "I hid under the bed to breathe, then someone walked in and lay on the bed — I couldn't move, so I stayed still, then someone else walked in and they started a conversation. It was Schmitt and Ian Anderson, both tripping. I can't remember the conversation, but I do remember the reaction as I joined in from under the bed — great party! Later in the evening, Vance Packer took a shit on that bed and stuck a toothbrush in it! it was Anderson's bed, and he went around the party threatening people for a while. Of course, we all thought it hilarious!"

A friend of theirs, Muffin, and another character called Kev Hyde and his crew, created more mayhem, having taken over the bathroom and initiating

Photo courtesy of Mia Lee and Kev Hyde.

Anderson and Kev Hyde, mid-1980s.

all who walked in with toilet water. Anderson wistfully recalls the chaos. "At one point," he says, "we piled three or four mattresses in the yard and people were jumping out of a window, onto the kitchen roof, then onto the mattresses, bouncing up, running up the stairs, and out again. That kept us trippers happy! Jesus — just about everyone we knew turned up at that party, starting at 4:00pm right through to next morning. There were folk from the punk scene, Helsinki's, Centre Bar, the Charlotte etc. — a mad house!"

HYDE AND SEEK & DESTROY

Kev Hyde had a wicked sense of humour and a love of hardcore punk. Anderson says that "Kev lived close by. I knew him and his crew a little, not well, but they always shared their draw, and there was always a crowd round there getting wasted — Hydey didn't seem to mind. That guy was so funny, I used to sit for hours just listening to their wisecracks — a bit like the Marx Brothers on acid! Robber started going around at the same time. One of the band's spiritual leaders, Muff, moved in next door, which helped the vibes a lot!"

Anderson and Robber had known Kev Hyde since the late 1970s, when all the young punks used to congregate in the city centre and hang outside the hip and favoured record shop, Revolver, next to Leicester market. Their paths crossed again when their respective punk bands shared the same bills. Robber was in Ha Fatto and says that Kev was always hinting he should join his own anarcho punk outfit, Church In Ruin. Although it never happened and both bands fizzled out, they remained friends.

Kevin Hyde was born in Leicester on 22nd January 1961, and for the most part grew up there. His family had moved to Birmingham because of his father's work. When Kev was 15 they returned to Market Bosworth, a small town 11 miles west of Leicester city centre. Kev left school at 17 and began a four-year electrician's apprenticeship in Desford. But almost as soon as he returned to Leicestershire, he was in thrall to the new exciting music phenomenon that had so captured the imagination of our other protagonists. "Since about 1976," Kev recalls, "me and a group of misfits in Market Bosworth had been closely following the rise of punk rock. Unacceptable to the ultra-middle-class inhabitants of the area, we opened our own club called The Hole at the back of a pub in the town, and gleefully jumped around to the new and refreshing sounds of The Clash, Sex Pistols, Ramones and Stranglers, and anyone else's vinyl we could afford to buy with our meagre paper round money."

As he got older and transport became more accessible, he and his friends would travel the Midlands, and whenever possible further afield to gigs in London. "The bands we would follow included 999, Slaughter and the Dogs, Skids, Damned, Buzzcocks, Theatre of Hate, The Ruts, Dead Kennedys, The Vibrators and Discharge, to name a few."

Kev started taking drumming lessons from a jazz drummer called Bob Nutt in Desford. He soon gave up jazz after seeing Buddy Rich play, thinking, "I might as well give up now," and adopted a rock style instead, playing along to his punk records. Having gained a reasonable level of competence, he joined a band that played Rolling Stones covers. "This was not good," recalls Kev. "At the first gig, the bassist came on stage wearing a canary yellow jumpsuit and I fell off the back of the drum riser and was damaged. My first ever gig. It had to get better!"

The next band he joined could hardly have been any different. Krud Deth were at least a punk band, but things didn't fare much better. Kev recalls, "After answering the ad, I met the bass player in Leicester. He said, 'We now need to find the singer.' This was not easy. It turned out the singer was a serious speed freak called Fast Ed, whose girlfriend was a prostitute — this paid for both their drug habits. When we eventually found Fast Ed, we got him to the rehearsal room and had to gaffer tape him to the mic stand to stop him falling over, giving him a Tesco bag to throw up in at regular intervals. Here's me at 22, never even smoked a spliff, so seeing this was a bit disturbing. I stayed with Krud Deth for a few gigs, but it was too much hard work."

As punk continued to mutate and adapt, Kev says that "attentions turned to the arrival of the anarcho punk scene, bands such as Crass, Flux of Pink Indians, and Poison Girls. These bands suited our rebellious punk/hippy lifestyles, turned us all into vegetarians, and gave us a tendency to wear black clothing." Goth was the order of the day for Kev's next band, Church In Ruin, who he now likens to Echo and the Bunnymen and Death Cult. Musically they were good, he says, and played regularly around Leicester, even supporting The Cramps and Hanoi Rocks. But a record deal eluded them and they split up before releasing a single.

Kev left Leicester in 1984 "with a girl called Su in a Morris Traveller". They had spent months renovating it and headed off to tour around Europe for a year. "Unfortunately," he says, "we broke down in Essex. So to allay the humiliation of returning to much derision, we managed to get to Su's cousin's in Llandrindod Wells, in bloody Wales. Turned out not so bad. I worked as an electrician in the day and sold dope to all the hippy artists who had dropped out there." Having picked up the travel bug from his earlier adventures in France and Amsterdam, Robber joined Kev in Wales and stayed with him for a while. It was a beautiful place, but it wasn't for Robber. "I don't think Robber was too impressed by the sedentary lifestyle," laments Kev. Robber soon returned to the grime of industrial Leicester.

NIGHT CLUBBIN'

Spurred on by Anderson's and Robber's tales of St Tropez, Mary decided to go grape picking in France with a friend the following summer. It didn't quite work out. Unlike Kev, he at least made it to France, but it was the wrong place at the wrong time. "There was no work," says Mary and prematurely ended up returning to England where he got another job at a graphic design company, this one in Kibworth, the village outside Leicester where his parents lived. The benefits of having such a relatively well-paid job may have enabled Mary to indulge in his love of gigs and clubbing on a regular basis, but these things aren't necessarily compatible with a nine-to-five job, especially as he was now having to do a 20-mile round trip commute each day. Secure in the knowledge that he had a vocational qualification to fall back on, should he ever need it, Mary quit graphics

3:00am eternal. Return from Rock City coach trip. Back row (L-R): Unknown, Caroline Pawley, Ian Hoxley AKA Mary Byker, Unknown and Jamieson. Front row: Martin, Sue Grogan, Barry Grogan and Sid Noot.

and, along with Robber and Ian Anderson, became even more immersed in the Leicester alternative music scene. They also travelled further afield to go clubbing. Mary says, "I was actually an original member of the Haçienda [club in Manchester] — I had a membership card! We used to just do a lot of clubbing. Our big thing was to go to Rock City in Nottingham. Sue Grogan and Ian Redhead used to organise these bus trips, so we'd all get on these buses, do loads of drugs, get completely twatted, and dance to Sisters Of Mercy and all that kind of rubbish."

Like most big cities, Leicester wasn't without an element of small town "shit kicker" mentality. Mary says that "If you went out with a silly haircut, you were likely to get your head kicked in." Fortunately there was a small circuit of alternative clubs and venues where the meathead townies, spoiling for a fight, could be avoided. "The only place we could hear decent music in Leicester was the Fan Club," recalls Ian, "and later Sector 5, rock night at the uni, the Charlotte, but not much else. Helsinki's and the Centre Bar were cool too." Vom picks up the thread. "Everywhere else was a townie pub where you tended not to go if you looked and dressed different to the usual beer swilling football hooligan. Unprovoked and violent attacks on 'weirdos' in Leicester were not uncommon at the time."

Robber says, "They used to have gigs on down the Centre Bar occasionally

— local bands — Johnny Seven played there… You'd go down the pubs 'til they closed, then you'd go to The Cooler or somewhere like that. We all used to go down the Fan Club, near the bus station. I think it's still going." Anderson recalls, "I used to virtually live my weekends at the Fan Club, leaning on a post near the dance floor, getting wasted and trying to pick up girls — usually asking 10 or 20 girls a night while Reverb DJ'ed!" Anderson later wrote a song about it for Crazyhead. "Reverb tells me Dragon City is what I used to call the Fan Club when there were lots of grim looking women — not very PC, and I was hardly a catch myself!" He fondly recalls the graffiti in the women's toilets at the Fan Club — 'Anderson has a big cock.'

Porkbeast was a punk DJ at the Fan Club between 1978 and 1980 when it was still Scamps. "It's where we all hung and did our first gig," he says. "I was also a DJ at the Never On A Sunday wine bar, and another place on the high street. We hung at the Fan Club, Cooler… Helsinki's was cool with the trendies but we went there, too, and they put gigs on."

"It was a bit of a gothie poser bar," Mary says of the Helsinki, "but it was one of the alternative places to go." Robber has a similar recollection. "All the trendy people used to get in there, and it used to be a bit more upmarket. We used to go because we knew other people who went there, but we were a bit more scuzzy so we'd end up down the Charlotte." By the mid-1980s, the most famous of these pubs was the Princess Charlotte on Oxford Street.

Apart from Leicester's most established venue, the De Montfort Hall, the polytechnic and university were the main places for gigs, especially in the punk days. But then there was the Princess Charlotte. Closing in March 2010, the Charlotte was a legendary Leicester venue that hosted many known and up-and-coming bands over the years. Primal Scream, Stone Roses, Radiohead and Oasis are among the many that played there. Particularly significant to this tale is the fact that it hosted the first (proper) Gaye Bykers On Acid gig.

NOT JUST ANOTHER BAND FROM L.A… LEICESTER AREA, THAT IS!

As noted, like many provincial cities and towns, Leicester established its own alternative scene following the emergence of punk in the 1970s. John Barrow, a bandmate of Reverb's when he was in Swinging Laurels, says in his autobiography, "There was a vibrant scene then. Other bands getting noticed were Raw

Deal — Dead Fly Syndrome — The RTRs — Robin Banks and the Payrolls — Disco Zombies — Farm Life and Sincere Americans."

Apart from hailing from Leicester, Disco Zombies are significant in that guitarist Andy Ross was later responsible for signing Crazyhead to Food Records when he was an A&R man there. (Ross also discovered a then little-known band from Essex called Blur, also for Food Records.) Formed in November 1977, the Disco Zombies released the *Invisible* EP and two memorable singles, the amazing Drums Over London and Here Come The Buts, backed by a paean to legendary British porn queen, Mary Millington. Drums Over London was a favourite with John Peel, and the song courted controversy after it was played on his show; some listeners misinterpreted the lyrics as pro-National Front, when in fact it was the opposite.

Andy Ross, the song's lyricist, told the fanzine *Safety in Numbers*, in May 1979:

Wraparound sleeve for Disco Zombies' single 'Drums Over London'.

Drums Over London is a sarcastic dig at the National Front, although some people got the wrong end of the stick, but I regard that as the price you have to pay if you don't want to be boringly extreme. I don't believe in SMASHING the Nazis/N.F. whatever, the N.F. love the idea, it makes them look the innocent victims. Anyway songs shouldn't need explanations as people can make out what they want.

Porkbeast certainly wouldn't have held any truck with the Disco Zombies if they'd been N.F. sympathisers. "Disco Zombies were around in 1978/9," he says. "I was their biggest fan and went to all their gigs at 15-years-old, but they were tolerant and bought me beers! Dave Henderson sang and later became a publisher, and their rhythm guitarist was Food Records sidekick Andy Ross. I met Gaz Birtles at one of their gigs supporting them in the Wendy Tunes, and was quite starstruck. He has charisma."

With Gaz Birtles on vocals and sax, the Wendy Tunes were a poppier new wave-oriented outfit, once compared to the Undertones in a *Melody Maker* review. They had a brush with fame when they began recording an album at The Who's Ramport Studios in Battersea, London. Unfortunately for them, Zilcho, the indie label to which they were signed, went under and the album was never completed. Birtles then joined another, ska-influenced, new wave band. The Newmatics achieved some success on the Leicester music circuit and supported The Clash before Birtles left to form a new band, The Swinging Laurels, with John Barrow, an old friend and musical collaborator.

And what of local Leicester punkers, Ronnie Slicker and The Banditz? They continued for a while, but never made it beyond the local circuit. Rob says, "We did a few gigs around Leicester, on various bills with other bands and a recording session at a studio in the Highfields, run by a Rasta called Wayne. Kev was involved in *S&T* fanzine [from the label of the same name], and it put out a compilation album of different Leicester bands — we got a track on it, called Disco Music. They were fun times. We got our first gig in London, the Hope and Anchor, supporting this really accomplished Bowie/Lou Reed type band called New Age. I was really impressed by them." ☠

CHAPTER TWO

SWINGING INTO A BRAND NEW AGE

THE BANDITZ CALLED IT A DAY AND REVERB JOINED THE Swinging Laurels, a band formed in 1980 by two members of the Leicester ska/rock group The Newmatics. Gaz Birtles and John Barrow had previously been in the brass section of fellow Leicester act Black Gorilla, who had a top 30 record in 1977 with the novelty hit Gimme Dat Banana. When Reverb joined in 1983, Barrow and Birtles had already experienced a degree of success as brass sessionists, and after working with the Special AKA's Jerry Dammers, and chart acts including Fun Boy Three, Musical Youth, Mari Wilson, Shakatak, and Classix Nouveaux, they found themselves increasingly in demand. They had also released two singles, the second, Lonely Boy, was produced by Culture Club knob twiddler Steve Levine, and Boy George had provided vocals that were removed at the last minute due to contractual objections. Nevertheless, Boy George's patronage of the Laurels led to them supporting Culture Club on

Swinging Laurels promo photo 1983 (Reverb, back row, holding film reel).

Photo by Hillary Patton, courtesy of Gaz Birtles.

Reverb on bass with the Swinging Laurels.

their 1983 March and December tours. Reverb was recruited in time for The Swinging Laurels' spring tour: "I got the gig with The Swinging Laurels after going for an audition. They said I was probably the worst bass player they'd tried out, but thought I'd fit in with the band. We only did a few small gigs before the Culture Club tour. They were really big at the time. Church Of The Poisoned Mind was their single at the time. We went down really well, the audience was mostly early teenage girls. We were probably the first live group a lot of the audience had seen. I remember being in the dressing rooms at the London Dominion that overlooked the car park at the rear of the theatre, it was absolutely packed with teeny fans. It was a real laugh to hold a hand or something up to the window and hear the screams."

John Barrow recalls the excesses of Boy George mania at its height. In his own memoirs, he describes how Culture Club had developed the art of avoiding hordes of teenage girls by making their exit "before the last scream had faded in the auditorium". He remembers how, in Cardiff, Culture Club had already made good their escape, and The Swinging Laurels, having made the mistake of hanging around too long, became the focus of attention: "We were swamped by hundreds of young girls. Reverb was pinned against a wall and they systematically removed of all his shirt buttons."

Following the Culture Club support slots, The Swinging Laurels' management booked a headline tour, which didn't afford them the luxury of the Culture Club tours. Life on the road was more cramped and monotonous, but at least they all got on well. According to Barrow, touring was made more bearable by Reverb, who had brought along "a thick telephone directory of a sex manual" that was chock-full of case histories of sexual fetishes. He had the touring party in stitches and kept them amused for hours, regaling them with the bizarre sexual practices in its pages.

Vom wasn't at a loose end for long following the demise of The Banditz either. Ronnie Slicker contacted him to say that local band, New Age, were looking for a drummer. New Age were headed by two brothers, Barry and Ian Morris (no relation to Vom). Vom explains, "Barry was the singer/rhythm guitar/sax player, and Ian the lead guitarist. They were a step up from people I had played with before ability-wise. I learnt a lot very quickly. These guys were serious about a career in the business."

Vom passed the audition with flying colours and joined New Age for regular gigs in Leicester and a couple of dates in London. Despite minor success on the gig scene, it soon became apparent that the Morris brothers wanted changes. They replaced the bassist and got rid of the keyboards. Rob recalls, "I put Kev's name forward, as he had just spent time playing bass with the Laurels and was now kicking his heels. He came down, tried out, and was in."

New Age secured a UK tour supporting London band The Playn Jayn. Rob says The Playn Jayn "were like a sixties psychedelic thing, and even though it was obvious where their influences were coming from, they were ahead of their time really. It was our first tour and I loved it, travelling in a transit van and sleeping on people's floors — if we got lucky!" The band's break came when they landed the support slot on a UK tour with West Coast alternative country/ psych band, The Long Ryders, fronted by Sid Griffin. Reverb says, "We were up for it and liked

Long Ryders and New Age at the Marquee (ad. 1986).

their LP — *Native Sons* — but they hadn't had much press and were unknown when we accepted the tour. By the time the tour started, The Long Ryders were flavour of the month. It became pretty obvious that a lot of the venues were probably too small for the crowds that were turning up."

Rob remembers how, at this point, he "decided to pack in my shitty postman's job and become a full-time skint musician". He continues, "That tour was amazing, because it had been booked prior to this big buzz, and the venues were jam-packed every night. The Long Ryders were great to us, and we would often end up in their dressing room at the end of the night, where we would eat and drink what was left of their rider. That tour was a massive learning curve for me personally."

THE BOMB PARTY AND THE JANITORS

New Age wasn't the only Leicester based band earning national recognition by the mid-1980s. The Bomb Party and The Janitors were also garnering attention from the British music press, as well as legendary DJ John Peel.

The Bomb Party allegedly took their name from the title of a Graham Greene novel, previously being on the fringes of the Leicester music scene for a few

Bomb Party (still from Youtube video).

years under the guise of Farm Life. They formed in the early 1980s when Milo Walsh, Andy Mosquera, Steve Gerrard, Dave Mitcheson, Mark Thompson, and Simon Crane were studying fine art at Leicester Polytechnic, and released just one single, Susie's Party, before splitting in 1984. Mosquera, Gerrard, and Thompson then invited Sarah Corina to join them on bass and they named themselves The Bomb Party. When their debut, the *Ray Gun* EP, was released in 1985, John Peel championed the opening track Harry The Babysitter. Their Cramps-meets-The Stooges brand of post-punk "gothabilly" struck a chord with hometown gig goers.

The Janitors had also been around since the early 1980s. Andrew Denton, Craig Hope, Amos Zamorsky and Phil Storey had met at Rutland Sixth Form College in Oakham, Leicestershire. Zamorsky's father ran a bar on an RAF base in the area, and the band used it to hold club nights. Denton recalls, "We had a shared interest in blues, rock and punk music, and spent our time playing covers and messing about with home-recording kits." Soon afterwards, Craig Hope started at Leicester Art College. Denton continues, "Myself and Phil would go over most weekends to see bands, go clubbing, or just get wrecked and play old rock'n'roll songs, usually finishing with a cranked-up version of the Everly Brothers' Bird-Dog, in the manner of our heroes, the Cramps."

The musical activity of this group of schoolfriends was put on hiatus when Denton moved to Newcastle in the summer of 1983. The following spring,

©jack daniels

The Janitors, circa 1985.

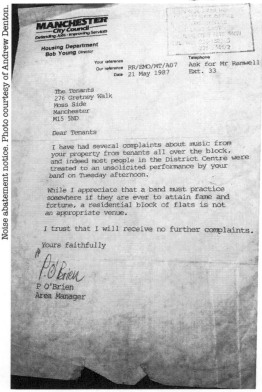

Noise abatement notice. Photo courtesy of Andrew Denton.

MANCHESTER
City Council
Defending Jobs - Improving Services

Housing Department
Bob Young Director

Your reference
Our reference RR/EMO/MT/A07 Ask for Mr Ramwell
Date 21 May 1987 Ext. 33

The Tenants
276 Gretney Walk
Moss Side
Manchester
M15 5ND

Dear Tenants

I have had several complaints about music from
your property from tenants all over the block,
and indeed most people in the District Centre were
treated to an unsolicited performance by your
band on Tuesday afternoon.

While I appreciate that a band must practice
somewhere if they are ever to attain fame and
fortune, a residential block of flats is not
an appropriate venue.

I trust that I will receive no further complaints.

Yours faithfully

P.O'Brien
P O'Brien
Area Manager

Craig and Phil sent a letter inviting Denton "to come and 'make a fool of myself on the microphone' in a new band they were getting together," recalls Denton. "I moved back to Leicester the following week!" Throughout the rest of 1984 they partied hard, although they also wrote songs occasionally. "It was at this time we met up with John Grayland from the band Yeah Yeah Noh. We played him some of the demos which we had recorded on an old eight-track and he was impressed enough to send them to his label In-Tape."

The Janitors were duly signed by In-Tape. Denton recalls that, "sadly at this point Phil Storey decided that he wasn't ready for pop stardom and opted instead to stay in the Leicester area. Myself and Craig Hope — now nicknamed Hoppy — left for Newcastle upon Tyne in the middle of the night, due to owing about three months' rent, recording our first single in Manchester in a one-off session on the way… The move to Newcastle opened up many doors for The Janitors."

Their debut single, Chicken Stew, was released in July 1985 and was warmly received by *NME* and *Sounds*, both awarding it single of the week, and it was regularly played on the John Peel show. By now they had replaced Phil Storey with Pete Crowe, who increasingly took on managerial duties, enabling Denton and Hoppy to concentrate on partying, which had become a favourite pastime. It wasn't long before John Peel invited them to record a session. Recorded at Maida Vale, London, in June 1985, and engineered by former Mott The Hoople drummer Dale Griffin, Denton says, "The session was well received, and played several times throughout the year, Peel even saying it was a favourite at the time."

TREAT WITH THE RESPECT THIS FORCE DESERVE!

Yours
Jim Khambatta

Still from Youtube video of Janitors John Peel Session.

Despite being largely based in Newcastle, Denton remembers how The Janitors spent a lot of time of time in the band's spiritual home — Leicester — over the next couple of years. The fact that they shared similar musical interests was not lost on the future members of the Bykers. Mary recalls, "We had a mutual love of Nick Cave and the Birthday Party. Hoppy, the guitarist, is now the guitar tech for Coldplay, of all bands — he was their first ever employee! He's an amazing slide guitar player. Anyway, they started getting these sessions with John Peel, and they were getting a bit of notice alongside The Bomb Party. I think those two bands were more similar to each other than we were really — they were the bands that ignited us!"

Anderson from Crazyhead also recalls the significance of these two Leicester bands: "GBOA, The Bomb Party, The Janitors, and us, were all mates. I think Crazyhead were closer musically to The Bomb Party than anyone else, especially in the early days. Mary, Robber, and I all used to go and see The Bomb Party in the early 1980s 'cos all the other Leicester bands were crap, well loads of them were good mates, but The Bomb Party were the shining light on the early scene."

Robber is more even-handed than Anderson when it comes to the relative merits of the Leicester bands and adds to the list the likes of Sister Crow, a post-punk/new wave band, and Chrome Molly, a heavy metal band. "Leicester always had a lot of bands," he says. "Everyone was in a band back then in the seventies

Photo courtesy of John Butler.

The Filberts around the time they changed their name to Diesel Park West.

and eighties. There were good bands and there were crappy bands, but even the crappy bands were good because you could laugh at them!"

Vom is less favourable. "There wasn't a buzzing Leicester music scene in the early to mid-1980s, really. New Age were a cut above maybe, and The Swinging Laurels got a deal, but they were just a pop band playing Three Blind Mice on a synth. There was also a band called the Sinatras that weren't bad." He refers to Diesel Park West as an exception to the rule. Diesel Park West were veterans of the local circuit, and included John Butler, who was a former member of Mott The Hoople offshoot Widowmaker, as well as David 'Moth' Smith, from late sixties Leicester hippy heavy band Gypsy. They originally called themselves The Filberts when they formed in 1980 after the street that was the home of Leicester City's football ground, and they were another bunch of Leicester musos, perhaps no less influential, but just as supportive of Crazyhead in the same way that The Janitors were with the Bykers. Vom stresses the importance of Diesel Park West on Crazyhead's development: "The Janitors were pretty good in their own way. There was also The Filberts, later to be renamed Diesel Park West, doing their own songs, as well as some West Coast hippy rock, they were good players. One of their guitar players is Rick Willson, who had a studio in Leicester. I recorded there with New Age, and all the early Crazyhead demos were recorded there as well."

It's hardly surprising that out of this disparate but thriving local music scene, inter-band relationships would form, and new friendships would develop. Mary would end up being a roadie for The Bomb Party, whilst Robber would drive New Age's van with their other roadie, Keith Penny. Penny also worked for Crazyhead before winding up as the Bykers' long-standing roadie. Less surprising is the fact that this growing coterie of friends would eventually start a kind of musical enterprise in their own right, by deejaying at nights they called The Great Red Shark, after the car Hunter S. Thompson drove in the classic of drug fuelled, gonzo literature, *Fear And Loathing in Las Vegas*.

THE GREAT RED SHARK

Featuring Reverb, Anderson, Robber and Mary at various times on the decks, the Great Red Shark ran three nights a week at The Chateau. The nights originally started as an excuse to play the music they liked, turn a few people on to what they were into, and, if they were lucky, perhaps even get paid for it in the process. Vom recalls wistfully, "Kev got together with Mary and Robber, and they would have these great DJ nights at this club on London Road, Leicester. They would basically do a load of speed and dope and play groovy garage music all night. I seemed to remember Mary picking up girls and taking them back to his place, which was around the corner. He would return 30 or so minutes later, looking for his next conquest! They were good nights!"

Anderson recalls, "We always got a crowd in on a Monday night in 1985 or '86, dancing to the better punk, metal and indie of the day, plus loads of fifties rock'n'roll, New York Dolls, Stooges, seventies punk — which it wasn't cool to play at the time — Funkadelic, and anything that took our fancy."

To this mix add a dose of garage rock, psychedelia, goth, rockabilly, funk and soul, and it's not too hard to imagine what the Great Red Shark nights were like. Says Robber, "We used to play the stuff we liked — Iggy and The Stooges, Cramps and stuff like that… Sisters Of Mercy for the goths, and Gil Scott Heron, you know, a bit of everything… when in doubt get The Passenger out. It was like 'Oh, let's get the goths dancing, let's put some goth music on now!' It was all a mixed crowd. Back then all the alternative scenes used to hang out together."

Another venue for the Great Red Shark night was The Cooler on Newarke Street. Reverb says, "It was a great place — me and Mary DJ'd there! Then the Fan Club opened, and that became the place to go. I DJ'd there from when it

The Great Red Shark in St Martin's Square, Leicester, 1985. Kev Reverb on guitar wearing shades (left), Mary Byker in black cap next to lamp post. Linda Knight in white dress, and Robber Byker on bass (far right), Rob 'Vom' Morris on drums is out of shot.

opened for a couple of years. A typical weekend evening would be early doors at Helsinki, perhaps going across to the Centre Bar — where I also DJ'd."

In his collection of stories from his time as a doorman, *No Time To Cry: Tales Of A Leicester Bouncer,* Jeff Shaw writes of the Centre Bar: "Over the years some people played and drank in there that made it pretty big in their little scene including the Meteors, UK Subs, Crazyhead, The Hunters Club, the Great Red Shark (who evolved into Gaye Bykers On Acid), Into a Circle and the Filberts (who became Diesel Park West)."

Reverb was in New Age with Vom and by now Robber was working as a roadie for them, so inevitably an all-star busking band was formed. Vom recalls, "We started doing these all-star busking sets in the middle of Leicester, called the Great Red Shark. They were good fun, and we would pick up some money as well. We would play I'm Waiting For The Man, I Wanna Be Your Dog, Louie Louie, stuff like that."

Robber recalls the busking band line-up as being "Kev Reverb, Rob (Vom) from Crazyhead, Simon, who was in Hidden Forbidden, and Ian and Baz — I think it was — from New Age, who played guitar and sax and stuff. We used to do Iggy numbers, and Velvet Underground stuff. Mary used to do the singing, and we did quite a few gigs like that." Gigs were sometimes chaotic affairs, as

Robber recalls. "We had all these songs, but we just used to jam through 'em really. I suppose Reverb, Rob and all the others were quite good musicians and knew the songs inside out, and I just used to go with the flow a lot of the time. We didn't really rehearse, we just went and did it!"

The Great Red Shark Busking Band would turn up in true busking style to play places like St Martin's Square in Leicester's city centre. But 'band' in this context is somewhat misleading. In reality, the Great Red Shark busking band was nothing more than a side project — most of its members had other bands that they concentrated their efforts on. For Mary though, his experiences with the collective gave him his first real taste of performing, and now he wanted a bigger bite.

"I'd tried various instruments over the years," Mary says, "but nothing really ever stuck. I think I had a bass guitar at one point — I played bass in one of the groups I was in for a while." A well-known face on the local music scene, Mary was a roadie for The Bomb Party and occasionally New Age. But until then he hadn't really been doing anything of significance in terms of performing in a band of his own. "The Great Red Shark was the first real music thing that I started taking seriously, and through that me and Robber decided to start a band." Things come back again to The Bomb Party. Mary reiterates, "The band we all liked most was obviously The Bomb Party and watching them also got us into wanting to get something of our own together."

BEWARE OF THE FLOWERS

The line-up of their new band, Petal Frenzy, varied before it settled on Mary on vocals, Robber on bass, Robber's old school pal, Craig Smith (otherwise known as Schmitt or Nut Roast) on guitar, and someone called Dave on drums, whose last name is lost in the mists of time. Robber recalls that, "I can't remember what his last name was, but he was a good drummer", whilst Mary remembers how "he was Sarah's [The Bomb Party bassist] boyfriend, but he was more like a jazz funk guy — he was a proper musician, and we were a bit crusty!"

Ian Anderson had tried out on guitar for a while and remembers, "I was in a couple of other bands with Mary and Robber that never got beyond rehearsal. The Plainsmen with Sparky — who was later the Crazyhead tour manager — and the Deadbeat Revival, in which I didn't play guitar, but just made a noise. This was 1984 or '85, I guess. I was later sacked from Petal Frenzy, 'cos I couldn't play

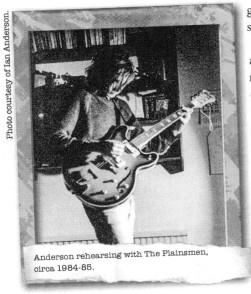

Anderson rehearsing with The Plainsmen, circa 1984-85.

guitar — true! Schmitt got the job of sacking me."

Schmitt became the guitarist for a while and the band changed its name to Petrol Frenzy, but ultimately decided against it because it sounded too much like That Petrol Emotion, an Irish indie punk band then doing the rounds. This prototype line-up never got beyond the rehearsal stage and Schmitt left the band. Anderson recalls, "A new guitarist, Tony Horsfall, was recruited shortly after — an ex-hardcore punk with an Andy Warhol image and grown-out mohawk, studying fine art at Leicester Poly — a fine axe man and painter both!"

Richard Anthony Horsfall was born in Huddersfield, West Yorkshire on 1st December 1965. Growing up, there wasn't a great deal to do entertainment-wise and, like many kids, he spent much of his time "skateboarding, climbing and making swings in trees, playing football and hanging around". His musical tastes included many of the top glam rock acts, such as Slade, Sweet, T.Rex, David Bowie and Gary Glitter, but he was also listening to non-glam acts such as the Wombles, ABBA, the Everly Brothers, Simon and Garfunkel, and the Beatles.

The Beatles played a particularly significant role in Tony's development as a guitarist. From the age of 12, he would study his father's copy of *The Beatles' Songbook* and play songs on an old acoustic guitar. Tony also practised along to old blues numbers on the radio, and even at this early stage was heavily influenced by Jimi Hendrix. When he was 15, he got his first electric guitar. "Then came punk rock," he says. "Sex Pistols, Dead Kennedys, but my all-time most favourites were Crass. Then later came sixties garage psychedelic bands and Hawkwind, Gong, Captain Beefheart, and Frank Zappa."

Tony had a natural aptitude for the guitar and was also a talented artist, with a particular interest in Pop Art and surrealism. He cites Francis Bacon, Piet Mondrian, and Jackson Pollock as some of his favourite artists. After leaving

Salendine Nook Secondary School in 1983, Tony headed to Leicester to undertake a degree in fine art at the Polytechnic. It was here that he met Mary, who in turn introduced him to the rest of the band.

Mary and Robber had been considering adding an extra guitarist to the line-up. When they visited Tony's student digs to meet the intriguing young guitarist with a Jimi Hendrix fixation, Robber didn't know quite what to expect. "I said, 'Can you play like Jimi Hendrix?' and he played some Jimi Hendrix, and I said 'Right, you're in the band!'" At that first meeting, Tony and Robber

Photo courtesy of Tony Byker.

Beach boy Tony Byker "In t'sand at Blackpool, or Scarborough... or somewhere". Circa late 1960s.

worked out a song that would eventually be called Go Go In Out, In Out Garotschka. Robber was impressed by Tony from the start. "I liked him," he says. "He used to wear dark sunglasses, even in nightclubs. It wasn't until later that he said, 'Oh no, these are prescription glasses!' that I actually realised. He used to look a bit like Andy Warhol because his hair was bleached too. He was doing an art degree at the poly, and I saw his artwork and I was impressed by that. He also had all his guitars painted up and stuff — he's quite psychedelic is our Tony!"

It was inevitable that the addition of a new member would cause friction in the ranks, at least as far as Schmitt was concerned. Robber says, "I think Schmitt got the hump and said, 'Oh you've got another guitarist? He's much better than me!', so I said, 'Well, if you wanna leave, fair enough, you wanna leave; you can stay if you want. But he bowed out."

Tony remembers how "the Leicester gang were all still involved in the cover band The Great Red Shark when I met them" and is of the opinion that the band wasn't named Petal Frenzy until after he hooked up with them. Whatever the exact circumstances, Robber considers it a small matter. Robber and Tony headed to Wiltshire for the summer solstice celebrations that usually took place at Stonehenge, as they had done since 1974. By the summer of 1985, Margaret Thatcher, still cock-a-hoop from smashing the near year-long miner's strike earlier

Art student Tony Byker (sporting love bite) in front of Mondrian inspired artwork. Circa early 1980s.

that spring, decided to declare open season on the so-called 'Hippy Peace Convoy', a bugbear to Conservative middle-England and the *Daily Mail*. Stonehenge was the pinnacle of the hippy travellers' calendar, and they congregated each summer to party, sell their wares, and celebrate the summer solstice. Their ranks were swelled by thousands more revellers from all over the country, lured by the prospect of partying on freely available drugs, such as cannabis, magic mushrooms, LSD, and speed, while being entertained by a diverse range of musicians and performers including the likes of Hawkwind and Here & Now, as well as more contemporary punk bands such as Crass, Poison Girls, and The Cardiacs.

The festival had grown and by 1984 was the largest it had ever been. Reports of people openly selling harder drugs like heroin, and incidents of hot dog vans and other rip-off food concessions being burnt-out had emerged that year and the authorities were no longer prepared to stand by and watch as nearly 100,000 people flouted the law. Police forces across Britain were called in, still fresh from fighting striking miners and their families. The new age travellers were considered an irritant by the government, and open season was declared on what Home Secretary Douglas Hurd would later label "medieval brigands".

On 1st June 1985, an advance party of travellers were heading in convoy to help set up that year's Stonehenge People's Free Festival on a site near the famous stones. After police blocked the travellers' route, they then began to attack their vehicles,

leaving the travellers no option but to attempt an escape across nearby fields. This played into the hands of the police, who effectively corralled them there. What happened next was one of the most brutal acts of state sanctioned violence in modern British social history. In what was dubbed The Battle of the Beanfield, Thatcher's boot boys proceeded to trash the travellers' vehicles, which were their homes, too, and beat up men, women, children, and their dogs. Many vehicles were impounded, and the travellers arrested to prevent them accessing the festival site. As news spread of the police brutality, other members of the convoy made their way to Savernake Forest, just outside Marlborough, to regroup, and were joined by many other festival goers, along with the inevitable media circus.

For the next three weeks, the travellers tried to rebuild their lives. The Earl of Cardigan, appalled by the treatment meted out at the hands of the police, provided the travellers with temporary sanctuary on his land. By the time of the summer solstice a few weeks later, their ranks had been swelled by many more expectant festivalgoers, still hoping to get to the stones. Again they moved on from Savernake Forest to Westbury White Horse Hill, under the watchful eye of Her Majesty's Constabulary. The ongoing four-mile exclusion zone around the ancient monument was rigorously enforced by police. Except for a few hardy fanatics, who braved the fearsome elements that solstice eve, few attempted to travel cross country and sneak to the stones under the cover of darkness. The majority of travellers and other festival goers remained on White Horse Hill. They were kept under close supervision by police helicopters that circled the camp, shining strong searchlights across it.

Greg Semple remembers that "Anderson, Robber and me made a Stonehenge Festival poster, 'Take Back The Land'. It was the festival's 13th year and if it had taken place an ancient law would have made it common land. That was the year the razor-wire went up, and the festival goers took on the police at Westbury Hill. Robber made it down with Muffin."

It was on the site of Westbury White Horse that Robber, Tony and Muffin found themselves on solstice eve, a windswept hill in the driving rain in a chaos that resembled a battlefield scene from *Apocalypse Now*. Although Mary had been to earlier Stonehenge festivals, he wasn't quite as "down with it" as Robber or Kev Hyde. "They were a bit more hardcore about it," he says, "because Kev was really bang into Crass and that anarcho punk thing. And they were vegans and had been quite politicised in a 17-, 18-, 19-year-old anarchist kind of way — not wearing any leather, just wearing canvas, you know the kind of thing."

Robber recalls how he and Tony "played an impromptu gig on an open stage with guitars and drums on it, with this amazing drummer — we had a great time

doing it. It was more of a jam."

The festival became more nightmarish when the pair sampled some of the LSD available onsite. "It was raining really hard," says Robber, "and this traveller came round with some white blotters — some of the strongest acid I've ever had. The next day the Windsor chapter of the Hell's Angels turned up and they started revving up their motorbikes around everyone. I seem to remember keeping me head down in a mate's car and keeping out the way of it all!"

Tony concurs on the matter of LSD. "Yes, I took a couple of those too, and admit I had no idea where I was, wandering round and round in a time vortex. I didn't dare stop in case someone spoke to me... I had my prescription tinted specs at night, and it was so dark and kaleidoscopic... large face syndrome... twisted cranial meltdown.... thought I was lost forever! Just getting back to somewhere familiar was like a Dream Quest of huge proportions."

Still, they managed to escape the festival site-cum-battlezone and marauding Hell's Angels with their heads relatively intact, even if their psyches were a little frazzled. Not so Greg Semple and Anderson, who had got a lift from Leicester with a girl they knew. Semple recalls being "so shitfaced on the way down we ended up at Glastonbury instead. We went through a hole in the fence and stayed there!"

The exceptionally wet summer that set the scene for this carnage slipped into autumn and was followed by a glorious Indian summer. Petal Frenzy were invited to play at a magic mushroom party near Aberystwyth in west Wales. The hallucinogenic mushrooms, known as Liberty Caps, or psilocybe pseminlaceata, were in abundance, and a good time was had by all. By now, the band had worked out a few songs of their own, as well as a smattering of cover versions, including the 1978 Hawklords classic Flying Doctor, about a drug-addicted Australian outback flying doctor, and an early version of what later came to be known simply as Edgar — two Edgar Broughton Band songs, Evil and Love In The Rain, bolted together and "linked with Jimi Hendrix's Gypsy Eyes."

The trip (in more ways than one) to the mushroom party is significant in that it could arguably be regarded as the Bykers' first ever gig, albeit under the name Petal Frenzy. (Robber thinks differently; the Bykers' "first real gig was probably at the Princess Charlotte, while the one at the farm was just a birthday party," he says.) The mushroom party is also where the idea to ask Kev Hyde to join the band came to fruition, "Kev played bongos with us while on stage at the mushroom party," Tony recalls, "which was the first time I met him."

Dave the drummer's days were numbered. Mary sheepishly recalls, "I started going out with Sarah [Corina], as a kind of ruse to half get rid of the drummer, 'cos she was his girlfriend... it was all a bit mean, but what transpired was that

Beware the flowers! Petal Frenzy at the magic mushroom party, near Aberystwyth, Wales, autumn 1985.

Photo courtesy of Gaye Bykers On Acid.

Kev was into the idea and decided to come back to Leicester, and from there we kind of got going."

Kev remembers that drummer Dave "wasn't quite what they were looking for, so Mary slept with his girlfriend, which made him leave the band, leaving an opening for me to step in... I'm not sure if it was my drumming skills, or the fact I had a Volkswagen campervan that swung it for me — the latter, I fear! But I left Wales and headed back to claim my place as a Gaye Byker — of which I was neither!"

On their return to Leicester, armed with a new drummer, they decided to rename the band, although they wanted one that had significance and meaning to them. A cartoon by Ray Lowry had recently appeared in the *NME* that depicted a Hell's Angel with 'Gay Bikers On Acid' written on the back of his leather jacket. Apparently, it upset some elements of the biking fraternity, and elicited numerous outraged responses via the letters page. The band were a fan of Lowry's work, but the reaction to this cartoon struck a chord with them, and with a couple of judicious modifications to the spelling, decided to call the band Gaye Bykers On Acid. Mary and Tony apparently came up with the name after idling away a few hours drinking beers down by the canal near Leicester Polytechnic.

The name played on people's fears and ignorance of minority groups, subcultures and drugs. Talking to Q magazine's Adrian Deevoy in late 1987, Mary explained for what must have been the umpteenth time that year, "It's all elements people are frightened of: gays, Hell's Angels and drugs. It's born out of ignorance."

Meanwhile, back at the house on Orson Street, Robber was now dossing on the settee after splitting up with his girlfriend. Anderson recalls, "Robber was a little sad. I could empathise. The same girl had dumped me a little before, and then fallen for Robber. It was a small scene!" Anderson also remembers how the housemates were all well into the then prevalent anarcho punk scene. "At the time, we were veggies and vegans, sharing food, shopping and cooking etc., but Mary and I were just veggie. I remember Mary imploring me to get some cheese or share it like it was some semi-forbidden habit, it was almost like he was talking like folk who became smackheads, whispering 'Let's get some. We both have the craving Ian, we both want it!'"

There was also a shared interest in drugs and music. Anderson continues, "Mary had lots of good records — The Doors' first album, the very first Chili Peppers, some Bunnymen albums, The Clash's *Combat Rock*, Shriekback, loads of sixties stuff and lots more. Schmitt had a pile of Hawkwind and Black Sabbath albums as well, for the grebe rock input." Of the emerging Leicester scene in the mid-eighties, he says, "It was good fun. There could be a little rivalry at times, but on the whole we all got on. Our mate, Muffin, had a practice studio where seven or eight bands used to rehearse together. It wasn't just the band, it was an extended family of roadies, wives, girlfriends, mates, dealers etc. — some real nutcases!"

A mutual friend on the scene provided "speed on tick so we could make money to buy musical equipment. We would go round his house and take lots of acid while watching *Koyaanisqatsi* with Butthole Surfers full blast… It was crazy, free, poor, and freezing cold, a wild experience. I just remember painting all the walls psychedelic and collecting firewood and interesting things from skips. 'Skip shopping' we would call it. Inviting friends round to party at any hour of the day and night."

THE END OF A NEW AGE

New Age decided it was time they and their friends found somewhere they could call a rehearsal studio of their own. Unit 66 on Vestry Street, an old industrial building in Leicester city centre, was located just around the corner from the

Helsinki Bar, near Humberstone Gate. They agreed to share the rent with the nascent Gaye Bykers On Acid and another local group, Hidden Forbidden. Vom remembers, "The idea was to build a control room in there, so we could start recording. I had a drug dealer mate who was a builder, and he came down and built this control room for next to nothing. I think he made a few quid when I introduced his business to the various musicians and hangers-on."

Everyone got along together just fine, that was until Barry and Ian Morris from New Age met an aspiring music producer-cum-wheeler dealer called Joe King who "fancied himself as a cross between George Martin and Simon Cowell," Vom recalls. "They brought him down to produce the band. I hated him the moment I laid eyes on him. I thought he was a pretentious wanker, who wouldn't know a good tune from a bad one. Of course, he brought down a drum machine saying this was the future, and people like me were soon to be redundant. Barry and Ian were totally taken in by him, I couldn't believe it!"

Reverb is equally scathing of King. "The guy was a fucking knob! Rob got replaced by a drum machine, and eventually my bass parts started to be played on a keyboard. We went along with it for a while for the 'greater good', but me and Rob started to get rather pissed off."

Vom and Reverb turned up for rehearsals one night, only to be told by the Morris brothers they were breaking the band up. Although they predicted something like this would happen with King on the scene, Vom and Reverb were still unhappy about the announcement. Says Vom, "I remember Joe trying to justify the decision. Kev lost his rag and I thought he was going to hit him. We managed to leave with no punches being thrown."

"We'd put a lot into the band and were obviously really fucked off," says Reverb, "but me and Rob decided pretty quickly that we'd get something together. I'd been hanging out with the Bykers socially for some time by now, and as I was getting more and more pissed off with my situation, I began to get inspired by their attitude."

Fuming from what had transpired with the Morris brothers at Unit 66, Vom went to a friend's house to try and unwind. It turned out there was a party of sorts going on, and he was reacquainted with Alex Peach AKA Porkbeast. Despite having gone to the same school, several years separated them and they hadn't seen each other since Porkbeast was in the Stazers, except, recalls Vom, "a few chance meetings at Wigston druggy type parties. I told him about New Age, and me and Kev being fired. I was really pissed off with the fact that my mate had built this control room in there and they just expected us to walk away, leaving them with this great rehearsal place."

The friend's house belonged to Baz the Postman, something of a central figure in what became the Leicester 'grebo' scene. Porkbeast (on Crazyhead's old Myspace page) recalls that Baz's home "was a great place to visit, relax, drink, smoke and chat at any time of the day and night, with a large and diverse group of revolving visitors. A good place to check out what was happening, just socialise and chill." As for meeting Vom there, Porkbeast says, "I was around Baz the Postman's having just passed my driving test and a glum faced Vom told me how him and Kev were redundant to New Age due to a drum machine sequencer new direction. I said give them one in the eye by being in a new band when they next turn up at Unit 66 rehearsals. So that was me, Kev and Vom. I picked up the bass instead of guitar and we were off."

Vom picks up the story. "After a long chat and a couple of joints, Alex and myself agreed that the two of us, and Kev, should just turn up at the studio and plug-in and make the biggest fucking row possible to stop the Morris brothers working. That way we could reclaim the studio!"

This they did, at 9 o'clock sharp the following morning. As arranged, Reverb and Vom were joined by Porkbeast and his Gibson SG Junior. The Morris brothers were already in the control room, but they didn't hang around for long. Vom explains, "We started to play this noise at full volume, it made The Stooges' L.A. Blues sound like the Nolans! After two minutes they were gone. Feeling pretty chuffed with ourselves, we decided to have a 'proper' jam. Kev [Reverb] said he had this song he'd written called Lovesick, and asked Alex [Porkbeast] if he could play his guitar and he could switch to bass. This was the very earliest incarnation of Crazyhead."

A similar scenario played out again the next day. During the jamming session that ensued, the still yet unnamed Crazyhead worked out a very early version of Buy A Gun, albeit without lyrics. On the third successive day in a row, Vom, Reverb and Porkbeast arrived early in the morning, expecting another standoff. But this time, the Morris brothers weren't there. "They never showed up again," says Vom. "We had our rehearsal space back. So we started rehearsing seriously. The three of us agree that we want to put a band together that is going to be groovy but aggressive, taking our influences from the Velvets, Stooges, garage bands from the sixties, and the punk movement. This would have been around January 1986." Reverb is more specific: "I can remember that me and Rob got chucked out of New Age on the 7th February 1986 'cos it was the day before my birthday."

Reverb and Vom wasted little time in expanding the new band's line-up. Porkbeast says, "We auditioned one other guitarist I think before Dick, and perhaps one vocalist before Ian." Vom remembers the other singer they tried

Early Crazyhead line-up, April 1986 (L-R) Vom, Fast Dick, Reverb, Porkbeast and Anderson.

Photo courtesy of Mike Dawkins.

before Anderson was recommended by the drug-dealer-cum builder who had helped them with the "control room" in Unit 66. "He said, 'My brother's got this mate, he wants to be a singer', and he came down with reams of paper — and I mean reams of it — and he was a bit mad, and he was younger than me, but he seemed a bit troubled, a bit vulnerable. We just had one session, and we all looked at each other and said, 'this ain't it, this ain't it', and he just disappeared."

(Fast forward 18 months to when Crazyhead are just breaking big. Vom is shopping for food in the Jesus Army shop in Leicester when he recognises the face over the counter as the guy who had auditioned for vocals. Vom enquires what the cashier has been up to since auditioning for Crazyhead. Says Vom, "It could've gone either way — Crazyhead or the Jesus Army.")

On Mary's recommendation, they recruited Ian Anderson, who had previously tried out for Petal Frenzy on guitar but lacked the necessary skills. At first, there were misgivings about taking on Anderson. Vom was particularly reticent. "I seem to remember it was Mary who suggested Ian Anderson as a possible singer for us. I wasn't so sure, because I always thought he was a bit of a flake, an unreliable pisshead with no discipline to be precise!"

Porkbeast offers an explanation as to why they chose Anderson. "He looked good rather than any particular singing talent — he was to grow into that." And grow into he would. Reverb and Vom were becoming increasingly strict taskmasters and soon set about whipping the shy and inexperienced singer into shape. The line-up was completed when a second guitarist was recruited, Richard Bell AKA Fast Green Dick — and a host of other pseudonyms, depending on whatever mood caught him. Fast Dick had a mutual love of bands like The Stooges and MC5, and was a known face on the Leicester alternative music scene. Previously, he was guitarist in Leicester rockabilly bands Johnny 7 and Return Of The Seven. His presence brought a rockabilly element to the set and is the reason Crazyhead always got one or two rockabillies at their early gigs. Anderson recalls that rockabilly was "massive in Leicester. Fast Dick — this stick-insect like, skull-faced drunken sulphate addicted Feargal Sharkey lookalike — walks in and we had a band!"

Richard Bell was born in Hinkley Road, Leicester, on the 24th March 1965, but grew up in Narborough a few miles outside the city, before returning aged 12. Although he finished his education at Brockington Community School in Enderby, he had cut his musical teeth earlier at primary school where he learned to play drums. When he was 13, he picked up his brother's guitar and started to play, remembering, how his brother "used to give me a slap when he caught me playing it. I used to plug the guitar into his stereo, put the cassette player in a paused record mode and overloaded the channel to give a distorted guitar sound... very clever at the time!"

His tastes ranged from David Bowie, through the Sex Pistols and Damned, to Deep Purple and Led Zeppelin, although his first band, The National Phoneys, played punk. Hailing from Beaumont Leys, a suburb of Leicester, the Phoney's were by Fast Dick's own admission "a very good four-piece punk band", and indeed came second in a local Leicester Battle of the Bands. Nothing really came of the National Phoneys though, and after leaving school Fast Dick worked as a painter and decorator, joining another band — one with rockabilly inclinations, or perhaps 'punkabilly' would be a more fitting description. Fast Dick's band were at the forefront of the thriving rockabilly scene in the city, which is how he first came to the attention of Crazyhead. He recalls, "Reverb and Vom saw me playing with Return Of The Seven at Abbey Park, and instantly wanted me in Crazyhead, as they said it 'looked like I was about to die." This also tallies with Reverb's version of events. "I think me and Rob had seen him playing with a band called Return Of The Seven, and thought he was a pretty good guitarist," says Reverb. "More importantly, he looked very close to death — rock'n'roll to the nth degree. We asked him if he liked curry, and he said yes — so he was in." 🐝

CHAPTER THREE

GOING DOWN

COMING UP WITH A NAME PROVED TO BE PROBLEMATIC. Reverb recalls how, at a loss over what to call the band, it was Mary who stepped in and helped out: "As far as I remember we got the name when we were out one night — Mary called us a bunch of crazy heads and it stuck." Thus Crazyhead was born. It was a compromise of sorts according to Porkbeast, who says they were nearly called The Scissormen. It was now time for the serious business of writing some songs and rehearsing.

According to Anderson, one of the first songs by Crazyhead was Down. It was about Harry Hormone, an old friend of theirs from Wigston: "He was an outrageous punk and druggy who used to live on Revs' sofa in his first flat. They were truly filthy, depraved people at the time. It's Revs' sad tale about watching his best mate drift deeper and deeper into drugs — hence the title. Harry got sorted later, so a happy end to this sad bluesy number."

Reverb agrees that their first song was Down but is less certain that it was about his old flatmate from Wigston. He has a clearer memory of another early song, Buy A Gun: "It was spawned by this TV advert for the *Sun* by Sam Fox. I think it was about a money prize they were offering. Her line was 'You'd know what to do with it!'... my reply was 'buy a gun and kill her.'"

The song led to accusations of misogyny and the band received criticism for condoning violence towards women. Anderson contests these allegations. "We got a lot of flak for it being misogynist," he says, "but it's actually anti-*Sun*/Tory TV propaganda. I remember

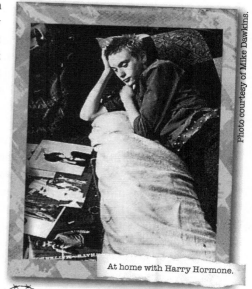

Photo courtesy of Mike Dawkins.

At home with Harry Hormone.

Explosive times! Crazyhead's first gig, supporting The Bomb Party. Poster courtesy of Kev Reverb.

the fan club
★★★★★★★★★★★★★
THE BOMB PARTY
PLUS· CRAZY HEAD·
Thurs 29th May
TICKETS·£2 Advance £2·50 door — 9·30pm—2·00
AVAILABLE FROM — AINLEYS · ZUZU · THE FAN CLUB

months later, after an early London gig, a very attractive woman was chatting to me when her two male friends got very angry, saying I was a misogynist and 'how did I feel that women would walk home fearing rape after one of our shows?' It upset me a bit, but I didn't show it. I tried to explain we were misanthropes, we hated everything and everyone — or close to — not women!"

Anderson remembers their dedication at that time. "The nucleus of Crazyhead, of Reverb, Vom and then Porkbeast, had been rehearsing for a while. Then I joined — I loved it! Reverb was writing all these great songs which we would build on at practice, and this we did three times a week for three months before our first gig."

By May, Crazyhead were ready, and played their first gig supporting The Bomb Party at the Fan Club on 29th May 1986. Considering that Reverb, Vom and Porkbeast had only jammed together for the first time in February, Reverb recalls without a hint of modesty, "Pretty impressive that we managed to get a set together by May!" Anderson recalls from that first gig, "We taped it. I hardly speak, mimicking anything Reverb says. Various Gaye Bykers On Acid and other mates can be heard heckling, especially Mary shouting, 'Why are you being so camp Ian?' We taped that first gig to listen to and work on making it better. I recall The Bomb Party played a blinder, lots of dry ice. They used a sixties colour oil wheel lightshow, great to witness, real showmanship!"

Anderson is less enthusiastic about another Leicester band on the bill that night, Hunters Club. "Great bunch of chaps but bloody awful, we nicknamed them 'Billy Bunters Club'. But to be fair they worked really hard and built up a

The Scissormen sessions. Early Crazyhead line-up, April 1986.

following, especially in Nottingham. They used to play a gig then drive to a traffic layby, park up the car and drop three tabs of acid each — nutters!"

One of Crazyhead's other early gigs was an anti-apartheid benefit. What made this show particularly memorable was the band having the plug pulled on them. Anderson recalls with amusement, "Our third ever gig was open air in Saffron Walden that Porky had arranged. We rolled up there in a tiny greeting cards van belonging to one of the Wigston heads, the back door opened, and we spilled out in a melee of greetings cards, dope smoke, and bottles of booze, to the dismay and horror of the promoter. We hit the stage as a ranting, drunken, speeding mess. After about 30 minutes, we were pulled off the stage as people from the area had complained about the swearing and abuse that was amplified around the sleepy town of Saffron Walden for about 30 miles. The local police told us to get off!"

GET YOUR KICKS AT UNIT 66

The industrial unit that New Age had originally leased with Petal Frenzy, Unit 66, became an increasingly important hub for both the nascent Bykers, and Cra-

Photo courtesy of Mike Dawkins.

Crazyhead at Unit 66, April 1986.

zyhead, as well as a number of other local bands, including The Bomb Party. The Morris brothers decamped after the bad blood between them and the newly formed Crazyhead. It was at this juncture that the Bykers and Crazyhead in particular seemed to take over Unit 66.

Mary says, "It was an amazing place in an old disused industrial unit, which was really barren. I think it was an old shoe factory, or an engineering place. It had one little door to enter it, and it was like a loft apartment these days." As well as a functioning rehearsal space, after breeze block bunkers were added, band members even took to living there on occasion. Mary recalls, "Kev [Hyde] kind of lived there half of the time. Crazyhead rehearsed there, and The Bomb Party rehearsed there too."

Anderson says that, in effect, the Bykers were trying to recreate the London squatting scene. He thought this was great and was thrilled to be part of such a happening scene. The Bykers were well read, and left books around the unit. Anderson emphasises that this coterie of bands was influenced by the likes of Hunter S. Thompson, Tom Wolfe, George Orwell, Jack Kerouac, JG Ballard and Hubert Selby Jr. Similarly, he pushes home the point about shared musical inspiration, "We all loved a lot of the mad sixties stuff, garage bands, surf bands and early psychedelia."

These musical influences were often reflected in their choice of songs.

According to Mary, the Bykers featured a number of cover versions in their repertoire, including Hawklords' Flying Doctor, Stone Free by Jimi Hendrix, and other material by the likes of MC5 and Edgar Broughton Band that would become staples of their live set. As far as Robber can remember, all the Bykers loved Edgar Broughton because he sounded so much like Captain Beefheart. "I think it was Mark [Thommo] from The Bomb Party who said 'have you heard of this guy? Edgar Broughton?'" recalls Robber. "And he played us some stuff, and then we were like, 'yeah, we like him, yeah!' So we kinda emulated their sound, basically taking their riffs and making them our own and stuff."

Tony is less certain about the covers they played: "I can't remember really doing any actual covers but selecting all our favourite riffs from all our favourite songs was the thing we liked to do." And their influences were legion: "There was a lot of sitting round watching *Star Trek* and a lot of sci-fi movies, loads of music — anything psychedelic, a lot of Butthole Surfers, lots of Funkadelic, and a lot of Dead Kennedys, they were a big, big influence". Says Mary of Jello Biafra, Dead Kennedys frontman, "We got to know the people from Alternative Tentacles, his record label in the UK. Kev, our drummer, was insanely into the Dead Kennedys, but Jello [Biafra] particularly, and the things he said and stood for. To us he was like a godhead, he was the all-seeing eye. It was like everything he said seemed to make a lot of sense to us."

Over the next few years, the band would openly champion Biafra's anti-censorship stance, and would become actively involved in the No More Censorship campaign. Biafra co-founded the campaign after he was prosecuted in America in December 1986 for obscenity, or more precisely, for distributing "harmful material to minors". This had nothing to do with the lyrics

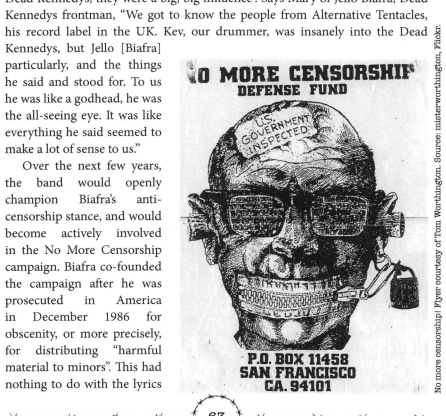

O MORE CENSORSHIP
DEFENSE FUND

U.S. GOVERNMENT INSPECTED

P.O. BOX 11458
SAN FRANCISCO
CA. 94101

No more censorship! Flyer courtesy of Tom Worthington. Source: misterworthington, Flickr.

or music contained on the Dead Kennedys album in question, *Frankenchrist*, but for the poster that came with it: H.R. Giger's *Work 219: Landscape XX* (more commonly known as *Penis Landscape*).

It was at Unit 66 that much of the Bykers' early material was developed. Mary describes the songwriting process: "We'd basically go into the room and do what we'd do... plug in and let rip, and whatever happened, happened. So, it was never like I just came up with a song... it was inevitable... Tony, or somebody's got a riff — Kev's got a drum beat, Robber's got a bass line, and it was very collaborative. It was never really one person driving it, it was all of us."

'Nam Vet was one of their own earliest songs. As the title suggests, the lyrics deal with the Vietnam war, a very popular topic in the 1980s, given the proliferation of war movies, magazines and comic strips that depicted the conflict. The other was Yellow Pack, which Robber says was about a budget range of food that the national supermarket Kwik-Save used to sell: "Basically, the song was saying you might as well just eat the packet instead of the food, as it's really crappy food." Neither song lasted long and few live recordings of either exist. Robber says, "'Nam Vet never really got off the ground, and they soon dropped it as they couldn't get the hang of it."

It was during this period that the band played their first gig as Gaye Bykers On Acid. An old friend, Dave Bartram, who later directed promo videos for the Bykers and Crazyhead, remembers that "It was amazing! They gave everybody a tab of acid on the way [into the gig], and there were manic strobes going on the whole time... it was very memorable!"

Robber, not confirming whether or not the band handed out acid at that first

gig, says, "There was always a plentiful supply of free acid throughout the Bykers' experience. We were the Merry Pranksters of the 1980s!" Tony's memory has faded somewhat, but he agrees that had they acid to spare, they would share it.

Unit 66 was within gobbing distance of a tower block called Goscote House, in the notorious Highfields area of Leicester, where many of the council's more "troublesome" or "problem" tenants were housed. People with varying degrees of mental health issues rubbed shoulders with violent offenders and other criminals, as well as misfits and those who just didn't care. Mary and then girlfriend, Sarah Corina, shared the flat in Goscote House with a couple of students, one of whom was Damian Swarbrick, a close associate of another Leicester band, Yeah Yeah Noh. With camera in hand, he was a well-known chronicler of the local music scene.

Crazyhead's Anderson was by now also a resident of Goscote House. Sarah Corina remembers how he "lived on the top floor and once threw a TV out of the window. He was always knocking on our door asking to borrow money!" Says Anderson, "I had a huge old 1960s TV which had bust, so Dentover [Janitors' singer Andrew Denton] and I chucked it out the window — after first looking; we didn't want manslaughter charges! I tell you, to see a big TV set falling 22 floors and breaking is an amazing buzz. In retrospect bloody stupid, we could have killed someone, but it was that rock star TV out the window thing —

Photo courtesy of Mike Dawkins.

Roof rats! Crazyhead at Unit 66, April 1986.

Gaye Bykers On Acid graffiti in Goscote House, featured in Leicester Mercury, 14th April 1987.

silly boys. Dentover always was a complete nutter!"

Anderson also recalls how the less than salubrious tower block and surrounding area were a rich source of inspiration for many of the lyrics he wrote for Crazyhead. In the space of a couple of months, Anderson came home on several occasions to find the fire brigade outside the tower block. "After about the fourth time I asked them why? 'Some guy keeps trying to burn his ex's flat down.' Good job I was always steaming when I returned at 2am or whatever — freaky stuff. That's how I wrote some of the lyrics to Tower Of Fire on *Desert Orchid.*"

Another early Crazyhead song, Cardinal Phink, is also about the Highfields area. The song title had its roots in the name of one of Robber's earlier short-lived punk bands. But Anderson used the name because he liked it. Although Diesel Park West are namechecked in the song, Anderson insists, "the only reason I wrote Diesel Park West in it was because it was a cool sounding name for an area. I didn't realise how big they were gonna get! The song really has nothing about them in it! It's all about Highfields nutters, including this hippy guy with a three-string guitar in denims who was always hassling people. Then I would see him in the town centre preaching, with his hair slicked back and black suit. He reminded me of the Wild West!"

Given its proximity to Unit 66 and Muff's flat on Orson Street, the Bykers made frequent visits to Mary's flat in Goscote House. Once Sarah Corina moved out, following The Bomb Party to London, it wasn't long before other band members began to move in. Mary remembers, "Robber came in, and then we just basically stopped paying rent. There was another guy in the flat called Nick, who was a really well-dressed guy. He hated it, and I remember him phoning my parents up going, 'Ian hasn't paid his bills', and my mum ringing up and going 'what's this about you not paying bills?' and I said, 'we're not ever paying for anything.'"

The Bykers also achieved some notoriety, not to mention publicity, when

the tower block was featured in the local newspaper, the *Leicester Mercury*. The article described how the tower block had a reputation as "a dumping ground for social misfits, drug addicts, drunks and criminals". The accompanying photograph shows the Chairman of the Goscote House Tenants' Association pointing at an example of the graffiti strewn walls of the building, which depicts a somewhat rudimentary but psychedelically inclined example of the band's name. In smaller letters underneath someone has charmingly scrawled 'MARY IS A SHITSTABBER' in black marker pen. Mary recalls that "Goscote House was the frontline in Leicester. It was pretty hardcore, it was where they basically put all the real sad cases on social security to house them, and at the bottom there was like a function room where they would have blues reggae parties — basically where you went to score dope. So, it was pretty edgy, yeah, but I mean at that age we didn't really care, and we were kind of grimy too. Do you know what I mean?"

MAD MIKE MILLER'S

In the spring of 1986 and on the recommendation of The Bomb Party, the Bykers booked a session in a small recording studio in Syston just outside Leicester. The owner, Mike Miller, had been a local "Mr Showbiz" type since the 1950s, and the Bykers wasted no time in nicknaming Miller "Mad Mike". Mary remembers, "We basically trolled up at this studio with this really straight bloke sitting at this very expensive console in a shed at the back of the house." Although Mike had been in the music business for years, he was more used to recording commercial jingles and demos for showbands, as well as Christmas medleys for the likes of local campanologists The New Parks Ringers Music For Handbells. It's probably no exaggeration when Mary says, "He saw us walk in, and I don't think he knew what had hit him… all us lot piling in with our long hair and dreadlocks, ripped up jeans and whatever… I remember him being pretty freaked out by our appearance." Mary continues, "I think we were all speeding our tits off, and then we just did it all really fast — it was really fast".

The Bykers took Mark "Thommo" Thompson and Steve Gerrard of The Bomb Party along to lend some support, as it was the first time the Bykers had been in a professional recording studio. Robber says, "We'd never done any recording before, so we took them to oversee what we were meant to do." But Miller's sense of bewilderment can only have been compounded when Thommo, also "speeding his tits off" according to Mary, sat next to Miller going, "You wanna

Music for Handbells
by the
New Parks Ringers

A Christmas Medley

THEME AND VARIATIONS   GAVOTTE – SOLDIERS JOY

turn that up mate! You wanna do this mate, ah yeah you want a bit of that mate!"

No matter, by the end of the session the Bykers had laid down four tracks: TV Cabbage, So Far Out (He's In), We're Gonna Change The World and All Hung Up On Ha-Penis. Tony says TV Cabbage "is that famous Hendrix Purple Haze chord. Used that a lot... Same kind of riff as Go Go really, just a bit more spacey in places. The title speaks for itself really." Mary elaborates, "Even at that point we realised people spent too much time watching TV and not doing other stuff and being brainwashed basically... you know people just vegging out in front of the TV and not really doing anything. That was an early anti-TV tirade!"

So Far Out was loosely based on a friend of Mary's called Larry, an early follower of the Bykers and other Leicester bands. "He was actually a roadie for The Janitors. Unfortunately he passed away quite early, but he was a bit of a character. I think there was a song called Larry The Revhead, too — there were a couple of songs about him. And, yeah, he was like so far out, he was in. Larry was on everything — he was a methadone user, an ex-heroin addict, he used to take acid, speed — everything. He was a proper character, and that whole thing about being into the sixties, and being far out, then it all comes back into fashion."

"He was so far out he was

Sarah Corina of The Bomb Party with Larry Revhead, the inspiration for Gaye Bykers On Acid's 'So Far Out (He's In)'.

Cover inlay and original cassette of Gaye Bykers On Acid's first demo, recorded at 'Mad' Mike Miller's studio in Syston.

actually fashionable!" concurs Robber.

Vaguely reminiscent of an adrenalised Johnny B. Goode, the third song, We're Gonna Change The World was a punked-up rock'n'roll style number that eventually became known as Go Go, In Out, In Out, Garotschka. With its "speeded-up sixties groove" Tony says it wasn't so much influenced by Chuck Berry as it was the Jimi Hendrix song Come On (Let The Good Times Roll).

All Hung Up On Ha-Penis sought to make a comment about macho male insecurity over penis size, evidenced in the title. Tony says it was "something about being too vain". Mary concurs, "Yeah, that's pretty much the size of it — it's a pun, a joke really... 'All hung up on a penis, and love's a word that doesn't exist...' But yeah, that's the kind of idea." With a country & western feel, albeit sped-up, this early version was quite a different beast from the one recorded for their debut album 12 months later. Mary recalls, "The psychobilly thing was big on the live circuit, so musically we were taking on board all different influences at that time. Everything was fair game to us."

Now armed with a handful of songs and an even larger supply of demo tapes, the Bykers set out on their mission to inject some life and humour into the indie charts. At this point they were still without a formal manager, with Mary largely managing the band's affairs. He'd spent his time as a roadie for The Bomb Party wisely though; not only had he and Robber been inspired to form their own

Photo courtesy of Gaye Bykers On Acid.

Early (possibly first proper) Gaye Bykers On Acid gig. Princess Charlotte, Leicester. Early 1986.

band, but Mary had picked up a lot of contacts on the way. "It was when I was roadie-ing for The Bomb Party," he recalls, "they were doing *NME* and *Sounds* interviews and I was actually meeting the journalists then — and I'd say, 'I've got a band called Gaye Bykers On Acid, you'll have to check us out!' So when we finally did come along, they knew the name and we had a bit of an 'in' with some of the journalists. There was nobody managing us, but because of the sheer brass neck that I had then, it was like, 'You gotta listen to my band, my band's brilliant!'"

A name like Gaye Bykers On Acid wasn't likely to be forgotten easily, and in those early days Mary arranged many of the band's gigs, thanks to some help from a photocopied list of gig venues circulated by Nick Toczek, an anarcho punk poet and musician from Leeds. Mary says, "He had like a database of gigs, and you'd send him a couple of quid and he'd send a big stack of photocopied paper with loads of venues and stuff." This was well before the days of the internet or email, and such a resource proved to be indispensable to any small alternative/punk band looking for a helping hand.

Punk promoter Nick Toczek explains how it worked: "I ran a strictly not-for-profit company called Twisted Pleasures and Drastic Measures — the name was taken from a line in a poem of mine, *West Yorks Nurse*, about the way journalists covered a rape and attempted murder. Through this company, I helped around 4,000 bands with advice, info and promotion etc. At one point I had to face a series of Inland Revenue tribunals because they were convinced I was making money — then it took me two years to find the £300 to pay the accountant who helped me to prove them wrong! Anyhow, one of the things I produced and sold for cost only was a huge loose-leaf info pack called *The Independence File*, that included contact details for venues, organisers, indie labels, indie distributors, studios, pressing plants, various advice articles I'd written, and whatever else seemed worth knowing if you were in a band. It was endlessly being updated, so there was never a finished item — however, I kept a copy of its final incarnation."

Since coming together in February and playing their first gig supporting The Bomb Party in May, Crazyhead had wasted no time in piecing together a set. Reverb is still impressed how quickly they managed it. So too Anderson. "When I joined Crazyhead," says Anderson, "it was already Reverb, Vom and Porkbeast, then known as Professor Peach. They practised three times a week for several hours, and Reverb had written these great songs. But he needed a singer, as that was the only

Nick Toczek's Independence File "included contact details for venues, organisers, indie labels, indie distributors, studios, pressing plants, various advice articles".

thing he couldn't do — although he sang to teach me, and also did four-track recordings where he played all the instruments and sang. They wanted to be a big independent band like The Bomb Party and get in the indie charts top 30, by playing and touring a lot. Vom and Rev had been playing in touring bands already for close to 10 years, so had a very serious businesslike approach to the music and promotion. We watched videos to give us ideas, Neil Young and Crazy Horse was a big fave of theirs, and they made me watch James Brown videos for ideas of showmanship. What came naturally to the gregarious Mary Byker had to be learned by this new semi-alcoholic, shy guy!"

Nick Toczek meanwhile had been the recipient of one of the Bykers' demo tapes. He was moved to book them as support for Zodiac Mindwarp & The Love Reaction, at Toczek's Grand Slam! club night at the Adam & Eve pub in Leeds on 17th June 1986. It may have been the first time the Bykers played with Zodiac Mindwarp but over the months their paths would cross again, and, along with other bands, their names would became inextricably linked — whether they liked it or not.

LONDON CALLING

Another breakthrough came in June 1986. After only a handful of gigs, the Bykers played Timebox at the Bull & Gate in Kentish Town, London. Bykers' drummer Kev recalls, "Tony came running in after the soundcheck with a copy of *Sounds*, and just inside was a picture of us, Mary at the front smiling like a demented Iggy Pop, and us behind sneering like twisted cartoon characters that had just crawled out of a skip — our first piece of press. I think at that point we knew we were onto something." The subsequent review of the gig proved to be even more pivotal for the Bykers. *Sounds'* Andy Hurt had this to say:

Methinks I detect a nasty smell in the air… funny isn't it, how nasty smells are always so much more *interesting* than the sweet smell of success, so all-pervading of late. Gaye Bykers On Acid are a positive *miasma*.

Flyer for Nick Toczek's Grand Slam! Club at Adam & Eve's, Leeds. Another early Gaye Bykers On Acid gig.

These creatures are a manifestation of John Selwyn Gumby's worst nightmare, the musical youth of the peace convoy swathed in Glasto-chic raiment and splattered with paint. The singer goes by the name of Mary and yet the four are to a man, well, *men*… young-ish specimens thereof, but almost certainly of the male ilk.

They quite possibly take drugs, but when I engaged them in a slurring match afterwards they were too drunk for me to tell. After a splut-

Gaye Bykers On Acid, Timebox at the Bull & Gate, Kentish Town, London, 1986.

tering wah wah liquid-light sound of a start, they vroom into hypersonic Stoogeophonics, Mary doing his very best Mr Pop with his right hand guitar man a dead ringer for the original axe-wielder of '1969'.

The crowd won't be as sparse as this next time. This lot know how to do the word of the year, and yea verily, that word is ROCK.

Not long afterwards, the Bykers supported Zodiac Mindwarp once again — this time in the capital, at the legendary Marquee on Wardour Street. The Bykers had 'arrived', but things didn't pass without incident. Mary, maybe overwhelmed by the occasion, or just drunk, stoned or both, saw fit to hurl abuse at Zodiac Mindwarp and his entourage. Not a particularly good idea, all things considered. Anderson wasn't above helping his old mates shift their gear and was roadie for the Bykers on this occasion: "Mary was being a twat, gobbing off at Zodiac and his big biker, ex-Forces crew. It was Penny and I who dragged Mary off when he was gobbing off to Smithy and the other Zodiac roadies who we later got to know. But they were real hard bastards — they would have battered Mary! I once had to split up Smithy and Dave Oldtight Greet, a brown belt and one of the original Leicester punks. Smithy was huge, but this would have been a nasty fight, and I managed to calm them down."

Back in Leicester, the Bykers and Crazyhead performed an impromptu

Photo courtesy of Mike Dawkins.

Crazyhead. An early live gig. Outside the Corn Exchange, Market Place, Leicester, August 1986.

open-air gig. A live video of the Bykers outside the Leicester Corn Exchange testifies to the raw energy and sheer chutzpah that the band exuded at the time. Robber recalls that he and Mary were both speeding, while Tony and Kev were tripping on acid. The band played all of the songs from the Syston demo plus a handful of other numbers including Yellow Pack and Space Rape, mainly to a small gathering of Leicester punks, psychobillies, a couple of mohicaned punk kids, and even more bemused passers-by doing their Saturday shopping in the adjacent covered market. The bands were presided over by the ever-present gaze of the statue of John Henry Manners, 5th Duke of Rutland. He would surely would have been spinning in his grave could he hear and see Mary leaping around in leather trousers, naked from the waist up, save for the words 'CANCER CHILD' scrawled across his chest, motormouthing between songs, and liberally punctuating his dialogue with swear words.

Despite a chaotic performance, beset by intermittent sound problems, it's apparent from the video that the Bykers had star potential — they certainly had the image, the sounds and the moves. Robber plays his bass like a furious rhythm guitarist and thrashes it to within an inch of its existence such is the ferocity of his strumming, whilst Tony lays down some tasty Hendrix-style licks on his customised paint-spattered guitar.

The ball was rolling. At the end of July the Bykers played at the 100 Club. A week later they were at the Croydon Underground where they were reviewed by *Sounds* again, but Jack Barron was more inclined to put the boot in, as opposed to Andy Hurt a few weeks earlier. Referring to them as "a slime trail of ineffectual thrash on a bad trip to the unenjoyment line", he proceeded to trample on them further, adding, "at the moment the Bykers have everything going for them except for the most essential ingredients: maximum music and scorching songs." Barron conceded that "they look[ed] good", before slamming them

Mary Byker with 'Cancer child' scrawled across his chest. Outside gig at the Corn Exchange, Market Place, Leicester, August 1986.

Photo courtesy of Mike Dawkins.

for having "no focus, no clarity, no charity of emotions, no dynamism, no laughter or lust, and, above all, no good songs — just a series of chain-linked riffs". He conceded that they had "blistering bursts of enthusiasm" and that it was still early days but concluded that "the day Mary forgets about aping Iggy Pop will be the day he gives an immaculate virgin birth to a music which really does tap into the acid-zap that the group's name promises. If they aim at altered states rather than worshipping at the altar of pure speed, then maybe their moped will turn into a Harley-quin."

Barron was charitable enough to acknowledge the band's potential, even if he didn't recognise it himself.

Throughout the rest of the summer and into the autumn the band enjoyed several more profile-building gigs, including the Klub Foot with Leather Nun and The Bomb Party. Jonh Wilde for *Sounds* commented: "Gaye Bykers pelt through highly-strung quips of loaded turbulence, slothful without being remotely effective, a bass-heavy wall of delinquency, sick from all the grease, dripping with scratchy streaks of powerhouse inelegance. As ticklish and becoming as a jackhammer up the rectum."

At this point in their career, even unfavourable reviews like these didn't do the Bykers harm and interest in the band continued to grow.

JUST SAY YEAH!

The 'grebo' tag was still some months away. The Bykers' next big break came when they were signed to a small independent record label from Manchester. In-Tape was formed by ex-Fall member Marc Riley and Jim Khambatta, the keyboard player in Riley's outfit The Creepers. Mary and Robber can't stress enough the importance of The Janitors, not only as an influence of sorts, but also their practical encouragement and help. It was The Janitors who gave Riley and Khambatta the demo tape that was instrumental in them getting signed.

It was about this time that the Bykers and Crazyhead were invited to lay down one track each for compilation album *Just Say Yeah*. The Bykers decamped to Driffield to record their contribution. Robber recalls "There was a guy called Si [Ord], who we nicknamed 'The Flash'. He used to look a bit like [comedian, actor, writer] Rik Mayall when he played the character 'The Flash' in the television series *Blackadder*. Si was a mate of The Bomb Party, who was putting this compilation album together and asked us to do a track."

The album was named presumably as a rebuff to the anti-drug song, Just Say No, that was sung by the cast of the popular children's television programme *Grange Hill* (inspired by a controversial storyline in which one of the lead characters slides down the slippery slope of heroin addiction). Just Say No was part of a wider nationwide moral panic at that time in the UK, about heroin use and teenage drug-taking in general. The phrase had been coined in the USA, where First Lady Nancy Reagan had endorsed the first 'Just Say No' campaign whilst doing her bit for Ronald Reagan's escalating War On Drugs.

Music press ad. November 1986.

The album featured mostly Leicester bands, with the Bykers, Crazyhead and The Bomb Party sharing company with post-punks and goths. With titles like After Suck There's Blow, I Don't Want That Kind Of Love and Fist Fuckin' Baby, *Just Say Yeah* was about as far removed from the wholesome and anodyne anti-drug rap as was possible. Crazyhead went into Rick Willson's small Leicester studio to lay down I Don't Want That Kind Of Love for the compilation. They ended up recording four or five more songs, all live in the studio, which they later used as a demo that got them a deal with Food Records.

After Suck There's Blow proved the band wasn't a one-trick pony. It differed from the rocking acid punk sound that epitomised the Bykers earlier demos. It was a shuffling, hypnotic beast of

Gaye Bykers On Acid and Crazyhead's first committed-to-vinyl recordings were on the Just Say Yeah! compilation album, 1986.

a song. Says Robber: "We went up there with no idea... sort of to just make something up in the studio. There was a bit of a Blue Monday influence — put a bass line down, stick a borrowed guitar line down and some sampled drums, and see how it goes sort of thing!"

Says Tony, "I still love that song — 'who's the infidel a sinner cries'... religious overtones and the corporate vacuum cleaner sucking everything up in its way. Just playing with words with 'blow' and 'suck', being high seemed to stick, the title came first, and then Mary wrote the lyrics around the suck and blow idea... and maybe Frankie Goes To Hollywood singing about coming."

"After Suck There's Blow was like a totally electro track," notes Mary. "Kev didn't play drums on it, he put something down on a drum machine and then played something like electronic drums on top of it. Whereas Everythang's Groovy was a total band thing that we'd written as a song, After Suck was a complete studio thing that we kind of wrote as we were going along. It showed at that time we could've gone in any of two directions. I think After Suck There's Blow is quite interesting, because if you listen to that original version it kind of almost gets into that Sheffield industrial territory. I think the producer had a vague connection with Fon Records which was Cabaret Voltaire's label. We liked all that stuff as well, so I'm quite proud of that in the sense that it showed we were experimenting with different things even then, when we didn't really know what

Jon Langford's cartoon of the Bykers, 1986.

we were doing! It's kind of what Ministry ended up doing in a way. If you listen to it, it's way before those guys were doing any of that, so, I dunno, it kind of was a bit before its time."

Mary has a point. It was certainly before the techno explosion really took off, and two years before the Acid House craze hit the headlines. It also predates similar efforts by dance/rock crossover acts; such musical styles were also evolving independently, albeit concurrently of one another.

Mary recalls that the day after the Bykers recorded After Suck There's Blow they recorded the song that would be their debut single, Everythang's Groovy. The band made the relatively short hop from Driffield in the East Riding of Yorkshire, to Offbeat Studios in Kirkstall, a suburb in northwest Leeds. The in-house producer for In-Tape was Jon Langford, ex-Mekons, who was then currently enjoying indie success with his post-punk band The Three Johns. Robber recalls Langford being a "top bloke, good producer and musician. He let us sleep on his floor when we recorded Everythang's Groovy."

The band clicked with Langford. Not only did Langford in turn design the cover of their debut single, he also immortalised the band in the cartoon that ended up on the back. Mary is even more effusive than Robber in his praise for the Mekon man, "Jon put everybody at ease. He's such an affable bloke… Basically, we walked into the control room after we'd done a couple of takes and he showed us this picture of us, which captured us completely — that cartoon I think was amazing! It shows you that that guy captured the music, captured us, and captured everything about us! For us he could do no wrong. It was a great experience."

FOOD FOR THOUGHT

Crazyhead had also built up a full head of steam since their formation in February 1986, and, like the Bykers, managed most of their own day-to-day band matters and business affairs. (To be more specific, Reverb and Vom managed them.) But after a while they opted to get someone else to do it. Si Ord, who had been instrumental in putting out the *Just Say Yeah* compilation, managed things for the band for a while. Reverb says, "Si was a nice guy, but I think he had different ideas to us about where to go; if I remember rightly, he wanted us to hold out for a major deal. It might sound crazy 'cos we'd only been together for about eight months, but there was also some internal pressure within the band about getting a record deal, 'cos the Bykers had already been signed [to In-Tape]." There was also some interest from Yves Guillemot, who ran the rare record shop Vinyl Solution on Portobello Road. Reverb continues, "Yves offered to put us into the studio with Craig Leon as producer." Leon had been instrumental in kick-starting the careers of some of New York's most famous punk-related acts and was notable for producing The Ramones' first album as well as Blondie's first two.

Crazyhead got their next break with their debut London gig at the end of August — albeit at the Croydon Underground, which was still just about regarded as being a London show. They were supporting veteran punks, Chelsea, very much "also-rans" by this time. Andy Hurt, who had championed the Bykers two months earlier when he reviewed their first London gig, was again in the audience. Although a poor turnout, this was in no way any reflection on Crazyhead, as they were the unknown quantity in London before this night. Hurt conveyed this in *Sounds*, lamenting that it was "a sad epitaph for Chelsea — the 'headline' band", and reserving his praise for the newcomers, likening them to napalm who "*fry* the intestines" of the outwardly unmoved audience. Hurt predicted great things for Crazyhead, once their confidence had grown, and concluded his review by stating they were "too good for Croydon".

It has since come to light that music journalist Andy Hurt was the nom de plume of none other than Andy Ross, PR man for Food Records (and former member of the late seventies Leicester punk band Disco Zombies). There is some suggestion that he might even have arranged Crazyhead's early London gigs. Another gig at the Croydon Underground followed shortly after. This time Crazyhead were supporting Robyn Hitchcock and the Egyptians. Hurt AKA Ross had been present at the previous Croydon gig, but Food Records label boss David

Crazyhead, Timebox at the Bull & Gate, Kentish Town, London, 1986.

Balfe went to see them for himself this time. More gigs followed. Timebox, the Bull & Gate in Kentish Town, Dingwalls in Camden. Says Porkbeast of the latter, "Lemmy was there and gave us the thumbs up."

On his first impressions of Crazyhead, David Balfe says: "I remember thinking that their music was very strong, really good songs, and fitted into the garage rock style that was having a resurgence along with the Zodiac thing we were doing. They had that *Nuggets*-style engaging primitivism to them. And What Gives You The Idea That You're So Amazing Baby? was just a song I absolutely had to put out. But I did think they were a right bunch of ugly, scruffy oiks, and that might be a major problem in terms of them ever becoming rock-gods! Which, unfortunately, proved to be the case. They were easily musically strong enough to be a lot bigger than they were, and live they could be awesome, but they had very little glamour — that much derided but nevertheless intrinsic element of rock'n'roll — which I think was the deciding factor in the end."

Anderson's memory of how the Food deal came about is as follows. "We rehearsed for three months, did a few gigs, sent out demos, and got signed to Food within six months. They wanted us straightaway, but we held out. Other indies were after us — Chapter 22 etc. — but Food had some cash, as well as just having done very well with Zodiac Mindwarp. In those early days, Dave Balfe and Andy Ross were absolutely brilliant coming up with plans and scams, yet

then fully realising it might take three or four albums to hit bigtime. I mean, everyone was telling us we were gonna become massive worldwide in the music industry. We just thought we were this little indie rock band that might make the indie top 30, if lucky!"

Reverb concludes, "In the end we went with Food. I guess because they had a bigger profile, and Andy Ross seemed to have the press in his pocket with their other acts at the time. I think we felt bad about turning Yves down 'cos he was so enthusiastic, and Craig Leon was a guy we'd loved to have worked with. We met him when he was producing Jesus Jones sometime later and thought he would have been great for us." It was not to be, however, and with Reverb and Vom at the helm again, they negotiated the deal with Ross at Food.

When Crazyhead signed to Food, they already had a deal with Polydor on the table, but ultimately rejected it because they didn't feel they would be a good fit for a major label. They weren't ready to be shaped to the label's whim and forced down the road of being a predominantly singles band. Vom says, "We weren't ever that sort of band, and we had a good conversation about this with David Balfe before we signed to Food, and he said, 'No, I'm happy to sign you on a five-year deal and let your career build. You can become an album band, or whatever, but I'm not going to put pressure on you to have hit singles.'"

Balfe can't remember the exact terms of the deal, but it is slightly at odds with Vom's version. "I think it was for one single," says Balfe, "with an option for another single, and then maybe options for three or four albums. I'm afraid I really can't say the numbers for sure. But it would definitely have started with just singles, and then definitely had album options, 'cos the plan was to try to get a major company label deal, and we had to have long-term options on the bands to do that."

GOSCOTE HOUSE HIGH-RISE

As one of the leading lights on the Leicester music scene, The Bomb Party had an inkling that they could make it, and so like many other provincial bands, re-located to London. With their departure, the Bykers ensconced themselves in Goscote House in Leicester. Goscote House is also significant in that it's where the Bykers and Pop Will Eat Itself first cemented their acquaintance.

Mary thinks it was after a Primitives gig at the Princess Charlotte. The Poppies weren't playing but had ostensibly come over from West Midlands to see The Primitives, and Mary infers that Poppies singer, Clint Mansell, possibly had designs on their lead singer, Tracy Tracy. If this was the case, it would appear that Mansell had no luck on this occasion, as the Poppies ended up hanging out with the Bykers instead, who invited them to stay at Goscote House. The Poppies were bewildered by their hosts' somewhat bizarre and unconventional abode in the tower block. "We invited them back to the place and they got pretty freaked out," says Mary. The Poppies walked into a flat that was covered in muslin sheets and spray paint, with televisions emitting static on the screens and white noise from the speakers. Coupled with the acid they'd taken it's hardly surprising it was something of a "headfuck". According to Mary, "It was all pretty psychedelic, you know?" It certainly was. Says Anderson, "I popped round in the morning… Mary introduced me: the Bykers were their usual manic cackling selves, our new friends PWEI — real pop stars on the indie scene — looked like confused rabbits — I later found out why — they'd been tripping with the Bykers all night on strong LSD! I met them again a few times over the years, nice bunch of guys, very down to earth, even when they became a big band."

The Poppies weren't so daunted by their night at Goscote House that they couldn't keep in touch. When the Bykers played a gig at the Birmingham Hummingbird a little while later, the Poppies reciprocated the favour and invited the Bykers to stay with them. These meetings were the first in a long association between the two groups and today Mary is co-frontman of Graham Crabb's version of Pop Will Eat Itself.

CHAPTER FOUR
EVERYTHANG'S GROOVY

WITH INCREASINGLY FAVOURABLE COVERAGE IN THE MUSIC press, it was only a matter of time before news of this strangely named band filtered through to the mainstream press, and at the end of November 1986 the Gaye Bykers on Acid were mentioned in one of the national inky tabloid red tops, the *Daily Mirror*. John Blake's pop column The White Hot Club reported that "there are some dodgy-sounding groups' names currently touring the UK, no doubt as a backlash to such oldies as Peter Gabriel dominating the charts". He included the Bykers as one of the most imaginatively named, along with the likes of Stitched Back Foot Airmen, Flowers In The Dustbin, and Smirking Hyenas.

Given the *Daily Mirror's* circulation figures, in many ways you couldn't ask for better publicity. But whether the average *Mirror* reader would prove to be receptive is debatable. Nevertheless, it wasn't long before the band was regularly gracing the British weekly music papers.

The fruits of the Bykers' hard labour were rewarded when Everythang's Groovy was released at the end of November 1986. It created a stir, shooting into the indie charts and reaching number six, where it stayed for 33 weeks. They had arrived! Everythang's Groovy b/w Space Rape and TV Cabbage, were three blasts of sonic mayhem.

Sounds' Mr Spencer said of Everythang's Groovy: "This one growls and festers, a rampant drug-riddled space beast on the lookout for unattended skateboards." He concluded that "with a splash of wah wah pedal and these

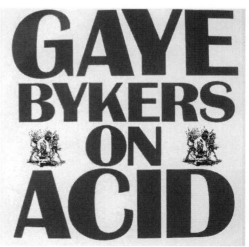

Gaye Bykers On Acid debut single, 'Everythang's Groovy', 1986.

unbelievably orbiting drums, it's tempting to describe Everythang's Groovy as a classic, but past experience says: resist! Let's just say it's a bit different and bit bloody bonkers".

Possibly the Bykers' first significant interviews appeared in the Christmas issues of *Record Mirror* and *Sounds*. Stuart Bailie referred to the new single as "a fine piece of looping, psychedelic mayhem, coupled with the equally alluring Space Rape". The Bykers had found an early champion in *Sounds* journalist, Mr Spencer — in an interview from December 1986, he describes the single: "... it makes you think of Hawkwind getting down with the Sex Pistols and feeling like they've known each other for years. It's a searing space rock bombshell, a brilliantly fraught mismatch of salivating basslines and Shaft guitars... it does awaken memories of Klingon raids on the star ship *Enterprise*, and more pertinently, Rod Serling's *The Twilight Zone*."

Spencer had a point — from the moment the needle drops onto the groove and the opening salvo of drums kick in, you know all the tracks are going to be killers. Tony Horsfall's demented Hendrix-grappling-with-Ron-Asheton -style-heavy-fuzz-distorted-psychedelic-wah-guitar onslaught is underscored by Robber Byker's thundering bass and Kev Hyde's drum rhythms, while Mary's vocals alternate between gruff Beefheart growl and Leicester-meets-transatlantic Iggy style howls... and so the template was set.

Side two opens with Space Rape — with its sci-fi influences and Dr McCoy samples from *Star Trek*, it's just got to be one of the most intense and demented space rock records ever! Then there's TV Cabbage, a searing indictment of

couch potato culture and the methadone metronome that is television — acid punk at its most furious and righteous.

Christmas 1986 proved to be a very merry one for both the Bykers and Crazyhead: the former's recent single was still garnering plaudits, while the latter were happy to have been signed by Food. As a later press release said, "Crazyhead received the best Christmas present ever."

Soon after, Crazyhead

recorded tracks for what would become their debut single, What Gives You The Idea That You're So Amazing Baby. Anderson recalls, "We went to record So Amazing at some famous but cheap studio in London, I forget where [It was Berry Street, Clerkenwell]. But they were really nice guys, and they wanted to recreate the vibe of the demo. So we drank loads of vodka, whiskey, snakebites and black, and did a shedload

what gives you the idea that you're so amazing baby?

Crazyhead's debut single, 1987. Photo by Donato Cinicolo 3.

of cheap amphetamines. The others smoked loads of really strong oil. I'd given up by then, just booze and the odd line!"

Crazyhead recorded all the tracks live, nearly all in one take. Porkbeast says of the session, "it was all very businesslike. We got in, thrashed it out, few overdubs, mixed — done! I can't remember anything except suggesting the guitar pan from speaker to speaker at the end of the solo. Wham bam thank you mam"!

To celebrate recording the single, the band trooped off to the psychedelic club that was the place to be seen on the scene, Alice In Wonderland, at Gossips on Dean Street in Soho. Anderson allegedly blagged them all in for free, claiming that they were the Gaye Bykers On Acid. With the recent release of Everythang's Groovy, the Bykers had begun to create a stir in the music press. Crazyhead were having a high old time, scrounging drinks and schmoozing with London's psychedelic and underground royalty, until Anderson, having had one drink too many, couldn't contain himself any longer, and let the cat out the bag: they weren't the Bykers at all, but another up-and-coming Leicester band called Crazyhead! When word filtered back to the door staff, they were unceremoniously booted out of the club.

Anderson also remembers a later occasion at Alice In Wonderland, when he and Porkbeast blagged their way in a second time. "I used to drink a small bottle of whiskey before I went out in those days. I remember we had a groovy time listening to The Doctor [of the Medics] spinning great music. We were approached by a Sun reporter who wanted to take our photo for a piece they were doing. He said we stood out with our heavy biker look. Alex maybe, but me? More New York Dolls camp biker look! We both ranted on about our hatred of the *Sun*, and he said 'forget the politics, get a picture in, promote your band, because it's obvious you're both in one'. We declined because of the *Sun's* history of evil, and years later, Hillsborough and the miners' strike — I'm glad we did."

Soon enough they would be welcome at the club, with Crazyhead's own star in the ascendant, not far behind that of their Leicester compatriots. Crazyhead's live performances were beginning to get them noticed and in January they were added to the ICA Rock Week, hosted in collaboration with EMI, at the Institute of Contemporary Arts in London. Ostensibly a showcase for the latest up-and-coming indie bands without contracts, it was also dubbed 'The Great Unsigned' rock week. Despite the fact they were now technically signed to Food, Crazyhead still hadn't released a record, and were added to the bill at the last minute, as a replacement for another band.

Still known by many of his friends as Ian, Food Records encouraged the use of Anderson as a name, and they helped to cultivate it in the press. "Ian was not very rock'n'roll," he laughs and, referring to arch prog rockers Jethro Tull's frontman, adds, "plus there was a slightly more famous Ian Anderson!" Adopting this 'new' name, Anderson joined Reverb in an interview for *Sounds* as part of its 'Great Unsigned' coverage. It was Crazyhead's first real press exposure. Anderson recalls the inclement weather on the day of the interview:

"I went round for Reverb. It was snowing heavily — bloody freezing! Reverb cheered me up, he had two women's fur coats — one a bizarre cowl he lent me — and we wore them on top of our black leather pants and jackets. We also had a good line of whizz to bolster us. We got the train, drinking cans of Stella and snorting more lines of speed, so we were out of our brains by the time we got to the interview, and the kindly scribe from *Sounds* took us down the pub and gave us more Stella. The interview was an amphetamine and beer fuelled rant, especially from Rev. But by the time of the photos we were completely pissed up, somehow all the booze taking over from the strong speed we had finished earlier. The piece came out in *Sounds* a week later, with Reverb and myself slumped in a doorway like a couple of leather-clad tramps grinning inanely, with the headline below 'You don't have to be drunk to like this band but it sure helps'!"

Anderson would be the first to admit he had a reputation for being a shiftless, lazy, drunken slob, and in the interview confided what he was like before Crazyhead. "I was in such a mess," he explained, "through drink and stuff, I couldn't walk down the street. Getting with this lot got me back together, it got me out of that. Mary from the Bykers suggested I went to see them. Apart from Kev, I think the rest took me as a bit of a joke, as I've got a bit of a reputation for being a drunken slob".

Anderson and Reverb also displayed a self-confidence and arrogance that wasn't necessarily just down to all the booze and speed. Rubbing their hands at the prospect of receiving £500 for their ICA gig, Anderson said, "I reckon a lot of these bands have pulled out because they just can't do it live." On the subject of their forthcoming single Reverb said, "our song is the best thing that has happened in fucking years. It's *not* about finding women and having a bonk — we reflect what's going on". He continued, "Who do we hate? All of them!

'You don't have to be drunk to like this band but it sure helps!' (L-R) Reverb and Anderson at ICA Rock Week. Photo courtesy of Greg Freeman.

Originally printed in Sounds, 31st January, 1987.

The independent scene is garbage. When the world hears our Baby Turpentine, they'll know…"

A week later, Neil Perry's review of the 'Great Unsigned' gig at the ICA appeared in *Sounds*. Crazyhead were sandwiched between opening act Hands Of The Virgin and headliners Head Of David, but such was his praise for Crazyhead, Perry hardly mentioned either of them:

> **Crazyhead were almost as good as the best sex you've ever had. Just four leather jackets and the bare arms of a frighteningly tight drummer; I swear Crazyhead blew the place apart.**
>
> **With the precision of Metallica and the righteousness of Motörhead, Crazyhead are The Ramones that Britain has never spawned. But they have 10 times the ability and 100 times the wit and suss, and they can't fail to become internationally massive.**

In the same week as the Crazyhead review in *Sounds*, the Bykers were given a full page by the *NME*. Steven Wells seemingly took a shine to the Bykers. At pains to distinguish the Bykers from the likes of other psychedelic rock revivalists at the time, like The Mission, Wells wrote:

The Bykers *must* be separated in your mind from such necrophilia, from the likes of Mr Mindwarp or, gawdhelpus, Dr And The Medics *if only* for the reason that they are raised above the turgid-cak-ophany of their fellow nouveaux long-hairs by the *cutting-edge* of their music; which is, like, *up there*, man!

In the interview that followed there was more than a little frivolity as the Bykers discussed analogies between US Presidents and *Star Trek* characters. Kev lowered the tone when he suggested, "we just can't wait to get between Uhuru's thighs and thrust upwardly," prompting Wells to call him "a prick". But Mary was quite serious in his explanation of what the song Space Rape from the new EP was about: "What Reagan's doing and what they're wasting money on — that's contentious isn't it? It's about the exploitation of space and the waste of money…"

As with Crazyhead, the Bykers were starting to feature more regularly in the weekly music papers. Thanks to their connections with In-Tape, their profile in the capital was elevated by a couple of gigs supporting other acts on the label: Bogshed and The Three Johns, just before Christmas of 1986, and Marc Riley & The Creepers in January 1987. The number of favourable reviews was growing, yet they weren't immune to receiving the occasional stinker too. At the Sir George Robey in Finsbury Park, *Sounds* scribe Roy Wilkinson was downright dismissive of headliners Bogshed ("In a word, they're boring") and was only slightly less disparaging in his summation of the Bykers:

The Bykers, four geeks who mix a high-tech fascination with the Dark Ages tinged altruism of a Hell's Angels chapter, have been reading *2000AD* and listening to 'Space Ritual' for the last five years. This quartet of walk-on parts from *Blade Runner* look great and have a nice if slightly overused state of the art concept behind them. Unfortunately, their sound in no way matches up to either their visuals or their brand of futurist manifesto. It's a bland if spikey rock out that leaves the Bykers with little credibility.

Nevertheless, the Bykers' single, Everythang's Groovy, was going from strength to strength, and there was a new EP on the horizon. It was no longer viable for Mary to continue juggling the responsibility of being the lead singer with managerial duties. "We went to see some cool people as far as managing the band was concerned," says Mary. In pursuit of a full-time manager, the band had "spoken to Andrew King, one of Pink Floyd's original managers, who was very interested in looking after us, but I don't know what happened. We had meetings with a few people." Ian Grant and Alan Edwards of Modern Management were among the other people the band met. Grant had managed The Stranglers in the 1970s, and, Mary says, "wanted to manage us at one point." He adds with regret, "maybe we should've! They were Big Country's managers, they were quite successful at the time."

Before they secured anyone with significant managerial pedigree, the Bykers crossed paths with a fast-talking, brash cockney, who shall be known from here on as Stacey Lafront. Her main claim to fame in the music business was that she had once managed a relatively popular English post-punk band which achieved some single and album success in the UK charts and to a lesser degree the USA too. It was February 1987 when the Bykers met Lafront at the Alice In Wonderland. The Soho club had built something of a reputation since the early eighties, and catered for a cross-section of alternative/underground subcultures, including goths, psychobillies and punks, but it was still predominantly renowned for being a psychedelic hangout. It was a place where the more famous rock cognoscenti happily rubbed shoulders with the average punter, and the likes of The Damned, The Cult's Ian Astbury, and Motörhead's Lemmy all featured amongst its clientele. It rapidly became one of the hippest parties in town, the place to be seen for any aspiring new band. So, when the Bykers were approached by the garrulous and truculent Lafront, with promises of all manner of fame, riches, and rock'n'roll stardom for little in return, it looked like a no-brainer.

The Bykers had just finished playing a set. Robber says that Lafront "came and introduced herself." Adopting a whiny cockney accent, he adds, "'I'm a manager, I can manage you and get you a record deal' and stuff like this — she was really, really gobby, and we didn't have a manager at the time, so I thought, 'Might as well give her a go, what harm can it do if she wants to do it for nothing and sort some gigs out and do some work for us?'"

Stacey Lafront seemed an ideal choice, possessing the requisite balance of front and business acumen. Hindsight is a wonderful thing. Mary says, "I never really trusted her from day one, but the other three, for some reason, really liked her... I don't know if it was because she was giving them drugs. Two of them, I think Tony and Kev, were living in her house at one point, and to be honest that's when it all started going wrong... for me."

The Bykers certainly wouldn't be the first band to fall for the spiel of a prospective manager promising the world, nor the last. Meanwhile, the Bykers' and Crazyhead's respective stars continued to rise, and both bands supported The Cult over two legs of their *Electric* promotional tour.

WHAT GIVES YOU THE IDEA THAT YOU'RE SO AMAZING BABY?

In February, Crazyhead released their debut single, What Gives You The Idea That You're So Amazing Baby?, on 7- and 12-inch vinyl. The sleeve design was the first of several Crazyhead releases influenced by the classic early 1960s Rolling Stones album and EP covers. On the front, the band posed halfway down the stairs of their recording studio basement. Glowering and resplendent in black leather, bowler hats and long, back-combed spiky hair, they looked every inch like mutant hybrids of *Dont Look Back* era Dylan and Johnny Rotten, circa San Francisco Winterland. The monochrome photos from the same shoot on the back of the sleeve depicted them in various states of disrepair in the studio itself — encapsulating the time, and the music contained in the record's grooves, perfectly.

Delivered with the precision and ferocity of a Stuka bomber's payload, What Gives You The Idea That You're So Amazing Baby? was incendiary — frantic heads down, no nonsense garage rock'n'roll with a hefty gob of punk attitude to boot. With lines like 'gonna take myself on a holy quest, what a rich bitch wants

Photo by Donato Cinicolo 3.

From the back cover of Crazyhead's debut single, 1987.

must be the best', the lyrics weren't just dripping in vitriol —the titular chorus was spat out with righteous indignation too!

The two tracks on the B-side could have been A-sides in their own right. Of Out On A Limb, Anderson says, "Reverb took some lyrics I'd scrawled about James Dean's life and death inspired by *Hollywood Babylon* — great book! — and turned them into a song, always a stage fave. Maybe it should've been a single." The lyrics for the other B-side song, Snake Eyes, were written by Anderson and Reverb. Anderson says that it was, in part, about a dealer they knew, as well as alluding to people in other bands: "It's about freaky looking people we knew on heavy drugs really." Reverb concurs that Anderson wrote most of the lyrics. "My contribution was mostly the music and chorus," he says, "which was more about new found evangelism."

The single received accolades in the music press. A review in *Melody Maker* by Mick Mercer described the Voice of the Beehive single Just A City as "cute", then contrasted it with Food labelmates Crazyhead's new release. Cute "is not exactly what you'd say about Crazyhead, not unless you want your face pushed in, which is *exactly* What Gives You... does. Though they may be rough-riding noise-boys, they've got control and melodic missiles to mess with. Supreme."

In *Sounds* it was awarded single of the week. Neil Perry's typewriter keys must have been on fire as he wrote, "So Amazing is simple and simply essential, if ferocious bass, guitars and drums ever made your spine tingle. A kick in the guts, a slap round the face... and now this *is* amazing: two cars and a brick wall have just inflicted serious damage on each other outside my window as I write. Get the picture? I wasn't even playing the record very loud." He concluded, "Crazyhead: such bravado, such gusto, such drunkards. Best of all, their amps have yet to reach 11."

The subject matter appears self-explanatory given the song's title, although there is a difference of opinion about what inspired it. Anderson suggests Reverb partially wrote the song about Mary Byker. Reverb is quick to dismiss the idea, although he doesn't refute it entirely: "When I started messing about with the chorus for What Gives You The Idea the working lyric was 'What Gives You The Idea that you're so amazing MARY?' though the song had nowt to do with him."

Despite members of both bands having been friends for years, Crazyhead and the Bykers were not above taking a swipe at one other in the music press. This was probably more for appearances sake, but despite such braggadocio there wasn't any real deep-seated animosity. That said, a sense of rivalry was now mounting, especially with each having to prove themselves on their respective support slots with The Cult.

Bykers with local constabulary backstage at Glasgow Barrowlands, on The Cult Electric Tour, March 1987.

Hitting the road at the end of February, the Bykers did the honours for the earlier dates. Beginning in Newcastle the tour crossed the border for several shows in Scotland before rolling back into the North of England. The Bykers made it between venues on a traveller's bus belonging to a friend of theirs called Tat, perhaps as much out of practicality's sake as to their ideological sympathies towards the beleaguered and so-called Hippy Peace Convoy. They played a further two nights at Birmingham Odeon, before the first leg of the tour concluded with three nights at London Hammersmith Odeon.

The Bykers supported The Cult on the first two of the three dates at Hammersmith Odeon, with Crazyhead taking over support duties on the last night. It might have been the perfect opportunity for both the upcoming Leicester bands to share the support slot, but it wasn't to be. Indeed, there were very few occasions when they did share a bill.

Whilst The Cult and the Bykers were playing at the Hammersmith, Crazyhead were the main support act for the newly reformed Pink Fairies, returning from a 10-year hiatus. The Pink Fairies were underground legends in the early 1970s, and this was the first date of their latest reunion, at an event called All-Day Explosion at the Town and Country Club in London. The Pink Fairies may have been associated with the hippies in the past, but they still had a loyal and fiercely partisan following. Porkbeast remembers the gig vividly. "We were very provocative at this stage, slagging off the audience to get a reaction," he says. "We were so broke I regularly used to order the audience to buy me a drink, and it usually worked. We played the Pink Fairies all-dayer, and called the London crowd a bunch of shandy drinking Southern poofters, and Anderson was threatened with a knife afterwards by an aggrieved Hell's Angel. He became a regular backstage member after that introduction! Our biggest London fan!"

The Hell's Angel to which Porkbeast refers is perhaps the same one Anderson mentions in regards to an early Crazyhead gig. "I opened by saying, 'Hello London scum,' in a drunken abusive rant," says Anderson of the night in question. "At the end of the show, three huge guys, a fully tattooed biker, and his rockabilly buddies, understandably gave me a hard time. I kept seeing the huge biker at our London shows, once when we played the Electric Ballroom, where he kept spitting at me and threatening me with his same big mates. I was shitting myself! Luckily one of Tommo's [Bomb Party drummer] mates was a real Hell's Angel and had a word. He never bothered me again. About a year and a half later he walked up to me backstage, shook my hand, apologised, said he used to take a lot of speed before, and even though he had nearly battered me, he was a huge fan! He was sharing a place with one of the guys from Jesus Jones at the time, who often used to come to our gigs."

Reviewing the All-Day Explosion gig for *Sounds*, Roy Wilkinson was so impressed by Crazyhead's performance that he didn't even bother to mention sets by the bands on the bill below them, or for that matter the headliners, the Pink Fairies. Heaping praise upon Crazyhead throughout the review, Wilkinson wrote, "pop will not be *allowed* to eat itself, because gangrene gobbed scumbag rock is on its trail and it's going to devour everything in sight. Hotly tipped as architects of this impending carnage are Leicester dirtball phenomenon, Crazyhead."

When die-hard Fairies fans showered the stage with beer glasses, Wilkinson admired the way Crazyhead dealt with it as "a testament to the most convincing display of onstage snottiness that I've seen in a long while". He goes on: "'Don't you tell

Pink Fairies reunion, supported by Crazyhead, 1987.

Gaye Bykers On Acid. On Tat's hippy bus during The Cult 'Electric' tour. (L-R) Tat, Tony Byker, Lindsey Jones. March 1987.

me how to do my job and I won't tell you how to sweep floors,' jibes singer and lead wag Anderson. He has the latitude for such obnoxiousness simply because Crazyhead have the songs to back up his boasting".

The night after the All-Day Explosion, Crazyhead took over on the last of The Cult's three nights at Hammersmith Odeon. There was an aftershow party at the trendy Kensington Roof Gardens, where, Reverb recalls, "There was a free bar, I remember that it was easy to identify the Leicester crew — Crazyhead, Bykers etc. — because they were the ones walking around with half a dozen bottles of beer in their hands just in case the world ended!" Anderson also remembers the incongruity of the occasion: "We just couldn't believe all this booze and food was free. We kept thinking someone was going to take it off us and throw us out. It was full of pop and rock stars… and us lot!" According to Anderson, "Mary was loud and drunk as usual and pissed all over a table of booze and food to impress a music journo, James Brown I think — the one who did *Loaded* magazine later. We thought it was a waste of good booze!"

Porkbeast has less fond memories of the party. "Yeah, it was a debauch in the roof garden with people shagging in the bushes, free booze and food. Muggins here was the only one who could drive so I was sober and taxiing the rest of the fuckers. I got bounced into it, so I was pretty pissed off really. They had that Punjabi Elvis

on at the time. The only incident worth mentioning was Rob Vomit living up to his name, puking out the window of the van just as I drove past a load of coppers!"

Andy Blade, from the original punk band, Eater, remembers things quite differently. In his autobiography, Blade recalls that

> The high point of the night, besides the Asian Elvis impersonator, was when Gaye Bykers' singer Mary, a boy with a girl's name, offered Boy George a little wrap of pepper he'd made up to look like a heroin deal. George, smelling a rat after having recently been through the tabloid mill over his drug problems, threw a tantrum and had his bodyguards eject him from the premises. Mary screamed at a paralytic Zodiac Mind-warp to come and help him but, slumped over a table, bottle of wine in hand, he wasn't going anywhere fast.

Within days, Crazyhead would appear at the Town and Country Club again, with another legendary musician, this time from New York — Tom Verlaine, formerly of Television. Then, just three days after the Television support slot, they appeared with the German proto-goth band Xmal Deutschland and homegrown goth folkers All About Eve, after which they resumed the concluding part of the *Electric* tour with The Cult. Anderson recalls, "I spoke with [Cult frontman] Ian Astbury a few times. One night he tongued me just before I went on stage, as he used to watch us every night. I've had fantasies about snogging pop stars before, but was thinking more Strawberry Switchblade, Danielle Dax or Voice of the Beehive — just the girls! We were treated great by The Cult crew and their soundman — great guy, but the name's gone, sorry! He worked for us later. Top sound, top chap!"

Ian Astbury was at the height of his 'Wolf Child' phase and had taken to wearing a rather large furry Davey Crockett style piece of headgear. Of course, it became the centre of amusement for Crazyhead and their entourage. Anderson remembers that Sparky had pointed out the hat looked like a cat. "Don't get me wrong," he says, "Astbury and co. were very cool to us, giving us a free tour etc. and treating us well, but that hat looked fucking stupid, we all agreed — even for the mid-eighties! And we all know Astbury could wear some very odd clothes and still look cool, but not in this case! We got obsessed with the cat-hat, even to the point where Sparky would wander around Cult soundchecks and backstage with a saucer of milk going, 'Here kitty kitty, here kitty kitty,' with no one but the Crazyhead contingent knowing the crack, which of course set us off in giggles of delight bringing tears to our eyes! I used to just say to any confused Cult crew, 'Oh he used to do a lot of acid.' It got worse when he started putting out cat food,

Photo courtesy of Sally Jones.

Gaye Bykers On Acid supporting The Cult, Birmingham Odeon, March 1987. (L-R) Robber, Mary, Kev.

which Reverb would dare him to eat for a Special Brew, which of course Sparky would! Rev would also buy dog food for Sparky which he would consume with relish."

Contrary to his bandmates, Porkbeast "thought The Cult were great, but the others were a bit sneery as I remember. They always thought my tastes were a bit too eclectic. I think *Electric* still sounds good and a wise move on their part to go very metal, but it was a bit counter punk ethic which is why the others were a bit dismissive."

Anderson remains grateful for The Cult support slot, as he does for the later Julian Cope support, too: "What I mainly remember about those support slots for Crazyhead is we didn't fuck around — these were free supports, very generous of both acts — we just got on and played good shows."

Crazyhead might not have had to buy their way onto the tour, as is sometimes neessary to land a support slot, but they weren't being paid much on The Cult tour, either. Anderson would ask the audience to throw money and run round between songs grabbing the small change. "It was an art avoiding being hit full-on by coins," he says, "whilst still grabbing all I could. Luckily, they liked us… We may have been the support act, but the audience gave us a lot of support! We got free booze and sarnies backstage as well. I seem to remember there being chocolate that would disappear very fast. But strangely, Porkbeast was always chomping on chocs like a biker Billy Bunter, no wonder he got so fat!"

A few days after finishing their stint with The Cult, the Bykers played a gig at The Comedy Store in Leicester Square, London. Numerous record company bigwigs were in attendance, much to Mary's chagrin, still struggling to come to terms with being flavour of the month. In an interview with Hans Peter Kuenzler later that year, Mary recalled how he didn't enjoy the Comedy Store gig: "before going on we were told there were lots of record company people down there, and I said, 'Why?', 'cos we just wanted to have a good gig. We didn't like the idea of being a puppet... so we just played badly... trying to be obnoxious, and annoying as many people as possible."

Duesi remembers the occasion: "I went with my friend Martin Goldschmidt who then, as now, runs Cooking Vinyl Records. I think he might have been mildly interested at the time in signing them, or he was friends with their manager, or something like that — I'm not sure. The gig was at the Comedy Store, I seem to recall dimly, and it was great. At the time there wasn't much rock music around that was actually fun and loud and more indie in spirit than metal, and not half as earnest as all that grunge stuff that was on the horizon. Wasn't 'Camden Lurch' [another music press constructed scene] about the same time? Bands like Milk, Swervedriver, Silverfish etc. — the Bykers were different again, more psychedelic and just plain daft. I remember a promo package at the time, a cardboard box containing various totally useless (of course!) items, including a can of turd spray. I tried it out on my toilet and discovered that the turds that sprouted from this can did indeed looking convincingly turd like — and it came complete with industrial odour effect. Only difference to the real thing — it wouldn't flush down the loo; too light, you see!"

Photo courtesy of Gaye Bykers On Acid.

PFX branded novelty fake deodorant shit spray — "The turds that sprouted from this can did indeed look convincingly turd like."

The Cult tour helped to expose both bands to music industry people, as well as a wider national audience. But the Bykers received an even bigger boost when an excerpt of Everythang's Groovy was shown on the *Old Grey Whistle Test*. As far as BBC rock shows went, this late-night programme had become something of a rock institution in the 1970s. By the mid-1980s it had moved to an earlier mid-week slot, perhaps in an attempt to appeal to a younger audience. Only a 30-second clip of the video was aired, but it got the band into the nation's living rooms on near prime-time TV, and helped raise their profile among a wider, albeit perhaps indifferent and somewhat bewildered audience.

The video had been made by Leicester Polytechnic graphic design student, Dave Bartram (no relation to the Showaddywaddy singer of the same name, also from Leicester). Bartram was not long out of college, having completed a degree in film studies, and the video gave him the chance to flex his film-making muscle, as well as indulging the Bykers in their creative fantasies. Bartram knew Tony Byker, who was studying fine art at the Poly at the time. It wasn't the first music video he'd made — that was Thunderhead Johnny for The Janitors, which, according to Bartram, has probably never even seen the light of day. (It features various friends of the band and other faces from the Leicester scene, including Mary playing — or, as Bartram has it, more likely miming because Mary couldn't play — bass in a scrapyard. The Janitors had not long been signed to In-Tape Records.)

There was no film or video course running at Leicester Polytechnic at the time, but there happened to be a video post-production suite in the basement that hardly anyone knew about. Bartram remembers he was given an animatic [simple animation] project one week when studying graphic design. "I found out there was a video technician there who was on the same wavelength as us," says Bartram, "so I bribed him to let us use the video camera and edit it all in the basement. So if it hadn't been for him it would never have happened."

A lot of the footage for Everythang's Groovy was shot in a burnt down Indian cinema on the outskirts of Leicester. Given its dilapidated state, Evington Cinema was perfect for what the Bykers had in mind, letting off fireworks and generally trashing the place. The whole process was on a shoestring, utilising whatever was to hand ranging from the video camera provided by the sympathetic technician at the poly, to some old 35mm film of a Bollywood movie that had somehow survived the fire and Bartram had found on the cinema floor. If you look carefully there's a shot of an Indian girl and a tiger flashing up sporadically. Bartram says, "everything was borrowed or stolen… there was a Raving Bonkers boxing game in there, just because that was lying around the house when we were students, and it was whatever you had to hand and something that made it different really."

Given the DIY proclivities and despite the circumstances surrounding

its production, the final product was pretty impressive. Filmed largely in monochrome, it was effect-heavy, in the kind of molten metal/flames way that was popular in 1970s videos. Bartram continues, "I was just trying out different techniques to see what worked… We threw everything we had into the mix to see what we could get away with, and I'm particularly proud, because on every drum beat there are flash frames which says 'Gaye Bykers On Acid' over and over again, which no way would you be allowed to put on air in this day and age because of people having epileptic fits. But somehow it made it onto the *Old Grey Whistle Test*, *The Chart Show*, and programmes like that!"

Also present in the video is a fleeting reference to Ted Moult. This continues the in-joke that had appeared on the rear of the single sleeve, which reads, 'Dedicated to Ted Moult (Out with a bang!)'. Moult was a familiar face on British television, appearing on the news show, *Country Game*, numerous panel shows and advertisements, although he is possibly best remembered as the face of Everest double-glazing. Moult had tragically taken his own life the previous year, and consequently became the subject of distasteful jokes, the sort that proliferate in schoolyards. The Bykers utilised Moult's grinning face in their video, which pops onscreen for about two seconds. Moult also can be found in Tony's personal scrapbook of Bykers ephemera, courtesy of an Everest coupon (with a picture of Ted Moult's face and the heading 'The rot stops here'), which has been filled in: "His Holy Divineness The Relatively Noble, Lord Teddy… OD'd On Lead '86."

WE HAVE A NOSEDIVE KARMA SITUATION ON OUR HANDS

The Bykers' TV appearance was more than enough to keep the momentum rolling until their next release, the *Nosedive* EP in May 1987. Available on 7-, 10- and 12-inch vinyl, *Nosedive* did not pass without controversy — not because of the recordings, but because of the cover. Ray Lowry, whose original 'Gay Bikers On Acid' cartoon in the *NME*, had unwittingly provided the band with its name, had now been commissioned to do the artwork for *Nosedive*. The finished cover was a collage of various clippings from magazines, including some from pornographic publications depicting breasts and the hairy pubic regions of naked women. In-Tape was forced to concede to demands by the distributor Red Rhino to reprint the cover with a black star strategically placed over the offending pictures. A spokesman for Red Rhino told *Sounds* they were concerned that 'major stores'

Uncensored cover of the Nosedive EP. Design by Ray Lowry.

might deem the sleeve offensive, and refuse to stock it, thereby hampering the band's future, adding that he hoped to reach some agreement whereby a limited number of unexpurgated copies might be released via the independent network only. As it happened, a number of such copies did make it into the wild and are highly sought after. Even uncensored, the pictures are quite tame by today's standards. One wonders whether it wasn't all part of a calculated publicity stunt, especially that there was supposedly a limited edition run of 1,000 collectors' copies on 10-inch vinyl, five of which featured a misspelling of the band's name. Naturally enough the hype generated a few column inches in the music press. Like the old adage goes, 'any publicity is good publicity.'

The EP was warmly received. Reviewing it in *Sounds*, James Brown wrote:

A drum beat Run DMC and the Beastie Boys would be scared of, and guitars that open like a Harley Davidson throttle over vocal wastelands.

The Bykers are perfect grebos, filthy little middle class kids with fertile imaginations and big mouths intent on being nothing but the dirtiest and best. Cruddy but entertaining live, pathetically shallow, and as grotty as they are groovy. The biggest cackle of it all is that the only real way to 'Nosedive Karma' is to dance like an amphetamine packed mod.

Also note the naughty sleeve handcrafted by the best rock'n'roll cartoonist since Michelangelo, Ray Lowry.

On 3rd May, the Bykers recorded a session for the *Janice Long Show* on BBC Radio One. Broadcast just over a week later it included live studio versions of tracks from the EP: Don't Be Human Eric — Let's Be Frank, Ruby Red Lips, Get Up To Get Down and Space Rape. Perhaps aided and abetted to some extent by the radio session, *Nosedive* stormed the indie charts, hitting the top spot later that

month. It remained there for the rest of the year. The four tracks were in a similar vein to their previous release, but there was a distinct hip hop undercurrent to the lead song, Nosedive Karma.

Breakbeats and yet more *Star Trek* samples collide head on with brain melting guitars and heavy punk riffage for what is arguably the Bykers' finest moment. Openly admitting to lifting the bassline from Michael Jackson's Billie Jean, the title track was a rock and hip hop fusion of titanic proportions. In addition, Robber has since admitted that the guitar riffs were lifted from AC/DC and the drums from PiL. The song itself was about "the state of the world," Mary says, "corporate interests and big business destroying little things. It was the beginning of our green consciousness, a kind of anti-everything song." Mary concedes that nothing really changes and uses an example of the song's lyrics to elaborate, "'Living for today, no looking back, if this was video, you could forward all the crap'. It's all crap! If life *was* like a video — great! — you could fast forward it all and get on with it… you know, living a nostalgia thing. I guess at the time we were looking to the punk thing and the sixties thing in equal measure, and for us it was the eighties. We'd lived through punk and been through the sixties, but what was happening musically and what was going on in the real world? It seems like nothing was really changing."

On the theme of nostalgia, Dave Bartram — who was again tasked with producing the promotional video — utilised Super 8 footage his father had shot of his family in the 1960s and 1970s. Commenting today, Bartram says, "I was doubling up to make it look more interesting than it really was, you know? Doing multiple layers, but of course in those days before the digital revolution as soon as you overlaid anything you lost a generation, so the quality's just dropping. Nowadays you've got first generation quality throughout, you can have as many overlays as you want." The video was not quite as immediate as its predecessor, but you had to give the band credit for doing as much as possible themselves. Well, at least within the orbit of their immediate coterie of friends.

Lyrically the other songs on the EP drew inspiration from recreational pastimes close to Mary and the other band members' hearts — getting intoxicated, thought-provoking sci-fi literature, and trashy sci-fi television. Mary says of Delerium, "The lyrics are about drugs and alcohol, and self-medicating," whilst Don't Be Human Eric — Let's Be Frank was inspired by the Iain Banks novel, *The Wasp Factory*, which Mary had recently read. He recalls, "it was a good book — when we signed to Virgin, I actually looked into buying the film rights to it, because I was quite interested in being involved in that. We didn't as it happens, but I remember Stacey [Lafront] talking to the publishers, and I still, to this day, think Banks is an amazing

Still from Star Trek episode 'The Way To Eden'. The Bykers based 'Golf Trek' on this.

writer — he died very recently. I was reading a lot of science fiction at the time as well, and I was a big fan of his, and that book was just, I dunno, sometimes you just read something and it's like 'raaaaahhh! — I'll write a song!' and that was it. So yeah, I was definitely influenced by that."

Golf Trek was a glorious adaptation of a song that had featured in the cult 1960s sci-fi series *Star Trek*. Originally broadcast on 21st February 1969, the episode titled 'The Way To Eden' featured a band of nomadic hippy space travellers who had been picked up by the USS *Enterprise* after their own space craft was about to break up. The hippies demand to be taken to a mythical planet called Eden, but Captain Kirk refuses, and under orders is told they must be repatriated to their own planets. The space hippies feel they have become prisoners of the *Enterprise* and encourage the crew to question the nature of authority. At one point, the space hippies have a musical jam session, before hijacking the *Enterprise* and setting a course for what they believe is Eden.

Despite its simplicity, the song contains lyrics rich in hippy type philosophy and the meaning of life. But musically the Bykers took it and turned it upside down, making it their own, with Tony's screeching wah guitar, Robber's funky bass, and Mary's strumming lip noises. The days spent on settees in various squats and dingy bedsits watching endless videos of *Star Trek* had not been entirely wasted, and Golf Trek became a firm live favourite with fans! If any other track

on the EP deserved its own video, then this was surely it. Alas it wasn't to be.

Nosedive Karma, with its elements of hip hop, signalled a shift. Also at this time, the band's friends and 'grebo' stablemates from the West Midlands were changing direction too: Released a week after the Nosedive EP, came the next Poppies EP. The Poppies had allegedly been moved by a Run DMC and Beastie Boys show in Birmingham to believe the way forward was to dispense with live drums and replace them with a drum machine and sampler. In doing so, Graham Crabb was free to join main singer, Clint Mansell, up front. Few could have predicted how far this direction would take them within such a short space of time. One of the highlights of the Poppies so-called *Covers* EP was a version of Hawkwind's Orgone Accumulator. But it was the lead track, a cover version of Sigue Sigue Sputnik's Love Missile F1-11, that really pointed in the direction the Poppies were headed. It appeared on a 12-inch as a 'Designer Grebo Megamix', reworked in the style of Run DMC's *Raising Hell*, and confirming the Poppies' shift away from the grungier guitar sound that first typified their sound.

Mary agrees. "The Poppies went completely down that route, they got rid of the drummer and totally became the hip hop thing. We didn't. We kept as a band… we could've gone exactly that same route as the Poppies at that point and said, 'Oh, fuck the drums off!'"

The Bykers would remain closer to the template of a guitar band although they were happy to experiment with new technology, hip hop, and various other styles and genres. Once again produced by Jon Langford, their *Nosedive* EP was engineered by Ian Caple, a freelancer at Berry Street Studio in Clerkenwell, London. Caple had recently made the acquaintance of Langford when the latter came into Berry Street to mix The Mekons' album *Honkey Tonkin*. It proved to be the start of a fruitful working relationship.

Nosedive was the first time Caple had worked with the Bykers, and he has good memories of it: "I loved mixing the *Nosedive* EP and really enjoyed working with them — it was always fun! Me and Jon both started in the punk days, and we both loved records with that raw energy. Through the eighties, records were getting more polished and safer, and many of the bands were being too po-faced and serious. The Bykers seemed to bring back that energy and irreverence we both liked". The sentiment is echoed by Caple, who says the Bykers "were great! They were full of wonderful ideas and they didn't mind working at it."

The respect was mutual, and Robber has nothing but praise for Langford and Caple. "They used to work as a production team, and we liked what they did for us. They kind of got us into early sampling, and stuff like sampling the drums. Before they had samplers, they used to do it on a Bel Delay unit, and they used

to put all these triggers down on the tape and turn the tape around, and get it to trigger this Bel Delay thing with a kick drum in it. It used to take them ages to put the kick drum and snare drums in because it was all really technical… yeah, they were a wicked production team!"

ST JULIAN TOUR

After The Cult's *Electric* tour, Crazyhead barely had time to draw breath before heading out on the road again, this time supporting Julian Cope on his 'St Julian' tour. Trading on the reputation they'd already built from some incendiary live performances and following on the heels of their enthusiastically received debut single, Crazyhead continued to wow audiences and members of Cope's entourage alike, including the Arch-Drude himself. Anderson recalls, "We got to know Julian Cope a bit, well he pretended to be a dog and bit me — not very hard — on the leg. One of his crew said 'wanker', but I thought it was pretty funny. Cope's band were really cool guys. I think they came and saw us a few times after… the crew were great too! We were playing footie once — Crazyhead v Crew, and I broke a huge crew member's nose, or maybe just a nosebleed after my kick rebounded off the lights and smashed him in the face. He was really cool about it and didn't seem too fussed, and we played on."

Crazyhead were fortunate in that they'd secured support slots on two fairly major tours in the space of a couple of months without even having to "buy on" them. Many bands starting out find themselves in the unenviable position of having to pay their way onto larger tours, to hopefully gain exposure. Porkbeast says Cope himself asked for Crazyhead to support him on that tour, but that they also had to share support with The Faith Brothers. They were "nice guys," says Porky. "We took the piss relentlessly. They were quickly christened the Goose Brothers. Goose was a generic label at the time, for some reason probably linked to that Norman Wisdom sex movie *What's Good for the Goose* that also spawned Screaming Apple [a track that appeared on the B-side of Crazyhead's 12-single, Rags]."

Porkbeast admits that things at this point started to go to their heads. "The first night we had a strop and nearly pulled the tour because Cope's entourage didn't give us enough time to soundcheck. Arrogant or what! It was sorted and we won the crew over pretty soon with our antics. Turning up pissed as farts on scrumpy for the Bristol gig and still playing a blinder won them over!"

As the tour progressed Crazyhead settled down and got into the party spirit of things — drinking lots more scrumpy, magic-marker-ing skulls and crossbones onto their cider containers for amusement's sake, and lots of accompanying onstage banter and piss-taking. Both the audience and crew loved it. But then things literally went to Porkbeast's head at Liverpool Royal Court Theatre when he was floored by an errant... pork pie! Launched less out of malice as it was respect, the miscreant happened to be a Crazyhead fan called Bobby Smith AKA Slime, who recalls the offending pie "impacting against his lumpy forehead. Poor Porkbeast, alas, concentrating hard on his four strings was taken by surprise and knocked to the ground. I must confess that I was horrified for a moment." Thankfully, "Porkbeast staggered to his feet, unhurt, whilst the rest of the band fell about laughing."

Scrumpy aside, Porkbeast arguably helped to nurture Cope's now well-known love of ancient standing stones and all things Neolithic. "Me and Julian got on really well," he says. "I had been into stones since I was 14 and being a bit of an info sponge had read all the books, especially the mystic ones. I was heavily shamanic at the time as well and carried a set of runes with me that I was always using, so we hit it off. I was the expert then, so he was into chatting and I told him lots of stuff... Julian was fascinated, and we had many long conversations on the subject." Porky concludes, "I go to academic conferences these days on the subject, and I'm a keen amateur. But Cope has way surpassed my little hobby. He remembers a story I told him, and it made it into [Cope's book] *The Modern Antiquarian*. The wife and I free camped and had a fire at the Rollright Stones, and the farmer chased us off firing shotguns over our heads. Cunt! I should have bubbled him to the cops."

During the tour, Crazyhead met Cope's manager, Martin 'Cally' Calloman. Cally had been in seventies punk band, The Bears, and cult band, The Tea Set, before moving into A&R and management. He signed Cope to Island, encouraging him out of acid-fried doldrums and reviving his career. Cally had already helped design the cover of the single What Gives You The Idea That You're So Amazing Baby?, and so was familiar with the band. But, following the tour, he was impressed enough to want to handle the band himself, still rudderless in terms of management. Crazyhead had parted ways with Si Ord several months previously due to a disagreement: the band chose to sign with Food Records, whereas Ord had been trying to negotiate a deal with Polydor.

Cally was, and still is, held in great respect by certain members of Crazyhead. Vom says, "We loved him, he really understood what we were all about. So he started being our manager. Him and Balfe used to have these meetings on our

Cally Caloman's post-punk band The Tea Set. Source: The Tea Set Facebook page. Photographer not known.

behalf that always descended into slagging matches; it was funny and pathetic at the same time."

Says Anderson, "Cally was a huge sixties garage and psychedelia fan and did us all loads of great mix tapes with such titles as 'Saucy Jack: A Rock n Roll Opera' from loads of obscure, but great, rock'n'roll from his huge vinyl archives. He had a whole room in his house chock-full of records! Astounding in their breadth of music. Cally also gave us loads of ideas about how to project ourselves as a band, getting each one of us separately to visit his home, where we talked music and image. As I said, a great visionary and talented guy! He showed Porkbeast videos of [actor] John Belushi and encouraged him to act out the demented overweight slob attitude — that wasn't difficult for Porky to adapt to! He told me I should never be seen offstage outside Leicester, so I would tie back my hair and mingle with the crowd in the early days listening to them talking about us, as we watched support bands, which included an early version of Inspiral Carpets, who later hit the charts."

Reverb remembers Cally's involvement with the band: "Cally had ceased to be Cope's manager and for a couple of months worked closer with us as 'manager' but wasn't with us long enough to get involved in the day-to-day running of the band." In summing up, Anderson says, "he helped us loads in a part-time way, and never took a penny for it."

GREBO GURUS

By the spring of 1987, it was apparent to the music press that a scene had emerged, and it began to identify any number of unkempt rag-tag bands that even vaguely projected a mutant biker chic look. Loosely typified by customised scuzzy leathers, denim and army surplus clobber, the bands' influences were eclectic, ranging from sixties garage, psychedelia, seventies heavy rock, thrash metal, punk and even hip-hop. But, while similar in appearance, in many respects, the bands greatly differed musically. In his review of the Bykers at Hammersmith Clarendon in April, Ron Rom referred to the phenomenon as "scum rock". He said, "dirt is now in vogue, bad BO is the new Aramis and greasy, chip pan hair is *essential,*" adding "We're talking scum rock, and Gaye Bykers On Acid with their animal noise and their surf axes tucked under their arms, are a dirtball's dream come true." Alluding to a wider movement, Rom also mentioned Crazyhead and continued: "We can theorise all we like but scum rock is the happening force in Britain in '87... The march of the smellies, with Crazyhead leading the way, will invade every neighbourhood in the country over the next 12 months, introducing to a new, spotty generation the joys of wild living."

On this evidence, the tag 'grebo' might just as easily have ended up being 'scum rock'. It came to be known as 'grebo', thanks, in no small part, to a music press eager to create the next big thing. James Brown, then a music paper scribe (at the time still some years away from being founder and editor of *Loaded* magazine), explains that 'grebo' "was an old word used as an insult for rockers or grease boys — 'gre-bo' — I found it on a track called 'Oh Grebo I Think I Love You' by Pop Will Eat Itself... I can't remember how it became a 'genre' but I did help

Photo courtesy of Mick Mercer.

Robber Byker at the Limelight Club, London, 17th May 1987.

James Brown, Sounds journalist and 'grebo' champion, and Beattie Bundle. Limelight Club, London, 17th May 1987.

promote it a bit because it seemed that with Crazyhead, Bomb Party, Pop Will Eat Itself, Zodiac [Mindwarp], and the Bykers, there were suddenly a clutch of bands with essentially greasy long hair and a load of noisy rock, who weren't metal." At the end of 1987 another *Sounds* journalist, Jack Barron, suggested the origin of the 'grebo' name was somewhat more prosaic. He might have had his tongue in his cheek, but he dismissed the Poppies' Oh Grebo I Think I Love You as the point of its resurgence. Said Barron, "Personally, I think it dates from two years back when I was interviewing The Bomb Party and Edwin Pouncey walked past and announced 'You look like a bunch of heavy duty bikers. Greboes.' At the time Mary Chunder-Lips-Star-Tripper-Golightly-On-Acid was The Bomb Party's roadie!" Regardless of how, when or where, James Brown must take a good deal of the responsibility for popularising the term. Following an interview with the Bykers in *Sounds* entitled 'Beer and Loathing on the Grebo Trail', he used the term five times, cementing the 'grebo' label.

Stuart Maconie points the finger at his erstwhile *NME* colleague, James Brown, too. In his 2004 memoir, *Cider With Roadies*, he describes how, having been headhunted from *Sounds*, Brown's recruitment had raised more than a few eyebrows among the *NME* staff:

There was a feeling among the older guard that there was something

crass and anti-intellectual about him. For one thing, he was at this point defiantly and unashamedly championing a style of music that he had invented and then christened grebo. The very name — Midlands slang for unwashed biker types — appalled some of the paper's ancient regime. Then there were the bands. Essentially, they were unwashed biker types from the Midlands: Pop Will Eat Itself, the Wonder Stuff, Crazyhead, Gaye Bykers On Acid. They made lairy dance pop and greaser rock for provincial tykes and James was keen on putting one or all of them on the cover at every opportunity. This disturbed those sections of the paper that wished things to continue as they had done for most of the middle eighties, where ideally each week's cover would feature Nick Cave and his new soundtrack to a Werner Herzog movie set in Berlin.

Although all manner of bands had the 'grebo' label foisted on them, geographically it was the Midlands that came to be associated with the name. As Brown points out, "Simply because of their hair length, lack of stylistic pretension and roughly similar geographic locations — the Midlands — it was easy to put the Bykers, The Poppies and Crazyhead into one group and call them a Grebo scene." Brown adds, "I'd never even heard that term [grebo] before hearing it in the titles of two Poppies songs. I knew there weren't huge gangs of new pop rock loving grebos roaming the land like mods, punks, rockabillies and rockers had when I was at school in the late seventies but it just gave me something fun to write about. I don't think it ever occurred to some readers who didn't like bands being grouped together that my freelance colleagues and I at *Sounds* were pretty skint young writers trying to make a living and 'inventing' a scene, as I was accused of, was just another way of getting to write more about bands we liked."

Brown's final words on the matter: "Something else I don't think some cynical readers ever understood. Sometimes you would want to write about bands because you liked the people more than just the music. And Mary and I got on really well. I liked him a lot — he was good fun. That's why I liked them apart from the look and the front, just Mary's personality."

The Poppies were at first a traditional guitar-led indie pop outfit, somewhere between Jesus and Mary Chain and Buzzcocks. In May 1986, their first EP *The Poppies Say GRRrrr!* was released. It contained five chunks of plucky, but perfectly formed indie pop punk, the lyrics topped with a large dollop of schoolboy humour. It was irreverent to the last, befitting the reputation the Poppies were earning for themselves in the music press. It was ironic that, despite disavowing the new label vociferously, the Leicester bands would come to define so-called

Bring on the frontmen: Mary Byker (Gaye Bykers on Acid), Andy 'Jesus' Mosquera (Bomb Party) and Anderson (Crazyhead).

'grebo', arguably more so than the band that had effectively coined the term. These bands could not know the media whirlwind that awaited them throughout the rest of 1987 and 1988, which would ensure the Bykers, Crazyhead, and Poppies would become synonymous with 'grebo'.

Anderson recalls the time he realised 'grebo' had begun to stick: "It may have been when James Brown did that *NME* piece about Gaye Bykers On Acid, Pop Will Eat Itself, and us," he says. "Pop Will Eat Itself used it a bit I think before that. When we were in London, James Brown was always hanging round licking Mary's arse and laughing and marvelling at all he said and did whether it was funny, or clever, or not. I thought he was a slimy character, like that Seething Wells tosser. Crazyhead didn't like either of them. I've been told they are both good guys by people I trust, but we didn't like them." Anderson pauses. "Didn't James Brown become a millionaire from that stupid *Loaded* magazine?"

For some the tag still rankles. Anderson continues: "Grebo is a pretty derogatory Midlands term for a weedy biker type from the seventies who *hasn't* got a motorbike. The publicity really helped us at first, but we were fucked up later by that tag, even though the Bykers, and especially the Poppies, escaped from it easier, I feel. We were always more a sixties or seventies garage punk band, but in the late eighties — listen to the music!"

Contrary, Mary Byker is in no doubt that Brown's media creation of 'grebo' helped them. Of the Poppies, the Bykers, and then Crazyhead, releasing singles in relatively quick succession, he says, "That was sort of when James Brown caught hold of it and then made this 'grebo' thing... that really propelled it. He was very much instrumental... I mean, people slag him off — 'He called you "grebos!" — but really without that, it wouldn't have happened quite so fast, I don't think. It *might* have happened anyway because we were already gathering momentum, but it was just like he saw something he could put a label to and create a movement, which was the kind of thing they [music journalists] used to do at the time."

Even the veteran disc jockey John Peel got in on the act, although he did stop short of using the name 'grebo' in a live review of the Bykers at The Garage in Nottingham at the end of May. Writing in the *Observer* on 6th June, Peel began his review, entitled 'Superscruffs', with more than a whiff of sarcasm:

1987 has seen the rise in popularity, perhaps in justified reaction against those sickly, sweet bands which meet in suburban bedrooms to write songs about peppermints, of a new generation of superscruffs, musicians eager to be styled 'bad boys of rock and roll', determined to let it be known that they have no hesitation in saying boo to a goose, anxious to give the impression of an easy familiarity of motorcycle maintenance.

Citing Zodiac Mindwarp as forerunners of this "superscruff" musical movement, he stressed the Bykers were "coming up fast on the inside". Peel commented that the relatively small crowd on the night of the gig largely consisted of "the painstakingly disreputable", and, for all of Peel's championing of experimental and leftfield music, including punk, it seems he never really understood the Gaye Bykers. In a gig bedevilled by sound problems, he said that it sounded like the Bykers were repeating the same songs at least twice in succession. However, they "rather wonderfully played a song from the all-but-forgotten catalogue of the Edgar Broughton Band". In a charitable mood, he said that he would be "delighted to see the Gaye Bykers, their studied muckiness, and dishevelled followers take centre-stage for a few months" as an alternative to the rampant celebrations to mark the twentieth anniversary of the release of *Sgt. Pepper's Lonely Hearts Club Band*. Peel concluded his review with the caveat, "If I was 16 and bored stiff, they would be the band for me and I would not worry about the incoherence of their live set."

It was clear that the Bykers weren't really Peel's cup of tea, further evidenced in the fact they were never invited to record a session for his radio show — except in a circumstance of mistaken identity just over two years later. More later.

Photo courtesy of Sally Jones.

Big Zap promotional photo, spring 1987.

At around this time, Mary Byker, Sarah Corina from The Bomb Party, Craig 'Hoppy' Hope, and Dentover, both from The Janitors, formed a side project called Big Zap! Aided and abetted on keyboards and production by Steve McIntosh, from one of the UK's leading soul bands at the time, The Cool Notes, they set about reworking The Temptations' classic Psychedelic Shack. It wasn't quite an entirely Leicester collaboration but one forged over a mutual love of Tamla Motown music, and a drinking session in the pub one lunchtime. The fruits of their endeavours would emerge later that summer.

PIN-UPS

By now, Crazyhead, and the Bykers, along with Pop Will Eat Itself, had begun to grace the covers of the music weeklies. Crazyhead made their first *Sounds* cover on 4th April, while the Bykers adorned it on 2nd May 1987. The headline proclaimed 'Gaye Bykers On Acid Picking Up The Tab: Interview Inside'. They looked every inch "like something that has dropped out of Judge Dredd's bottom", as James Brown would describe them in the interview. He also referred to the Bykers as "culture mongrels", before reeling off an exhaustive list of popular culture characters and groups that the Bykers had cited during their conversation with him. The list included, "Salvador Dalì, New Order, Tom Wolfe, Oliver Reed, Hunter S Thompson, The Pet Shop Boys, Fungus The Bogeyman, Jimmy Stewart, Jimi Hendrix, Max Ernst, Judge Dredd, Kurt Vonnegut Jr., Ozzie Osbourne, Peter Gabriel, Ian [sic] Banks, Ray Lowry, Bobby Sands, Jimmy Tarbuck, Crazyhead, Tom Jones, Frank Miller, Philip K Dick, Frank Zappa, The Furry Freak Brothers, Age of Chance and Michael Aspel."

Brown said, "Like most of the other disease-ridden grebo worms falling out of the Midlands, the Bykers feel they have not the right to preach but a duty to entertain." He recounted that it had taken nearly an hour to get beyond the schoolboy banter about "homosexual band orgies, and recalling the amounts of drugs and women they were doing when they first met". He then cited Mary's professed admiration for Salvador Dalì and the great surrealist's fascination with excreta, sex and Dalì's fantasy to sodomise his father on his deathbed. An off-colour exchange between Mary, Tony and Robber ensued about IRA hunger striker Bobby Sands, before returning to

Crazyhead's first major music press cover, Sounds, 4th April 1987. Photo by Russell Young.

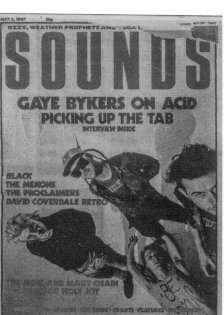

Gaye Bykers On Acid's first major music press cover, Sounds, 2nd May 1987. Photo by Peter Anderson.

Dali's scatological predilections. This apparent preoccupation with all matters faecal and other juvenile frivolity belied intelligence and self-belief, not to mention a rapier wit that many journalists would fail to comprehend at their peril during the coming months. Brown, perhaps more than anyone, was astute enough to understand the Bykers from the off, even if he didn't champion them for too long. He knew that what made them "triumph over their weedy peers in the bowl-headed land of anorak pop [was] through their characters." He admired them, and recognised their self-deprecation as their strength: "they'll ridicule themselves before they'll attack others, they won't get embarrassed when they admit their parents own swimming pools and villas in Spain, and they'll thrive on the fact they are genuinely uncool."

Brown concluded his interview by nailing home the 'grebo' message one more time: "In a year's time Gaye Bykers On Acid will either be presenting *Blue Peter* or serving time on obscenity charges. In the meantime this goofy bunch of sex morons are going to chain whip your parents, rape your big brothers and penetrate your eardrums with their heavy hippy hop metal krush grooves. Get hip to some beer and loathing on the grebo campaign trail." The die had well and truly been cast.

Gaye Bykers On Acid and Crazyhead were featured in the same issue of *Melody Maker* on 9th May. Both bands were interviewed by the Stud Brothers — Dom and Ben — well known for their acerbic comments and caustic style of journalism. Perhaps the Stud Brothers' reputation preceded them because the Bykers were somewhat more truculent and facetious than usual. Stating that the Bykers had "a reputation for being stroppy" at the outset wasn't the best of starts. The Stud Brothers continued in much the same light: "The Gaye Bykers dress like Martin Amis' punks of the post-apocalypse. We were reliably informed that they also smell appalling but, as we'd been exchanging a cold for the last few weeks, we were obliged to ask whether they were really dirty, smelly and horrible."

The Stud Brothers were keen to highlight a tendency for a current crop of bands to exhume rock music's illustrious past, "ex-punks who belligerently amplify guitars under the names of The Cult, The Mission, Zodiac Mindwarp and Crazyhead to mention but a few." They went on to describe Crazyhead as "a bastardised version of the white-faced, sunken-eyed rock'n'roll gypsy" whose music was "loud, brash and pleasure-seeking." Crazyhead, they wrote, "look like a group, the way The Rolling Stones unconsciously decided groups should look."

The piece continued in much the same vein, with the Stud Brothers pointing out that despite Crazyhead objecting to being ghettoised, they were "happy with the attention it's earned them." The band's "schizophrenia", noted the

Gaye Bykers On Acid Melody Maker photo session, 16th April 1987.

Stud Brothers, was predictable but also pardonable. Crazyhead were said to be handicapped by their own sincerity and "have a visible, audible purity that only the innocent and the honest can possess". Charitably, they conceded that, "Crazyhead are as revivalist as Coca-Cola Classic and therefore as new. They deserve to be as popular".

The issue of contemporary 1980s rock and indie bands appropriating sixties and seventies music was something of a hot topic. In his review of a Bykers' gig at The Clarendon in Hammersmith that April, Ron Rom observed the cross-section of subcultures and youth factions from different eras: "Hell's Angels with their leathers and oily denims, punks with blue mohicans and studded belts and hippies with long beads and tabs of acid. They merged together into the nastiest mishmash of wild abandonment I've seen in a long time." At the end of May, *Melody Maker* also ran a feature called 'Rock Of Ages' in which various members of Gaye Bykers, Crazyhead, Bomb Party, Batfish Boys, sixties psychedelic revivalists Voodoo Child, goth rockers Rose of Avalanche, and All About Eve, went head-to-head in a summit chaired by *Melody Maker* scribe Mick Mercer. Mercer was primarily concerned with the escalating trend for bands to exhume and regurgitate aspects of 1960s and seventies rock, as if punk had never happened. There was also a sixties psychedelic revival in full swing, largely centred on the Alice In Wonderland club. Coupled with the ever-increasing popularity of goth, it was inevitable there would be some comparison with the 'grebo' upstarts.

Phil Morris of Rose of Avalanche found the association with the 'grebo' scene "appalling" and was vocal in his dismissal of the Bykers and Crazyhead, accusing them of "reverting back to shit punk, not even good punk". Mary Byker took it all in his stride, countering such accusations with "You know what 'shit' means? It's a Freudian message for gold." Mercer acknowledged the merits of the bands and yet was disparaging at the same time. "All good things come to those who hate," he wrote. "Take a good look at what's happening and marvel at what a hopelessly lacklustre 'happening' it is…"

If music critics were divided on the merits of a propensity to pillage rock music's illustrious heritage, it was certainly hard to ignore the Bykers or Crazyhead. By now, thanks in no small part to music journo James Brown using the tag at any opportunity, 'grebo' was gaining common currency throughout the music press. The major record labels couldn't fail to notice the increasing media scrum and, after courting several majors, the Bykers signed to Virgin for a six-figure sum.

Photo courtesy of Sally Jones.

Gaye Bykers On Acid – signing to Virgin, 5th June 1987.

VIRGIN MARY

Even if the Bykers weren't everybody's cup of tea, there was certainly a great deal of interest in them. Mary recalls that "CBS were sniffing around, and there were various other labels interested too". Virgin were eager to get a piece of the so-called 'grebo' action. "We liked the idea of Virgin because of the Sex Pistols," says Mary. "I think that was the bottom line, it was like 'Oh yeah, the Sex Pistols were on Virgin' and because we kind of came from that punk sort of background... and Virgin really was more of a musicians label... they had a better back catalogue and they had some pretty cool old psychedelic stuff, and there was a history. You thought at least maybe they actually *liked* that kind of music." He continues, "I think Simon Draper, the guy who ran the label, was into that slightly psychedelic kind of stuff, so yeah, we went with them. And I think our big pitch was that we wanted to make a film as well. And so Stacey's [Lafront] big mouth... she sure had a big mouth, she talked the talk, but she pissed a lot of people off, but I think she just went in and did the deal — great!"

WHEELER DEALING

The deal was actually brokered by Hedd Records, a subsidiary of Virgin, run by Ian Grant and Alan Edwards. They also ran a PR agency, Modern Publicity, managing The Cult and Big Country, and representing the likes of Blondie, The Rolling Stones, and David Bowie. Lafront had already done business with Grant and Edwards when she secured a support slot for the band on The Cult's *Electric* tour a few months

Meet me at the crossroads... Mary Byker signing to Virgin, 5th June 1987.

Photo courtesy of Sally Jones.

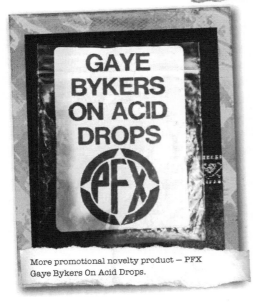

More promotional novelty product — PFX
Gaye Bykers On Acid Drops.

earlier. With Stacey perhaps playing the various labels off against each other, Virgin were seemingly anxious not to let them slip away and signed them on 5th June for just over £100,000, and agreed to the terms allowing the Bykers to use their own Purple Fluid Exchange (PFX) label. The label had been mooted as early as 1986 when Stuart Bailie spoke of the band's grand ambitions to the *Record Mirror*.

Mary explained the reasoning behind PFX to Paul Narvaez and Jackie Zahn of *B-Side* magazine: "If we're going into corporate business, we decided we'd have our own corporate identity. We have it on our records. We wanted to do toothbrushes, wash and brush-up kits and lunch boxes. I'm taking the piss out of American marketing, that was the idea."

Robber recalls that the label name came first and that the band "wanted to use it for something, so we came to Virgin and we said, 'Can we have like our own label, stick our own labels on the records and stuff, rather than having the Virgin label?' and they said, 'Oh yeah, you can do that. Whatever!'"

Having their own label under Virgin didn't give the Bykers total control over what was released. More crucially, perhaps, the band and Stacey got Virgin to agree to fund a film, one of their long-time aspirations. Even before signing to Virgin, the Bykers had ambitions for making a movie, and to some extent also appearing in one. Talking to *Melody Maker*, Mary insisted, "I do like to be taken seriously as an artist though, I really *do* want to be a method actor when I grow up. I want to be an actor just like in the tradition of rock'n'roll. Do a bad film."

Today, Mary reaffirms the band's movie ambitions by explaining how the Bykers had always been into keeping themselves busy, painting, drawing, and making music. To make a movie "was a logical extension". Little did they know at the time, this would have far-reaching repercussions.

Gaye Bykers On Acid at The Venue, Edinburgh, June 1987, "only tempered by the news that Margaret Thatcher was on course to be voted into power for a third successive term of office."

Photo by Jan. Source: The Edinburgh Gig Archive

THE LAST TOILET TOUR

On signing to Virgin, the Bykers embarked on The Last Toilet tour that had been arranged by Stacey. The tour name was a wry comment on the state of many of the venues they were playing, as well as a hint at being on the verge of hitting the big time, so to speak. Supported by The Bomb Party, the tour began on 3rd June at the Woolwich Tramshed in London and concluded nearly a month later at Hammersmith Clarendon.

The UK General Election was a backdrop to the tour. Penny Kiley, reviewing a Bykers' gig at Liverpool Planet X for *Melody Maker*, was not buying into the hype, even if much of the music press and bigwigs were. Kiley opened her review: "You've got to laugh. On the eve of an election, what can you take seriously? More noise?" She wasn't impressed by the irony of the Bykers coming onstage to the strains of Tom Jones' It's Not Unusual belting out through the PA, and exiting to Delilah, also by the raunchy Welsh crooner. Her disapproval continued: "This group are offensive only to the inner ear. Hurtful only to guitars, which swirl and scream and batter and laugh in a controlled incompetence. Music that's crawled from under a pebble, in the shadow of the greats (Dolls, Stooges, Cave, Morrison)."

The Bykers' reaction to this po-faced summation is not recorded. But likely they would have delighted in it. On election night itself, the band played a storming gig at the Venue in Edinburgh, albeit the post-gig party was tempered by the news that Margaret Thatcher was on course to be voted into power for a third successive term of office. After finishing the Scottish leg of their tour, the next date was in Cardiff. On the way to Wales, they dropped in on Ray Lowry in Manchester, to discuss the storyboard for their film, the reality of which was becoming much more tangible having signed to Virgin.

The highlight of the tour surely had to be when the Bykers attended the Glastonbury festival for the weekend and played the second stage on Sunday afternoon.

GLASTONBURY

The 'grebo' triumvirate of Crazyhead, Gaye Bykers on Acid and Pop Will Eat Itself made an appearance at that Glastonbury festival in the summer of 1987. Crazyhead played the second stage on Thursday, which was the day before the official opening of the festival. According to one account, Porkbeast had clods of mud hurled at him throughout the entire set. Anderson recalls, "Yeah, there was lots of mud. We hit Stage 2 after a long trip, including being stopped by cops and searched. Fast Dick and I were on snakebites and a bottle of whiskey, Dick said, 'I've hidden 200 tabs of acid in my arse' and was promptly strip searched nearby! I think someone got busted for personal whizz, but I forget who, I could be wrong. There were about 2,000-plus people watching, mainly sat down, one of the best gigs ever. I said, 'Wake up you dirty hippies and take some speed. If you like us, dance, if you don't, throw things — we thrive on reaction!'"

Anderson continues, "A few people danced, including some mohawk glue heads. Mud, bottles, cans — we were dodging all kinds of shit being thrown. I was being all pantomime yelling, 'Missed!' loads of times, being a cock really, huge ego on speed and booze. Then a huge clod of mud hit me in the face, and the largest applause of the gig went up from the crowd! Mic stands were kicked over by Dick. We came off to huge applause, pumped up high on adrenaline amongst other things, only to meet the head of Stage 2 threatening us, saying we smashed his gear up. We denied it. He said, 'I just saw you do it.' He and Dick squared up at each other, Reverb tried to break it up, but the guy went for Rev and got a 'Reverb handshake' — a headbutt sending him down. He disappeared

One part of the 'grebo' triumvirate: The Bykers backstage at Glastonbury, 1987.

very fast. Then every other member of the stage crew came and shook our hands, and said he was a dick and deserved it! Oh yeah, I forgot to say one of the glue head mohawks invaded the stage and grabbed the mic. I thought about bottling him, as he was huge and I had a bottle of whiskey in my other hand, but the crew got him finally. Glad I didn't, not nice, and an audience of 2,000 witnesses, not cool behaviour. I was a useless fighter anyway!"

Among those "2,000 witnesses" was a budding actor called Simon Pegg, who was not only attending Glastonbury for the first time but also experienced his first acid trip that weekend, too. Making it his mission to see "as many bands as possible, the future *Shaun Of The Dead* and *Star Trek* actor says in his autobiography, *Nerd Do Well*, "Crazyhead were amazing!"

Pegg doesn't say if he also saw Gaye Bykers On Acid that weekend, but Crazyhead hung out and stayed to see their Leicester compadres play the second stage on Sunday evening. Earlier that same afternoon, the Poppies also played a set. Coming on after the MC had announced, "OK grebo fans, please welcome Pop Will Eat Itself," the Poppies launched into Oh Grebo I Think I Love You. Clint Mansell replaced the 'grebo' chant in the song with the word "hippies". As if in confirmation that 'grebo' was now something of a phenomenon, the Poppies played another number from their canon — Grebo Guru. And no Poppies set at this time would have been complete without a cover of Hawkwind's Orgone

Photo courtesy of Sally Jones.

Mary Byker "putting on an exaggerated drippy hippy-dippy accent like Neil from The Young Ones," Glastonbury 1987.

Accumulator, somewhat fitting given the festival's origins.

Once again, the Bykers came on stage to Tom Jones' It's Not Unusual. Mary was in fine fettle, motormouthing as usual, and greeting the crowd with an ironic and none too subtle, "Helloooo Stonehenge, yeeeeah! Let's hear you shout yeah, yeah, yeah!" and launched into the countdown for set-opener Space Rape. He baited the audience between numbers throughout the set, throwing in references to Woodstock, and comments like "fuck the sixties!" Mary continued to play the devil's advocate. Halfway through Dog (AKA Tolchocked By Kenny Pride), which he dedicated to "every dead pop star that died in the bath, with a barbiturate overdose," he verbally attacked a couple of rock's sacred cows, whose affections would have been close to the heart of a cross-section of those watching — "Jim Morrison was as wanker 'cos he's dead, [he] was as much a wanker as Sid Vicious…"

Mary teased the audience by asking, "Do you honestly think what we're doing here now is going to ban the bomb?" and, in an exaggerated drippy hippy accent, like that of Neil in The Young Ones, "like if we all grow our hair really long?" This could have been interpreted as a sleight against CND, the main beneficiaries of the festival in those days, but it was probably more a case of drunken badinage rather than any malicious intent. Sounds summed things up neatly: "Classic festival material (bored middle-class brats), the Bykers, embrace the stuff of psychedelic legend but kick the whole thing into cartoon dimensions and spend the time mocking its transience."

Musically, the band wasn't as tight as they had proved they could be. Hardly surprising, given the temptations frequently afforded by festivals back in those days. A group of skateboarding punks from Bristol (who ran a fanzine called The Skate Muties From The 5th Dimension) and friends of the Bykers, happened to be working security at that year's festival. They introduced the Bykers to numerous flagons of strong scrumpy cider. According to Mary, the 'Muties' were daring everyone to drink the West Country gut rot. "It was pretty strong, so we got completely out of it to be honest."

Drunk as as well as chemically enhanced, the Bykers rose to the occasion. Despite Mary's hippy-baiting comments, the Bykers owed as much to their 1960s and seventies festival forebears as they did to contemporary sources. Befitting a festival steeped in rich counterculture heritage, the band deviated into elongated jams worthy of their Hawkwind and Edgar Broughton Band influences, particularly on the track, Edgar. Here, Mary howled and growled (as much in imitation of Edgar Broughton's vocal delivery as Broughton's was in honour of Captain Beefheart's), whilst Tony's

Robber Byker, in best, wasted, Sid Vicious pose, backstage at Glastonbury, 1987.

Photo courtesy of Sally Jones.

guitar spewed out swathes of heavy psychedelic wah wah across an audience that Mary had spent the last half-hour insulting — who were as dumbstruck as they were in awe. *Sounds* summed the performance up: "Gaye Bykers On Acid are boredom breaking out into brilliance and a parody of festival history. This'll do for now... this is the end of civilisation as we know it."

A couple of days after Glastonbury, the Bykers rounded off the Last Toilet tour. On the penultimate night, they played a venue called Central Park in Burton On Trent. Mark 'Wag' Wagstaff had been following the Bykers round the country for some months and had a got to know the band well, to the extent that he landed a job driving for The Bomb Party. He remembers, "You know what the scene was like with the Bykers and all the dancing. It was all a bit roughneck, people throwing each other around and all that kind of stuff, and the bouncers at this club in Burton weren't really prepared for that. So they got a bit rough with us, but this one guy walked all the way home and got a starting pistol and reappeared at the gig and shot me in the groin with it!"

Why the wronged punter took his revenge on Wag is anybody's guess.

Mary and Tony Byker, 1987.

Although not seriously injured, the blast from the starting pistol was powerful enough to make a hole in his leather trousers. When Wag aired his grievance about the assault to the already antsy club bouncers, he received a beating for his trouble and was thrown downstairs. Stacey Lafront was adamant that the police should be called and she, Wag, and the Bykers, all gave statements. Wag returned to Burton to give evidence a few months later, where the individual wielding the starting pistol was found guilty of assault. The bouncers were acquitted.

The night after Burton was the tour finale, and the Bykers were back at the Klub Foot at the Hammersmith Clarendon in west London, with support from new labelmates the Blood Uncles, Bomb Party, and the 8-Track Cartridge Family. Tellingly, where once the Bykers and Crazyhead had supported the likes of The Bomb Party and The Janitors, the roles were now reversed. Mary had gone from being a roadie for The Bomb Party, to a frontman of a band in his own right. Furthermore, it was a band that now topped the bill. Mary says, "The classic thing for me was the Hammersmith Clarendon, which was always a great gig, usually with four bands on. One night we supported the Leather Nun. I think we were bottom of the bill, and The Bomb Party were second from top… but then, in the space of about four or five months, we went from bottom of the bill, to second, to headlining. For us that was like a gauge of success, headlining in London at this place which was an 800 or 900 capacity venue."

Things were also moving along with the album. Soon after signing to Virgin, and throughout The Last Toilet tour, the hunt had been on for someone to produce their debut long-player. Mary remembers how they "nearly ended up with Slaughter Joe, you know Alan McGee's friend?" Slaughter Joe was more than a just a friend of McGee's, though. Along with McGee and Dick Green, he founded Creation Records in 1983, and had a hand in producing The Jesus and Mary Chain, Primal Scream and My Bloody Valentine, amongst others. Mary says that Slaughter Joe "would have been a spot of genius… or not. But it did seem

like he was too out to lunch, but yeah loads of people's names were mentioned…"

One of the other names was Howard Gray. Gray had been an engineer at Virgin's prestigious Townhouse Studios, working with renowned producer Steve Lilywhite, before going on to produce the likes of UB40, Simple Minds, and Terence Trent D'Arby. He was a sampling pioneer, having used the Studio 440 sequencer with rock/dance crossover act Age of Chance, contemporaries of the Bykers and Pop Will Eat Itself. Mary enthuses how "Howard was great. He was on the list of people to produce the first Bykers' album… but for some reason our destiny didn't go there." Also on the shortlist was Rick Rubin, the founder of Def Jam Records and a producer of some renown whose clients included Public Enemy, Beastie Boys, Run DMC and Slayer. He had also recently produced The Cult's *Electric* album. Another candidate was Rick Browde, but unlike Rubin, he was more known for his involvement with the glam side of the American rock scene, and had produced Poison's multi-platinum album *Look What The Cat Dragged In* the previous year. Tony Byker recalls that "It was all very annoying trying to decide about a producer."

Making the decision was made all the more frustrating because the A&R man at Virgin, Andy Woodford, was more interested in going off to play squash, according to Mary. Woodford, he says, would be sitting at his desk swishing his squash racket around, itching to be on the court. The Bykers would suggest potential producers and Woodford would agree to contact them. Two days later they'd get the reply, "He's not available." In the end, the band plumped for Alex Fergusson. Fergusson had co-founded post-punk band Alternative TV with Mark Perry of *Sniffin' Glue* fanzine in 1977, and later went on to form Psychic TV with Genesis P-Orridge, after proto-industrial experimentalists Throbbing Gristle had split up. Fergusson had produced an Alternative TV live album, and a smattering of singles mainly connected to the Scottish indie record label, Postcard. The Gaye Bykers' album would be his first major production job… and his last.

The Bykers, now rehearsing for the forthcoming album, *Drill Your Own Hole*, had to familiarise themselves with the technology Fergusson and Philipp Erb, the programmer, had in mind. Two days after the Last Toilet Tour climaxed at the Hammersmith Clarendon, they decamped to Spaceward Studios in Cambridge. The Bykers weren't particularly focused. Robber says, "We were meant to be writing songs for the album, but basically we sat around getting off our heads." One account suggests the band spent more time playing pranks on studio cleaners and bringing local girls back from the village pub than getting to grips with the samplers Fergusson had hoped to utilise on the album. A visit from the *NME*'s Gavin Martin illustrates the point:

Source: Punk Music Catalogue. Photographer not known.

Alternative TV, featuring 'Drill Your Own Hole' producer Alex Fergusson (2nd from left). 1977.

… attempts have been made to incorporate the technology of the future into the band. For the practice sessions at Spacewood [sic] they hired, at considerable expense, a sampling machine. Now 10 days later, it lies, still a source of bemusement, largely unused.

'We couldn't really work it out; we wanted to sample TV themes and excerpts from the news.'

'There's this one here but that's just you making burping and farting noises.'

And that's all you got out of it?

'Yeah, half a grand for a burp and a fart.'

I'M NOT AMERICAN YET BUT WHAT A STATE I'M IN

It was around this time that the fruits of the Big Zap! sessions were released. The music press didn't miss the opportunity to refer to the project as the "world's first grebo supergroup". The name was derived from Mary and Sarah's housecat, Zappa, who, Sarah told *NME's* Steven Wells, had been named after "legendary

Vietnam chopper pilot and marijuana smuggler Frank 'Zapper' Harris". The record itself was a cover of The Temptations' Motown classic, Psychedelic Shack. Despite being described by Wells as "crap, the world's worst greeb track ever" it isn't actually that bad a remake, featuring a big sound with a pummelling bass and driving guitars. Recorded at Hollywood Studios in Birmingham, and produced by keyboard player Steve McIntosh, it was backed by a self-composition called Zap Attack. It also serves as an early recorded example of Mary's rapping, a freestyle rhyme that makes reference to the band members. It may not have been as immediately appealing as the A-side but it is an interesting Bykers-related release.

Extracurricular activities such as Big Zap! were seen by some in the band as another example of Mary's increasing appetite for attention, and nothing more than gratuitous self-aggrandisement, a detriment to the band. Robber said in 2013, "I love Mary, but he sure did wind me up with all that bollocks... We wanted commitment for the band first, turn up to rehearsals on time... if at all sometimes. It got so bad that we rehearsed stops in the songs so it made him look like a cunt on stage. I think he got the message after a few live numbers! The only thing he turned up for was a press interview on time... or a poxy photo shoot!"

In mid-July, the band jetted off to New York for a prestigious gig supporting The Cult, at the Felt Forum Theatre, Madison Square Gardens. Hastily arranged by The Cult's management, Hedd Records in the wake of signing the Virgin deal, it was only a whirlwind visit, as part of the New Music Seminar being held at various venues throughout the city. Apart from Mary, none of the Bykers had visited the United States before, so naturally there was an element of trepidation. Tony recalls butterflies in his stomach, but was excited nevertheless, despite being "hungover and feeling shit on the way to the airport". Arriving in the US, manager Stacey Lafront had difficulty keeping the band together at check-in. To maintain their equilibrium on the flight over, they had washed down Valium with Blue Label

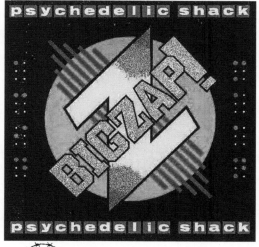

"World's first grebo supergroup" – Cover of Big Zap! 'Psychedelic Shack'.

In yer face! Tony and Mary Byker, 1987.

Smirnoff vodka, and puffed away on cigarettes (smoking was still permitted — even on planes!). Tony recalls, "It was hot when we arrived. The initial blast of humid air when we exited the airport was overwhelming and awaiting us was our white carriage — our very first limousine ride. That was quite something, hanging out of the windows and sunroof!" Given the Bykers' streetwise image and raggedy clothes, they still stood out like wide-eyed tourists. According to Tony, "We couldn't help but look upwards at the skyscrapers while walking down the street, a sure-fire giveaway that we were freshers, paranoid of all the potential pickpockets and muggers."

Tony still found time to take a bite out of the Big Apple's seamier side. "I remember trying to go on the subway once, but it was pretty shitty down there, so I came back up and got a cab instead," he says. "One night I remember walking down a dark street and then realised I was surrounded by strange freaks in the shadows. I think I found a crack alley."

The stretch limo was the stuff of any aspiring young musicians' wildest rock'n'roll fantasy, and this was no small thing in the second half of the eighties; limousines weren't available for any gaggle of giggling hens or strutting stags to rent on a weekend, as they are now. But what expectations were built up by the luxury ride to the hotel were quickly let down by the hotel itself. Tony remembers the hotel as "a little shabby with cockroaches in the TV, and the air-con and bad

CHAPTER FOUR

Gaye Bykers On Acid. Kev and Tony in the limo. New York City, July 1987.

[TV] shows were on all the time!" He adds, "The drug delivery guy reminded me of that scene in *Taxi Driver*: 'uppers , downers, acid, shrooms, mescaline, weed, hash, coke, crystal meth? what do you need?'... 'er, what's crystal meth? I'd never heard of it until then, so I had to try it. I didn't sleep properly for three days."

The venue for the gig itself was awe-inspiring. "The Forum was huge, very daunting," remembers Tony. "We appeared to be miles away from each other on stage, my amplifier on full blast sounded like a tiny transistor radio, and I couldn't hear anything the others were playing. When Mary walked down the long catwalk at the front of the stage, I almost couldn't see him anymore."

The Bykers had spent the afternoon embellishing cardboard boxes so that they looked like Marshall stacks. They painted on the Marshall logo, and, at the end of their set, proceeded to smash them up. Tony explains, "We knew that The Cult were going to do that [for real], and we thought it rather silly and wasteful."

If the Bykers' last major appearance, at Glastonbury the previous month, had been lacklustre, they were firing on all cylinders for the New Music Seminar. The Felt Forum gig acted as a kind of barometer to measure how far on the scale of rock'n'roll stardom the band had come. Tony recalls the surreal situation backstage. "Stacey Lafront was in her element, talking shit to everyone, flirting with Hedd Records [The Cult's management], and trying to find potential producers for our 'upcoming debut album'. I remember meeting Poison's

Gaye Bykers On Acid and their "very first limousine ride". New York City, July 1987.

producer, who had some grand ideas for our future sound. And there were a few *Spinal Tap* Artie Fufkin Polymer Records, you-guys-are-great-kick-me-in-the-ass types."

Robber was had his own problems backstage. Having scored speed earlier on, he says, "I didn't realise it was meth speed, did a massive line of the stuff and freaked out. I asked Mary to throw the Beastie Boys out the dressing room. When we went onstage somebody threw a bottle at me, it hit me on the head, I carried on playing, I didn't feel a thing! I was awake for four days solid!" Alienating himself from what he called "The Cult crowd," telling the audience that it was stupid to like The Doors when Jim Morrison was dead, Mary was showered with missiles. But while Mary's comments antagonised some quarters of the audience, the Bykers were warmly received by others — as corroborated by Jim Bessman, who wrote in *Sounds*, "if anything, the Bykers' amelodic punkadelia was tight and rhythmic enough to warrant as good a reception as that given to The Cult."

The Bykers arrived back at Heathrow on Friday 17th July, 7:50am local time. Barely able to shake off their jetlag, they were whisked away to Loco Studios in rural Gwent to lay down demos and rehearse for the forthcoming album. Like the session at Spaceward, things didn't quite go to plan. Despite having once snubbed him as a producer for the album, Stacey Lafront had no choice but to call on the services of Jon Langford for the demos, because of his ability to deal with

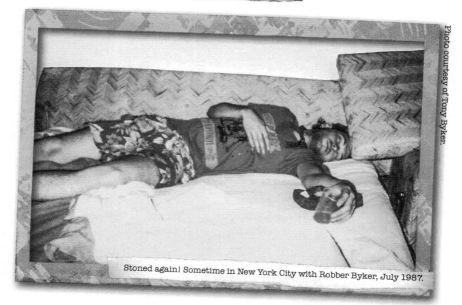

Stoned again! Sometime in New York City with Robber Byker, July 1987.

the Bykers. Langford recalls "this insane manager called Stacey, who wouldn't let me produce the first album for Virgin but would call me in desperation to go down to the demo studio and help them write songs. They were at a place called Loco near my mum's house, nice studio in the countryside where they sat around and did nothing for days on end. I went down there and bought them some beer. I remember seeing Kev miles away in a field cross-legged next to a boom-box as I drove down the lane. We drank the beer and I left them to it."

Less than a week after arriving back from the States, the Bykers were on the front pages again. This time for a "Grebo!" special in the *NME*. James Brown had by now jumped ship from *Sounds* to the *NME* and brought his 'grebo' baby with him. It's unlikely the *NME* would have given these bands such extensive coverage otherwise. The cover was a blaze of eye-catching orange and yellow hues and blonde hair — Tony's and Mary's! From beneath the headline, 'GREBO! "A BURST OF DIRTY THUNDER" GAYE BYKERS ON ACID', Tony stared intently from behind round, reactolight, John Lennon specs, whilst Mary rested his head wearily on his shoulder. It was a photogenic, if hardly 'grebo' defining image. The cover also boasted other 'grebo'-related headlines: 'THE POPPIES' GUIDE TO GREASY GODS' and 'CRAZYHEAD GET LOUD AND LOUSY'. Inside was a page-and-a-quarter Gaye Bykers On Acid interview with Gavin Martin and a tongue-in-cheek feature entitled 'Pop Will Eat Itself's Guide to Grebo'. On

NEW MUSICAL EXPRESS

GREBO!

25 July 1987   50p   US $1.95 (by air)   ISSN 0028 8362

"A BURST OF DIRTY THUNDER"
GAYE BYKERS ON ACID

+ THE POPPIES' GUIDE TO GREASY GODS
+ CRAZYHEAD GET LOUD AND LOUSY

BOY GEORGE WYNTON MARSALIS
PAUL JOHNSON 'NAM COMICS BIG ZAP

"A Burst of Dirty Thunder" Gaye Bykers On Acid cover stars of NME's "Grebo!" special, also featuring Crazyhead getting "Loud and Lousy".

the inside back cover, the satirical Dick Nietzsche column was devoted to 'Ten Things You Want To Know About Mary From Gaye Bykers On Acid', followed by a piss-take quiz ('Are You Grebo?'), in which the scores ranked you as Zodiac Mindwarp, Terence Trent D'Arby or Aled Jones. Elsewhere, James Brown found another opportunity to slip in the g-word, this time in a review of Junior Manson Slags at the 100 Club ('Carry On Grebo'). According to Brown, the band's press release proclaimed that "the Manson Slags exist to take the money that hasn't been wasted on the Bykers and Zodiac". But the centrepiece of the "Grebo!" special was a double-page centrespread. 'Q: Are We Not Men? A: We Are Grebo!' is disdainful and laudatory in equal measure, focusing on the Bykers, Poppies and Crazyhead, evidently considered by Brown a cut above their contemporaries. He considered The Primitives, The Stupids, Bad Dress Sense, Frankfurter to be "all the same band", while Zodiac Mindwarp was "too serious, too worried about his credibility". Brown argued that it was "wit, attitude and personality" that set the triumvirate apart from "the grungy glut of cock-rockers in leathers that are jumping at, but missing, the bandwagon and the point".

If it was possible to ignore 'grebo' before this point, the NME changed all that. Whether you loved 'grebo' or loathed it, there was no escaping it now. The 'grebo' special was something of a watershed, and arguably polarised opinion in the ensuing frenzy that spread like a rash across the pages of the British music press. In the long run, the hype proved detrimental to the reputation of these bands. 🦋

T WASN'T ALL SONGWRITING, RECORDING, AND scriptwriting. The summer was also punctuated by high-profile festivals. During the time they spent at Loco Studios in Wales, the Bykers made the first of two appearances at the Super Tent in Finsbury Park, London, on a bill that included The Fall and Psychic TV with Siouxsie and the Banshees headlining. Despite the presence of Gaye Bykers On Acid at the bottom of the bill, *NME*'s Len Brown seemed relieved that the event was a largely "grebo free zone" predominated as it was by the other bands he referred to as "punk wars vets".

Such was the urgency to cram some final rehearsal and demo time in before they started recording, the band were whisked back to Wales on the same day. They stayed another five days and then returned to London for a long weekend break, prior to turning their attention to the recording of their debut album.

Another trip to Wales was booked, a provisional three weeks from the beginning of August at a different location: Rockfield Studios, near Monmouth. But the studio was changed at the last minute. Maybe they felt they'd already spent

Ad for Under Canvas, the first of two Gaye Bykers On Acid appearances at Finsbury Park Supertent, summer 1987.

far too long in rural environs? Whatever the reason, the actual recording of *Drill Your Own Hole* took place at Orinoco Studios in London, with Alex Fergusson producing, Ken Thomas taking on the engineering duties, and Philipp Erb as programmer. Tony says, "We chose Alex because of his Psychic TV connection, and because he was going to make everything digital, and we liked the idea of becoming more technological. However, we just lost the raw rock edge instead."

The recording sessions were considered a soulless experience. According to Mary, the Bykers were hardly ever in the studio, busy as they were with promotional exercises and executing plans for the forthcoming movie. Previously, the band had all been present and each member provided input at recording sessions, but now they were distracted by other commitments. Each member would arrive at the studio to put their backing tracks or other parts down, before rushing off to other engagements. "We'd come back in three days and Fergusson had already got it done," says Mary. "They [Fergusson, Erb and Thomas] spent a lot of time, what we would say nowadays, doing the engineering production on the computer."

The band's biggest bugbear, especially Kev's, was that Fergusson "kind of took all the drums off and programmed it". The process was new to the band. "We worked with a producer who didn't really know what he was doing, and the technology was really new." Mary says that Fergusson and his production team changed the nature of the band on *Drill* rather than bringing out the best in them: "I think he kind of knew what to do, but I don't think he was particularly experienced himself even. He was, for sure, the wrong guy for that record."

Mary doesn't believe the finger of blame should point entirely at Fergusson and the production team, and that the band must be held accountable for not having monitored the production of the record more closely. He says, "Had we been sitting in the studio all the time there might have been a point where we would've all sat there going, 'do you know what? This sounds shit! This isn't what we really want to hear'. We never had that moment because we weren't really around, which is our own fault as much as anybody's." The band had taken their eyes off the ball, carried away with the media whirlwind and their obsession with making the movie.

Ultimately, Fergusson et al were left to their own devices. They might have been better equipped to understand what the band wanted and coax the best out of them had the Bykers been around more. The results may have been very different. As it turned out, Robber was so disappointed in the final production that he insisted the original version of TV Cabbage (from their first ever demo at 'Mad' Mike Miller's) was included on the album. "I was like, 'I want that track

putting on it!', and I fought for that track, 'cos I thought that's what we were meant to sound like!" The album proved an expensive learning exercise. Mary adds, pointedly, that the band would always be present at recordings that followed, admitting that *Drill* "was a bit of a schoolboy error. We were young and didn't really know what we were doing."

One of the more unlikely songs to emerge from the recording sessions was Afternoon Tea With Dave Greenfield. It's a keyboard drenched piece, similar in style to that of Dave Greenfield, The Stranglers' keyboardist. Pressed on whether Greenfield himself had appeared on the recording, Kev Byker responds enthusiastically:

"Yes indeed, it was the legendary Mr Greenfield. Quite why this happened is a mystery. I think one of the engineers must have known him, and we said for a joke, let's get him in to do a song. Before you know it, the next day he turns up in his Porsche and gets a keyboard out of the boot. I remember him asking what we wanted, and we requested that he play those twiddly keyboard runs he plays on all The Stranglers' songs. Yes, I can do that, he says. After listening to the track for the first time he declares the drums were completely out of time — something I am very proud of still today! But he played it anyway — what a pro — and we named the track thus, even though we never thought he would actually turn up. We were never told just how much he charged us, I imagine it was not a cheap whim at all, but I assume Virgin Records paid it. After that I thought, 'Hey we're on a roll here, can we give Ozzy Osborne a call and see if he will come down and give us a glockenspiel solo on the next track?' Sadly this was not to be!"

Crazyhead meanwhile played a homecoming gig at the Abbey Park Festival, which would become a regular summer event in Leicester for years to come. Anderson recalls the day was somewhat marred when a notorious gang of Leicester City football hooligans called the Baby Squad turned up and "split a few heads". This was a firm of football hooligans, renowned for slashing their victims with Stanley knives. So, it was lucky things were not much worse.

But the pen is sometimes mightier than the sword, or in this case, the Stanley blade. Another kind of Stanley — Bob Stanley, *NME* journalist and future St Etienne band member and musicologist — exacted more harm to Crazyhead than the blades carried by the Baby Squad. Stanley wrote of the gig in context of the violence that had erupted: "To the left and right of me fights are breaking out which prove considerably more interesting than what's happening on stage." To add insult to injury, "As Crazyhead became gradually more pissed off with the lack of response they lurch into Cher's Bang Bang missing out all that song's camp humour".

Crazyhead backstage at Abbey Park festival 1987.

Contrary to Stanley's disparaging review, video footage filmed from the back of the stage proves that Crazyhead were on fire performance-wise, with the crowd boisterously jumping around and moshing furiously to a super-charged version of What Gives You The Idea That You're So Amazing Baby? Cans of industrial strength Tennents Super lager sit conspicuously on the top of a speaker as the camera pans across the back of the band and over the audience. Anderson grabs a can of equally strong Carlsberg Special Brew from the drum riser for a few thirsty gulps. He then turns round to face-off the audience, stock still with his hands behind his back, before becoming animated once more for the final flourishes of the song as it explodes into a sudden

Crazyhead's Anderson at Abbey Park Festival, Leicester, August, 1987.

ending. This is clearly a band at the top of its game, thoroughly enjoying itself.

Despite Stanley, much of the hype in the music press at the time was credible and accurate. Anderson notes that Crazyhead headed to London the day after the Abbey Park Festival. He says, "I remember we headlined two nights at the Marquee club, selling out both nights, with queues round the block. The gigs were like a sweatbox, kids going ape-shit crazy of course, a wild time was had by all. Reverb took care of managing at the time and I'll always remember

Crazyhead's Fast Dick takes a swig of Tennents Super AKA Electric Soup.

walking through a really rough part of Soho full of drunks and lowlifes, just the band and Sparky, Reverb walking down the street counting the £400-odd in gig money in tens and twenties. Lucky there were five leather-clad Crazyheads plus Sparky in his Vietnam *Apocalypse Now* look." Further hijinks ensued when the Crazyhead entourage decided to go on a spray-painting frenzy in central London. Towards the end of the night, Anderson admits to getting into the spirit of things, "completely pissed out of my head," and decorating another wall when a police car screeched up and collared him. The cops berated him for being so conspicuous, therefore forcing them to arrest him when they could have been trying to catch

Crazyhead. Anderson and Vom at the Marquee, August, 1987.

real criminals. Although the police had tried to pin graffiti on Anderson from earlier in the day ("Porkbeast for President" had been sprayed on a wall next to the Houses of Parliament), he was only charged with defacing one wall in the end. Anderson recalls that "the Duty Officer that signed me in the cells proudly told me that he had nicked Topper Headon from The Clash for smack — very proud he was!"

Anderson was released on bail the following morning and the band returned to the Midlands for a gig in Birmingham, before heading up to Scotland for dates in Ayr and Glasgow. The Bykers, meanwhile, still busy with their forthcoming album and preparations for their movie, had been booked to play Acid Daze in Finsbury Park on Saturday 23rd August 1987. This was a celebration of the continued resurgence of psychedelia from the 1960s, as well as featuring music from contemporary bands. Co-promoted by Christian Paris from Alice In Wonderland, the line-up included the Jimi Hendrix-influenced Voodoo Child, Ozric Tentacles, 'grebo' rabble-rousers Pop Will Eat Itself, and the Bykers. The old guard were represented by headliners Hawkwind and the recently reformed Pink Fairies. Bridging the gap between were The Damned, who appeared as their garage band alter ego, Naz Nomad & The Nightmares, with a suitably psychedelically sixties-charged set, peppered with covers of the Electric Prunes' I Had Too Much To Dream (Last Night), Nobody But Me by The Human Beinz, and The Doors' Riders On The Storm.

Mary wistfully recalls Acid Daze and the summer's other festivals: "I do remember feeling quite excited by the whole thing, because it seemed at that point we were really taking off, especially when you start getting onto the bigger

Photo courtesy of Linda Knight.

Robber and Tony backstage at Acid Daze flanked by friends (L-R) Colin Woodland and July Tafy.

stages. It really starts hitting home to you, especially when you're on stage and you're supporting bands like Hawkwind, and obviously even Siouxsie... they were big bands to us, and all of a sudden we're on the same stage as them... You find yourself thinking 'What are we actually doing here?' So, it's a mixture of astonishment, and you get a pretty good feeling about yourself. I don't know if that's good for anybody's ego, but in those early days when everything was going so fast it's all just a buzz."

The event was typically lambasted by the trendier elements of the music press, and the Bykers' set was chaotic and unpredictable — or maybe not for those who had witnessed their performance at Glastonbury. Video footage shot by one of the Bykers' entourage suggests that they got pretty wasted before going on stage, where they were joined by an equally inebriated Clint Mansell from Pop Will Eat Itself. Mansell proceeded to skank away to the Bykers' version of Call Me A Liar by the Edgar Broughton Band with his trousers round his ankles, stopping short of completely going commando by keeping his underpants on. Some accounts likened the event to a "sports day in hell". Indeed it was a sweltering hot afternoon, with very little respite from the summer sun. Even the relative shade of the Super Tent didn't escape the humidity and reeked of sweat, stale booze, and cannabis. The barely adequate portaloos had overflowed by the early afternoon, adding to the unpleasantness.

NME derided the event. David Quantick and Barbara Ellen co-reviewed the day's performances. Quantick disparagingly commented: "Who are these people? Who goes out to see Hawkwind, The Pink Fairies, Pop Will Eat Itself, Gaye Bykers On Acid, Doctor and the Medics and, in the name of God, Ozaric Tentacle [sic]? Is this the reappearance of a counterculture? No, it's a lot of dirty hippies in purple t-shirts with stupid scrawling make-up round their eyes. They stand or sit and chew mental gum, eyes glazed and bored, becoming animated only when a song ends and they clap and go *Wayy!*" Whilst Quantick went on to focus his review on Ozric Tentacles, Pink Fairies, Naz Nomad and Hawkwind, Barbara Ellen concentrated on Voodoo Child, Pop Will Eat Itself, Doctor and the Medics and the Bykers. Crazyhead's Anderson had a brief dalliance with Ellen a few years earlier, when she was living in a small village in Leicestershire, hanging out with Hoppy and Dentover from The Janitors. Treating the Bykers with little more than indifference, she wrote:

> Gaye Bykers On Acid have their own-Freak show to flaunt for half an hour… Mary has forsaken his Off-the-Peg Stonehenge for a Jello Biafra anti-censorship t-shirt. The rest of the Bykers look as deranged as ever, denim tacked together with cat-gut. Tony plays guitar and I listen, my senses awaiting instructions. Cave and Iggy can rest easy, but with comics currently so popular this white-hot clout of drama could run and run.

Following with some sarcastic comments about Mary, Ellen concluded the review curtly: "Something happened and it wasn't rock'n'roll."

Peter Kane from *Sounds* was equally dismissive:

> Already very big in a very small way, Gaye Bykers would have you believe that they really don't care. Signs are though that they actually do. Considered by some to have a pretty wit, their noise has the finger-printed smudge of shredded punk all over it and in the few minutes allotted they come over as a desperate howl for attention. Attitude and shorts score maximum points though.

In the same issue of *Sounds* was Motörhead's Lemmy. Asked whether he considered Motörhead the godfathers of 'grebo', Lemmy replied: "No, I wouldn't have said so. Things like Gaye Bykers On Acid you mean? Their music is different to ours. That's a brilliant name though, because the way they spell it makes it look like a girl's name, *and* there's a geezer in the band called Mary!"

It might be coincidence that just over a month later the Gaye Bykers would be the main support act for Motörhead at their Hammersmith Odeon dates. On top of that, they also secured a prestigious support slot on a European tour by The Ramones.

DON'T GET SICK BABY

Crazyhead's second single Baby Turpentine was released a few weeks before Acid Daze. In the wake of its release Anderson and Porkbeast were interviewed in *Sounds* by Ann Scanlon, who was moved to describe Porkbeast as "a perfect gentleman… despite the gross implications of his name." Porkbeast explained how their cover of Sonny and Cher's Bang Bang was nearly released as an A-side, but ultimately the band "didn't want to bring a single out that wasn't an original, so we decided to stick it on the B-side with That Sinking Feeling instead."

Of the A-side, Baby Turpentine, Scanlon describes a single built on "renegade rockabilly and social awareness… dedicated to 'heartless Tory scum'". Porkbeast declares the band's socialist credentials before giving a potted history of his own family heritage: a grandfather who was a member of the IRA, and another who was a socialist agitator from the East End of London.

Although Scanlon did not mention 'grebo', it was infered when she wrote: "Rather than herding along with the next five minute movement, Crazyhead are aware that they're out on a limb of their own. They sneer at lazy revivalism and take wholesale pickings instead, from everyone from Howlin' Wolf and Chuck Berry through early Stones and sixties garage music to The Stooges and Ramones." Pressed on how they would describe themselves, the band reprised an epithet they had used earlier in the year when talking to *Melody Maker*'s Stud Brothers: "urban bastard

Baby Turpentine cover. Photo by Russell Young.

Anderson on stage at the Logo Club, Hamburg, 8th September 1987.

blues." Porkbeast explained they'd always lived in the city and were bastards, if not as individual people, then at least as they would be judged by society's standards. As for the blues element, he elaborated: "We're the sort of people that get into all the weird things that you're not supposed to get into, like drugs and alien jungle rhythms. And blues because that is the basis of all rock music and of what we're doing."

Jane Solanas, in *NME* the following week, was surprised that Crazyhead didn't live up to the dirty, uncouth, sexist, drink and drug fuelled Mad Max inspired "cartoon fantasy known as Grebo" that her music press cohorts had created. She was instead impressed with the respectful way the band treated her when she travelled to Leicester to interview them, after which they insisted their "tattooed roadie Sparky" escort her to the train station to make sure she arrived safely.

Solanas was more than eager to bandy around the word 'grebo' throughout her interview, but not so naïve to realise that the label could have implications: "if Grebo the cartoon has been a derisive diversion for everyone else, it has left Crazyhead feeling bemused. Lumped in with the swine, fed mescal and snakebite by the press, Crazyhead are now fighting off their grubby Grebo identity. They sit in a shack of a Leicester studio convinced they are 'the greatest band in the world'." Seemingly without sarcasm, she added, "they probably are."

In the Solanas interview, the band again described their music as "urban blues", to which was added the now familiar references to The Ramones, Stooges et al. She called the band "a raucous, nasty shriek of defiance from the bowels of boring Leicester". Their sound, she said, was "gloriously dumb, raw and honest. It has nothing whatsoever to do with the manufactured efforts of Grebo amateurs." Baby Turpentine was an "explosive masterpiece". Solanas went on: "Everything Crazyhead have committed to vinyl so far has been perfect. In terms of energy there is no one to touch them, and in Anderson they have a vocalist who has restored the snot-nosed whine of real emotion to British music."

At first, Baby Turpentine's opening salvo appears cryptic:

'When life is unfair good people don't grow old and Valium pours from the TV screen, always in the red, always in the cold and hardly room to swing a tiara here, baby's looking mean waiting for the love machine (don't get sick baby don't get sick baby), baby's doing fine, baby, baby turpentine...'

Described at the time as an "anti-royalist statement", Anderson now says, "Reverb tells me he tried to write a fast punky song in the style of early Dylan if he'd been unemployed — as Reverb was — in Thatcher's late eighties Britain." Reverb confirms this: "Baby Turpentine was a kind of reflection on the life I was living at the time, and the demise of the National Health Service."

Sounds' Mr Spencer called the single, "A monster! Seriously... these greasy slobs could soon be providing Motorhead with some very real competition in the battle for 'grebo' supremacy... I'll say it just one last time, they could be huge." David Stubbs, a vociferous detractor of both Crazyhead and the Gaye Bykers, was not in the slightest enamoured of it though. In his review for *Melody Maker* he wrote: "To Baby Turpentine *bollocks* would be entirely inappropriate, for the tragedy of Crazyhead is that they are all dick and no testes. Spilling to the bar at the Marquee for more tinned lager in spindly tanktops, as illuminating as a slash against a lamppost. Groups like Crazyhead seems [sic] to crop up every two or three months, spurious proof of rock's capacity for self-regurgitation. But this is doggie vomit."

Gigs had been lined up for early September, a series of live dates in Holland and Germany, which would have provided useful exposure for Crazyhead and the single on the continent. They all fell through, apart from one gig in Hamburg. Says Reverb, "It was at the Logo club... It wasn't a financially viable gig to do as a one-off, but [Julian Cope's manager] Cally

Porkbeast in full flight at The Boston Arms, London, 23rd September 1987.

Photo courtesy of Pen-Åke Warn.

Photo courtesy of Nuala Bugeye.

"Another night on the streets. Bug Eyed Monsters after a 'good night's sleep' Bedford Bus station 1987 — the things you do to see a band..."

Photo courtesy of Fifi Faiza Ariech.

Daye Trippers with Mary Byker (with arms raised) and Tony Byker (in front in floral frock and face-paint).

said we should consider doing it for a 'jolly', so we did. We took an overnight ferry from Harwich to the Hook of Holland. We booked cabins but spent the majority of the trip in the bar of course. It took ages to drive to Hamburg. Can't really remember much about the gig itself. I do remember that four of our followers made it to the gig."

Porkbeast recalls a little more. "It was a great gig," he says. "The journey was even more fun. Nuala [one of a hardcore group of Crazyhead followers, later known as the Bug Eyed Monsters] came along and set the t-shirts on fire on the way back. We stayed up all night drinking Blue Label Vodka on the ferry and the drive to Hamburg was the most uncomfortable ever, sat on a Marshall combo, hungover and delirious."

BUG EYED MONSTERS
AND DAYE TRIPPERS

Members of the Bykers and Crazyhead have their own take on the popularity of their respective bands. Mary Byker has said that the Bykers were never well supported in their hometown, once they'd left to find fame and fortune in London, while Anderson, says, with seemingly characteristic deprecation, that he always thought the Bykers were "hugely more popular than [Crazyhead], in Leicester and everywhere else… except for, maybe around the time of the Time and Have Love singles." The general consensus was that Crazyhead remained more respected in Leicester because they never saw fit to desert it as the Bykers had done. Maybe there is some truth to this, but whatever their popularity in Leicester there can be no doubt that both bands had built up a small but rabid group of travelling followers. Crazyhead's followers were known as the Bug Eyed Monsters, or BEMS. The name derives from the sleeve of Crazyhead's debut single, on which the band is referred to as "FIVE Bug Eyed Monsters from Venus", in turn a derivation of a Captain Beefheart song (Bug Eyed Beans From Venus). The Bykers' contingent of loyal hardcore fans were affectionately known as the Daye Trippers. Some of them built up such a friendly relationship with the band over time that they even began working for the Bykers, as drivers, roadies and selling merchandise for them at gigs.

"You're either on the bus... or you're off the bus" — Daye Trippers in the area!

MOVIE MADNESS

There wasn't really a moment's rest for the Bykers that summer. Just over a week after Acid Daze, they topped the bill at Nottingham Rock City, which also included Pop Will Eat Itself, a Leicester band called The Hunters Club, and two other bands, Salvation and The Longest Day. It would be the Bykers last gig for five weeks. But outside of gigs, they wrote and recorded material for their forthcoming album, and continued to be sucked into the maelstrom that was going to be their film epic. It had been one thing employing the services of Dave Bartram to make a couple of three-minute videos for their first two singles, but a full-length feature movie was another matter entirely.

Ray Lowry was again called upon — this time to help with scriptwriting and drafting a storyboard. Wanting to maintain a certain amount of creative control and input, the Bykers fed him ideas and discussed the direction they wanted the film to take. The Monkees, Monty Python, and *The Young Ones* crossed with *Mad Max* and the state-of-the-art SFX movie *Tron* were cited by both the press and the band as influences, along with *The Blues Brothers* and *Fear and Loathing in Las Vegas*. The overarching plot was an allegory of sorts about an up-and-

coming young band trapped inside a video game. Based on decisions they make in the game, the band try to negotiate their way through the cutthroat trials and tribulations of the music business, and the attendant perils — ultimately to find fame and fortune in Las Vegas or, if they fail, landing on the "could've been contenders" scrapheap.

"Virgin, of course, thought we needed a video to promote the single," says Tony. "But instead of making individual videos we decided to make a movie that had all the songs included. We had to convince Virgin Vision about this. But in order to get the cash we had to put up half of our cash."

While the Bykers were making plans for their movie, Crazyhead employed Dave Bartram to make the video for Baby Turpentine. Anderson recalls that Bartram was "a student of film we knew down the pub, who was studying at Leicester poly. He had also made the Everythang's Groovy video for the Gaye Bikers on Acid. We managed to accidentally erase all the action shots of me, that's why I'm lying on the floor for the whole video, as that scene was all he had! Typically, cheapskate Dave Balfe at Food got the finished video off him first, then said he would only pay him half the original agreed fee!"

Bartram is not entirely sure whether the action shots in question got erased but says there was certainly no money to go back and reshoot anything. He says he got paid £400, and adds, "All the gear was blagged, and mates would help us out, so it didn't really cost us anything to make it apart from time."

The promo's black and white footage was shot at Crazyhead's rehearsal rooms, while the colour footage was shot in the Leicester Polytechnic basement studio. Once again Bartram experimented with different techniques, and particularly favoured solarisation effects. He admits to making a conscious effort to keep the look of the Crazyhead promo different to that of the Bykers'. "Not as lairy, because it was a straighter kind of rock sound." He considers the Byker's promo much more of a "performance video".

But the Bykers had their sights set higher than just a promo, or at least Mary did. The idea of a Gaye Bykers On Acid movie had been a twinkle in Mary's eye ever since the band's inception, but the Virgin deal had afforded them the opportunity to make it a reality — with the band having gotten their solicitors to draft a clause to that effect in their contract. Scouting for ideas, Mary and Kev travelled to see members of the Mutoid Waste Company at the Edinburgh Fringe Festival that month. The Mutoid Waste Company was a collective of anarcho travellers-cum-urban squatters with a propensity for making post-apocalyptic looking sculptures out of vehicles, and other scrap metal and materials. The Mutoids had already earned themselves a level of notoriety having displayed

Photo courtesy of Tony Byker.

L-R: Mary Byker, cat, Dave Bartram and Ray Lowry sketching ideas for Drill Your Own Hole.

their metallic creations at the previous year's Glastonbury festival. As well as static sculptures, they were also a dab hand at customising vehicles. It was with this in mind that the Bykers wanted to employ their talents to make a *Mad Max*-style vehicle to use in the movie.

The trip to Edinburgh was more than an exercise in securing the services of the Muties though. Mary says they managed to "kill two birds with one stone" by also employing a new scriptwriter. Paul B. Davies had written for television comedy programmes like *Alas Smith and Jones*, *Spitting Image*, and Jasper Carrott. His impressive CV also included a nomination for a Perrier Comedy Award at the Edinburgh Fringe Festival in 1985. Davies had once been involved in a number of alternative theatre productions in the West Country, including the Crystal Theatre Company, which sometimes featured comedian Keith Allen, known in the late 1970s and early eighties for his stand-up supporting punk gigs in Bristol.

At the Edinburgh Fringe in August 1987, Paul Davies was performing in *Slave Clowns Of The Third Reich*, which he describes as "a deliberately avant-garde show which involved me talking to television monitors". Of the meeting with Mary and Kev, he says, "Somebody told a friend of mine that they needed a writer, and they recommended me, and they said, 'Can you do it?'... Because they suddenly had all this money from Virgin, they flew up to Edinburgh to check me out. So they came to see this show I was in and obviously decided I was suitable, partly because they didn't know anyone else and partly because the show I did demonstrated a certain… it was kind of out there, it was quite imaginative and strange. I had a drink with them afterwards, we got on alright, so I think they figured, 'OK, we'll have him!'"

With the movie deadline scheduled to coincide with the completion of the debut album, early in the autumn, time was now counting down fast. Ray Lowry may have been a brilliant artist and ideal for the storyboard, but he couldn't get his head round how to write a screenplay, according to Davies. As soon

BROGUE MALE PRODUCTIONS PRESENT

PAUL B. DAVIES IN

SLAVE CLOWNS
OF THE
THIRD REICH

PROD. R. WILLMORE

NOV 3-22 (not Mondays) **8.00pm**
CORNER THEATRE (Hen & Chickens Pub, Highbury Corner, N1)
TICKETS £3.75 (£2.75) + 25p Ann. Membership
BOX OFFICE ☎ **226 3724**

Poster for Paul B. Davies' Edinburgh Festival production, Slave Clowns Of The Third Reich.

as he got back from Edinburgh, Davies set about writing the screenplay while fine-tuning the earlier efforts of Lowry and the Bykers.

"It was all seat of the pants stuff, but crazy fun! And it was all being done in a mad bollock scramble!" claims Davies. Just hours before shooting was due to commence, Davies was still writing the last of the script, in the Maida Vale flat of then producer, Max Bruno. "I was basically locked in this room, in the sense that Bruno was very keen that I stayed there until I finished the script, and to encourage me, he discouraged me from coming out by giving me the sort of things one needs in order to maintain one's energy levels, as well as the Scotch whiskey that I was slugging quite a lot of."

Davies finished the script in the early hours. A dozen or so copies of the script were required before arriving on the set in just a few hours' time. This was still an era of typewriters, and while London may well be a city that never sleeps, it was not easy to find a 24-hour copy shop at such an hour. But as luck would have it, Bruno was friends with the manager of Heaven — the gay nightclub near Trafalgar Square had a photocopier! Wired, the two of them hightailed it across the West End to arrive at the club at around three in the morning. Bruno adjourned to the manager's office to run off copies of the script, while Davies found

Courtesy of Dave Bartram.

First and second page of Ray Lowry's storyboard for Drill Your Own Hole.

himself standing on the club dancefloor, and "feeling very strange, while all these guys in their leather cowboy chaps with their bums out gyrated around me".

Mission accomplished, they made it to the designated rendezvous point of Belvedere car park, behind Waterloo Station, before heading to Kent with the assembled cast and crew. The first day of filming had arrived. Even Mary remembers being daunted, contrary to his usual boundless confidence and enthusiasm. "It was when the catering buses, lighting trucks all arrived at the set that we actually saw the scale of the thing," he says. "It was like 'Jesus Christ, what have we let ourselves in for?' So, we'd

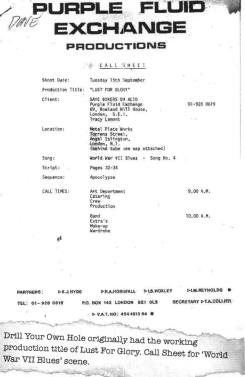

PURPLE FLUID EXCHANGE
PRODUCTIONS

CALL SHEET

Shoot Date:	Tuesday 15th September
Production Title:	"LUST FOR GLORY"
Client:	GAYE BYKERS ON ACID 01-928 0619 Purple Fluid Exchange 69, Rowland Hill House, London, S.E.1. Tracy Lamont
Location:	Metal Plate Works Torrens Street, Angel Islington, London, N.1. (behind tube see map attached)
Song:	World War VII Blues - Song No. 4
Script:	Pages 32-34
Sequence:	Apocalypse
CALL TIMES:	Art Department 9.00 A.M. Catering Crew Production
	Band 10.00 A.M. Extra's Make-up Wardrobe

PARTNERS: ▷K.J.HYDE ▷R.A.HORSFALL ▷I.S.HOXLEY ▷I.M.REYNOLDS ●

TEL: 01-928 0619 P.O. BOX 142 LONDON 5E1 OLS SECRETARY ▷T.A.COLLIER

▷ V.A.T.NO: 454 4513 54 ●

Drill Your Own Hole originally had the working production title of Lust For Glory. Call Sheet for 'World War VII Blues' scene.

bitten off more than we could chew really. But at the same time it was like the spirit was 'We'll give it a go!'"

The working title for the Bykers' film was *Lust For Glory*, although Ray Lowry's storyboards suggest a more *Spinal Tap*-esque alternative: *Thrust For Glory*.

The following Tuesday, 15th September, the so-called "Apocalypse" sequence was filmed at the Metal Plate Works in Islington. A new song had been written especially for the film, called World War VII Blues. The band played themselves (obviously), while the extras were largely made up of friends and members of The Janitors and Bomb Party. The same cannot be said of the "Roadhouse" scene, in which the band performed All Hung Up On Happiness. Filmed on location at The Salisbury Arms, a pub in Barnet, the sequence required more than just a few friends and so the band called on the services of some locals to make up the numbers, a sort of rent-a-mob from Barnet. Bartram recalls, "They were a famous notorious local crew that came, and they were just smashing everything

Tony Byker and girlfriend July Tafy on the set for 'World War VII Blues'.

up!" To compound matters, the furniture and fittings were real rather than balsa, as is usually the case on film sets. It may have added to the realism, but only a barrier of flimsy chicken wire stapled across the pub's stage served to protect the band from the onslaught. It didn't do much for the band's nerves. Laughing at the memory, Bartram says, "I think it probably comes across in the performance that they were shitting themselves!"

A week later, cast and crew adjourned to the Hackney Empire where After Suck There's Blow — or the Vegas Song, as the call sheet calls it — was filmed. Here the band are supposedly performing live at Caesar's Palace in Las Vegas, the pivotal "shit or bust" moment in the film's narrative when the Bykers realise their ambitions, or not. Shooting the scene proved to be less fraught than "Roadhouse". But complications arose on another sequence, Motorvate. Production was delayed when the Mutoid Waste Company vehicles that had been commissioned failed to materialise. Shooting was due to take place at an industrial quarry in Westerham, Kent, with the vehicles playing centre-stage. Dave Bartram found ways to work around the setback. Nevertheless, it was an inconvenience, and just one of many disruptions during the six-week shoot.

There were rumours that the Mutoids had been arrested en route to the quarry, but Bartram thinks the truth is rather more mundane, and has more to do with a certain managerial faction withholding payments: "I suspect the Mutoids probably wouldn't release the vehicle until they'd been paid. I think they may have rescued it back until they got their final 50% too. Ray Lowry had similar problems. We all did!" Other reports suggest there were problems paying some of the professional actors and extras, who threatened to strike and refused to turn up until band manager Stacey Lafront found the money to pay them. But by and large the extras consisted of the Bykers' friends. Sally Jones was Robber's girlfriend at the time. As well as being the band's unofficial photographer, she also acted as an artistic director of sorts. Shuddering, she recalls, "Drill Your

Photo courtesy of Sally Jones.

Mutoid Waste Co. vehicle used in the video for 'Motorvate' from Drill Your Own Hole.

Own Hole… they certainly did! Yes, I remember many bits from that fiasco. I was roped into helping out after the art director dropped out. I was rushing around trying to make props with whatever came to hand. The whole idea was great, but in reality it was madness, and pretty much bankrupted them — though I have no clue where the money went, certainly not on the scenic department! More than likely embezzled by management and spent on powdering noses!"

With everything that was going on around them, it was easy for the band to take their eyes off the ball. It was not entirely unreasonable for them to expect that their best interests would be taken care of, having employed Lafront to act on their behalf. Today, various members of the band and associates say that, unbeknownst to them, Lafront was allegedly wasting huge amounts on drugs and God knows what else. Tony thinks that Lafront was allegedly snorting much of the band's advance money up her nose. Says Tony of one particular stuntman, "Oh yes, Cocaine Nose — it had rotted away so he had Teflon implants so he could keep snorting. What a dodgy guy. He and Stacey 'Speed Freak' Lafront snorting away our money, and the champagne lunches that were taken in the editing room by the editors. Dave Bartram was very cool, and he did a good job, but I think it was difficult for him to control the crazy crew and the ball that seemed to be rolling."

Dave Bartram says that Lafront was the "worst kind of nightmare" to work

"Lots of friends were extras, such as in the punk scenes/hippy bus."
Kev Byker (far right). On the film set of Drill Your Own Hole.

with: "She wrote a cheque for £30,000 from the production budget but couldn't recall who she'd made it out to or what it was for. So a third of the budget disappeared early on. She then turned up at the shoot with a sugar bag full of coke the following day, so we all know where the money went!"

Sally Jones adds that "It was fun too. Lots of friends were extras, such as in the punk scenes/hippy bus etc. The continuity is terrible — which was hilarious. The Bykers just turned up each day, wore what they wanted, and paid no attention to the continuity girl. I can't remember who she was, but she wasn't getting anywhere with them. We were struggling to get things done last-minute with no materials, and I remember we had to make the jukebox out of the wood we used for the clapperboard — if you watch the film, when the jukebox gets pulled apart in the roadhouse scene you can see the painting of the clapperboard on sections inside it. The clapperboard turns up later in the film — the minstrel bit, I think. In another scene, my hand pops out of the fruit machine — accidentally — and when Tony sees it he squeals — 'a hand!' Very funny, it was all ad-lib. Also, in the big stage scene at Hackney Empire, we were supposed to get lots of friends and fans turning up to be the audience, but the advert didn't get put out — usual incompetent management. Any of us who were available working on the shoot had to be the audience, so you see the same people in different areas of the audience. We would move between shots." Jones wistfully concludes, "I think the

The Ken Kesey/Electric Kool-Aid Acid Test-styled school bus used in the 'Zen Express' scene in Drill Your Own Hole.

whole film was kind of a cross between The Monkees' film and early Beatles, with a bit of Monty Python thrown in."

Dave Bartram admits that the Bykers could be hard work at times. "The Bykers wouldn't take acting lessons because they wanted to be themselves," he says. "They deliberately changed clothes during a scene because they wanted 'jump cuts'... they'd walk through a door they'd be wearing a hat one side and not the other, but in order to do things like that you have to plan them... shoot accordingly, and they didn't really get their heads around that, so, in one scene they're talking in a Yorkshire accent and then in the next one it's Northern Irish... it just jumped all over the place, but then that's just the nature of the beast... you know? Working with a band like that you get what you get!"

One of the more memorable moments is the "Zen Express" scene, which featured two buses, one a Ken Kesey/Electric Kool-Aid Acid Test styled school bus, and the other a Sex Pistols' 'Nowhere — Boredom' bus. Again, most of the extras were friends of the Bykers, dressed as hippies or punks, depending on which bus they were riding. Mary spoke of this sequence and the inspiration behind it a few months later. He told Peter Mengede of *Rockpool* magazine, "The video is a cross between The Monkees and *Electric Kool-Aid Acid Test*. The whole thing is a homage to the Pranksters and the madness that Kesey and the bunch got away with. It's important to acknowledge the phenomenon that is acid and that it changed a great many people's way of seeing and thinking. What we had was this one nihilistic punk bus where everyone was vomiting gloomy doom, and this Hippy Dippy bus. They just smash into each other, collide and no lesson was learned by either generation, and they still aren't learning."

As autumn rolled on, the film had run well over the projected budget and was behind schedule. Reports filtered through to the music press about it being a cursed film, a curse that targeted the producers specifically. One producer's eardrums were allegedly perforated by an exploding television, while another contracted some mysterious tropical disease. The third had his Porsche stolen, and then the art director broke his foot when a clap-o-meter fell on it. All this was said to have happened at the script-reading stage, before production was barely out of the blocks! Dave Bartram brings some clarity to the roll call of producers: "[Stacey Lafront] wanted to produce the film herself at some point, but obviously that was never gonna happen… The original producer was a guy called Max Bruno. He was totally inept and lost the plot. I think he was the one who broke a leg. He was replaced by Debbie Mason's husband for a week or two — Adrian, I think — who quickly realised he was out of his depth working with such a chaotic outfit of misfits, then Debbie took over and finished the job!"

With the squat scene filmed on location in and around the flat that Kev shared with Stacey Lafront, it was inevitable that the presence of a 20-strong film crew with attendant articulated lorries, catering vans, and cables would be cause for complaint. The council allegedly contacted Lafront's mother to try and talk some sense into her — all this was on day one of the shoot.

The misfortune continued. Lafront's car then got broken into, two cars got destroyed that weren't meant to, and one of the buses the Mutoid Waste Company had provided for the "Zen Express" scene would not carry out a roll over that was necessary for the shoot. On top of that, Kev allegedly filled the other bus with diesel as opposed to petrol and had no choice but to leave it stranded outside Tower Bridge Magistrates Court. To cap it all, £3,000 was wasted on the 12 hours of lost production caused by the Muties failing to deliver the vehicles they had customised. On this occasion, after a two-hour crawl through rush hour traffic from London to the quarry where several scenes in the movie were scheduled, the Bykers were not in the best of moods. As dusk fell and it became clear they wouldn't be shooting any scenes that day, they retreated to the nearest pub. Here, Mary and Tony spent the rest of the evening talking to *Melody Maker* journo Carol Clerk. But Kev and Robber made their excuses and left. Robber left a life-sized cardboard cut-out of himself in his place, a prop from the film. A general tone of weariness replaced the usual upbeat demeanour of the remaining two

Bykers — hardly surprising given the day they'd just had, but also indicative perhaps of the toll of the punishing daily schedules and the pressure it was placing on the band.

Adding further to the catalogue of woes, Ray Lowry's original artwork for the album cover disappeared for a spell. According to the music press, Virgin press officer John Best ordered everyone out of the Virgin offices to search for it and eventually found the work "sandwiched between a stack of old Mike Oldfield albums and congealed coffee grounds".

Photo courtesy of Sally Jones.

Robber and the life-sized cardboard cut-out used as a prop in the film (and band interviews).

Lowry's cover art featured bright streaks of thickly daubed oil paint spelling the band's name on a background of what looked like the mess of colours on an artist's palette. It may not be as iconic as his *London Calling* cover for The Clash, but the inner sleeve was unmistakably Lowry, adorned with illustrations representing a number of songs on the album, which were used as part of the original storyboard for the movie. Tony says, "We had an idea about the feel of all the songs of course. We knew all the movies and scenes we imagined, but Ray Lowry wrote the basic script and storyline, tying all the songs together to fit the plot, and then many cartoons to go with the scenes... I wish I'd

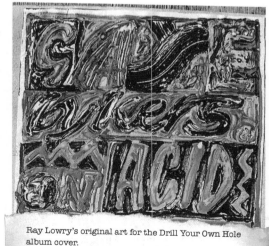

Source: Tony Byker's Gaye Bykers On Acid scrapbook.

Ray Lowry's original art for the Drill Your Own Hole album cover.

No cucumbers were hurt during the filming of this scene. Mary Byker with "banned" cucumber.

kept all those originals now. I don't know where they went. We spent quite a lot of time with Ray, meeting to put things in place. He was a nice guy." Lowry died suddenly in October 2008. His contribution to the world of music is immeasurable and his distinctive art style iconic.

Lowry also provided cover art for the singles culled from *Drill Your Own Hole*. The first, Git Down, was mooted for release on 5th October. The release was put back a week possibly because of delays in finishing the promo video (from the work-in-progress movie), or because they hoped to capitalise on the support slots for Motörhead at Hammersmith Odeon. The 12-inch version was backed by two tracks, purportedly recorded live at Eyres Monsell Working Men's Club in Leicestershire. They were fast and furious versions of a couple of early Bykers' songs, Go Go In Out, In Out Garotschka, and Dog, retitled Tolchocked By Kenny Pride. This was a moniker bestowed upon Kev Hyde by the owner of Unit 66. Kev recalls that the owner "couldn't remember my name so any time he saw any of the others he would shout over to them, 'Aye up you's lot, 'ave you seen that Kenny Pride, tell 'im I wants me rent money!'"

The A-side was a monster of heavy metal funk that opened with a bludgeoning variation of Black Sabbath's Symptom Of The Universe riff, over which Mary screams the immortal line 'Yowzah, yowzah, yowzah', originally from Chic's disco classic Dance, Dance, Dance. Amidst Robber's thundering bass and Tony's wailing guitar, the song incorporates sampled strings to great effect too. Talking to Carol Clerk, Mary explained that the somewhat cryptic lyric was about double standards. The scene that accompanies the song in the film, says Mary, "is directed against a lot of music journalists and a lot of crap they come out with. They're in a position of responsibility, they can be helpful I know, but there is a double standard." He cites what he sees as "so much inverse racism" prevalent in the music press, whereby

Cover of 'Git Down (Shake Your Thang)' the first single taken from Drill Your Own Hole.

sexuality in songs is treated differently according to a person's race or colour. "If it's a black man singing about sex, if it's Prince or Terence Trent D'Arby — they can sing dirty and get so much media attention. But a music journalist doesn't like a white person singing that way. They can't handle it — 'That's indecent.' It's all very well for a black guy to sing 'Ease it in gently baby', he can get away with it."

The scene in question is none too subtle in putting this point across, depicting a room full of arrogant music hacks spouting forth invective — of a type hackneyed critics are prone to use — while watching a band supposedly at a talent show. The band is introduced as the Lesbian Dopeheads On Mopeds but is actually the Bykers "blacked up". Dressed as a black American 1970s soul band, they go through all manner of salacious and suggestive moves on stage before the song is over. The video draws upon *The Black And White Minstrel Show,* a British television variety show that featured many of its singers and dancers "blacked up". It ran from the late 1950s to late 1970s, before being deemed unsound and cancelled. The Bykers ended up in hot water with the censors, but not for connotations of Minstrel-style racial stereotyping — they were obviously being satirical in this respect. Instead, it was for a line in the song's lyric, "put me in my place, sit on my face," and the suggestive use of cucumbers in the promotional video. Mary spoke about the censorship issue to Adrian Deevoy in Q magazine that autumn: "I'm singing into a plugged-in cucumber and the bassist's got another one stuffed down his trousers. Why? It's all to test people's preconceptions and perceptions... and because we're really stupid." With typical flippancy Mary concludes that "this vegetable oppression is symptomatic of the corrupt system we're attempting to undermine... which is an amazingly articulate statement for a smelly pouf who plays second rate heavy metal."

Mary was more serious when talking to Lisa Tilston in *Record Mirror*. Although it can't have been easy keeping a straight face discussing the "phallic symbolism of the humble British cucumber", he appeared genuinely aggrieved that the satire and what the Bykers were trying to say was lost on the powers that be. He was also indignant that their work should be deemed more offensive than the out-and-out sexism of many 'acceptable' MTV videos. "The video hasn't been officially banned, it's just that nobody will play it," Mary lamented. "I can't believe the amount of censorship and the double standards operating in the media at the moment. I find women in suspender belts with heavy metal bands behind them much more offensive than our video. Something like Mötley Crüe singing Girls Girls Girls is just sexploitation, really crass and tacky, but it's so institutionalised that people take it for granted."

Tilston was disarmed by Mary's charm, erudition and wit. She saw how humour had been used by the Bykers "as a weapon against the slow-witted, giving them a reputation for being difficult interviewees. I was expecting smart-arsed comments and endless *Star Trek* conversations". Tilston was certainly not the first journalist to be surprised at just how articulate Mary and the other Bykers could be when they wanted to, nor would she be the last. The band's quirky humour was as much a self-defence mechanism to mask their own insecurities as it was a form of mockery. Unfortunately for the Bykers, what had been regarded as endearing at first, soon became perceived as churlishness by the wider music press. They couldn't quite square their honesty and intelligence with the buffoonery of their cheeky chappy personas.

London *Time Out*'s Nick Coleman was not far off the mark when he observed: "the Byker's insistent infantility can be a bit wearing. Don't they realise that a pinch of mystique is not only good for sales, but also ensures long life."

Andy Darling, writing for *City Limits* that autumn, summed up the wider journalistic perception of the band when he said of Mary: "His loquacious bemusement borders on bewilderment." Darling was just plain confused by the Bykers frontman wildly zigzagging from one subject to another, which ranged from "inverse racism", through censorship, comics like *2000AD*, Salvador Dalì, the Socialist Workers Party, and being "one of the top sprint cyclists in the country".

The four main British music weeklies received the single warmly, though not without reservations. Shaun Phillips, writing for the usually beneficent *Sounds*, said, "Mary blubbers, guitars scream, the sky caves in and Big Audio Dynamite's beatbox tries to crash the party. Nothing much at all is mixed to great effect." In the *NME*, Sean O'Hagan complemented it as "a pig ugly brute of a record", adding, "I like it a lot… especially when the big mouth bastard on lead vocals swallows his tongue and lets the screechy guitar, psychotic strings and throbbing elastic bass hum collide in masterful mayhem. When all this gels, you can see why the dirty filthy, dreggy, drug addled sons of post-punk Britain dress in rags, dye their straggly, dreadlocked hair and git down to the sound of hardcore post-acid metal mayhem."

Carol Clerk, for *Melody Maker*, was more forthcoming with her plaudits: "I have to report that having lived with this bizarre piece of music for the last month, it keeps on getting better, pisses all over everything I've heard in the last *three* years! And so even in the face of assassination threats from my esteemed colleagues, I'm duty bound to put this single where it deserves to be: in a class of its own." Putting the single in its own 'Gaye Bykers On Acid Section', *Record Mirror* bestowed the honour of Top Of The Tree upon the single. Guest reviewers for the week Steve Mack and Réamann Ó'Gormain from That Petrol Emotion had obviously never been moved by the Bykers prior to this. Réamann was surprised at how much he liked it, saying he thought the Bykers were a complete shambles last time he saw them, before proclaiming, "I think it's a great pop record. It should be in the charts."

Unfortunately, the record buying public thought otherwise, and the single stalled at number 54. It was at this time that the Bykers secured their prestigious support slot on The Ramones' European tour.

HEY HO, LET'S GO!

The Ramones support slot was only a short tour, but it gave the Gaye Bykers On Acid their first major exposure to European audiences. Travelling to Denmark on 4th October 1987, they played Copenhagen the following night, and then proceeded to play successive nights in Hamburg, Amsterdam, and Düsseldorf, before returning to London for a couple of whistle-stop gigs supporting Motör-head. The Bykers then promptly rejoined The Ramones for the last two dates on the European leg of their 'Halfway To Sanity' tour.

Poster for Gaye Bykers On Acid supporting The Ramones in Zurich.

CAMEL

GABBA GABBA HEY WITH:

RAMONES

special guests: **GAYE BYKERS ON ACID**

Montag, 12.Oktober '87, 20 Uhr
VOLKSHAUS ZÜRICH
Kasse + Türöffnung: 19.30 Uhr
Einziges Konzert in der Schweiz !!!
Vorverkauf:

It may have been some years since The Ramones' heyday, but they were still regarded as godfathers of punk. To be mentioned in the same breath as the revered "bruddas Ramone" was kudos enough, but what young band with punk aspirations wouldn't give its eyeteeth to share a bill with them? The Bykers couldn't believe their luck.

From the outset, the Bykers were given a stern warning, as Mary recalls: "Basically we were told by The Ramones' management not to go near Dee Dee [Ramones' bassist] or let him get involved in any pharmaceutical type of activity. So what's the first thing you see as soon as you get to the dressing room? Dee Dee's there waiting for you, asking you for everything under the sun. So what are you going to do? This punk rock legend's asking you for a smoke. I mean you're like 'alright', so invariably we ended up in his room, and he's like 'Check this out!', and he's getting his hairdryer out of his suitcase and getting a screwdriver out and opening his hairdryer up and all this stuff falling out, and Dee Dee's going 'Check this out maaan!'"

Robber picks up the story. "It was like an Aladdin's Cave of pills and all sorts, that he used to take just to keep him straight. He had loads of hash and got us really stoned. I thought it was really funny after the tour manager had said all that — but I suppose he meant it was heroin they were really trying to keep him away from."

The tour also afforded other opportunities for the Bykers to indulge in

alcoholic and narcotic excess. On one German date, Robber recalls coming round in the hotel flowerbed, while Amsterdam sticks in Tony's mind. Says Tony, "I had been before, purely to enjoy smoking ganja and explore. I couldn't quite shake the feeling that it wasn't illegal. I kept looking over my shoulder. I am so used to avoiding authorities, I find it hard to smoke in public! I had lots of space cake, wondering if it was going to work… and of course it did! It was very weird walking down the red-light area with all the different windows and women on display, and the little self-service fast food drawers. Lots of strange characters wandering around at night."

The Ramones treated the Bykers well and they got along fine for the most part. Johnny Ramone was another matter. "We didn't really speak to Johnny," says Mary, "but Joey and Dee Dee were incredibly friendly, in so far as hanging out with us and talking to us." Robber concurs: "Johnny was well known for being a Republican and a tosser, so nobody spoke to him."

Often the Bykers had to pinch themselves in such legendary company. Joey Ramone had already introduced himself to the Bykers when they played at the Felt Forum in New York several months earlier, and Mary struck up a friendship with him that would continue whenever they met over the years. Says Mary, "I actually hung out with Joey Ramone in New York, which was weird, because he was one of those people who, when he leaves his house, has to count the number of steps and not stand on the cracks in the pavement. So he had one of these personality disorders that means if it doesn't tally with what it's supposed to, he goes home and starts again. He was quite a strange character, but then again, a lovely, lovely guy. But you know you find yourself sitting in a bar with somebody like that, or go to the toilet to share some sniff with them, and it's all unreal. Do you know what I mean?"

Even now, Mary still feels privileged to have played with The Ramones: "On reflection you're like, 'What was all that about?' 'cos they were pretty amazing times… it was pretty nuts, because The Ramones were obviously a seminal band, and to find yourself sharing an environment with them for a couple of weeks was great, you know? You don't necessarily realise how big that is whilst you're doing it but suffice to say they were really good guys."

The Bykers were well received by the European audiences and headliners alike, but the same could not be said of the two support gigs for Motörhead.

NO SLEEP 'TIL HAMMERSMITH

The Bykers forsook the Italian gig on The Ramones tour, despite their name being on the posters, and dashed back to support Motörhead at the traditional venue for their UK tour finales, the Hammersmith Odeon. However, the Bykers found themselves somewhat between a rock and a hard place. Motörhead had, until Lemmy's death in December 2015, a rabidly loyal following that included the Hell's Angels. Lemmy was particularly friendly with the London Chapter, as Mary recalls: "I'd seen Lemmy out and about in Soho, but I'd never really spoken to him, and I think he kind of knew who we were — he'd always be in The Ship [famous pub frequented by rock stars since the 1960s on Wardour Street]."

This being home turf, the Bykers were aware that the Motörhead entourage would include a number of Hell's Angels and that a name like Gaye Bykers On Acid would not go unnoticed. The source of the band's name had already incurred the wrath of the biker fraternity when Ray Lowry used it in a cartoon for the *NME*.

"We basically thought we were going to get our heads kicked in at that gig because of our name!" says Mary. "That was like *their* gig, their one big gig. Motörhead had done the live album, *No Sleep 'til Hammersmith*, and along with The Ramones, we were also big fans of Motörhead too, so it was weird again."

It was with some trepidation that the Bykers arrived at the venue. In a show of bravado, they brought along two Rottweilers that belonged to a drug dealer friend of theirs from Leicester. Outside the venue were rows of motorbikes, the Hell's Angels having showed up for the sound check. Mary remembers, "It was like 'Oh shit, the Hell's Angels are gonna stomp us for sure because of our name!'" Although Lemmy had given the Bykers his seal of approval in *Sounds* back in August, his endorsement didn't assuage Mary's fears. He recalls, "It was kind of scary, and all I can remember is going down to the soundcheck with one of these Rottweilers on a chain and as I was walking up to the stage, coming down the stairs towards the dressing room was one of the famous Angels. I think his name was Crazy Charlie. He was like the President of the All-England Hell's Angels, and he was slightly surprised seeing me with this huge dog… There was an aftershow party, and a couple of Angels came up to us and said, 'We really liked you guys, you really held your ground well.'"

They may have earned the respect of Motörhead's inner sanctum but winning over the crowd was a completely different matter. Heavy metal audiences are

notorious for being fiercely partisan towards their favourite band, and as for Motörhead fans at Motörhead's spiritual home? Well, that was something else again! The fact the Bykers were popular on the indie and punk scenes didn't wash with the heavy metal fans.

Says Robber, "Yeah, that was quite a tough gig, we played two nights. There was another support band — a typical poncey metal act — so it was a typical metal crowd, weren't it, and we weren't a metal band! We were kind of out of place, but it was cool to meet Lemmy and play with Motörhead."

While the crowd gave them a hard time, the Bykers managed to deflect the abuse and missiles hurled at them and got on with the job. On the one hand Robber says it was "quite a tough gig", on the other he says, "I don't think it was *that* difficult. It may have been a bit hostile, but because the audience is so far away from you anyway it's like, they ain't gonna get to ya! So you just get on and do your thing… You're booked to play there for a certain amount of time, so you get on there and get through it and get off." He adds, "I don't think we got an encore though!"

Tony is more pragmatic. "The Motörhead gigs were shit," he says, "playing to a metal audience really early didn't go down too well. Sword, the band that supported them throughout the tour, would have been on first because of us, so Lemmy came backstage and asked us to go on first instead. How could we say no to the guru of rock?"

Tony was not alone. Jon Wilde in his review of the gig for the *Melody Maker* mercilessly slagged the Bykers off. Among the epithets Wilde used to describe the Bykers were "mediocrity", "stupid", "hoodlum racket", "shambolic din", "witless wonders", "yokel self-parody" and "transparently opportunistic". He dramatically concluded his write up of the Bykers: "Tonight, like condemned men, they walked their last mile. Motörhead fans at least know what makes for great oblivion, and this faint coma was not about to be suffered gladly. Rubbish bovine rubbish. Treat it to a slow death."

That the other support act wasn't even mentioned in the review, or that Motörhead received only a salutary paragraph (less than a quarter of the word count), speaks volumes. The Bykers were obviously doing something right, even if it was only raising hackles. Reviews in both *Record Mirror* and *Sounds* were similar in that they concentrated on the Bykers rather than Motörhead, such was the media focus at the time — even in a heavy metal friendly publication like *Sounds*. Pete Paisley's review in *Record Mirror* referred to the Bykers as "the Bad News boys of grebo". He likened their music to "cheap fast and agonised chaos-metal", and said, if anything, their "new material" was getting less accessible than

ever". He concluded, somewhat curiously, that "the Gaye Bykers still make music to break into dilapidated squats by".

Cathi Unsworth, writing for *Sounds,* emphasised how the Bykers bombed in front of the rabid Motörhead audience. The stage had been "set for disaster" from the moment the band bounded onto it, with Mary facetiously announcing they were the Beastie Boys. Launching into Nosedive Karma, things got more excruciating as the sound deteriorated and, amidst a barrage of heckling, the Bykers gave up on trying to pull their set out of the mire. Eventually they left the stage in darkness, with only the sound of a feeding-back guitar trying to compete with the crowd's dissatisfaction and chants of "Motörhead! Motörhead!"

Unsworth had a point when she said the Bykers were "out of their depth supporting Motörhead". Who wouldn't be at the Hammersmith Odeon? However, she was perhaps uncharitable when she concluded the review, "all their clever gimmicks cannot hide the fact that they just don't know how to rock".

In her report of the second of the two nights for *Kerrang!,* Alison Joy said the Bykers "drew little response from the hardened Hammersmith hordes", with the only two memorable things about their set being "the bass player [...] mysteriously covered in fluorescent orange stick-on bits, and secondly that the vocalist seemed to spend most of his time either crawling along the floor or shuffling around bent double." Joy, like the audience, was less than impressed with the spectacle, and added, "the Bykers provided little entertainment for the gathered metallers as they stood bathed in strobe lights, bashing out blasts of psychedelic guitar." She describes Mary regaling the crowd with "stories of his mother's spleen operation." Her closing comment on the Bykers was "I shan't be seeing them again. (I hope)." This being *Kerrang!,* a magazine devoted primarily to heavy metal, Joy reserved her praise for Sword and, naturally enough, Motörhead.

The Bykers had more than proved their worth on other occasions and they rose to the challenge on this one, too, holding their own on both nights in front of the fiercely hostile biker audience. Mary reflects, "As far as the gig was concerned, we didn't go down very well, but we did it — we'd played with The Ramones, then played with Motörhead at Hammersmith, ticked it off the list kind of thing."

Unscathed aside from a few dented egos, the Bykers returned to Europe for the last two dates of The Ramones tour (Zurich and finally Paris, on 13th October), *NME* journalist James Brown went out to meet them in Paris where he interviewed Mary and The Ramones. Echoing Mary's earlier sentiments, Brown recalls, "It was great being around the original cartoon punks and my memory is Mary and I were in awe and thrilled to be in and around The Ramones dressing room." Unbeknown to them though, outside, a near full-scale riot was underway as the show was taking place. Brown remembers, "When The Ramones gig finished Mary and I went out of the venue through the front doors and there was still tear gas in the air and all the huge glass doors had been smashed in with French punks trying to get in to see The Ramones. Inside the gig had been so good we had no idea what was happening outside. It was a shock to be crunching over lots and lots of broken glass and seeing mangled barriers and still a few riot police getting into vans."

Photo courtesy of Beki Field.

Beki Field, Bykers' keyboardist had previously played piano on The Chameleons' Strange Times album.

The Bykers returned to the UK and had a week off before embarking on their first major headlining tour since signing to Virgin. The band had no opportunity to wind down, being occupied with press interviews and pre-production duties for the *Drill Your Own Hole* movie. Now they also had to prepare for the tour and meet their appointed keyboardist/sample operator.

Beki Field had been working as a tape-operator at Jacobs, the famous residential recording studios in Farnham. Chameleons' guitarist Reg Smithies overheard her playing a classical piece on the studio's grand piano, during a day off from recording their 1986 *Strange Times* album. Impressed with the 16-year-old's skills, he asked her to provide piano on some of their songs. She contributed to Seriocity and two songs that would become bonus tracks on the album's CD release (covers of David Bowie's John I'm Only Dancing and the Beatles' Tomorrow Never Knows). Says Beki, "I even ended up shouting on Mad Jack. I was so proud of that experience but carried on with everyday life."

The following year Beki had a call from Ken Thomas. Thomas had worked with *Drill Your Own Hole* producer Alex Fergusson when he was in Psychic TV and would later work with The Sugarcubes. Thomas remembered Beki from The Chameleons recording session and asked if she'd be willing to play keyboards for the Gaye Bykers On Acid's forthcoming tour. Beki recalls, "I had heard of the band but was unfamiliar with their music. I had to meet them in London for an audition… I was put in the hot seat — something like *Mastermind* — and surrounded by the band. The fact that I liked Hawkwind seemed to be the most important thing to them."

Mary asked Beki if she could play a combination of Hawkwind and the Pet Shop Boys. She replied yes and was given the job. Beki remembers, "With little time to rehearse on my two-year-old piano, and a week in France with a boyfriend who really didn't want to listen to Gaye Bykers On Acid on repeat in his campervan, meant little practice time. I remember practising while my mum was doing the ironing — God knows what she thought of the lyrics! Maybe that's why my dad actually chopped up my piano with a pickaxe for firewood! One session in a rehearsal studio and the photoshoot, and we were off!" ☠

CHAPTER SIX

SOFT TOILET PAPER AND
LOCKS ON THE BOG DOOR

THE TOUR WAS NAMED SOFT TOILET PAPER AND LOCKS ON The Bog Door, a send up of the grandiose names that some bands gave to tours, and a wry comment on the marginal increase in status that the Gaye Bykers on Acid had enjoyed by signing to a major label. Explaining the name to the *Scottish Sunday Mail* on the eve of the tour, Mary said, "It's just a bit of a joke really. All these bands put stupid names to tours, you know 'No Sleep till Christmas Tour' or whatever… This is possibly the first tour we're doing where we will get soft toilet paper and locks on the toilet door. Our new upwardly mobile status had been realised at last." As recently as six months ago, the band was supporting the likes of The Janitors and The Bomb Party, but now the Gaye Bykers on Acid were headliners. Returning the favour, they asked both their erstwhile mentors from Leicester to support them on the tour, with The Janitors as support on one half of the dates and The Bomb Party the other half. Virgin obliged the Bykers by letting them choose their own support acts, but insisted that another Virgin act, The Blood Uncles, would be the main support band. The Blood Uncles were already earning themselves a reputation, and featured former Exploited bassist Big John Duncan, who went on to play with future Garbage singer Shirley Manson in the Scottish band Goodbye Mr McKenzie, before ending up as a roadie for Nirvana in 1993.

The Soft Toilet Paper (sometimes Soft Toilet Roll) Tour kicked off on 21st

"LET'S SHAKE SOME ASS" – The first of two music press ads for Git Down single.

"REACH CRITICAL MASS" — The second of two music press ads for Git Down single.

October 1987 at the Diamond Suite in the Irish Centre, Digbeth, Birmingham. Arriving at the venue at about 2:30pm, the Bykers soundchecked, before heading off to be interviewed by Jenny Wilkes at BBC WM Radio at Pebble Mill. They returned to the venue for a solid first night performance of the tour.

Their newly elevated status afforded more than Soft Toilet Paper And Locks On The Bog Door — the Virgin deal also enabled the band to enhance their stage show: Psychedelic oil-slide projections were accompanied by near epilepsy inducing strobes and fluorescent tube lighting, while banks of television screens — glowing red and green — flickered away and variously displayed snippets of pornographic movies, white noise interference, and even speeded-up footage of supermarket dashes — perhaps symbolising the increasing rampant consumerism endemic of Margaret Thatcher's Britain of the 1980s.

Beki made her live debut playing keyboards on the opening night of the tour. Mary introduced her on stage in Birmingham, and, in typically thoughtless and impulsive fashion, described the band as "child molesters". On those early dates, there were technical difficulties with the keyboard and sampler, and Beki also suffered a spot of the nerves. Says Beki, "All I'd ever played was classical apart from The Chameleons, so it was hard. I was only 18 when we went on tour. It was scary but very exciting. I turned my volume down and everyone was telling me to turn up!" If Beki wasn't quite up-to-speed due to her lack of rehearsal time, she admits that Tony was always on hand to help out, "shouting and pointing every time I had to play helicopter noises or bomb noises."

Health and safety also proved to be as much an issue as the keyboard volume and technical difficulties. Only three dates into the tour, Beki recalls that when the band arrived at the soundcheck at the Louise in Glasgow, the venue was deemed too unsafe to play. The road manager took one look at the stage and noted that while high enough to prevent people from climbing onto it, was worried that those at the front of the audience could have their necks crushed against the stage in the event of a surge. Not only that, but the dodgy electrics could also have caused an unintentional "fireworks display". Consequently, the Bykers' got the evening off and went to see The Damned, also in Glasgow that night (playing at Strathclyde University).

The following night's gig at King George's Hall in Blackburn was sparsely attended, according to Stuart Maconie for *NME*. Maconie was indifferent towards the support that night from The Janitors and Blood Uncles, and noted that most of those in attendance were "doing the sound or selling t-shirts." Over-egging the 'grebo' connection, Maconie derided the Midlands

Rare picture of Beki Field with the Gaye Bykers On Acid. Photographer not known.

("the spiritual home of kipper ties, ropey football, and heavy metal. It is the land where it is forever 1973. Something as endearingly gormless as grebo could never have been spawned anywhere else."). He seemed to enjoy the band's set and latest single, Git Down, but overall wasn't enamoured: "GBOA celebrate the cheap and pointless in a manner unheard of since Mud and The Glitter Band, loud and silly and obnoxious. It's the perfect soundtrack to the fag end of a low and dishonest decade." Ambiguous to the end, Maconie bemoans the fact the Bykers arrived too late for the olfactory phenomenon of what was the 'Golden Age" of the Scratch and Sniff Sleeve'. "These records," he writes, "should come inside covers that stink of piss and snakebite [...] Pop has eaten itself. Are we living in a land where beer and shagging are the new gods? Yes, I think we probably are."

Songs like World War 7 Blues and Zen Express were showcased for the first time on the Soft Toilet Paper tour. The Bykers also incorporated another Edgar Broughton Band song into their set, Call Me A Liar, at the expense of Evil/Love In The Rain, which they had started to play live earlier in the summer.

Beki throws some light on what life was like on the road with the Bykers and the individual personalities at play. Kev commandeered the tour bus VCR. Being the only female on the bus was an eye-opener for Beki. "What Kev picked to watch on the bus TV was a bit of a shocker for a young girl from the back of beyond like me!" she says. It's not too hard to guess the sort of material in question, given Kev's penchant for porn videos and *Spinal Tap*. Beki admits, "But I didn't mind *Spinal Tap* over and over!" In Leeds, Beki recounts that Kev brought back a chicken to his hotel room. "I was a bit worried being a vegetarian, but I didn't hang around to see what that was all about!" Even stranger, Kev was also a vegetarian, so quite what he was doing with a chicken is anyone's guess. Of the other bandmates, Beki recalls that, "Mary was so enthusiastic about everything, and took me under his wing, letting me stay at his house with his talking cats! Tony was the sweet one... a bit more calm and realistic, but very sweet. Kev and Robber were the mad ones — it was like the boys — Tony and Mary — and the men — Robber and Kev. Robber was the one to play tricks, like winding up my boyfriend when I phoned him, saying things like 'Ohhhh, great blowjob' in the background".

Then there were the groupies. Beki took pity on some of them and put them up in her hotel room on occasion. By and large though, she adds that it was "all quite innocent — no one ever complained. The band were all nice guys, letting male fans jump on the tour bus from one town to the next."

Sandwiched between gigs in Manchester and Nottingham, the Bykers were booked to play the Futurama Festival in Deinze, Belgium on 31st October on a bill that included Dinosaur Jr., Wire, Pop Will Eat Itself, Christian Death, The Godfathers, The Young Gods, Zodiac Mindwarp, The Leather Nun, and PiL. Although they'd made a similar dash from Europe and back for the Motörhead gigs earlier in the month, they pulled out of the Belgian festival. Perhaps the rigours of the last few months were starting to take their toll, or maybe it was something to do with their record label, Virgin. Jack Barron in *NME* reported with a hint of relief: "Today was heavily tipped towards the Grebo end of the body fat scale, with planned appearances by Pop Will Eat Itself, the big smelly Zodiac Mindwarp & The Love Reaction, and Gaye Bykers On Acid. In the event the Bykers never turned up, likewise their labelmates PiL. Did this amount to a conspiracy of chasteness by Virgin?" It transpired that PiL pulled out because the stage was too small. But at least the Bykers were rewarded with two unexpected days off in what was fast becoming a punishing schedule.

On Monday 2nd November, it was back to business as usual for the last seven consecutive dates of the Soft Toilet Paper tour. It wasn't all plain sailing though, and they ran into trouble with Exeter council, which objected to the band's name and banned them from playing the city's university. Another gig was hastily organised in Port Talbot, Wales, before the band concluded the tour in London at the Town and Country Club.

Here, the Stupids were added to the bill alongside support acts The Blood Uncles and The Bomb Party, who had taken over the second support slot from The

Janitors halfway through the tour. They were a British skate punk band currently enjoying a certain degree of success on the UK alternative scene. Roger Holland in *Sounds* made reference to Kentish Town, location of the Town and Country Club, being rammed full of "8 million" people wearing baseball caps, and that "even two hours before the door opened it was clear that we were on the verge of a happening… the only question was who or what was happening." He was more single-minded in his pot-shot at the Bykers: "The Gayes were the headliners with the big record deal. But their record is Hackneyed and Hammersmithed, and all Mary could do was stand outside selling fanzines."

DRILL YOUR OWN HOLE
OR DIG YOUR OWN GRAVE

During production, the title of both the LP and the movie were changed from *Lust For Glory* to *Drill Your Own Hole*. A marketing ploy was concocted whereby a limited-edition number of copies of the record would initially be made available without holes in the middle, the premise being that unsuspecting recipients would be required to emulate the title and furnish the record with their own hole for the turntable spindle to go through. Dave Bartram thinks this gimmick was instrumental to the name change. He says, "so the film was also called that to fit in with the album really, but I think the album was written around the premise of the film… songs for certain themes."

Initially the *Drill Your Own Hole* album was planned to coincide with the release of the video and was also mooted for airing on the British television station Channel 4. *Drill* was ostensibly intended to be the soundtrack for the album, including as it did a mixture of older, but reworked originals, as well as several numbers written especially

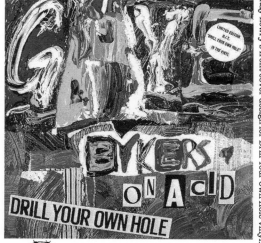

Ray Lowry's front cover design for Drill Your Own Hole vinyl.

Inner gatefold sleeve of Drill Your Own Hole album.

for the film.

It became obvious that when the band were due to set out on the road to promote the album and their new single Git Down, the video wouldn't be ready. Even as late as 16th October, the band were still recording incidental music for the film, less than 24 hours after arriving back from the last of their European dates in Paris with The Ramones. The schedule was gruelling for everyone.

Finally released on 2nd November 1987, *Drill Your Own Hole* polarised opinion and continues to do so. Robber finds it hard to listen to: "Some folks love that first LP, but I hate that *Drill* record! There were some great songs — All Hung Up, So Far Out — ideas that we had played live since we started were ruined by being overproduced into bad techno turds. You cannot polish techno turds, what's the point of sequencing all the drums then using the boring kit sounds you sampled off Kev's drums? Why not use an 808 Kick or Janet Jackson snare like we did with Jon Langford on the In-Tape sessions? To Kev Hyde's credit, he was a tight drummer anyway! What were we thinking? I think Stacey Lafront was keeping us far too busy touring for us to get a grip on the musical creative side of things... that and the *Drill Your Own Hole* film we made at the same time, which although was quite a laugh to make, cost us a small fortune... and distracted us all."

Jon Langford considers *Drill* a "mistake" and goes on to explain that the band

"had real momentum after *Nosedive*. They should have done the first album on an independent with me and Ian [Caple] but their heads were full of PFX and making a movie by then. Stacey had some producers who wanted to sample everything and just bleed all the life and energy out of a truly great shambolic rock band — *Drill* is a very un-grebish sounding record".

Similarly, Ian Caple has misgivings about *Drill*: "I saw this a lot in the eighties, a new exciting band gets signed to a big label and have the energy produced out of them by an expensive producer. This happened so many times. I must admit I was a bit disappointed when I heard *Drill Your Own Hole*. It just didn't sound like the Bykers. They were, first and foremost, a really great live band, and what Jon and me tried to do was to capture the energy and the vibe of the band, so most of the time we recorded them all together — vocals and all, and then added the electronics and loops etc. on top, whereas a lot of eighties producers were taking the band apart, making them play along to their sequencers etc. Nine times out of 10 this will kill the vibe stone dead!"

Perhaps Dave Bartram has a point when he says, "It was basically 'a difficult second album' — a concept album in a gatefold sleeve, that most bands go through." Laughing, he adds, "but the Bykers did it as a debut!"

Critics were also divided. It was apparent that media opinion was turning against the band, more forcefully than before in any case. That's not to say there wasn't some sympathetic reviews, but even these had a degree of ambiguity. Dilemma was a noun bandied around by at least two reviewers. Despite awarding it four out five stars, Mr Spencer still wasn't sure of the album in his review for *Sounds*. "Not so much brilliant as... Not bad. Not bad," he wrote. "Gaye Bykers On Acid have long been a source of dilemma, their cracked minds and the resultant spillage of sex and tack, skateboards and space travel, have always far exceeded their actual accomplishment."

On the one hand, Spencer considered *Drill* in terms of "Mad Max with a rocket pack and a head full of hallucinogenics", while on the other "exactly like being at a Bykers live show". He considered the album, "Bewildering, amusing, a bit boring towards the end, then picking up nicely for the big climax." He concluded: "think concept hard enough and you've got a classic."

Billboard, the American entertainment trade magazine, was confused: "We don't get the 'Gaye' part, 'Bikers On Acid' is just what this album sounds like: MC5 energy coupled with less-than-zero production values and ripped-off riffs from the Kinks to Zeppelin. A good listen for the open-eared. Includes the UK charted single Git Down (Shake Your Thang)."

Robert Sandall, writing for *Q* magazine, attributed the album's charm to a "freewheeling, cacophonous energy which propels the Bikers [sic] way beyond the cynical and safe guitar bashing of the metal merchants and does a lot more than recreate the heady days of heavy acid rock as well". He considered it "Leicester's best effort since Roger Chapman and Family," and admitted to "a manic inventiveness that I was beginning to think that rock had grown completely out of".

A relatively new UK national daily broadsheet newspaper called the *Independent* was also complimentary in its summation of the album: "More interesting and just as contemporary is the way the lads have guerrilla raided the editing techniques of hip hop and the base [sic] lines and vernacular of funk to top up the novelty value of their ferocious psychedelic funk-rock. The energy is infectious and, incredibly, even sulky journalist types like a good laugh. Buy this and believe that Fat Freddy's Cat can dance."

Alas, most critics and the record buying public didn't appreciate the album quite as much as the *Independent*. Stalling at number 95 in the album charts, *Record Mirror*, *Melody Maker* and *NME* all routinely rounded on it, and savaged it.

Nancy Culp of *Record Mirror* opened her review by begging the question of the band, "Oh why didn't their mothers drown them all at birth and save me the trouble of saying something that I'll maybe regret in two months' time?" The "noisily trumpeted" Gaye Bykers' debut album, said Culp, put her in a dilemma, particularly "the squealy but maybe tongue-in-cheek guitar solos, I abhor the way it so often becomes a flimsy excuse for 'energy'! It also thinly disguises the fact that the Bykers don't appear to have any idea of what a good tune sounds like". Much of *Drill* reminded her of the "Edgar Broughton Band on ricicles [sic], or worse Jethro Tull on Reeboks". Perhaps this barbed comment was less venomous than Culp had intended, given the Bykers' propensity for the Broughtons and the fact that a more than commendable version of Call Me A Liar was covered on the album. Culp gave *Drill Your Own Hole* 1½ stars.

The Bykers seemingly had a firm ally in the *Melody Maker* camp with Carol Clerk. However, David Stubbs was not so forgiving. He opened his *Melody Maker* review with the sardonic comment, "I feel the Bykers aren't completely hopeless", and proceeded to maul them without mercy. He suggested the band ought to change its name to "Thick Bykers On Beer" and decried what he considered was the Bykers' attitude problem, particularly when it came to Mary. This over-confidence was self-consciousness, he lamented, and made a comparison intended as disparaging but actually the Bykers wouldn't have had any issue with: "if the Bykers had been born in America they could have

Mary Byker and Carol Clerk at The Oporto, London, 1987.

Photo courtesy of Mick Mercer.

been the Butthole Surfers, *completely* moronic, floating as blearily as bromide, abstractedly abrasive, their brains leaking, and their bloated bodies oozing. As it is the Bykers are too fatally sussed to produce a giant dung masterpiece like *Locust Abortion Technician*." Part of the Bykers' problem, noted Stubbs, was that "they're never up in the air, never bowel-deep". He likened their performance on World War 7 Blues to "Judas Priest with a small, blunt instrument instead of a dick".

Neither did Stubbs appreciate the gimmick that his review copy of the record was missing a hole. "A mere prod of my pen," he lamented, "was enough to puncture one." The marketing ploy behind the album had not quite realised the ideal, and although it *appeared* you would need to make your own hole to render the disc playable, the reality fell a little short. The myth still persists today, but as Stubbs pointed out, this was not the case. Only the label itself, not the plastic, had to be 'drilled' on these limited-edition copies.

If the Bykers thought things couldn't get any worse, they needed to look no further than Bob Stanley. In his review for *NME*, Stanley wrote that, "Git Down and Zen Express smack of a group discovering studio technology for the first time, pressing every button in sight and hoping for the best." Stanley was more merciless than Stubbs when he described the Bykers as the "hideous mutant offspring of the Jimi Hendrix Experience", and just to allay any possible ambiguity,

Drill Your Own Hole... or at least poke a pencil through the label.

Stanley elaborated: "The tunes are non-existent. The resulting mishmash of everything plus the kitchen sink is akin to mixing all the colours in a paint box. It comes out turd brown." He didn't stop there. He considered the songs "overflowing with suitable rock clichés" and cited "the interminably long All Hung Up" as a prime example. The list of insults went on until he twisted the knife one final time. "*Drill Your Own Hole* should have come in a scratch and sniff cover — I'll leave it up to the reader to choose the relevant odours." Stanley awarded the album a score of two out of 10.

Stanley's comment about the album's production wasn't without merit. Even Mary was not averse to criticising aspects of the production. Asked by American music magazine *B-Side* if there was anything he would change about *Drill*, Mary replied, "The drums. They're not at all like how [Kev] plays live. We had to put them down on an electric click track machine because they're in the movie. Having said that though, I listened to it the other day and it really didn't sound that bad. When I'm here, it sounds like a section of it is different. American people seem to like it because the album is more popular here than it was in England."

Mary stands by this opinion today. Although he looks back on *Drill* with affection, he still has issues with the production. "Most bands were interested in seeing how pointy their shoes were and the like," he says. "We weren't, although everyone thought we were concerned about our image and stuff — well we kind of were, but — we were really a quite creative bunch, you know? We really had so many different ideas that we were trying to cram into this one thing. And when we came to make the record, I just think we were all a little disappointed 'cos it didn't really show us as a live thing — they should have just recorded us live.

Fold out promo leaflet for Drill Your Own Hole movie.

Well, they kind of did and then they took all the drums off and programmed it, and the process was all new to us, and so I think we weren't entirely happy with the way it turned out. But I think now when I look back on it, yeah, it's pretty good!"

At the time of release, perhaps due to increasing media scrutiny and criticism, Mary appeared to be more concerned about being misinterpreted by the press. This was highlighted in an interview with *Melody Maker's* Carol Clerk. Mary featured on the cover of the issue in question, thumbs hooked louchely in his belt, resplendent in a bright red retro 'reefer madness' t-shirt and gazing coyly towards the camera beneath a 10-gallon hat. In the interview he describes he now had to be more "introspective" and think before he replied to questions from journalists for risk of offending people. "We didn't realise that we have to articulate to people that much. We did credit people with more sense, probably," he told Clerk. He then highlighted one dichotomy the band faced since signing to Virgin: "We lived in a squat a year ago. We're now employing 40 people. That's enough of a head trip for anybody. Margaret Thatcher would be well proud of us. People can say 'Oh you're a product of Thatcher's Britain'. Yes, yes, yes, yes, that's what we're doing, but it sucks. The position we're in is the most frustrating position I've ever been in. It's the most pressure that anybody could ever have. It's really, really, really hard, because we are now by the very nature of what we're doing setting ourselves up as sitting ducks. The album is called

Purple Fluid Exchange in association with Virgin
Invite you to 'Lig' at their movie premiere of

"DRILL YOUR OWN HOLE"

on
Friday December 4th
at
The Town and Country Club,
9/17 Highgate Road, London, NW5.

Doors open: 7pm 'til late

Reverse of invitation to Drill Your Own Hole movie premiere. Courtesy of Dave Bartram.

Drill Your Own Hole. It's like dig your own grave really".

James Brown was one of the few people privy to a preview of the Bykers' movie prior to its premiere and was ambiguous in his summation. He admired the Bykers for their determination, and wrote in the 7th November issue of *NME*, "They don't play the most creative or inspired music in the world — many of you will understandably never see it as anything other than crap — but what they have is an unstoppable drive of energy, determination, and enthusiasm. Such qualities disappeared from the mainstream with the demise of Two-Tone." But Brown expressed his disappointment in the movie: "The plot was as frail as a baby's skull but the high-colour multi metal musical performances were more than enough to keep it breathing." The Bykers' acting ability, or rather lack thereof, was one of the main drawbacks, noted Brown. This was an accusation levelled at the Bykers in subsequent reviews of the film.

In *Sounds* the following week the Bykers received a two-page spread and were interviewed by Andy Hurt. He had been granted access to a short clip of the forthcoming *Drill* movie and therefore unable to "pass judgement" because, he said, "the Bykers' manager deemed it a smart promotional move to hold back the finished item with a view to squeezing further press to coincide with its release." From what little he did see, Hurt was reminded of the anarchic TV show, *The Comic Strip Presents....* Mary readily agreed, citing *The Young Ones* as an influence, but not as much as Hunter S. Thompson's *Fear and Loathing in Las Vegas*. Hurt also made a comparison to the movie *Tron*. "The obvious analogy with the film is the band's relationship with the music business," Hurt wrote, concluding, "they are inside the machine whether they like it or not."

Hurt reflected on whether the Bykers' career had been "manufactured". Mary refuted this of course. "Everyone seems to think we're a real hype, but if we are, it's a *natural* hype, rather than a contrived business kind of hype," said Mary. Hurt wasn't shy of pointing out the potential contradictions raised by signing

to Virgin while at the same time flaunting a "brash, anti-star attitude", not to mention the band's stance against censorship and "a desire to sell records". Mary argued that rather than be banned in the States because of the band's name, he might compromise by abbreviating it to simply "On Acid". It was also evident in the interview just how much the Bykers were tiring of the fickleness of the music press. "I don't hate the music press," said Mary, "I just don't like people who abuse their position."

It was amidst all this ratcheting media coverage — good and bad — that arrangements were made for the premiere of *Drill Your Own Hole*. But this wasn't without problems. In addition to the various production and post-production issues that had plagued the movie, rumour has it that producer Debbie Mason refused to hand over the master copy until the production team and actors had been paid in full. Other rumours posited that the hold-up was an attempt to generate press coverage, or that Stacey Lafront had allegedly held back preview copies in order to try and extract more money out of Virgin. The film's director Dave Bartram says that Lafront had taken "a VHS copy of the film with the time-code across the bottom and stretched the picture to crop out the time-code, and she tried to sell that to somebody, or gave that to Virgin and said, 'you're not getting the real thing until you give me more cash'". Robber thinks that in all likelihood, all the scenarios are true to some degree. After a delay of a month, *Drill Your Own Hole* premiered at the Town and Country Club on Friday 4th December. Given the rocky road of its production, it seems hardly surprising that the premiere failed to run smoothly. The usually sympathetic Carol Clerk couldn't ignore that fact that the whole thing was a disaster. "Something had to go wrong," she wrote in *Melody Maker*, prophesying that the premiere would screw up:

> In the event, it got screwed up very badly. The picture, for a start, was hardly as sharp as it could've been, and the sound remained so muffled it was impossible to understand any of the dialogue. The audience were as baffled at the end as they had been at the beginning when the Bykers climbed into a washing machine and set off on their time-travels. It was necessary to watch the video to grasp any idea of the 'plot' which, briefly, finds the Bykers as participants in a computer game, their actions dictated by a pair of disembodied lips, their goal to find 'fame, fortune and everything you've ever dreamed of'.

Dave Bartram recalls of the premiere: "It wasn't a big do at all, it was only on a video screen, and again it was lots of the band's mates that were there. It wasn't

the big movie premiere it should have been. It was a bit of a damp squib from what I remember."

Paul B Davies says he fell asleep during the screening, not so much out of boredom but because he was "out of it". He adds wryly, "I'm probably not the only one who fell asleep during it!" The film, he added, "didn't go through much professional discipline, put it that way. It was all pretty wacky and out there. Nobody quite knew what they were doing. They certainly didn't do what you should do with a film, which is not film it until you've written several drafts and honed and refined, and it wasn't even professional by music video standards."

David Quantick's 'Gaye Bykers On Acid Movie Lig' review in *NME* was surprisingly favourable given Quantick's disdain of the Bykers and their ilk at Acid Daze a few months earlier. "The dialogue," he said of the movie, "leans heavily on *The Young Ones* for its content and *The Monkees* for its style." He went on: "The acting is of a standard that recalls the glorious moments of *The Double Deckers* and clips from Children's Film Foundation movies as shown on Michael Rodd's *Screen Test*." Quantick concluded the film to be "crap, basically" but admitted to having liked it.

Drill Your Own Hole was passed 18 without cuts by the British Board of Film

Classification (BBFC) and released on video by Virgin Vision. Robber admits that "In hindsight, I wouldn't have done the film. I would've spent the money on a recording studio and somewhere to live above it… something a bit more tenable. But you don't think like that when you're 20, do you?" Robber is mystified by the BBFC's 18 classification, which restricts the film to an adult-only audience. "We didn't swear in that film, and there's nothing really that outrageous in it and they classed it as an 18 because of [the wording] 'On Acid'! There's a lot worse things than that ain't there, really?" Even in the 1980s, a verb alluding to drug-taking was enough to offend some and consequently the video sleeve replaced 'Acid' with asterisks. As Robber points out, by comparison "The records never got an 18 certificate or parental guidance stickers, or whatever else!"

Dave Bartram is also puzzled by the asterisks on the video sleeve. "I don't know why that happened… it must've come from Virgin Vision rather than Virgin Records." As for the certificate, he states, somewhat incredulously, "it was an 18 certificate! And the only thing in there… a hippie in the bus [during the Zen Express scene] says 'shit', but that was about the only bit of swearing in it, so I'm surprised it got an 18!"

Adrian Deevoy pilloried the movie mercilessly in Q magazine. He describes a "horrific barrage of Bobby Davro-style non-jokes" and casts aspersions over the band's acting capabilities. His parting shot: "After seven songs and an hour of self-consciously wacky behaviour the impression left is that of a primary school nativity play: the naivety and embarrassment is almost endearing, the enthusiastic amateurism is charming, but the whole project cannot, under any circumstances be assessed as a considered contribution to the arts. In many ways, *Drill Your Own Hole* digs its own grave." He awarded the video two stars.

Sam King liked it. In *Sounds'* end of year round-up of videos, King wrote that

> *Drill Your Own Hole* sees the Bykers shattering the now complacent stereotype of rock videos, while at the same time flattering by imitation the entire host of subversive, underground movies that inspired them in the first place. This is pop psychology at its best, combining the brilliant plagiarism of films like *Videodrome* (the obvious initial inspiration), *The Blue Brothers* and *Koyaanisquatsi* [sic] with an astute sociopolitical outlook that manages to incorporate subjects as diverse as American capitochristian evangelism and the banal reality of today's TV gameshows.

As other reviewers, King commented on the performances, but for him the film was "Aided rather than hindered by the Bykers' excruciating attempts at acting (*The Young Ones* meet *Terry And June*) it's a superb example of modern grebo culture. Less of a video in fact than a way of life."

Record Mirror described the movie as "Tacky, crass and in places a bit heavy on the gratuitous shock tactics (blood and guts)". The anonymous reviewer wasn't far off the mark in stating the film to be "something the *Comic Strip* might have come up with had they got into greboism" and considered it "rather entertaining if only because the Bykers are such bad actors and the plot's so naff!" In conclusion, the film was "more preferable to the usual sort of live footage that's trundled out in tandem with an album release".

The Bykers were unable to glean consolation from the majority of reviews of *Drill Your Own Hole*, but some shared the idea that theirs was a novel approach to music videos. David Giles in *Number One* magazine agreed that it was a cut above the usual promo video: "An hour long film of the GBOA album as opposed to yer average run-of-the-mill video…"

Music Week, a trade paper for the UK record industry, was almost ecstatic in its praise: "Probably the best thing that could have happened to rock video is that someone like the Bykers should come along and break all the usual rules." *Music Week* made the usual comparisons but rather than an overt dig at the acting, surmised that "The Bykers are not professional actors but they've managed to create a cohesive screenplay… giving *Drill Your Own Hole* every inch of vitality that was lacking from the album of the same name… Sales forecast: with the right publicity this will sell really well and should re-promote interest in the LP. Eventually it'll be shown on Channel 4 but an initial cheap price should secure early buyers from their legion of fans."

Unfortunately, *Music Week*'s projection fell woefully short of the reality. Despite pre-publicity fanfares that mooted the movie would be aired on Channel 4, MTV and nationally in cinemas, none of it materialised and in the end countless copies of the VHS could be found languishing in the bargain bins of Virgin Megastores up and down the land. It was an ignominious fate for a project that, only a year prior, the Bykers and Virgin had such high hopes for.

Tony regrets the money pit that the movie had become: "It was strange going from being on the dole and squatting to then getting some cash. However, I must say that 100 grand [£100,000] doesn't go that far between five people! We only got 50g [£50,000] up front, and we each took 5g [£5,000], so that's 25g [£25,000] gone to begin with. Then we bought some equipment. The rest we had to put towards making the movie, 'cos Virgin Vision wouldn't spend that much unless we invested some. So, then we were back to zero again!"

Tony continues: "I remember that we were all pissed off 'cos the extras in

the movie were getting paid more than we were! We were still signing on and hanging around literally all day long wasn't that much fun. When the next 50g came, the shit hit the fan because of the trouble with Stacey. All of these unpaid bills that we thought she'd paid. The cash had to go to a professional accountant in Swiss Cottage, who held onto it, to keep the tax man from bankrupting us. So that was that. Back to nothing!"

Back to nothing indeed. In an interview that appeared in the short-lived music monthly, *Underground*, the band discussed the film with Alex Kadis. Said Robber: "Basically, it was us making a film about us making a lot of money and overspending by about £100,000! That's what it was about!" Kev corrected him: "We spent £200,000! We now owe £50,000, and we now have no money. THAT'S what the film was about!" Mary was uncommonly guarded and admitted that "certain people did take advantage of us". But Robber had qualms about identifying who he considered the real beneficiaries, "namely Debbie Mason who had champagne dinners; namely Mike Pike who edited it and who f***** us off and Dave Bartram who took the piss out of us even though he was our friend. But I'm not squabbling about it. THE FILM WAS SHIT!!!" It was obvious that the experience of making the film had left a bitter taste. Kev likened the band's present attitude to being "more pessimistic than someone waiting on Death Row". Mary announced, "OK — get this down — we'd like to just say that the film industry *is* full of more shit than the music industry and the music industry *is* full of shit!"

The music industry may well be full of shit, but the Bykers, whether they liked it or not, were still up to their necks in it. The second single to be released from the album, coinciding with the movie premiere, was the significantly reworked version of All Hung Up. Anyone reading the reviews could be forgiven for thinking the single was lifted from a different album to the one that had been mauled only a few weeks ago. Lisa Tilston made it 'Top Of The Tree' in *Record Mirror*, writing that, "Yup, it's a funny old world where the Bykers get Single Of The Week, but this mows down everything in its path on the way to the top". Tilston went as far as to say that it wasn't even the best song on the album.

Mr Spencer referred to All Hung Up as "one of the stronger songs" from *Drill* and made a point of "someone's foot being pressed down on the wah wah pedal throughout. The tune itself, despite being perfectly reasonable, is soon forgotten amidst the delicious spiralling chaos". Working against the single was the fact that it was released at Christmastime, a time of frivolity and asinine pop tunes, otherwise Mr Spencer believed "it could be a hit."

Nonetheless the end of year music press reviews devoted a great deal

Music press ad for Gaye Bykers On Acid All Hung Up single.

of column space to the 'grebo' phenomenon. *Melody Maker* referred to the movement as being not much more than a liberal baiting nucleus comprised of bands with "long hair… from Leicester (or thereabouts)", all of whom "extolled the virtues of yobbery and sexism as if yobbery and sexism were a startling new polemic in rock's ongoing dialogue." After some disparaging remarks directed at the bands in question (including The Bomb Party, who had rhymed Grandma with crowbar in one of their songs), the anonymous writer admitted that Crazyhead had released two of the best pop singles of the year in So Amazing Baby and Baby Turpentine. But this failed to save 'grebo' as anything but a meaningless aberration from which the bands couldn't wait to extricate themselves.

Things were a bit rosier elsewhere in the same issue of *Melody Maker*. Carol Clerk, who had shown her undying love of the Gaye Bykers On Acid when reviewing Git Down in October, listed three Bykers tracks in her top 10 picks of 1987, with All Hung Up at the top slot. Also included were Crazyhead's What Gives You The Idea That You're So Amazing Baby and tracks by The Cult and Zodiac Mindwarp.

Carol Clerk wasn't blindly following the pack or participating in the wider-brewing backlash. Nor was Ron Rom, who in his

end of year summation for *Sounds* described the 'grebo' phenomenon: "The grebos were a vile and gloriously loud response to a music industry in which y'average rock'n'roller was old enough to be somebody's granddad, and where new music was as cold and calculating as the CD/Filofax generation for which it catered." Rom posited that 'grebo' was an alternative to things being too safe. "It was brewing up behind the bike sheds of the indie charts at the end of last year, with bands like Gaye Bykers On Acid, Pop Will Eat Itself, and Crazyhead, busy vomiting all over the twee, lovesick, shambling class of '86. These groups had borrowed traditional rock values like megalithic guitar solos, even longer greasy hair, biker chic, casual laddish sexism, and mixed it with acid, some primal punk. *Kick ass* adrenalin."

Blaming The Cult for the rise of 'grebo', Rom believed it was up to the likes of the Bykers, Poppies, and Crazyhead to now make it a credible force. He stressed the significance of a largely Midlands based phenomenon and not one from the "fashion conscious streets of London". However, Rom also seemed to suggest that 'grebo' had already had its day: "The grebos were animals. They were generally scummy, had chip pan hair and bad breath. They were vulgar. The grebo is now a part of rock history in which the old style became the new style. Rock is dead, long live the grebo! Excuse me while I fart!"

Earlier in December Ian Astbury had defended so-called 'grebo' bands. In answer to a question put to him by Billy Duffy in the *NME*, Astbury said:

> I remember grebo when I was 12 years of age in Liverpool in 1972…
> Then it wasn't detrimental, it meant greasy bikers and if you saw a guy
> on a Triumph or a BSA with his girl on the back covered in leathers and
> horrible grease then he was a grebo, and they'd listen to Zeppelin, Pink
> Floyd, Deep Purple.
>
> The people who call the Gaye Bykers, Crazyhead, and Zodiac, grebos
> are old people who were never seen on a bike ever. I think it's sad that
> people put this tag on kids because they've a lot of potential and are nice
> kids. They slag us off but we couldn't give a shit because we like them.
> And they only slag us because we're their peers.

Duffy added for good measure, "And much more fucking famous. Ha!"

Jack Barron, with reference to the Bykers, Crazyhead, and Pop Will Eat Itself, noted that 1987 was the year bands of the 'grebo' ilk "set light to their farts, took a lot of drugs, acted like complete spamheads, but above all made a racket that you couldn't ignore". He described the *Drill* project as an "LSD-psychosis cut-up-

voice classic" but one that had "disappeared down the toilet of eternity without trace helped along by the idiot pen of every miserable critic ever to wear an anorak."

Sam King made *Drill* one of *Sounds'* albums of the year. He framed the album in the wider context of the 'grebo' phenomenon. King noted that 1987 was remarkable for "the emergence of the sampler and the cut-up, re-recorded record (the external manifestations of pop's love affair with technology)" and also the resurgence of "the rock guitar". The Cult had already picked up the mantle where Led Zeppelin had a left off almost a decade earlier, said King, and the time was right for a "grebo renaissance", which he considered was "the immaculate product of a union between contemporary hippy hedonism and progressive guitar playing." Gaye Bykers On Acid were "leaders of the pack" because "Their lively genius lies in the marriage of the despotically ancient with the ultra-contemporary." Unlike many of his music journalist peers who were damning of their debut album, King liked *Drill Your Own Hole*. "Loud, brash, impeccably attired and vocally prescient, Gaye Bykers picked up where the goths left off, introducing a whole new generation to the (dubious) pleasures of the retrospective overindulgence of guitar solos and intellectual (mis)adventure. Undeniably Hole-y."

So it wasn't all bad.

The Bykers rounded off the year by playing Les Trans Musicales Festival, an annual festival held each December in Brittany, France. Beginning in 1979, over the years the festival has earned itself something of a reputation, either rightly or wrongly, for showcasing the "next big thing". The Bykers shared a bill on the same night as Stump, Head and The Young Gods. Despite having been so busy for the past few months filming, recording their new album and touring it was apparent the Bykers had found time to write new material. In his festival report for *Sounds*, Jack Barron commented that the Bykers "premiered their new golfing song Fairway To Heaven in all its gonzoid glimmery".

Mark Wagstaff was at the festival selling Bykers' merchandise. He recalls an incident on the overnight crossing by ferry: "We

Gaye Bykers On Acid advent calendar Christmas 1987.

broke into the bar and stole some bottles of vodka and whiskey etc. I somehow managed to get back to my cabin. God knows what had taken place! When I woke up with an awful hangover, I made my way off the ferry only to see the whole band lined up in front of the Captain being severely reprimanded! 'You'll never travel on this line again!' sort of stuff! Hilarious!"

Given the lukewarm reception to *Drill Your Own Hole*, both album and video, it must have seemed to Virgin executives that the Bykers had already passed their sell by date. For a band that had promised so much less than six months prior, it was a bitterly disappointing end to the year.

For Crazyhead, 1987 ended on a quieter note. Their two singles had been well received, but unlike the Bykers they didn't have a movie to promote, let alone an album. They did however pay a visit to Jackson Studios in Rickmansworth to record Dragon City with the legendary Vic Maile producing. Reverb describes a confused session: "Vic started talking about his ideas for the song. It took a while before we realised that he was talking about Time Is Taking Its Toll On You. Food had sent him a tape with both songs on, and with Time being the first on

the tape he thought he was meant to be recording that one and had been getting ideas for that song."

With the matter of the correct track having been sorted, Food shelved any further sessions with Maile and decided not to release his version of Dragon City in any case. Reverb says that Food, or at least Balfe, "had already decided that they wanted us to sound more 'polite'". (Maile's version of Dragon City would eventually surface on a self-released compilation CD, *Fucked By Rock*). It would be several more months before Crazyhead recorded again, by which time major developments had occurred for the band.

WINTER OF DISCONTENT

Following a year in which the Bykers' fortunes and popularity had roller-coastered, thanks in no small part to the vagaries of the British music press, they were able to step back from the maelstrom that had engulfed them. Their time wasn't spent completely idle though, and they had already started to hone new songs in preparation for the forthcoming US tour in spring.

The band had already visited the States supporting The Cult in New York, and Tony returned in January 1988 on the back of his royalties: to the exotic climes of the Pacific islands of Hawaii for a holiday. A keen street-surfer on his skateboard, it was in Hawaii that he began to ride waves and developed a life-long love of the ocean (becoming an experienced SCUBA diver and dive instructor). "I thought I had better take a holiday while I had the chance and some cash," says Tony. "That was the only break I remember. I think we only took a month off, and then began writing and practising again." With good humour, Mary concedes: "Tony was actually a quite sensible Northern lad with his money. I think he actually saved it and used it a little bit wisely and did something with it!"

The other band members stayed in London, where Mary revelled in his newly found notoriety, frequently hanging out with Graham Crabb and the other Poppies. "I was living the life of Riley in London, ligging, going to the opening of any envelope," Mary admits. "I'd be standing next to Lemmy in The Ship, watching him play the one-arm bandits. At that point I could actually walk into any gig or nightclub pretty much for nothing, so I probably *was* disappearing up my own arse!" Mary is quick to point out, "I was always very sociable and liked a drink and to be out at night."

Contrary to what might have been assumed, given their large advance from Virgin, the band were not receiving a huge personal income. Most of their money had been channelled into the movie and equipment. But Mary found a means to supplement his basic income and maintain the lifestyle he was becoming accustomed to, by selling records. He would catch the bus to the Virgin press office on Harrow Road and "sit in the press room with the press officers and they'd say, 'Do you want to take some records out of the stock cupboard?' and I used to go and get 25–30 records and sell them down at Record & Tape Exchange. They

Tony Byker on holiday in Hawaii.

used to look forward to me coming in because I'd bring them all this brand-new stuff and promos, too. I used to make £150–£200 each time, something to go down the pub with — that'd be a long weekend in those days!"

Mary says "a lot of the bands used to do that", but adds ruefully, "I mean why didn't I hold on to some of those great records? Some of those early Virgins like Gong and Steve Hillage, real classic early seventies originals."

Meanwhile, some members of the band were becoming suspicious about how their finances were being handled. Stacey Lafront's brusque managerial style had ruffled more than a few feathers in the music industry, and her business acumen was now raising eyebrows in the Bykers, too. Robber remembers an occasion when Lafront was away on holiday, and he was sitting in the office room of her flat when the telephone rang. He answered. On the line was a company that had provided the band with a set of custom-made purple flight cases, and now demanded payment. "What do you mean you ain't been paid?" replied Robber. "That was six months ago! So, I started making a few enquiries with rehearsal rooms, and the others started making a few enquiries, and then after some deep digging, we turned up loads of stuff that hadn't been paid for!"

The band decided Stacey had to go. Robber continues the story, "After she had ripped us off by not paying any bills, or for flight cases, rehearsal rooms etc. and totally fucked all the finances up after the *Drill* film, we had a meeting up the

West End… I think it was in the World's End pub. Anyway, the discussion got very heated between me and Stacey Lafront, resulting in me jumping across the pub tables sending all the drinks flying, tables upturned, and strangling her with both my hands around her scrawny cockney neck. I had to be pulled off her."

Tony Byker shudders at the mention of Lafront's name: "She was a shocking speed freak bitch who 'might have potentially helped' in getting what we initially wanted as regards the deal and gigs, but she was a terrible representative for the band, made enemies in the music industry, and embezzled our money. We all now completely disown and avoid that creature at all costs!"

Mary continues in a similar vein: "Stacey had a big mouth. She talked the talk, but she pissed a lot of people off, so she went in and did the Virgin deal — great! But once you've done the deal you've got to execute it, and you've got to be nice to people, and you've got to get things done the right way instead of pissing everybody off."

Soon after she was sacked, revenge was apparently uppermost on Lafront's mind. She allegedly threatened any other potential managers that went near the Bykers with legal action, and worse. "She started to become a real nemesis, and no other manager would touch us," says Robber. He claims that Lafront even resorted to blackmail. "She had some videotape of us skinning-up joints and stuff like that and threatened to show it to the American Embassy to stop us getting into the USA, and all sorts, man. She was really vindictive." He laughs about it now, but the threat in his eyes was serious. As he says, the band were about to embark on their first major headlining tour of the USA, and anything relating to drugs would have jeopardised their visa applications and chances of entry into the country. It was one thing to be associated with drug-taking, but it was another matter entirely for hard evidence in the form of videotape to land in the hands of US Immigration Officials.

In the end Lafront didn't bubble them to the US authorities, but it was certainly not the end of their trials and tribulations with regards to their ex-manager. A few weeks after the sacking, Mary remembers being in The Kit Kat Club in Leicester Square with one of the roadies, Deptford John Armitage, when a commotion at the door drew their attention. Lafront and a bunch of biker heavies had arrived, according to Mary, who he was convinced they were there with the intention of beating him up and kidnapping him. Deptford John grabbed Mary, threw him over his shoulders, and hightailed it into the night.

Despite the adrenaline rush, for the rest of the night Mary couldn't shake off the paranoid feeling that Lafront's henchmen were going to track him down and bundle him into their van at any moment. Thankfully for him, this was the last

time Mary would encounter Stacey in person. But the fallout would last for years. In 1989, Lafront allegedly threatened the Bykers with legal action, claiming it was the band that owed her money, not the other way around. Nothing came of this as far as Mary is concerned. "I was never contacted by anyone regarding the case, and so can only presume she lost," he says. Even as late as 2001, Lafront was allegedly still ripping the Bykers off. "She sold our dodgy Virgin demo to Cherry Red in 2000 for £3,000," says Robber. The demo was released as a Cherry Red compilation entitled *Everything's Groovy*, which featured outtakes and rehearsals from the *Drill Your Own Hole* album recording sessions. Robber and the other band members have distanced themselves from the album. Cherry Red did eventually make amends, and Robber now says the label "did bung us all a wedge a few years back to make up for it". To say the Bykers' experiences with Lafront left a bitter aftertaste is something of an understatement, and Mary now says, "Her actions really affected the way we all began to negatively view the industry in general." For his parting shot, Mary adds: "You know? In Brazil they have an expression 'sem graça' — 'without grace'! There was nothing nice about her…"

Without Lafront, the Bykers prepared for their US tour by writing and rehearsing new material, which included Animal Farm, Ill, Teeth and No Justice, Justice Just Us (AKA Crime), the latter a thinly veiled broadside against Lafront. Some of this material was lined up for the band's next album. It was clear the band would not be returning to Alex Fergusson as producer, following their dissatisfaction with their debut album.

GAYE BYKERS OVER AMERICA '88

The Bykers had tasted the States back in July 1987. This time, however, they were headlining a full tour. Before departing, they played a handful of pre-tour warm-up shows in London. Two of these gigs were reviewed in the British music weeklies and are indicative of how the press now distanced itself from the Bykers and 'grebo' in general. Even *Sounds*, perhaps the most sympathetic towards rock and punk style bands, had seemingly grown weary of the 'grebo' hoopla it had helped create — and benefit from — over the previous 12 months. The title of Sam King's review of the Bykers at The Mean Fiddler in Harlesden on 8th March summed up this attitude: "Crisis Time for Grebo." The review began: "As grebo — surely the least appealing division of the current rock revival — transcends its infancy, attaining the plateau of maturity that falls between first and second albums, it becomes evident it has already reached a crisis point." King had seemed an avowed champion of the Bykers just a few months previously, but here was sounding the death knell on 'grebo', as well as serving notice on the Bykers. He bemoaned the appropriation of "American football garb" and "biker trappings", arguing that it "indicates nothing more than the restyling and retooling of obsolete rock extravagance for the modern audience".

While King did concede that "Mary is still rock's most beguiling and aggressive frontman", he also inferred that the band was a one-trick pony, whose Nosedive Karma was the only real song of merit. "Just as Zodiac's sexual antics have become tired and tiresome so Gaye Bykers' message of redemption through rock is wearing slightly thin," he wrote. "Something hard, powerful and fast is needed now if they're to rise above the stagnating isolation of the present, and a tried and tested dayglo cartoon imagery just isn't going to be enough."

Chris Roberts, in *Melody Maker*, was clearly only at the gig at the Hammersmith Clarendon on 10th March to see the opening act, The Seers. He didn't even bother with the middle band, Boys Wonder, facetiously commenting that he "rushed out to set the video for *Cheers*" while they were on. He saved his worst scorn for the headliners though. "Moronically, you allow duty to retrieve you to observe Gaye Bykers On Acid taking another club-footed welly-shod step back into the least glamorous kind of oblivion", lamented Roberts, adding, "Gaye Bykers tonight offer no spark, wit, style, nothing." There was more. "How small-brained this bass-heavy rumbling of tunelessness is, how unerotic, how unfunny their one joke. What was it again? Ah yes, *grebos*. Yes, well that was a durable howl wasn't it?" Roberts admits to having left before the end of the show, because "elephants like to die in privacy, among their own kind".

It was on this note that the Bykers set off for America.

Arriving in the States on 4th April 1988, according to their tour itinerary they had a "production day", before playing the first gig of the tour at the Club Revival, in Philadelphia, Pennsylvania on 6th April, supported by New York band, B.A.L.L. Although the 'grebo' phenomenon was out of favour with the British press, Jonathan Tankiff writing in the *Philadelphia Daily News* some days before the Bykers arrived in America, considered it "the latest musical catchphrase and fad out of Britain. It denotes a grungy, Gothic, heavy metal-meets-psychedelic brand of rock, with some inklings of social relevance. Converging the spirits of Steppenwolf and AC/DC, the genre is represented with contemporary British groups like The Cult, Zodiac Mindwarp and by Wednesday's Revival headliners Gaye Bykers On Acid."

Another Philadelphia newspaper, *The Inquirer*, noted that the Bykers were

billed as "the wildest band in Britain" and would be "doing numbers from its recent album, *Drill Your Own Hole*, which is short on tender ballads". The latter point was no understatement, but along with songs from *Drill*, the set also had many new songs. With its catchy opening Eddie Cochran style riffola, Nero Fiddles got the first gig of the tour off to a lively start. Mary barked his way through the verse ("I know that prevention is better than the cure") and chorus ("burn baby burn, burn, burn, burn baby burn"), with Tony's wah guitar refrain shimmering throughout — the result being one of the Bykers' greatest songs never to make it on to an official album release. The Bykers then proceeded to romp through a selection of old favourites, including Git Down, All Hung Up, and Everythang's Groovy.

Evelyn McDonnell, writing in the *NewPaper* prior to the Bykers' gig at the Living Room in Providence, Rhode Island, was enthralled by the band's name. "*Any* band with the verve to call themselves Gaye Bikers [sic] On Acid is all right in my book." McDonnell didn't consider the debut LP as striking as the band's moniker but believed "it does fulfil its promise of British pop-meets-heavy metal-meets psychedelia. And it does so with enough grunge and good humor to make Gaye Bikers [sic] On Acid more than just a gimmick."

McDonnell was off the mark in assuming the Bykers were "indeed gay, as in homosexual". Given the band's name and the fact Mary was male, not to mention the album title, McDonnell wouldn't be the only journalist to make this assumption. However, she was closer to the mark in describing the album as "very eighties sounding" what with its sampling and other studio trickery. She wasn't enamoured of *Drill Your Own Hole* for the most part, likening the Bykers' sound to "an extended joke without a punchline". She reserved praise for the last track: "Fortunately, the LP ends on a positive note with the unmixed, unproduced TV Cabbage, a wonderfully rough, absurdist gem… If the rest of the album could tone down the hyperbole like TV Cabbage does, Gaye Bikers [sic] On Acid could even live up to their name."

McDonnell's comments must have resonated with Mary. Stepping on stage at the Living Room he announced, "We're the Lesbian Dopeheads On Mopeds," and dedicated the opening song, Motorvate, to McDonnell, asking if she was in the audience. Mary made another reference to McDonnell at the end of the song. On her assumption that they were gay, he asked, "How can you say such things? You don't even know us!… we're all virgins from behind I can tell you that." When the band started the introduction to Don't Be Human Eric — Let's Be Frank, he added, in an exaggerated masculine American drawl, "We're men, and we like to do what men like to do, hey honey? Know what I mean?" Mary made a pretence

Gaye Bykers On Acid, Silver Dollar Club, Toronto, Canada, 1988, "the audience appeared somewhat subdued."

Photo by Derek Von Essen.

of being hurt, but Evelyn's comments evidently rankled. The band had had their sexual orientation questioned over the past 18 months, and the matter appeared to have come to a head for Mary, who alluded to McDonnell's comments again at the beginning of Call Me A Liar: "If I say I'm not gay, you think I'm a liar."

Along with Motorvate and Call Me A Liar, the Bykers performed another new song, Space Cadet. The rest of the set varied little from that of Philadelphia, or the following night at The Ritz in New York City. They trod the same tour circuit that other Brit bands like Zodiac Mindwarp, Screaming Blue Messiahs, and Balaam and The Angel were also working that spring. The Bykers were supposed to have been joined on some dates by Pop Will Eat Itself, but the Poppies were apparently refused visas at the last minute. Tracy Sigler's a fan who drove for three hours with her boyfriend to see them at the 9:30 Club in Washington D.C. seem to think the Poppies were refused visas due to "lack of artistic merit". The Bykers were billed that night as "Gaye Bykers On Parade" and Tracy has the ticket stub to prove it. She says, "Maybe having a drug reference in your band name wasn't conducive to getting visas, or bookings, or something."

A week into their North American tour, the Bykers made the short hop over the Canadian border to play at the Silver Dollar Room in Toronto. They were supported by an aptly named local punk band of some repute, The Almighty Lumberjacks Of Death. Judging by photographs taken at the gig by

Derek Von Essen, the audience is subdued, sucking on bottles of Moosehead beer, and seated round cabaret-style tables at the edge of the stage. This was as far as the Bykers' excursion into Canada went. The following day they crossed back over the border and headed into the industrial heartland of the Midwest, Detroit — Motor City as its nickname has it. The motor industry that was based in Detroit was already in decline, as was its population. But Detroit had a rich musical pedigree, spawning not only Tamla Motown, but many influential rock bands.

Two Detroit bands that had been a major inspiration for the Bykers were The Stooges and MC5. For the US tour, the Bykers had taken to performing a cover of Ramblin' Rose in honour of MC5 (who in turn had covered Teddy Taylor's original R&B version from 1965). This was a somewhat canny move on the part of the Bykers, which possibly helped win over a partisan Detroit crowd, and Neil Perry of *Sounds* reported that the 300 strong Detroit audience were "genuinely enthusiastic". Perry was impressed. "One thing is certain," he wrote, "this is not the same band who died, slowly, in front of 2,500 impatient Motörhead fans last autumn, and nor is it the same band who had fiddled about so frustratingly on *Drill Your Own Hole.*"

Being on a tight schedule, the Bykers were chauffeured to a live interview with a local college radio station at around 2am, much to the bemusement of the radio station employees tasked with driving them there. According to Perry, Mary, being Mary, and probably still buzzing from the Bykers' performance that night, took to shouting "Vote Jesse Jackson! Vote Jesse Jackson!" out of the car window through a megaphone. Bearing in mind that Detroit was a city in rapid decay and had the dubious honour of being the US murder capital at that time, it wasn't necessarily a wise idea for a bunch of freaky white guys to be attracting unwanted attention on the eerie, seemingly deserted streets of Detroit. Mary caused further consternation when, at the radio station, he adopted an exaggerated American accent and proceeded to mimic a cop, bellowing out that the building was surrounded and that the occupants should come out with their hands up. According to Perry, the radio station employees only relaxed when they and their English guests were finally admitted to the building "after 10 minutes of furious bell-pushing". The DJ really didn't know what to make of Mary and Robber, according to Perry, "both her head and her neat schedule scrambled by the two Bykers' stream of semi-inane, semi-hilarious psychobabble."

The Bykers departed Detroit the following morning and arrived in Chicago after a five-hour journey. The venue, The Metro, was not full, but Perry considered

Photo courtesy of Tony Byker.

"She turned up with a gay fluffer in case we were gay!" Cynthia Albriton AKA Cynthia Plaster Caster shortly before casting Mary Byker's penis, Chicago, 1988.

it a good turnout, given that at half-capacity there were several hundred people in attendance. The Bykers played three encores for the appreciative Chicago audience. "Onstage at Chicago's Metro club… Gaye Bykers On Acid turn on whatever it was they so badly lacked last year," Perry continued to rave. "As Tony's guitar fills the hall with deep moans and banshee wails, Kevin and Robber plunge into the bedrock intro of Teeth." This was another one of several new songs the Bykers had written over the winter. The Bykers informed Perry that once they returned to the UK they planned to work with Vic Maile, who

Photographer not known.

Mary Byker's member is on the far left and Jon Langford's is on the far right. Source: Nardwuar vs. Cynthia Plaster Caster website.

In the hotel car park. DJ Fontana (Elvis's drummer) with his band and the Bykers, Chicago 1987.

Photo courtesy of Gaye Bykers On Acid.

had produced Motörhead's *Ace of Spades* and had worked on The Who's *Live At Leeds* albums — as well as with Crazyhead but with mixed results.

In Chicago, the Bykers met a couple of legends from different ends of the music spectrum. Cynthia Albritton, better known as Cynthia Plaster Caster, was part of a coterie of groupies who gained notoriety in the late 1960s by making plaster casts of visiting rock musicians' penises. Cynthia and the Legendary Plaster Casters of Chicago had cast the cocks of Jimi Hendrix, MC5's Wayne Kramer, Anthony Newley and the like, beginning in the late 1960s and continuing in the decades since. She turned up at the Bykers gig that night at The Metro, pointed out by the band's American road manager, Mitch. Robber was at a loss as to who she was, and what she was famous for, but Mitch enlightened him. "She turned up with a gay fluffer in case we were gay!" says Robber. Not all the band were keen on having their cocks immortalised in plaster. According to *Sounds*, Kev chickened right out, but Mary jumped at the chance — although he is reticent to recall the matter.

The morning after the gig, as they were leaving their hotel, the Bykers encountered another celebrity in the form of DJ Fontana. Again it was Mitch who enlightened them, as Robber recalls in a mimicking American accent, "'Hey you guys, you guys, check this out, this is Elvis's backing band maaan!'" Despite their age difference, and the Bykers' outlandish appearance, DJ Fontana

Photo by Keith Penny, courtesy of Andy Purple.

Robber overdid it on the margaritas and tequila slammers. The Mexican mushrooms were quite strong too.

and his band of "good ol' boys", as Robber puts it, were very affable and friendly towards the Bykers. Such are the vagaries and whims of the music industry, it was somewhat telling that time-served old veterans, such as this, left the hotel car park in a battered old truck, while the Bykers had the luxury of speeding off in a limousine. Says Robber, "Thinking about it, that's kinda wrong really isn't it? They should have been in the Winnebago or limousine!"

For Robber, meeting Cynthia Plaster Caster and DJ Fontana towards the end of the tour perhaps helped him take his mind off some of the more demanding distractions associated with life on the road. *Sounds* reported that Robber had given up drugs and alcohol when he almost died following a heavy tequila session the week before the Chicago gig. Pressed on the matter, Robber says, "Yeah, I kind of overdid it on the margaritas and slammers, and I think there were some sort of Mexican mushrooms involved that were quite strong. I remember waking up in a car park later, and someone chucking me in a cab back to the hotel. I woke up looking out of what I thought was a porthole, but it turned out not to be that... I actually had my head down a toilet!"

By the time they got to the West Coast, the Bykers discovered that the first of several dates scheduled for California had been cancelled — the Fillmore in San Francisco, no less. Robber was largely eschewing interviews at this point. Having to meet the "right people and do radio interviews" was boring, not to mention tiresome, but Robber was not able to switch himself for a life-sized cardboard cut-out as he had the previous year, when the Bykers had been the press darlings of the 'grebo' scene.

Picking up Robber's interview duties Tony talked with John Penner of the *Anaheim Bulletin*

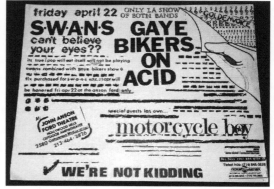

Flyer for Swans and Gaye Bykers On Acid. Los Angeles. April 1988.

about issues of censorship. He cited the Bykers' Git Down promotional video as an example, where shots of Mary singing into a cucumber had to be cut for it to have any chance of airplay in the UK. Commenting on what he saw as hypocrisy in the media, Tony told Penner, "Git Down ended up being more controversial among the British press after it was released, simply because GBOA was a group of white kids singing a song dealing with sexuality. It really [upset] English journalists for some reason, if you're white and you sing about your [sexual organ]… but they think it's OK for a black man to do it." It was for this reason the band had "blacked up" for the video. "It was a political statement as well." He then hammered home the point about how the Bykers were staunch advocates of the anti-censorship movement. "We definitely have things to say about the world," he told Penner. "That's part of your obligation as an entertainer, I think. We're not gonna change the world maybe, but we might change somebody's attitude."

On the penultimate date of the tour, the Bykers played the John Anson Ford Theatre in Los Angeles, with New York noise terrorists Swans. Craig Lee in the *L.A. Times* described it as "the underground mismatch bill of the year". This was the Swans home turf, while the Bykers according to Lee were "loose 'n' woolly trash-mongers" and "this month's plaything from England". Lee described the Bykers as "members of a scene called grebo — a blanket term for a mix-and-match melange of trash-consciousness filtered from the excesses of the last three decades, combined with rude behaviour". Their sound, he said, was "rather routine garage punk… camouflaged by manic, psychedelicized guitar and a very funny, sexy, frenetic, hoarse male singer named Mary whose magnetic stage presence Friday almost redeemed such sophomoric ploys as basing a song on George Orwell's *Animal Farm*. Following the sonic precision of Swans' morose bombardment, though, the Bykers seemed tinny and minor, better suited for a

small basement club than a large outdoor stage."

On the final date of the tour in San Diego, Mary was interviewed for local music fanzine, *Lively Arts*. He made no secret of how much he and the others were distancing themselves from *Drill Your Own Hole*. Asked by Kenzo, the interviewer, how he felt about the album, Mary responded bluntly, "We used the wrong producer for the album. We're not really satisfied with the album at all." He added that it had to be listened to while watching the video to fully understand its relevance. "There's a lot of social comment on the album," he said, "especially concerning evangelism and America's paranoia of the Middle East." Prescient words indeed.

GAYE BYKERS OVER EUROPE

On their return from the States, the Bykers began preparing for their follow-up to *Drill Your Own Hole*. Throughout May, they also played a handful of live dates in the UK, which served as a warm-up for an extensive forthcoming European tour. The first of these shows in Bradford was received warmly by *Sounds'* man in the provinces, John Anthony Lake, who described their set as "a coursing, punishing exhibition of GBOA 1988". He added, "Each song takes off at the pace of a rocket swooshing up rock'n'roll's fundament and it works its way up to a climax somewhere in the deepest innards."

Ellie Buchanan was quite ambiguous in her appraisal of the Bykers at Govan Town Hall in Glasgow. The Soviet headliners AVIA had failed to show, but despite the sparse crowd and sound problems, Buchanan was charitable enough to declare that the Bykers' image and antics would ensure them "a place in the history of rebel rock".

Back in the capital the anti-grebo feeling was still gathering apace. Dave Jennings for *Melody Maker* covered a Bykers show at ULU, for which Spaceman 3 and Hook 'n' Pull Gang were support. Jennings had displayed a weariness towards the Bykers two months previously, not long before they left for the States, and his attitude hadn't changed. (Although to be fair he was equally scathing towards Spaceman 3.) "The only things that distinguish the Bykers from a thousand dodgy post-punk pub rock bands are their inspired choice of name and their colourful period costumes," wrote Jennings of the ULU gig. "And, though Mary *did* look terrific tonight in his dayglo mini-dress — GBOA's psychedelia is clothes deep. Nothing in music could be less consciousness expanding than this soulless, unimaginative, mind-numbing noise."

Support for the European tour was fellow Leicester band, The Hunters Club, with the addition of various bands local to each city scattered across the dates. After opening in Copenhagen, the Bykers were scheduled to play seven dates in West Germany, but Cologne and Munich were the only ones that survived according to an extant tour itinerary. Robber can't remember much of the tour, but believes the cancellations were down to poor advertising on the part of the promoters.

Photo courtesy of Sally Jones.

Robber Byker. Melkweg, Amsterdam, Gaye Bykers On Acid European Tour, June, 1988.

Ian Redhead, singer of The Hunters Club, says that a major international football tournament had something to do with the cancellations; specifically the hooligan element among England's travelling football fans with a reputation for causing trouble. Redhead told the *Leicester Mercury* in 2012, "we were in Germany at the same time as the European Championships. That wasn't good. Three venues just called it straight off because they knew we were English. I think we did about 13 gigs, maybe less, in three-and-a-half weeks."

The tour took in Vienna, Paris and Amsterdam, while a video recorded in Groningen, the Netherlands, shows the Bykers were on blistering form. Concluding the tour in the Netherlands, at OJC Dingus in Venray, the Bykers then returned to the UK to prepare demos for the new album. Some of the fruit of these sessions included several songs they had honed on their recent US and European tours, such as Nero Fiddles, Space Cadet, Why?, Shit Happens and No Justice, Just Us. They approached veteran producer Vic Maile. At this stage, Virgin was still behind the band, and Mary says that A&R readily agreed to the studio time with Maile, and probably suggested they do an EP. Having adopted a back-to-basics approach, the band decamped with Maile to Jackson's Studios in Rickmansworth. Mary recalls that the stripped-back attitude was a conscious decision modelled after punk rock and playing with The Ramones. "It doesn't have to be complicated to write good songs — three chords you know? Punk

Photo courtesy of Sally Jones.

Tony Byker. Melkweg, Amsterdam, Gaye Bykers On Acid European Tour, June, 1988.

rock!"

As for Maile, Mary has fond memories. Maile would often interrupt proceedings by saying, "Hold on chaps, do you mind if I just —" and then whip out a syringe and inject himself with insulin because he was diabetic. "Even then he was kind of old school, and I can remember the desk at the studio. It had this one great knob in the middle, and it didn't look like a normal recording studio." Alas, things didn't work out, arguably because Maile didn't provide the input the band expected.

Only one new song was recorded during the Vic Maile sessions, Animal Farm, the subject of which is still open to conjecture. Robber has inferred that the song was inspired by the infamous bestial pornographic film 'loop' of that name. Mary thinks there may be a kernel of truth to this, and that the band may have encountered the video in a sex shop while touring Europe with The Ramones. But the song could be read as a statement about totalitarianism, in keeping with George Orwell's titular novel, which seems the case in an early live performance at The Ritz in New York's East Village. Here, Mary dedicates the song "to the George Orwell novel" and references Margaret Thatcher and Ronald Reagan, before declaring "the divide is becoming wider — someone's shitting on you!" The lyrics are ambiguous enough to suggest either interpretation though. ☠

CHAPTER SEVEN

TIME IS TAKING ITS TOLL ON YOU AT "HOTEL GAYBOY"

WHILE THE BYKERS WERE EMBROILED IN A MANAGERIAL dispute with Stacey Lafront, Crazyhead were finally taking a breather from the rigours of touring. Apart from the demos and forays into Berry Street recording studio, Crazyhead had been on the road virtually from the moment they played their first gig, almost two years earlier. Anderson, in particular, was in need of a break and told Mr Spencer in an interview for *Sounds* in July 1988 that he'd seen a psychiatrist. He had started to believe he was hearing messages from ice-cream vans when walking the streets. Thankfully, as he told Spencer, he had fully recovered from this paranoia.

Crazyhead did not stop playing live altogether during this period. John Robb of Blackpool punk band The Membranes also worked as a writer for *Sounds*, where he drew unfavourable comparisons between Crazyhead and their 'grebo' contemporaries: "Whereas Gaye Bykers and Pop Will Eat Itself take rock clichés, amplify and then trample them underfoot in a gleeful orgy of naff stupidity, Crazyhead just recline stoned, into a huge vat of rock excess. Lacking any glamour or excitement." Robb seemed to pick up on the tour fatigue that was perhaps symptomatic of Crazyhead's gruelling schedule: "As the grebo bandwagon which they and The Bomb Party unintentionally kicked off in the first-place creaks out of town, it looks as if Crazyhead will have to dig deep into their souls to find the crazed rock monster that undoubtedly lurks there."

In the meantime, Dave Balfe was busy negotiating a deal with EMI for Food, whereby the band were signed to Parlophone sort of by the back door. In practice, Crazyhead would be able to enjoy the financial backing a major label might offer, while retaining their indie identity. Asked by Spencer if they were prepared to be accused of "selling out", Anderson countered by saying he'd had his fill of shit jobs and was sick of being on the dole. If it meant he would soon be in a position to earn a similar wage to a building labourer, then the association with a major label was "fair enough" as far as he was concerned.

It didn't quite pan out like that according to Vom. Within a year of Crazyhead signing to Food, Balfe had "sold a 51% controlling stake in Food to EMI, so

Front cover of Crazyhead's 'Time Has Taken Its Toll On You'.

in effect *we* ended up being signed to EMI, which we didn't want, but had no choice. The reason he did it — you know Balfey being Balfey — was the dough! And the simple reason EMI did it was because they wanted Diesel Park West!"

Diesel Park West started to attract interest after the release of their debut single on Food, When The Hoodoo Comes, and it wasn't long before they caught the attention of Nick Gatfield, head of A&R at EMI. Vom recalls that Gatfield had "heard their first album. It's got great choruses on and you could imagine it being in big stadiums in America, you couldn't deny that. But we weren't really like that, so we just came as part of the package."

In order to record the new single and debut album at Music Station in Fulham, Balfe relocated Crazyhead to London. Unlike the Gaye Bykers On Acid, Crazyhead were resistant to the idea of moving to London. But Fast Dick had a girlfriend in north London and the band soon adapted to life in the capital, even if they returned to Leicester to see friends and family at weekends. Initially Balfe had booked the band into "a dreadful travellers' hostel", Anderson recalls, going on to say, "As per usual Dave Balfe said, 'It's bloody cheap, it'll save us some money.' All the TVs were faulty, the sheets were tatty and there was that crappy hard toilet paper you used to get at school. We had recently seen The Comic Strip's *A Fistful of Travellers Cheques* on TV, where the main characters stay in a scummy Mexican hotel, run by a character played by Keith Allen [who incidentally ended up directing the video for their next single]. We started doing the characters… 'You want soft toilet paper? You go to the Hotel Gayboy' routine in a cod Mexican accent."

In the end they could take no more of the hostel and complained to Balfe, who found them "a really nice but cheap hotel", only a short hop across the road from the hostel. This turned out to be Philbeach Hotel, one of Europe's premier gay hotels, which, under the circumstances, the band found highly amusing and christened it the "Hotel Gayboy". The band's entourage was not so amused. According to Vom, the roadies were outraged and got "all homophobic", refusing to stay there on the first night. The band had no such qualms, which was just as well as the hotel would become their home for the next three months.

Time Has Taken Its Toll On You was the title of the next single. Anderson explains: "I wrote the song lyrics from awful hangovers and looking in the mirror the day after." If any of the band thought that life in the recording studio would prove a respite from the rigours of the road they were mistaken. Their first two singles had been recorded quickly — basically live takes — and they naively assumed they could continue in the same vein for the album sessions. Balfe apparently hated the quirky elements of the band's songs, referring to them, according to Reverb, as "the Beefheart bits". But, Reverb continues, "it was those bits that had taken us loads of work and stopped us being just a straight garage rock band!"

Balfe's attitude towards what he envisaged as the band's direction changed with Time Has Taken Its Toll On You. Reverb says that, "Up 'til then our recording sessions had been basically picking the best take and adding a bit of fairy dust. They then became drawn out affairs where almost everything was done separately, and we pretty well became divorced from the proceedings."

Vom was particularly aggrieved by Balfe's perceived megalomania, wanting to turn Crazyhead into Bon Jovi. Shortly before the recording sessions for their debut album, Balfe went as far as to play Bon Jovi's hit, Livin' On A Prayer and telling Vom to play like that. Vom laughed at the suggestion but looking back considers that Balfe was entirely serious. Appointed producer Mark Freegard had been present during Balfe's proposition, which Vom now considers was no accident. "Unbeknown to us at the time, Freegard was under strict instructions from EMI to turn our songs into a polished AOR type thing, to make it palatable for mainstream American radio."

Matters became worse during the recording session itself. According to Vom, Balfe "totally took over" and announced he was going to produce the single. What particularly galled Vom was being told by Balfe that his drumming lacked "precision" and that the band should use a drum machine instead. Anderson recalls how the band was dead against Balfe's insistence on using a drum machine on the track.

Balfe's fascination with Bon Jovi became even more apparent while recording the album. Reverb says that the stadium rock sound became an "obsession" of Balfe's, one that "was completely incongruous with what Crazyhead were about". The session rolled on. Taking a leaf from an interview he'd apparently read with

Adam and the Ants producer Chris Hughes, Balfe invested a lot of time on the sound of the drums. Hughes had intimated that the secret of his success had been not to compromise and to keep recording until you got it right. "That was where the multitrack madness began for us," recalls Reverb wearily. "I worked out that Time took 21 studio days to finish."

Vom is disdainful of Balfe's logic. "Balfey spent *two* weeks programming a drum machine to play *exactly* my parts," he says, "a track that I could have laid down in three minutes! After that, the others laid down their parts on the track and that was that." Vom describes the recording of Time as "a turgid and fun free affair". He recalls another occasion during the recording sessions for Desert Orchid when Nick Gatfield, head of A&R for EMI, walked into the studios. "We just played him what we'd been doing that day," says Vom. "He listened to a couple of the tracks and just walked out — he didn't even say a fucking word to us — he just turned round and walked out, and we knew then, 'well the writing's on the wall ain't it, if that's what he thinks of us!'"

But Vom concedes that Balfe's intentions might not have been entirely mercenary. If EMI saw the wholesale purchase of Food as a means to obtain the object of their real interest, Diesel Park West, perhaps Balfe was out to prove that Crazyhead had their own worth. In a brief conciliatory moment, Vom argues: "Fair play to Balfey, I think he saw it as part of his own personal crusade — 'No, I'm gonna prove EMI wrong, and that Crazyhead are capable of having hit singles'… and that's possibly why he tried to commercialise us."

Rick Willson and John Butler of Diesel Park West provided a welcome distraction when they came down from Leicester to provide backing vocals. There were a few other moments of light relief too. One such occasion was during the remixing sessions for Desert Orchid at Townhouse Studios in Shepherd's Bush. It was here their paths crossed with Queen, who were working on their album, *The Miracle*. Anderson recalls an incident involving Queen's drummer, Roger Taylor and his son, while the band were hanging out during some downtime: "There was a recreation room where most of the band played pool with ex-members of Frankie Goes To Hollywood… Roger Taylor of Queen also played some pool, and he was a nice bloke. He had a precocious son though who played pool with Sparky after Roger Taylor went off. The 10-year-old brat had a tantrum when he lost and said, 'My dad's Roger Taylor from Queen and I won, I'm telling my dad!' Sparky replied, 'I don't give a shit who your dad is you can piss off!' leaving Roger's brat to storm off in tears. Roger Taylor came back 10 minutes later, and to his credit apologised for his son's brattish behaviour. We may not have been Queen fans — bloody awful — but the drummer was ok!"

The respite was only fleeting though. Says Vom, "we were all pissed off in one way or another at this point, and we did not have the emotional and mental skills to deal with it really. Balfe recognised this and saw it as his mission to take total control." Balfe called a meeting with the band at the studio, allegedly turning up with 10 pages of notes, and a ready answer for anything Crazyhead had to say. Unlike Balfe, the band hadn't prepared anything, and ill prepared as they were, Balfe walked all over them. Reverb states bluntly: "The bottom line from Balfe was the old cliché 'my way or the highway'. With hindsight we should've called his bluff and left — we were in a good position with a couple of well received singles, a great live reputation and a great and photogenic frontman in Anderson, so I think we would've easily got another deal."

If things weren't bad enough, the band would also lose their manager around this point. Warner Brothers had been sniffing around Cally Calloman and offered him a plum A&R job. Legend has it Cally demanded a huge wage and a rare 1960s sports car as a joke — much to his surprise, Warners agreed. Vom says, "He couldn't turn it down, so he was gone." Reverb adds with genuine sincerity, "It couldn't have happened to a nicer bloke. He told us he'd be taking it because he had a wife and family to support." Not wanting to leave Crazyhead in the lurch, however, Cally helped them look for a new manager, and was happy to act in an advisory capacity in the meantime. He came to the studio on their behalf to meet with Balfe but would end up arguing and nothing was resolved.

Arguably, things may have been different if Crazyhead had not lost their manager and had stood their ground against Balfe. But hindsight is a wonderful thing. The band was now on a wage and the possibility of going back on the dole didn't appeal to them, so they begrudgingly accepted Balfe's ultimatum and got on with the task at hand. To compound matters further, Balfe was also applying pressure on the band to take a new manager, following Cally's departure. True to his word, before Cally left he recommended a replacement, Andrew Cheeseman. At first, it seemed that Cheeseman would be the ideal choice. Anderson says they were impressed he had started out as Jake Riviera's bagman at Stiff Records and had worked for Elvis Costello and The Damned when they were enjoying success during the 1980s. Reverb however sees things differently: "Andy Cheeseman was managing The Men They Couldn't Hang. They were signed to Magnet Records, that was bought by Warner's, which was how Cally came to know Cheeseman. We were getting pressure from Balfe to get a manager. We were recording Desert Orchid in Fulham at the time, and Cally arranged for us to meet Cheeseman at the studio. I remember we missed the first meeting we were meant to have with him and got told off like naughty

schoolboys by Balfe and Cally. After the meeting, we decided we didn't think he was the right manager for us, but Balfe did his 'my way or the highway' routine, and pretty much forced us to take him on."

Reverb doesn't deny that Cheeseman was keen on the gig but adds, with cynicism, that "he didn't have anything to lose. The hardest job for a manager has got to be getting a band a recording contract — we already had one! We also had two indie hit singles, and a good live following, and were recording our first album — a ready-made meal ticket!" Reverb concludes, "I don't think he was overly keen on the music we made."

Cally's role in the band at this point was that of a kind of spiritual adviser and musical guru, until the arrival of Cheeseman. Reverb largely took care of the day-to-day duties usually associated with a manager. "I liaised with the record company, agency, accountant, lawyer etc. and, with the help of Sparky and the AA B&B guide, organised the tours," says Reverb. "The band agreed to fund a phone for me so I could do this 'cos it was impractical to spend hours waiting outside phone boxes for return calls."

With upheavals in management, EMI's lack of interest, and Balfe applying pressure with regards to recording and production, fractures within the band were inevitable. Says Vom, "People were getting out of their heads for the wrong reasons — not to create, but to medicate, so to speak. There were one or two girlfriend issues, you know personal stuff."

It was a far cry from the carefree days of bashing out demos in Rick Willson's studio in Leicester's Barkby Road, or for that matter the first two singles. If the recording sessions weren't always as straightforward as they might have hoped, at least the Philbeach Hotel afforded much needed relief. After spending a day in the studio, the band would return between midnight and 2am. The hotel was party central, and there was no shortage of colourful guests and interesting goings on. Crazyhead were embraced with open arms by the hotel owners and predominantly homosexual clientele. Vom recalls that sometimes there would be crates of beer and food waiting for them on their return from the recording studio, but even when there wasn't, the bar would be open. "It was wonderful," says Anderson of the hotel, "it had a lounge with plants and a huge Buddha statue, and a basement bar that sold us beer 24 hours a day! We loved it! When you went for breakfast high-energy disco would blare out, and I remember sitting for breakfast with Rick from Diesel Park West after a heavy night recording on whizz… very surreal!"

Early into their stay at the Philbeach, the band attended the launch party for *Tattooed Beat Messiah*, the debut album of Food labelmates Zodiac Mindwarp and the Love Reaction. Vom recalls that at the party the band "got totally wankered. There was shit loads of booze, and we got the roadies, Sparky and Scotty, to ferry out loads of it into our van throughout the evening." Bringing the party back to the Philbeach, the Crazyhead entourage proceeded to break into the booty they had liberated from Zodiac Mindwarp. Vom continues the story: "It was obvious it was going to get messy. I seem to remember cans of beer being shook up and opened randomly, and then full cans being thrown around the room at each other, pictures

Photo courtesy of Ian Anderson.

'PLENTY OF FUCK AND SUCK IN ROOM 21 — BRING PLENTY OF AMYL.' Crazyhead's Anderson and Fast Dick with Batch, a sound engineer (in foreground), at the Philbeach Hotel, AKA Hotel Gayboy, Earl's Court, London, 1988.

smashed, beds wrecked, just wanton vandalism." This incident sticks with Vom because it was, he says, one of the only times where the band "did the clichéd smash up the hotel routine". The next day, Vom was convinced they would be thrown out of the hotel: "We had mad nights before, but there was nothing on this scale!" Heading sheepishly to the studio, they were still expecting the worst on their return, only to find that it was as if nothing had happened — the rooms had been tidied as best they could and no one on the staff said a word.

Vom recalls another incident at the Philbeach: "Anderson woke up to Sparky pissing over his head. Anderson had a massive go at him saying 'You are pissing on my head,' 'No I'm not chap' came the reply, 'I am pissing in the sink' — while still emptying his bladder over Anderson's pillow!"

Crazyhead got to know a number of the other guests at the Philbeach. One was an ageing transvestite called Fergie, who, by day, was a High Court Judge. They nicknamed another guest the Scary Stair-Creeper, because, according to Anderson, he "would haunt the stairs, cruising, dressed in little more than rubber shorts with the bum cut out." Often while Anderson was having a bath, he would receive a knock on the door and was politely asked if he "wanted any company", to which he would reply, "No, I'm having a bloody bath, go away!"

Crazyhead's roadies sometimes played pranks on the other hotel guests as well as on the band. Anderson recalls, "As the nights wore on and the late-night partying increased, Sparky really didn't help one night by pinning a note on the toilet door, 'PLENTY OF FUCK AND SUCK IN ROOM 21 — BRING PLENTY OF AMYL.'" Unaware of the note, the band spent the night answering the door to a succession of "cruisers" asking if they wanted company. "Scary Stair-Creeper, not so shy, just sidled in in his leather bum cut-out pants, spied a very, very stoned [Fast] Dick, sat beside him and put his arm around him. Transfixed, really stoned with a look of extreme fear and terror on his face, Dick told him, 'Oh no chap, you've got the wrong end of the stick.'"

On another occasion, Anderson adjourned to the hotel lounge after a day's recording. He got chatting to a couple of resident transvestites "off their heads on mushrooms". He politely declined an invitation to indulge in anal sex, telling them that he was straight. The irony was not lost on the Crazyhead singer as he "sat there dressed head to foot in black leather with girly hair halfway down my back, looking like — well, a gay biker on acid I guess!" Anderson made his excuses and staggered off towards the familiar sound of Hi NRG disco music emanating from the breakfast room as dawn broke.

The band felt protective of the Philbeach. On yet another occasion Anderson was drunkenly wandering through the streets of London, back to the Earl's Court hotel, when he bumped into Keith Penny, the Bykers' roadie in chief. Penny was accompanied by a couple of his face-tattooed skinhead mates from the Leicester Oi! band Clockwork Soldiers. Clockwork Soldiers had been notorious for the violence and trouble they attracted at their gigs earlier in the 1980s. Says Anderson, "They were all completely off their trolleys... Penny, with that glazed look of a tortured, angry bull in a bullfight. I knew that look very well. This was a rare appearance of the usually jokey, affable Penny's Mr Hyde!"

The upshot was that the drunken Penny demanded Anderson take them back to the hotel and put them up for the night. Anderson didn't think it would be a good idea: "Penny and his Clockwork Soldier skinhead mates off their fuckin' trees in Europe's biggest gay hotel? Not a good idea." Stuck between a rock and a hard place he told Penny no and was "smacked full in the face out of the blue, his two mates chuckling." Luckily for Anderson that was the end of it, and he made a sharp getaway. "I didn't want to stand up and try and fight Penny in his mad bull phase — or any other time for that matter! I mean, this guy had been arrested at a football match for headbutting a police horse!"

This was the night of a Bykers gig in the capital. Anderson later discovered that Penny and his mates had been hassling other members of the Crazyhead entourage to stay at the Philbeach over the course of the evening. "It must have been the last straw for Penny, wandering the empty streets of London without even a floor to kip on, deserted by his mates," reflects Anderson. "We couldn't have taken them back to Hotel Gayboy, especially in that state, it would have been a bloodbath!"

Alternating their time between the recording studio in the daytime, and the "Hotel Gayboy" at night, creatively it was a very productive period. Crazyhead not only recorded their debut album, but also made videos for their next two singles in anticipation of the album's release.

Food initially came up with a short list of possible directors for Time Has Taken Its Toll On You, and it included Keith Allen. Reverb picks up the story: "We were big fans of *The Yob* by The Comic Strip, so we pushed to use him. Food arranged a meeting between us, Keith, Food and, I think someone from EMI." According to Reverb, the somewhat mercurial comedian "turned up late and obviously a bit strung out," before apologising and putting it down to the large amount of magic mushrooms he'd taken the day before. "After the pleasantries, he was asked what ideas he had for the video. His answer went something like, 'Yeah, I can see it, it's great.' 'What can you see Keith?' 'The band rocking… and all this is happening and it's great.' 'What's happening Keith?' 'You know… it's all going off, the band rocking,' etc, etc. It wasn't the most coherent storyboard ever delivered, but his enthusiasm and charm seemed to win the company people over. We didn't really care, we knew it would be a good laugh working with him!"

Anderson has a similar recollection: "The normally verbose [Dave] Balfe and [Andy] Ross sat in bewildered silence as Keith ranted out his maniac master plan. We all burst out laughing and were overjoyed, but Balfe and Ross looked very worried!"

Shooting the video took place on 1st June 1988, a day Reverb remembers for one particular reason. "I know this 'cos me and Sparky were really into horse racing and liked to have a flutter, and it was Epsom Derby day. I really fancied this horse called Kahyasi. We asked Scotty [another Crazyhead roadie] to nip down the bookies for us. Keith heard what was going on and had a flutter himself. Kahyasi romped in at 11/1, I don't remember what we or Keith won."

The band did indeed have great fun making the video with a cast of extras dressed as mods, rockers, teds, skinheads and so on, all apparently inspired by Allen's mushroom trip the day before the meeting with the record company big knobs. In addition to friends from Voice of the Beehive and *Kerrang!* journalist Krusher Joules, the video also featured the UK's number one George Michael impersonator — a fact Allen was proud to tell the band. Reverb also recalls how Allen kept making frequent trips to his office and returning "inspired".

Video still from 'Time Has Taken Its Toll on You', directed by Keith Allen.

Anderson witnessed Allen's wicked sense of humour at close quarters while he was relieving himself in the gents. Allen burst in and, according to Anderson, "leered and grunted in a yobbish way, 'OK Anderson it's just you and me alone sunshine, now I can have my evil way with you!'" It turned out that Allen was joking but for a moment had unnerved the pretty-faced singer. Anderson admits, "Allen was quite a big and intimidating fella."

Crazyhead headed out on the road for the first time in over six months, to promote the forthcoming single. Warming up at The George Robey in London's Finsbury Park, they took in another 14 dates in Wales, the North of England, and Scotland, before heading back to London and concluding the tour at the Electric Ballroom in Camden. Scottish audiences have a reputation for being fanatical and are often unforgiving of even the slightest slip. But both Crazyhead and the Bykers always went down well north in Scotland. Vom says, "the further north you went the more wild it got, but we used to really enjoy playing Scotland because they just loved it, and they seemed to like soak it up, you know? We always went down well, and we always had a good fan base there."

But while fans were good in Scotland, the same wasn't necessarily true of the bouncers. Crazyhead were booked to play the notorious Rooftops club in Glasgow, where the bouncers had a fearsome reputation. Vom says, "It was a great venue, but I was always really nervous about going there, simply because the bouncers were just animals… they were all in the black suits, with the black dicky-bows and the white frilly shirts. All fucking super-hard Glaswegian guys, you could tell they were all from Easterhouse and the Gorbals. And there were loads of them. They were just there for violence. You could just tell they loved violence, especially on somebody who wasn't so good at fighting. They were fucking heavy guys, and I remember when we got there you just got a vibe off 'em."

Vom relates an earlier gig at Rooftops in which a drunken Scottish fan, helping to shift equipment at the end of the night, had the temerity to get "lippy". Says Vom, "The bouncers gave him a good working over. They methodically stomped him, completely pulping him to a bloody mess in the process." With this in mind the band approached gigs in Glasgow, and particularly Rooftops, with a certain wariness. Now the band were back at Rooftops again. According to Mr Spencer's review in *Sounds*, when Crazyhead came on stage Porkbeast mischievously quipped, "Hello Wales!" The Glasgow audience had already embraced Crazyhead and were "game for a laugh". It was fortunate that the bouncers were well behaved too. While Porkbeast's light-hearted jibe hadn't gone unnoticed, they didn't appear to take exception to it. But later things got tense when somehow Vom and Porkbeast were left behind at the venue after the gig. For whatever reason, the Crazyhead rhythm section found itself stranded backstage, and to compound matters they then got lost trying to find their way out of the venue. Describing the backstage area as a "labyrinth", Vom recalls how the pair kept going through door after door until stumbling into what looked like a doormans' convention. They found themselves at the top of a spiral staircase, a bouncer on each step all the way down to the bottom. A head doorman was giving the other bouncers instructions for that evening's club night. Conscious that all eyes were now on them, Vom mumbled, "Sorry, we're in the band, we've got lost, we're just trying to get out. It was just quiet, and the head bouncer went, 'OK, come down,' and we had to walk down that spiral staircase past all those bouncers, and I thought 'What the fuck's going to happen?' All he did was open up this massive back door, and we just walked out onto the street and the door closed behind us. I just thought 'Thank fuck for that!'"

The band did themselves no favours a couple of days later. Porkbeast remembers: "We were big in Aberdeen, and the local radio came down and invited me and Vom on. We went on about how good James Brown's rhythm section was, and how modern pop music was rubbish. We slagged off local heroes, the very shit Deacon Blue, and complained that you could not hear the female singer's vocals… probably because she was crap, and she was going out with the singer." The station's switchboard was immediately bombarded by calls from irate locals,

Photograph by DC3, sleeve design by P. St. John Nettleton.

Reverb sporting Viz comic's Finbarr Saunders t-shirt. Source: Back cover of 'Time Has Taken Its Toll On You' single.

furious at Porky and Vom's remarks about their hometown heroes.

Reverb took great delight in wearing a pair of tartan Bay City Roller baggies in Scotland, which he had picked up at a sale in Leicester in the late 1970s. "He took the wretched things on tour," says Anderson, "and when we got to the venue in Aberdeen or Glasgow, he wore them for the soundcheck, doing a crap Scottish accent. To say the local crew were not amused would be an understatement. He also insisted walking down Sauchiehall Street on a Saturday afternoon and early evening in his Bay City bloody Roller trousers!"

The band crossed back into England for the three final dates of the tour to coincide with the release of the single. The promo video for Time Has Taken Its Toll On You first aired on the Saturday morning television programme *The Chart Show* on 11th July, and while it proved to be the band's highest charting single, it nevertheless stalled at 65. Given the more commercial appeal of the record, and the major clout the band now had behind them, this seems surprising. Certainly Time Has Taken Its Toll On You was more accessible than Crazyhead's first two singles, a fact that did not go unnoticed with Nancy Culp. Writing for *Record Mirror*, Culp considered the likeness to The Monkees' (I'm Not Your) Stepping Stone. There can be no denying the similarity. She alluded to the more polished sound being the result of the band signing to Parlophone, and awarded the single "A cautious thumbs up because commercialism for its own sake is an ugly

accusation and one I wouldn't want to level at them." Richard Cook for *Sounds* also heaped praise on the single: "A stroke of greatness. A moment to cherish. Five sick men join the angels."

Reviews were generally favourable, but there were some dissenters. James Brown, whose 'grebo' pets had been the Gaye Bykers, dismissed the single, paraphrasing the lyrics in his review for the *NME* before concluding: "And so continues the grimy life and times of Anderson and his muckers." Chris Roberts for *Melody Maker* was more blunt: "Crazyhead are a pile of shite, always have been, always will be. QED."

The photograph of Crazyhead on the back of the single sleeve caught the eye of *Viz* cartoonist Simon Thorp. Reverb happened to be wearing a 'Finbarr Saunders and His Double Entendres' t-shirt. Saunders was one of Thorp's most famous creations for *Viz*, and, as the comic strip's title suggests, the titular hero had a penchant for misinterpreting even the most innocent of comments. Thorp was suitably moved by Reverb's patronisation to draw a caricature of Crazyhead. At the time, the UK adult comic magazine was almost at the peak of its success, and to be immortalised in ink by one of its main artists was honour indeed for Crazyhead. Allegedly the band were unaware that Thorp had taken it upon himself to draw them until the cartoon appeared in *Viz*'s own version of a singles chart. Anderson says the rights to it were subsequently bought outright by EMI for the band to use for promotional and merchandising purposes. It would be emblazoned across Crazyhead t-shirts by the end of the 1980s.

It was almost certainly a Crazyhead t-shirt that saved Bobby Smith from a kicking after a Leicester City vs. Wolverhampton Wanderers football match. Smith, an avowed Crazyhead and Wolves fan had left Leicester's stadium on Filbert Street. "The game was a drab nil-nil draw," he recalls, "enlivened only by the red card Steve Bull received for nutting his nemesis, Steve Walsh... After the match, however, the real action started. I was walking back to the station, knowing all too well the dodgy hooligan element that had attached itself to Leicester. Dressed, as ever, in my punk bondage pants and leather jacket, I kept my head down and walked fast, eager to avoid the agro that normally followed a Leicester match at that time. As I turned a corner, I ran into a group of knuckle-dragging Leicester skins, intent on dealing out distress to any passing Wolves fan. They ran up to me shouting 'kill the Wolves fans'. Oh, I thought, I have had it now. However, rather than inflicting pain upon me they ran straight past. The reason, I realised, was that I was wearing a Crazyhead t-shirt — they must have

EMI

had me down as a Leicester fan! So, I can honestly state that Crazyhead saved me from a good kicking. Not many fans can say that, I'll wager."

Concluding the summer tour, Crazyhead headlined the Camden Electric Ballroom in London, with support from Soul Asylum and Birdhouse. Writing in *Melody Maker*, Chris Dawes AKA Push related how Crazyhead's set was beset by sound problems. Not even Baby Turpentine, So Amazing Baby, or the reviewer's

own personal favourite, Time Has Taken Its Toll On You managed to escape the sound engineer's shortcomings. But Dawes was charitable enough to point out that, although the performance was under par because of the technical hitch, "their sense of fun shone at the heart of the madness." After the relative monotony of all-day-long recording sessions, Crazyhead were glad to be back on the road and playing live again. What Dawes presumably didn't know was the distinct lack of fun the band had experienced in the recording studio, particularly Vom in light of Balfe's drum machine. Alas, animosity over the use of drum machines would raise its head again soon enough.

RAGS TO RICHES

According to Reverb, Rags was the first song he'd written using a different guitar tuning: "the version that was released on the album was a lot 'straighter' than the way we'd been playing it." As with its predecessor, Time Has Taken Its Toll, Balfe complained again that it was too "Beefheart" — a favourite expression, according to Reverb. He adds, "We recorded one version for the album, but Balfe wanted it to be a single and hence the released version was somewhat ironed out."

Employing the talents of legendary soul singers P.P. Arnold and Katie Kissoon on backing vocals, the band also utilised the services of a brass section. Their old pals, John Barrow and Gaz Birtles from Swinging Laurels, provided the saxophones and brought along a muso acquaintance of theirs, Tony Robinson, when it was apparent that a trumpet was also required.

Dave Balfe had previously used brass with some success on Teardrop Explodes eight years earlier, and evidently was trying to replicate the winning formula on Rags. It had been Balfe's idea to call on P.P. Arnold and Katie Kissoon, of which Anderson says, "we all agreed wholeheartedly... Balfe liked the way the song had a bluesy/souly/Motowny feel and wanted to get some great girl backing vocals on the track." Reverb gives Balfe his due. Of the backing singers, he says, "They were really good, dead professional. We didn't have much input into what they did really, Balfe asked them to do lots of variations and they just knocked them out."

Anderson adds, "They were great, but the producer had to stop them and do a retake because their bangles were jangling loudly as they moved around getting into the tune! It was great watching the two stars strutting their stuff, and those voices! They looked stunningly attractive as well."

Crazyhead on top of a high-rise office block in the heart of the City of London.
Source: Video still from 'Rags', directed by Tony van den Ende.

The band certainly wasn't against a brass section or employing the services of the soulful backing vocalists. But, says Anderson, "The same couldn't be said of using a drum machine on the track." Balfe was becoming increasingly forceful about how he thought things should be done. As with Time Has Taken Its Toll On You, Balfe obsessed about using a drum machine. Says Vom, "The pattern was what I'd written, what I'd worked out, but Balfey took it and just put it into a drum machine! And he spent two weeks — *two weeks!* — putting all the drum patterns… two weeks, fucking stupid, into a drum machine right, two weeks! And then the drum machine crashed, and he lost it all and then he insisted on doing it all again!"

The band made another promotional video for the forthcoming single. This time they employed the directorial services of Tony van den Ende. Unlike Keith Allen, van den Ende had a proven track record, having directed promo shorts for The Cult's She Sells Sanctuary and The Mission's Wasteland, among others. He was a sought-after director for alternative rock music promos in the UK. Reverb says that Food/EMI chose van den Ende, and admits he was a more "legit video director" than Keith Allen. Reverb also remembers how much van den Ende reminded them all of Allen's character, "the luvvie" music video director, in *The Comic Strip Presents… The Yob.*

The band were filmed at night miming to Rags on top of a high-rise office block in the heart of the City of London, near where the Gherkin now stands. Vom says the actual location was next to the Lloyds Building. It was the height of yuppiedom and the video was interspersed by cutaway clips, highlighting the huge gulf between poverty and affluence that still persist in society. Crazyhead took van den Ende up to Leicester, where he filmed Super 8 video footage in two of the most deprived areas of the city. Reverb recalls with wry amusement, "I think Tony found the poverty quite romantic — 'Wow — poor people!'" But adds with affection, "Nice chap though." The location shots in Leicester included glimpses of inner-city life in Highfields, as well as the ingrained poverty of a rundown council estate in Braunstone. This was contrasted against the highrollers in the capital, with clips of Rolls-Royce cars, city workers, and gleaming tower blocks.

Given that the theme of the song as an indictment on the widening gulf between rich and poor, it is ironic that the video shoot ended up being an excessive cocaine session… for Anderson at least. He says, "I got a paranoid moment halfway through the night and confided in Tony I was really coked up in central London. His reply: 'Everyone is coked out of their minds, we are doing a 12-hour night-time video shoot in London, dear!'"

It wasn't simply paranoia on Anderson's part, however. The presence of a film production company in the city drew undue attention, and executives at the Lloyds Building tried to get the shoot shut down. Despite these complaints, filming was completed without intervention.

With the promotional video in the bag, there was the matter of photography for the cover art for Rags, as well as the impending album. The photographer was renowned snapper Laurie Lewis, and the location of the shoot was an office tower block in the City of London, once again. This time the run-in was not with irate bankers but construction workers on an adjacent building. Anderson recalls, "It was a chilly day in London, and I was on one of the highest rooftops with a pair of giant angel wings attached to my back for a Wim Wenders influenced shoot. As I tried to balance in the wind, vomiting over the side in-between shots, with a mammoth hangover, a bunch of builders shouted abuse from the next rooftop, 'You fackin' ponce!' I waved my arm in an angelic manner and replied, 'I forgive you my sons, for you do not know who you mock.'"

Rags was released on 30th August 1988. If its predecessor Time Has Taken Its Toll On You had marked a subtle shift in direction from the all-out garage punk assault of the first two singles, this was even more of a departure. The three major weekly British music papers gave it reasonably favourable reviews, even if *Melody Maker* was more indifferent than praiseworthy. Paul Mathur referred to Rags as "A spirited outburst from the boys that turned grebo into a verb."

Anderson wearing "giant angel wings" — front cover of 'Rags' single. Photo by Laurie Lewis.

But for Mathur there was "a tad too much banal preaching" and he concluded his review on a puzzling note: "when they twitch a bit, the world is their oyster should they wish to live in a shellfish."

Robin Gibson, for *Sounds*, gave Crazyhead the benefit of the doubt, calling Rags "a damn good single... fine alcohol fuelled rock'n'roll with a breathless horn section and some inspired backing vocals." His parting shot was undoubtedly meant as a compliment: "These chaps are already across the water, routing Aerosmith at their own game."

Stuart Maconie, for the *NME*, said it was "Equal parts axle-grease, lurex and Cherry B," while the "very idea of a bunch of oikish White Midlanders trying to get sassy" filled him with glee, as he said it should the readers too. Maconie inferred a likeness to Ashton, Gardner and Dyke, an early 1970s power rock trio with brass led inclinations. With Rag's blaring horns, foot stomping refrain, and soulful wailings from Arnold and Kissoon, Maconie wasn't far off the mark. The song was as catchy as hell.

But it failed to make a big impression on the charts. The comparatively lavish presentation didn't help boost sales: A limited edition 12-inch picture disc of Rags came in mottled shades of blue, turquoise and black vinyl, in a screen-printed plastic sleeve that featured Thorp's caricature of the band. One explanation for its poor showing was that BBC Radio One, the UK's make or break station at the time, had decreed it unsuitable for widespread airplay. And yet at the same time it was too mainstream for the likes of John Peel. Consequently it stalled at 78 before dropping out of the top 100 a couple of weeks later.

The single's inglorious departure from the charts roughly coincided with what *Sounds* journalist Neil Perry would later call "a day of equestrian mania at Newbury racecourse — thinly described as a launch party for Crazyhead's debut LP *Desert Orchid*." The single's failure didn't bode well for the album's chances, but this didn't prevent Crazyhead from having a party.

On the morning of 17th September 1988, the band along with an assortment of journalists met outside the Parlophone office and piled onto a coach. They were headed to Berkshire to spend a day at the horse races, where they had hired a marquee for the day. Crazyhead must have looked an incongruous sight dressed in smart grey morning suits, wearing

'Rags' 12-inch picture disc single and Viz screen printed clear plastic cover.

shades, and with long scruffy hair tumbling out of their top hats. Reverb was something of a racing buff, so was relatively seasoned when it came to betting. Porkbeast, on the other hand, had no luck whatsoever. Anderson says wistfully, "The new LP launch was a lavish affair… free booze for everyone, and a few lines of whizz for some of the band. I could barely walk I got so wasted, though I do remember someone giving me a £10 note to burn for a photo."

It wasn't only Anderson who was wasted. He continues, "Our manager's even drunker wife started tonguing me, to the anger of Andy Cheeseman who started threatening me! 'Not my fault if your wife fancies me mate, she snogged me!' was my reply." The band took advantage of the record company hospitality. "There was a free bar," says Reverb. "Towards the end of the afternoon I think we decided that we ought to get our money's worth and hit the bar hard, I can remember drinking half-pint glasses of whiskey. Needless to say, the drive back was very messy."

Anderson picks up the story. "A Food Records bigwig, who had an iron Keef Richards constitution for strong dope and LSD — a lot of which he did while working with us in the studio — was totally whammoed on about four cans of weak lager, snogging a female journo on the way back and berating us, 'C'mon lads get chatting up those female journos!'"

Arriving back in London, the band went to a club except for Reverb, who had other ideas. He picks up the story: "I was very, very drunk but somehow decided

"A day of equestrian mania at Newbury racecourse – thinly described as a launch party for Crazyhead's debut LP 'Desert Orchid'", September 1988.

Photo courtesy of Mary Scanlon, originally printed in Sounds, 1st October 1988.

it would be a good idea to get the train back to Leicester. I managed to buy a ticket and get myself on the right train. Next thing I knew, I was being woken up by the guard asking for my ticket. He looked at my ticket and said, 'this ticket is for Leicester'. 'Yeah, I'm going to Leicester." The train conductor replied, 'We've just passed Wakefield.'" Reverb had to get off at the next stop, which was Leeds, some eighty miles past Leicester. "No train back until Sunday morning," says Reverb. "I was pissed, dressed in a morning suit, staggering round Leeds at midnight."

In addition to the day out at Newbury racecourse, ostensibly a press junket and photo opportunity, the band decided to hold another, 'official' *Desert Orchid* album launch. For this they returned to the Philbeach Hotel. According to Anderson, the band "loved the luxury, mixed with the madness and sleaze" but somehow neglected to inform invited press and record company executives about the hotel's reputation. They watched with amusement as the party was bolstered by some of the more "bizarre and exotic" guests and visitors to the hotel. The launch started in the hotel's basement, but as the night progressed drifted upstairs and into individual rooms. The hijinx got out of hand at one point. Says Anderson, "We hung our mate and journo Mr Spencer out the hotel window from three floors up by his legs, as he giggled drunkenly. He was a mate of Lemmy's, so I guess the young guys wanted to treat him to some good natured rock'n'roll drunkenness. I believe Spike was to the fore, as usual, along with Sparky Pearson."

WE ARE THE ROAD CREW

Many roadies and technicians passed through the ranks of Crazyhead and Gaye Bykers On Acid over the years, but three names crop up with regularity: Spike, Sparky, and the indefatigable Keith Penny — or just Penny. Anderson relates how he first got to know Penny in the Leicester punk scene of the late 1970s: "He was big, loud and mouthy, dressed in brothel creepers, drainpipe jeans that were really short and a leather jacket." Penny had been in various Leicester bands himself before ending up as a roadie, including Tone Deaf and Clinic 6 — the latter named after Leicester's VD unit. Clinic 6 later became Rabid, a name lifted from a David Cronenberg horror movie. Rabid were arguably Leicester's foremost punk band in the early eighties, entering the indie charts with their *Bloody Road To Glory* EP in the summer of 1982. Rabid have continued to play and record over the years, albeit with various personnel changes. Their most recent incarnation featured one Robber Byker on bass!

Penny then drummed for Clockwork Soldiers, a band that, as noted, had a large skinhead following. Penny frequently got into fights in those days. Anderson admits to being wary of Penny at the time, but concedes, "Later, Penny turned out to be a lovely guy who would protect and die for you on tour." Anderson got to know Penny better in the mid-eighties at the Princess Charlotte. Penny had largely divested himself of his skinhead past by this point and was in another band called Focker Wolf. He was also the main crew for New Age, a band that included Reverb and Vom. After Reverb and Vom parted ways with New Age, Penny went with them to Crazyhead. "He was fast and coordinated for such a big guy," says Anderson, "and moved and set up kit really fast. At this time he also worked for Gaye Bykers On Acid, eventually ending up with them full-time."

Another notable member of the Gaye Bykers On Acid road crew was 'Deptford' John Armitage. He was originally the bassist for infamous skinhead Oi! band Combat 84, who gained notoriety when they appeared in a controversial episode of the BBC television documentary series *Arena*, in which lead singer Chris Henderson expressed certain far right sympathies. Armitage has always refuted the racist accusations. He later played bass with UK Subs and The Exploited, before crewing with the Bykers. Armitage has become a renowned guitar technician and tutor in his own right, and has worked with artists as diverse as Paul McCartney, Motörhead, Slayer, Take That, Spice Girls, Annie Lennox and more. He also runs the guitar maintenance workshop, The Guitar Hospital.

Kev Byker and Keith Penny.

Old friend and Janitors' guitarist Craig 'Hoppy' Hope crewed for the Bykers after The Janitors split in 1989. Hoppy was with the Bykers through their final year and accompanied them on their second American tour. He continued to work as a roadie and has been guitar technician for Coldplay's Chris Martin for many years.

Sparky Pearson is another legend of the Leicester music scene. Anderson recalls how Sparky had, for many years, drummed in local bands: "I remember first meeting him at a punk night in Scamps in 1979 or 1980. He was the drummer in The Observers, a post-punk act with Steve Pierce from Wigston on bass. They had a single, Crisis, on a local label." Sparky had also been in a pre-Bykers and Crazyhead band called The Plainsmen,

Former Combat 84 bassist and subsequently Gaye Bykers On Acid roadie, 'Deptford' John Armitage.

with Mary and Robber Byker, which never got beyond the rehearsal stage. He had also been in Leicester rockabilly band, Johnny 7, whose line-up included Christina Wigmore, Porkbeast's replacement in Crazyhead in 1990, and another infamous name on the Leicester rockabilly scene, Nev Hunt, who once drove for Crazyhead. But the band had to let him go, because, according to Anderson, "he got really drunk and tried to CS gas the security at a gig."

Sparky would become Crazyhead's full-time roadie

"Heavy metal oil!" – Clockwork Soldiers with Ian Roche and Penny (far left and second from left).

after Penny left for the Bykers. Anderson says they were taking a bit of a chance employing him, because "friends on the local post-punk rockabilly scene said

he would fuck things up. He was a great drummer, but his solid partying had lost him band work, I heard. When we took Sparky on, he swore he'd cleaned up his act. From 1986, or maybe '87, he was our man, and bloody good at it, wisecracking as he chain-smoked his way down the M1, Reverb by his side doing the same, cracking up the van with their sick, twisted humour... Orgasmatron or Leadbelly cassettes blaring out loud, plus various tapes done by band members, mainly seventies punk, sixties garage punk, or old rock'n'roll. New

Craig 'Hoppy' Hope – Janitors guitarist, Gaye Bykers On Acid roadie and now guitar tech for Coldplay's Chris Martin.

Photo courtesy of Ian Anderson.

Sparky Anderson, Crazyhead roadie — "from 1986, or maybe '87, he was our man, and bloody good at it".

faves were The Godfathers' *Hit By Hit* LP, and later on The Pixies." Anderson adds wistfully, "Like Penny before him, Sparky did a great job for a couple of years, working like a dog for peanuts, at least in the early days."

The band first met Spike AKA Michael Hall, backstage at a gig in Birmingham. It wasn't long before Spike relocated from Coventry to Leicester and started working for Crazyhead. Anderson recalls that "Spike was a jolly character who racked out huge lines of top whizz for us, as well as himself. He became our second main crew member with Sparky — a fine double act, dressed in army fatigues on tour, quoting lines from various 'Nam movies — it was the eighties remember! These two would work their way through a couple of years of heavy touring with Crazyhead, up and down the UK. I could just imagine Sparky and Spike creeping through the jungle wearing beads of human ears!"

John Barrow, of Crazyhead's erstwhile brass section, says in his memoir *How Not To Make It In The Pop World*, "Spike did an awful lot of graft behind the scenes. He re-strung and tuned guitars, looked after the whole of the backline and shifted gear around. He was worth his weight in gold and was a real larger than life character. Road crew are often dedicated unsung heroes, without whom proceedings would come to a grinding halt."

SURVIVAL OF
THE FILTHIEST

Taking its name from a much loved and highly rated race-horse, Crazyhead's debut album was released almost a year after the Bykers' own debut. The long gap between the media furore that had surrounded 'grebo' the year before, and the eventual release of *Desert Orchid* in October 1988, ensued that much of the hype had died down. Anderson lays the blame on David Balfe, but

Spike AKA Michael Hall, Crazyhead roadie —
"Spike [was] a jolly character who racked out
huge lines of top whizz for us, as well as himself."

also recognises that the original plan was rather optimistic: "The whole original Food deal was to have one LP, even two a year, and release a single every three months, like the punk days in the seventies and the sixties mod/rock bands. It all changed."

As to the meaning behind the album's title, Vom, talking to Hans Peter Kuenzler in November 1988, said that *Desert Orchid* was derived from the "cultural wasteland" that is Leicester and the band as "the orchid growing out of it." Reverb offered his own, more down to earth explanation: "Apart from the idea that we're a bloom flowering in this barren wasteland, the greatest steeplechase horse is also called Desert Orchid. He won a couple of good races last year, and the first time out this year, last week, won by 15 lengths." Reverb's enthusiasm for the racehorse was such that as early as September 1988, according to Fast Dick, he had already backed it to win the Cheltenham Gold Cup in March 1989.

The irony inherent in the title was not lost on some. Neil Perry wrote in *Sounds*, "After two and a half years, a thousand sweaty gigs, four singles and a pile of enthusiastic press, now comes Crazyhead's first LP, *Desert Orchid* — in honour of that very special supersonic racehorse."

In terms of production, *Desert Orchid* didn't capture the raw immediacy of the band's live performances, or their early singles. Reviews were mixed but generally favourable. David Cavanagh, writing in *Sounds*, utilised horse racing terminology when he noted that "in the age of the dodgy debut, it's reassuring to find that Crazyhead can stay the distance at 40 minutes". He reserved particular praise for What Gives You The Idea That You're So Amazing Baby, which he said benefitted from its makeover: "Its flawless construction and massive guitar kick make it an early morning must. See if *your* neighbours agree." In conclusion, Cavanagh called *Desert Orchid* "a thoroughly convincing first album".

Andrew Smith for *Melody Maker* said, "there's something healthy (if that's the word) about the amount of riff pilfering that's going on here: this, surely, is what rock'n'roll is all about." Smith was enamoured of the riffs. "We've heard them all before of course, but like the war, we need to be reminded of them every so often. In any case, the riffs in question are put to good use on *Desert Orchid*." Citing the first side as the stronger, he posited that the riffs combined with Motown rhythms resulted in "pop classics" and that a number of the tracks "wouldn't sound out of place on daytime radio… without ever sinking to a level that makes them likely to *get* played. Brilliant!" Smith was more guarded in his summation of the album as a whole, pointing out that it was a significantly different beast from the Crazyhead live experience: "What you don't get with *Desert Orchid* is a sense of abandonment, of the mania that these songs will be accompanied by live. But allowing for this intangible fact, it's a good listen. Hear in it what you will."

Record Mirror was also complimentary about the album, if dismissive of the spectre of 'grebo'. Wrote Tony Beard,

> So far grebo has yet to live up to last year's hype. A new spirit of rock, they claimed, while offering us nowt but a mug of rancid Jack Daniels and a flash of tattooed flesh. This is different. What Gives You The Idea…? wipes the grease from the grebo myth with a single splash of the Pork-beast's sword. It's a frantic rush, a melee of biker chic riffs and Red Leicester whiffs, while Rags is oceans apart, a brassy splurge over a grossed out metal buzz that spells diversity. Crazyhead excel because they mix grunge with style. They're not afraid to glance back at the hellish past, relishing all the sixties has to offer in the way of shit-kickin' depravity.

Henry Williams for *Q* gave *Desert Orchid* a score of four out of five. He mentioned "last year's 'grebo movement'" and, like Beard, alluded to how Crazyhead had been tarnished by association. More crucially though, he made a clear distinction between Crazyhead and other bands of their ilk, suggesting they were a cut above: "[Crazyhead's] marriage of sixties pop, punk and heavy metal actually has little in common with groups such as Gaye Bykers On Acid and Pop Will Eat Itself." Williams went on to describe how all 11 tracks were "delivered at the same breakneck pace", seemingly oblivious to the many mid-tempo numbers. Nearer to the mark perhaps, he likened Time Has Taken Its Toll On You to "an after-hours meet between The Monkees, Byrds and Jimmy Page where all parties were convulsed by drunken fits of giggling." After mentioning Porkbeast's passion for pagan sites, Williams concluded obliquely that Crazyhead had "made one of the year's most comic LPs".

Sounds journo Neil Perry said, "*Desert Orchid* is a near flawless collection of 11 songs — each as comfortable on an LP as it would be as a single — and a record that will finally trash the warped, still-lingering notion that Crazyhead are just drunken, talentless minor league oiks."

At the time the band appeared as satisfied with the album as many of the critics and were quick to defend the inclusion of several previously available songs. These included the most recent singles (Time Has Taken Its Toll On You, Rags) as well as remakes of other songs (What Gives You The Idea That You're So Amazing Baby?, I Don't Want That Kind Of Love). Reverb justified the inclusion of the latter by saying the remakes were of songs originally recorded and released when they were on an indie label, and argued that "a lot of people will be hearing us for the first time with this LP." The idea of reworking songs certainly didn't bother Anderson, who was still not entirely happy with the re-recorded version of I Don't Want That Kind Of Love. "We may do it again and again until we get it right, so tough shit!" he said. "If people want to buy the LP with different versions, fine; if they don't, they can always tape what they want off their friends. That's what I always do…"

Anderson says, "some of *Desert Orchid* was great" before reiterating the beef the band had with Balfe about overproduction. Pausing to consider the matter further, Anderson concedes, "Apart from that, I think at least half of it is great, and I think Mark Freegard and Cenzo Townsend did a great job."

Reverb agrees with Anderson about Mark Freegard: "It wasn't Mark Freegard's fault. He had never seen us play live when he started recording us. When he finally got to see us at the Town and Country Club [March 1989] he got rather tired and emotional, and said he'd have made the process very different if he'd known how good we were live."

Vom is less charitable. He considers their cover of Richard Berry's 1959 hit, Have Love, Will Travel, to be the best song on the album — and not because of Freegard, who was absent on the day they recorded it. Freegard was at a dental appointment, recalls Vom. "We started messing around, and we'd been playing

Music press ad for Crazyhead's Desert Orchid album and The Survival of The Filthiest tour.

Have Love, Will Travel at soundchecks and stuff like that just for a laugh… It was the only time in that whole session where we really played as a live band, and we put it down. When Mark Freegard came back, he went: 'That's brilliant that's great!', 'cos when we put it down originally, we just thought it was going to be a B-side, and he said, 'No, that's great, that's great', and when we played it to Balfey, he said, 'That's got to be a single!'" In light of this, an exasperated Vom says, "*Well why didn't you let us fucking get on with it?* That was basically our argument, and [Have Love, Will Travel] was right at the end of recording the album. We'd more or less done it all, and that was one of the last things. We all felt it was such a shame, because if we'd just been allowed to play as a band in the studio and let us develop the album without any interference, we'd have done a great album."

The final word on the matter is left with Reverb: "I've always regretted that we never recorded the songs on *Desert Orchid* the way we would've wanted to hear them, to release at a later date."

To promote the album the band embarked on 'Survival Of The Filthiest', a relatively short tour of the UK. John Robb was at one of the first gigs at Manchester International. He opened his report in *Sounds* with the observation that "Leicester's Crazyhead are poised tentatively on the edge of the big time boogie precipice", and, in all earnestness, considered how they were "just a hit single away from that handshaking walk through rich pastures into tax exile". Unfortunately, the band was beset by technical gremlins on the night, or, as Robb put it, "a PA sound that was total plasticine-in-the-speakers-mush". Crazyhead didn't hit their stride until after at least five songs, but Robb gave the band the benefit of the doubt when they launched into their cover of The Stooges' TV Eye, commenting that "Anderson took off at this point". In conclusion, Robb considered Crazyhead to be less crazy than "fellow Leicester leather renegades Gaye Bykers On Acid" but believed that "persistence and hard work will eventually pay off in a handsome sense".

Having utilised the services of a brass section on the Rags single and elsewhere on *Desert Orchid*, Crazyhead invited John Barrow, Gaz Birtles and Tony Robinson to accompany them on some of the tour dates. In his autobiography, Barrow recalls how liberating it was to be playing live session music once again, freed from the responsibilities that entails being in a band of one's own. Straight after the Survival Of The Filthiest tour, Crazyhead manager Andy Cheeseman then invited Barrow, Birtles and Robinson to join the band on a prestigious support slot on the European leg of Iggy Pop's Instinct tour. This was not without its problems though. Barrow had not long been in a new day job and had already asked for time off for his ongoing extracurricular band activities; a whole month on the road might be pushing his luck as far as his employer was concerned. Still, Barrow felt that supporting a music legend was too good an opportunity to miss. So, once again he had to grovel to his employers who, to his relief, grudgingly allowed him the time off, with the warning that they would not be so accommodating in the future.

To say that Crazyhead were excited to be supporting Iggy Pop would be an understatement. In an interview with Ian Gittins of *Melody Maker*, Porkbeast and Anderson spoke of the impact that Iggy and The Stooges had on them as teenagers. Porkbeast had played *Raw Power* to Anderson in his bedroom, and the proverbial seed was sown. Anderson is alleged to have said on first hearing the album, "Fucking hell! Wouldn't it be great to be in a band?" Over 10 years later here they were, about to embark on a tour supporting one of their idols and major inspirations. Iggy Pop was the Godfather of punk and a bona fide rock legend. Says Reverb: "I remember getting on the plane to Berlin for the first date of the tour and saying to myself that if this was as good as it gets then fair play." Not surprisingly, Reverb considers the Iggy tour as the pinnacle of Crazyhead's career.

INSTINCT

Following the end of the UK tour, Crazyhead had almost three weeks to pre-pare for Iggy Pop. On 4th November 1988, they flew into a bitterly cold Berlin to play the Tempodrom, a circus tent situated in the shadow of the Reichstag. It had huge icicles hanging from the guy ropes. Barrow recalls, with just trailers for changing rooms, the band was "half frozen". But Iggy played a "blinder" of a 90-minute set "full of raw power and energy", and Crazyhead as support was well received too. There was hope among the Crazyhead entourage that David Bowie might make a guest appearance, given that Berlin had been the location for so many of his and Iggy's former collaborations and past glories. It was not to be though.

Anderson always found Reverb an amusing tour companion, if bizarre and complex at times. While staying at a rather upmarket hotel in Berlin, Anderson knocked on the guitarist's door to see if he fancied joining him for a beer, only to be greeted by the sight of a stark-naked Reverb, facial hair shaved into a Hitler moustache, with "his cock and balls pushed between his legs... He was Sieg Heiling of course! Oh dear. So here I was in Berlin, face-to-face with a female Hitler/Reverb from hell's worst nightmares!"

After the Berlin gig, the tour headed into the lowlands of Belgium and the Netherlands. Barrow recalls that the Crazyhead entourage hit the bars following the show at Amsterdam's Paradiso. Unfortunately, when they returned to the tour coach, they discovered that an opportunist thief had gone through their luggage while the driver had caught some shut eye. Tony Robinson's trumpet was among the things stolen and so, on arriving in Copenhagen, much time was spent traipsing around music shops trying to find a replacement. However, Barrow says Robinson seemed more concerned about a fresh pack of y-fronts that had also been stolen than he did his trumpet.

Oslo was next, followed by two nights in Sweden. The English tour party had been warned about the astronomical price of alcohol in the Scandinavian countries, particularly Sweden, and had stocked up accordingly before leaving Amsterdam.

Whiling away the hours of boredom on the tour coach, the band and Spike instigated a tequila session in which they plied relative newcomer Robinson until he was sick, forcing him to spend the rest of the journey with his head down the toilet. This was the least of the brass section's concerns though. More worrying was Spike's threat to "get" them before the end of the tour. Not knowing whether he was joking, the threat was a lingering concern for the brass section for the rest of the tour. Luckily, Spike never made good on his threat; a bottle of plonk was enough to placate the roadie.

The brass section earned themselves the nickname The Space Bastards on the Instinct tour. They had started the tour as The Phantom Horns, the name that had appeared on the sleeve credits for *Desert Orchid*. But Anderson had different ideas and introduced them under a different stage name each night. He frequently had the brass section in stiches,

Cover of Crazyhead's itinerary for the European leg of Iggy Pop's Instinct tour. Courtesy of John Barrow.

calling them Dirty Birty and the Over Thirties, or The Space Leather Rats, until eventually The Space Bastards stuck. It always took a few moments for the brass section to regain their composure and a relative level of decorum was restored.

Heading back into Germany, the tour took in Hamburg, Berlin again, Offenbach, Düsseldorf, and Munich. Crazyhead were met in Germany by a film crew, although there is a difference of opinion as to which live performance they documented. Reverb thinks it was Offenbach near Frankfurt, while John Barrow recalls Düsseldorf. The band were also given Super 8 video cameras by the film crew to obtain footage from the rest of the tour. The band agreed to film themselves miming on the tour bus, with a view to using the video as a promo for the future single Have Love, Will Travel. The band complied despite feeling fragile from the night before, after Reverb had hooked up with an old friend and they all ended up getting stuck into Vom's supply of Stroh rum back at the hotel. No one got much sleep because Reverb's pal was having loud conversations with

The Space Bastards, Crazyhead's brass section: Gaz Birtles (far left) and John Barrow (3rd from left), on the Iggy Pop Instinct tour, Germany, November 1988.

himself in his sleep in German. Reverb now says, "You don't have to look too hard at the finished video to see how rough we look."

The tour rolled through Austria, where Crazyhead headlined their only show of the tour as Iggy and his band had a day off. Then it was off to Switzerland for a show in Zurich, before Italy, Southern France, and the warmer climes of Spain, where they played Barcelona, Madrid, and San Sebastian. The band wasted no opportunity in the bars of Barcelona capitalising on the footballer Gary Lineker's name, Leicester's biggest export and a hometown they shared. Lineker was one of Barcelona football club's favourite adopted sons. A show of support, not to mention a tenuous link, certainly went some way in securing the Crazyhead entourage muchos gratis cervezas! Barrow recalls how the band also took advantage at that night's show at Studio 54: "On stage we got a lot of mileage from Lineker's name, the crowd loved it."

Iggy Pop had given up drinking and drugs and was, apart from the occasional relapse, clean by the time of the Instinct tour. Maintaining a respectful distance from the others, he largely kept himself to himself, and generally turned up just before a show and left straight after it. That's not to say he didn't take the time to get to know the band. Boozing was banned before gigs, at least among Iggy's tour musicians, but Crazyhead got on well with his backing band, and were occasionally afforded the opportunity to socialise with them on days off, or when not travelling through the night straight after a gig.

Among the members in Iggy's backing band on the Instinct tour were Hanoi Rocks guitarist, Andy McCoy, and UK Subs bassist Alvin Gibbs. "Andy McCoy was like a cartoon of a rock star," recalls Anderson, "always shivering, wanting more smack, always with an attractive groupie in tow the next morning, and *always* drinking Jack Daniels. He managed to live like this and yet still be a fairly down to earth guy, in a fucked by rock kind of star way."

On one occasion, Anderson joined Iggy's band — "minus the mighty Iggy" — and blagged his way into a Dave Lee Roth show. "Iggy was playing big halls, but this place was a huge arena!" says Anderson. "The show was spectacular in a Spinal Tap kind of way, with Roth being pushed through the crowd on a giant surfboard, supported by metal struts and on wheels, then leaping into a boxing ring to shadow box."

Unfortunately, Crazyhead's shows in Spain were bedevilled by timeslot gremlins, and on at least one occasion the band was scheduled to go on before the doors had even opened! Despite a three- or four thousand capacity venue, in San Sebastian they ended up playing to just eight people because of this stage time cock-up. Anderson told *Sounds*: "I actually went out and met the audience and said hello and learned their names."

The band headed north, over the Pyrenees, and into France for the last leg

Ticket stub for the last night of the Iggy tour.

Poster for Iggy Pop and Crazyhead Spanish dates, November 1988.

24 NOVIEMBRE BARCELONA 25 NOVIEMBRE MADRID 27 NOVIEMBRE SAN SEBASTIAN

IGGY POP + CRAZYHEAD

of their great Euro jaunt. Playing Bordeaux, the tour party rolled into Paris on 29th November to play two final shows at La Cigale. But even if they had "learned how to burn and keep burning", as *Sounds* journalist David Cavanagh put it the following February, tour fatigue had perhaps begun to take its toll 25 nights into the tour, along with an element of homesickness. Reverb confided in Stuart Maconie: "Ah Blighty. It'll be great to get back. The tour's been great… But it'll be nice to get back home. Leicester's got this unreal image thanks to the Bykers and grebbo [sic] you know."

On the penultimate night, further evidence of tour madness was displayed, when Fast Dick and roadie Spike were ejected from a trendy nightclub after a glass table was smashed. On their return to the hotel, Spike then drunkenly proceeded to decimate the hotel by first kicking a door off its hinges. The entourage were forced to leave and find new accommodation, but not before the unrepentant roadie was grudgingly made to pay for the damage. Anderson recalls that this was somewhat par for the course for Sparky, Crazyhead's other stalwart roadie, too, and his approach to tour fatigue: "He was drinking a bottle of Jack a night, plus God knows how many drugs, and always doing a sterling job somehow."

NME sent Stuart Maconie to Paris for the final night of the tour. It took a while for him to track the band down, due to their ejection from the arranged meeting place at their hotel that morning. When he found them, he instantly hit it off with Reverb and Anderson, interviewing the pair in a sleazy bar in

Montmartre's red-light district. Anderson reflects: "We were amazed, as he was from the *NME*, and was actually down to earth and seemed to like the band... most of the *NME* journos we met were a bunch of stuck-up pricks. I really think the *NME* lost the plot in the late eighties — very anti rock'n'roll — unless you were from Manchester of course!"

Apart from a cursory mention of the legendary headliner, Maconie directed his praise towards Crazyhead. Sprinkled with favourable epithets, Maconie concluded his review, "I have seen the future of rock'n'roll... and it lives in the East Midlands." In a later, more comprehensive feature about his trip to Paris, Maconie wrote how he had "watched Crazyhead blow... Iggy off the stage and into the middle of next week. There was something truly gratifying in seeing five East Midlands rowdies teach the old goat a thing or two about making records that kick ass and wear a mile wide grin."

The Instinct tour proved to be a learning curve for Crazyhead, with its highs far outweighing the lows. Talking to Bataille Fidol for *Sniffin' Rock* magazine the following year, Reverb summed it thus: "If we learnt anything on that tour it was how to keep together!" 💀

CHAPTER EIGHT

28 TABS AND STILL ON THE BALL

N THE AUTUMN OF 1988, LAURIE RUSSO INTERVIEWED Robber and Kev for *House Of Dolls* fanzine. It was apparent in the interview that the band's now parlous financial affairs were cause for concern. Without being drawn too deeply into the matter for legal reasons, they made it clear they were broke following dealings with Lafront. Kev revealed they had been busking to make ends meet, and Robber said they had had absolutely no money for nine months: "All this stuff about how much we signed for in the last year, hundreds of thousands of pounds — it all got blown. In a certain way which really can't be revealed without being libellous." On leaving Leicester, lamented Robber, "We had nothing, then we got something, now we have nothing again!" The irony of having come full circle financially didn't go unnoticed. Kev continued, "When we were living in Leicester, to eat we used to have to go down to Leicester market every night to get free vegetables, and that's funny because

Photo courtesy of Sally Jones.

"they enjoyed dressing up as their transvestite alter-egos, Lesbian Dopeheads On Mopeds" that's what I was doing yesterday in Hackney! I've been so poor I have to beg for vegetables!" It was a Catch-22 situation, with no money but not in a position where they able to sign on, either.

On a positive note, Robber admitted "we're probably more inspired when we're poor". Matters then turned to transvestism, moreover the Gaye Bykers' alter ego, Lesbian Dopeheads On Mopeds (LDOM). The name had first cropped up in a scene in *Drill Your Own Hole*. At that point, they had yet to come up with the idea of dressing in drag when playing under the LDOM moniker. One of the band's sound engineers, an Australian cross-dresser called Geoffrey Perrin, was undoubtedly the inspiration. "He liked cross-dressing!" Mary affirms. "Perrin was one of the reasons we used Aussie/New Zealand accents as the Dopeheads." Sally Jones took a number of photos of the band in October 1988, dressed in drag during rehearsals and sessions for their next album. She says they probably wanted to sort out their wardrobes before playing live as LDOM.

Soon after this, they made what is probably the first documented gig dressed in drag as LDOM. With reference to the Lesbian Dopeheads' supposed place of origin, New Zealand, Neil Perry wrote: "This female four-piece from the land of lamb cutlets — Roberta, Marlene, Heidi-Hi and Toni — are to Women In Rock what the Sinclair C5 was to motorised transport, yet they still turned out some of the finest grunge-pop-metal of the decade." Although patently not

hoodwinked by the thinly veiled pantomime, Perry was happy to go along with the ruse and had fun with it in the process: "For the Lesbians, the signs of a rollicking rebirth would be very good indeed if you could ignore one highly significant factor... After listening to an advance tape, just the other day, it seems the new Gaye Bykers On Acid LP has beaten them to it." Perry was possibly referring to demos the Bykers had recently recorded.

Virgin weren't entirely convinced by these new Bykers demos either, but for different reasons. Robber says they turned

Photo courtesy of Sally Jones.

Mary Byker as his Lesbian Dopeheads On Mopeds alter ego Marlene Dopehead.

them down, possibly because they were too punk for the direction they wanted the Bykers to pursue. Mary concurs, and says that a compromise with Virgin was reached: Since Alex Fergusson had failed with *Drill Your Own Hole* and matters hadn't worked out with Vic Maile, the band were allowed to choose Jon Langford as producer again. Mary says: "Langford had already worked on stuff that had done alright, and Virgin knew that he was probably the man for the sound that we were going for."

It was also around this time the Bykers enlisted the services of Martin Elbourne. He wasn't their manager, but he did everything he could to help them. Elbourne had been a booking agent for Rough Trade and represented the likes of New Order and The Smiths. He had also been involved with co-promoting the first ever WOMAD festival, before becoming the major booking agent for the Glastonbury festival. It was through Mike Hinc, another connection the Bykers had with Rough Trade, that they became involved with Elbourne.

Elbourne was instrumental in the band's dealing with Lafront. Other potential managers or agents might have been put off by Lafront's bluster in the wake of her sacking, but not Elbourne. According to Robber, Elbourne had said that he would help the band out — unofficially. "'I don't care, I ain't scared of her'... yeah, he was dead sound Martin was, and he did help us out a lot."

Elbourne only vaguely recalls Lafront and certainly doesn't remember being intimidated by her. If she had made any threats, he states it would've only made him more determined to help them. Recalling his first impressions of the band, Elbourne says, "The good thing about the Bykers was they were all really interesting, nice people... They weren't exactly going to take over the world, but at that time they still had a major record deal and a new album about to come out."

Mary recalls the sense of relief that came with Elbourne: "Once we'd got rid of Stacey, Virgin were happier... we were still a live draw and they were still behind us at that point. I think Martin Elbourne was talking to Virgin, and I think they were happy that we had someone relatively sane looking after us. So, we still had their support up until *Stewed To The Gills* was released. I think they thought, 'Oh let's see how the Bykers do with a normal record that hasn't got a film to go with it...'"

If nothing else, it was a marriage of convenience. The Bykers had made themselves at home in Alaska Studios near London Bridge, and Elbourne lived in Deptford, not a million miles away. The band settled into a routine and concentrated on writing, rehearsing and recording their second album. Mary remembers how they approached the task, "When we went to make the second album with Jon Langford it was like, 'OK. We're a rocking band. These are

Caple at the controls, with Gaye Bykers On Acid and friends behind, Walworth Road, 1988.

instruments, forget the electronics, let's use the guitars — let's get back to basics! And that's what happened. We had some new influences on board for the second album. We were listening to a lot of Bad Brains and stuff like that... a lot of American punk, which was a lot more musical. We were just listening to some different styles, and we'd been out on the road, and we knew what was working and we were much more satisfied with the way that album turned out."

Engineer Ian Caple recalls the determination with which the Bykers' approached these sessions: "I think we wanted to prove a point — to show what the previous album could have sounded like. I had been to see them live a few times and had a good idea of what they were capable of. By the late eighties I was also working at another London studio, Terminal, in Elephant and Castle. It was a brand-new studio — bigger than Berry Street and it was above ground with windows and daylight! We [Caple and Jon Langford] had just made The Mekons' album *Rock 'n' Roll* there and liked the sound of it. So we recorded all the basic tracks there, setting up the band in the room together. I also set up a guitar amp to run the keyboards and samples through to rough up the clean digital stuff. We worked hard, but Jon was very good at keeping the vibe very relaxed and stress free."

The sessions weren't without humour or excess. One notable incident involved Kev Hyde, and the band's friend and drummer for The Bomb Party,

"He's the Georgie Best of rock'n'roll, 28 tabs and still on the ball" – Bomb Party's Mark 'Thommo' Thompson.

Mark 'Thommo' Thompson. Various members of the Bykers and Crazyhead had joined some of The Bomb Party and indie/goth outfit Balaam and The Angel for libations at a seedy bar in Kings Cross. Thommo had brought with him a supply of acid, some of which was to be distributed amongst the assembled throng before they headed off to a gig at the Sir George Robey. But before Thommo had the chance to distribute the acid, several of Her Majesty's finest trooped into the hostelry. "They didn't look like they'd popped in for a half," Kev recalls with amusement. It was a raid. Everyone in the pub was marched outside and ordered to face the wall for a search. Kev noticed that Thommo was surreptitiously rummaging in his pockets. Kev says, "I thought 'throw the evidence onto the floor, the bastards will never be able to pin that on us, and we might even get them back.'" But Kev was wrong and he watched in horror at what Thommo did next: "Hang on that's not the floor that's his mouth! What lunacy is this he's just put 22 tabs of acid in his gob for safe keeping!"

After the disappointed coppers had left empty handed, Kev set about trying to make Thommo throw the psychedelic stash back up before his stomach began to ingest it. Already quite inebriated, Thommo failed to grasp the magnitude of the situation. All attempts to induce vomiting failed, including feeding Thommo a cup of salt water procured from a nearby kebab shop. It was probably too late to do anything to save Thommo from the inevitable psychedelic onslaught by this point, and Kev concludes by saying, "The only thing to do now was to treat this as some kind of experiment. Thommo was known for having a strong constitution for most things, so this would be the ultimate test."

Accounts as to what followed are muddled. Robber recalls that the somewhat freaked out and bewildered Bomb Party drummer turned up at Alaska Studios later that day a gibbering wreck, with Kev leading him by the hand. "We got him back to the squat in Hackney," recalls Kev. "Lo and behold, after three days

of close monitoring and a lot of hash and Brandy — the obvious vaccines — he began to start talking sense." Robber, on the other hand, recalls that Thommo's hair turned grey and he returned to Leicester, where he was watched over and had to take large quantities of Valium for weeks before he recovered. Mary says that the incident changed Thommo, "I can remember Thommo being pretty spaced out. He was never really the same after that."

The unwitting "experiment" was later immortalised by Mary in the lyrics to Mr Muggeridge, a track on the Bykers' third album, *Cancer Planet Mission*: "He's the Georgie Best of rock'n'roll, 28 tabs and still on the ball."

IN A JAM WITH VAN THE MAN

The Bykers finished recording *Stewed To The Gills* and were putting the final touches to the album at Virgin's Townhouse Studios in Shepherd's Bush. According to Ian Caple, it was the top studio in London at the time. In its previous incarnation it had been a film studio. Richard Branson bought it in the late 1970s and converted it into a three-studio recording complex. The Bykers were booked into Studio 1, while Paul Weller was in the studio next door. Tears For Fears had been in Studio 2 for the best part of the previous year, recording their 1989 opus *The Seeds Of Love*.

There wasn't a great deal for the Bykers to do while the album was being mixed, and, says Caple, they were bored. Hearing that one of the studios was due to be redecorated soon, the band were inspired to do a little decorating of their own. Says Mary, "We redecorated one of the mixing rooms with beer can sculptures and stuff… There was a look of horror on the face of the studio manager when he came in and said, 'Paul Weller's going to be here tomorrow." The band threw a party and asked Paul Weller to join them, but he declined. In an article for *Record Mirror*, Jon Langford offered an impenetrable take on what transpired next on that evening of October 26, 1988. According to Langford, Robber had "attacked [Weller's] recording session" armed with "a well primed fire extinguisher. Asked to elaborate on the matter today, Langford is still reticent: "I would only confuse the issue if I was to comment." Robber is equally evasive if blunt: "It was because he was a cunt," he says. In all probability, Robber, in a somewhat inebriated state, was piqued by what he perceived to be a snub on the part of the Modfather and returned to the studio to trash it. Although he hadn't witnessed it himself, Caple corroborates this story: "Robber had staged

Photo by Peter Anderson.

Something fishy going on. Virgin promo photo for Stewed To The Gills.

an assault on the studio next door… bursting in on the poor unsuspecting Mr Weller and spraying him with a fire extinguisher!"

Caple relates another anecdote about the mixing sessions at the Townhouse. Soon after Paul Weller had finished using the studio, Van Morrison arrived to start work on *Avalon Sunset*. At one point, the Irish singer-songwriter was joined by Cliff Richard, who ended up duetting on the single Wherever God Shines His Light. By now the boredom was stultifying for the Bykers, and they continued to find ways to occupy their time. They discovered that the long sloping corridor that ran the length of the building was perfect for skateboarding. The Bykers were skateboarding when Cliff arrived at the studios. They desisted briefly to listen in on Van's session with Cliff, which, according to Jon Langford, was "some rather smooth white gospel stuff." The skateboarding soon recommenced though, resulting in them being reprimanded by the studio manager, who told them to keep the noise down as they were disturbing Van. Caple recalls, "One evening I was busy mixing when I heard a loud commotion outside the studio door. Mary came running in, looking nervous. He slammed the studio door shut and we could hear a lot of shouting and swearing in a loud Belfast accent coming from outside."

As one might imagine, the irascible Ulsterman was getting wound up by the rumbling of skateboards outside his studio. But, Caple continues, "what had really pissed him off — literally! — was an incident in the gents' toilet. Van had got dressed up in his best suit for a photo shoot in the studio with Cliff. Mary was standing at the urinals having a wee and Van came in and stood at the next urinal. Mary saw who it was, and in his excitement turned round quickly, said 'Fookin' 'ell, it's Van Morrison!' and pissed down Van's left leg!" Laughing, Mary says, "I'm not entirely certain if I pissed on Van Morrison's leg or not, but I do remember some incident with him in the toilet."

Promotional photos for *Stewed To The Gills* were taken by Peter Anderson. The shoot took place in London's East End. Of the props used in the shoot, Tony recalls, "We went to Billingsgate Market early one morning and got a shit load of mackerel, which were the cheapest, and then a few extras like the squid on Kev's head. We got an old door and cut four holes for our heads and then covered it in the fish. We stunk for days after that and we all took the fish home and ate it. I really got sick of mackerel. I put so much in the oven one time, and it is a greasy fish, and the smoke that filled my kitchen was shocking… lingered for days!"

In January, several live dates were announced to celebrate the completion of the new album, for a tour that was tentatively called 'Radio KRAP', a dig at "radio for being crap, being ironic, you know?" according to Mary. On another level Mary intimates that this working title was in deference to Radio Clash. But in any case, the live dates were postponed until February, after it was discovered that Robber had contracted a gastro-intestinal infection as a result of sitting in a silo filled with raw fish for the album's photo shoot. This made good copy, but it transpires had been nothing more than a publicity stunt, according to Tony. On 4th February the Bykers featured

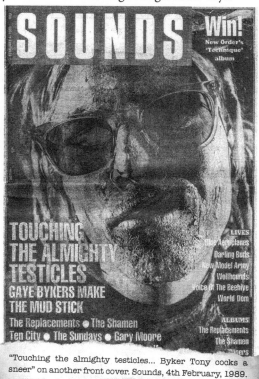

Photo by Steve Double.

"Touching the almighty testicles… Byker Tony cocks a sneer" on another front cover. Sounds, 4th February, 1989.

G.B.O.A.
STEWED TO THE GILLS...

on the cover of *Sounds*. It was the first time they had graced the front page of one of the main British music weeklies since touring the USA nearly a year earlier. *Sounds* scribe Mary Anne Hobbs was of the understanding that the Gaye Bykers were "supposed to be about the con? About selling shit?" Mary's response to Hobbs: "Yes, it was about the con… But the con was only ever that we signed to a major company and got loads and loads of money. We always wanted to write fantastic songs."

Hobbs didn't disagree and described *Stewed To The Gills* as "a grubby, euphoric, guitar-groovy testament to the brilliance of Gaye Bykers' swerving, irreverent, skewered chaos… This is the album that Gaye Bykers On Acid had to make to shake their arrogant, talentless delinquent status. They've done it and everyone is surprised."

Also in the same issue of *Sounds*, the lead single from the album, Hot Thing b/w Rad Dude, was described by Keith Cameron as the best material the Bykers had recorded since the *Nosedive* EP — thanks to the return of Jon Langford behind the production desk. (Cameron was less enthusiastic about Pop Will Eat Itself's new single, Can U Dig It? "Don't kid yourselves. This is the sound of two years ago.") Other reviewers, however, Phil Cheeseman and Stuart Maconie among them, mercilessly slated the single. Cheeseman was scathing enough to say, "If there was justice in the world GBOA would be signing on the dole while Tyneside shipworkers and Liverpool labourers queue up for their pay cheques." He added that the band had "embraced dance music in a desperate attempt to get hip and have made even bigger prats of themselves in the process." Cheeseman is considered an early chronicler of the new dance music scene in the British music press of the 1980s, but Hot Thing hardly fits this bracket and was never one of the Bykers' more dance-oriented offerings in any case. At least Maconie realised the single wasn't a stab at dance music, even if he was less than charitable in describing a band "wallowing in their own muck and making snotty derivative rock crap".

It was left to Mick Mercer of *Melody Maker* to redress the balance. Mercer had been torn by the Bykers in the past, both praiseworthy and critical of them. Of Hot Thing he wrote, "Gaye Bykers in Great Record Shock? I'm afraid so. Having wasted all the early attention by being fussily tendentious, psychedelically obtuse, they scamper back onto the straight and narrow, and it's worked wonders. Concise to the point of atom-splitting, they open with a scream funnelled into charging noise, and shape the mayhem around you. A highly potent, *fertile* experience and about fugging time too."

Photo by Peter Anderson.

Virgin promo photo for 'Hot Thing'.

With lines like 'Cut the crap get on with it, just take me to bed' it's not surprising that some people considered the lyrics to Hot Thing sexist. It was in fact a salutary warning about the perils of casual sex and the risk of AIDS, still very much the number one global public health scare at the time. Speaking with Mary Anne Hobbs in *Sounds*, Mary admitted, "I've actually had girls say that to me… I am crushed that I've lusted after that kind of eroticism and now that AIDS has taken hold it's something I've had to reconsider." Mary was equally concerned about how the threat of AIDS might be exploited by the pillars of the establishment. "AIDS is a disease to end all diseases. It's something that Christians are using to persecute gay people and encourage rampant government homophobia."

There was a serious undercurrent running through the whole of *Stewed To The Gills*. Mary cites the tracks Ill and Teeth being about health care and privatisation. The UK's National Health Service is seriously under threat and stretched to its limits, a demise that had begun nearly 30 years ago when the Bykers highlighted its precarious state in the hands of Margaret Thatcher's Tory leadership. There are also songs on the album with environmental themes, such as Harmonious Murder, while M.A.D. takes its title from the acronym for 'Mutually Assured Destruction', a military strategy whereby two or more opposing nuclear powers would obliterate each other in the event of a nuclear war; none of the sides is inclined to instigate all-out war, yet none has the incentive to disarm either. This track is as much an allegory for mankind's environmental rape of the planet as it was destruction by mass warfare. Mary expressed these concerns to Hobbs in his interview: "Mother Earth, provider of everything is being destroyed... And OK, perhaps this is very serious, but if we don't get serious now, we're not going to have a future to be stupid in."

Today, Mary speaks of the album emerging at a time when people were beginning to talk "about the possible effects we were having on the environment, and I think with us all being anarchistic youngsters we were sensitive to that kind of information." He speaks of a party thrown by an *NME* journalist in which he got into a heated argument with someone who knew little about global warming, and cared even less. "I remember being angry about why they didn't know, and why it was important and why wouldn't that be important to an *NME* reader... I got really angry and started ranting about the environment. We were really all quite aware of it, and it was something we felt strongly about."

Another topic that came under scrutiny on *Stewed* was censorship. The track It Is Are You? took its name from an advertising slogan for the British newspaper, the *Independent*, which launched in 1986. Mary recognised the importance of the freedom of the press and the influence of the press on society. The lyrics question press impartiality: 'Patrons of the 4ᵗʰ Estate, now it's down in black and white, any loss of liberty means that we just have to fight... Clasps are tightened up, we've lost the freedom that was speech, you could play the easy game to practice what you preach.' But if the *Independent* was a relatively even-handed newspaper, the motives of tabloid organs such as the *Sun* and *News of The World*, which belonged to media baron Rupert Murdoch, were more questionable. It was this abuse of power and wider journalistic Machiavellianism that Mary railed against. The music press wasn't so different from the mainstream media, and It Is Are You? also reflects Mary's frustration on this matter. Having been press darlings not so long ago, the Bykers were now the victims of a media backlash. The lyrics level accusations of treachery against the fickle music press: 'Is that a pen in your hand, tell me what to think, designers all to the future hail to the King of Ink.'

With various references to drug-taking and dance crazes, either real or imagined, Better Off Dedd clearly had hedonistic overtones. Mary says, "That's about just being out of it, I guess... having a good time and not conforming. I never felt more alive than when we were doing so many drugs, and it was so full-on, drinking and drugging, and you almost felt like, 'how the fuck am I actually still alive through this?' You know, having a great time, but you know

it's killing you." With lyrics that namecheck populist songs (Monkey Spanner, Boogie Nights, Rock Lobster, Blue Suede Shoes, The Bump), and a chorus that warns, "It's a new sensation sweeping across the nation — don't believe the hype," some might consider Better Off Dedd a comment on the burgeoning "drug fuelled" acid house boom, the attendant media hysteria surrounding it, and its inevitable commodification into the mainstream. The late 1980s were a turbulent time: Society was under attack from Thatcherism, nationalised services were privatised, the NHS was weakened, and the much-reviled poll tax bill was being rolled out. Better Off Dedd was also self-reflective, a case of fiddling while Rome burned. A contemplative Mary admits, "We thought then it was bad, but on reflection it wasn't, it was a kind of more naïve time, I guess. So, that's what that was all about really."

Better Off Dedd also included a sample from the classic Vietnam war movie, *Apocalypse Now*. "Charlie don't surf" was a line barked by Robert Duvall in one of the film's many surreal scenes. Mary explains its use in the song: "*Apocalypse Now* was everybody's favourite movie. It was such a good film, and that whole going to war and it all being fucked up. Basically when US troops were going to war, they were doing more drugs than the hippies were just to survive it. So, you had these people who were supposedly going to war and supposedly toeing the line of being under orders and they were all getting out of it. And again, it was like — what's the point of it all?"

Hair Of The Dog, the title of another song, is self-explanatory. Mary says, "At that point, whatever anybody else says we were doing, as far as chemicals or whatever, we were drinking more than anything... Obviously we were still taking things to keep us awake and doing the obvious." This excess feeds into the album's title, *Stewed To The Gills* — along with the band's concerns for the environment. "The water levels were said to be rising dramatically and we were all going to be underwater," reflects Mary, plus "*Stewed To The Gills* is a great analogy for being drunk".

Testicle Of God (And It Was Good) is a somewhat tongue-in-cheek number. With its bombastic celestial opening lifted from the Sisters Of Mercy's This Corrosion, the inspiration behind the song soon becomes clear. "I think we had this riff, and it was a bit gothy, I guess it's a bit of a piss-take to be honest!" admits Mary. It was an affectionate one, however. The first time Mary saw the Sisters live he thought frontman Andrew Eldritch was "the coolest thing I'd ever seen." Eldritch was also an easy source of amusement because of his deathly serious "Prince of Darkness" persona. But there was another influence at play here too. Before becoming the outspoken television presenter he is today, Piers Morgan

Patricia Morrison (left) and Andrew Eldritch...
"the coolest thing I'd ever seen".

was in 1988 a rookie reporter for the *Sun*. One of the stories Morgan had a hand in writing appeared under the headline, 'Three Rock Fans Die in "Devil" Pact'. The story was a variation on a familiar theme around that time, of the negative influence of heavy metal songs and so-called "satanic" lyrics on vulnerable young rock fans. The story by Morgan and Martin Smith detailed how "three teenage fans of a bizarre British rock cult" were said to have killed themselves in a suicide pact and that police were concerned that "at least 10 other youngsters" might try to copy the victims.

The story claimed that "teenagers, who dress in black, follow the sinister Gothic pop movement which glorifies death and devil worship," and cited how they "worship bands such the Sisters Of Mercy, Jesus and Mary Chain, Cult and Gay Bikers [sic] On Acid."

Sisters Of Mercy took the brunt of the blame for the suicides, which reportedly took place in New Zealand. A spokesperson for the band is alleged to have said: "We're very shocked, but we can hardly be held responsible for these deaths." The seriousness of the suicides aside, the shock-horror sensationalism of the report is risible enough, but also begs the question whether the authors were deliberately being economic with the facts and demonising bands with provocative names for the sake of good copy. Probably. Tony and Mary concur that the news story inspired one line in Testicle Of God: "Go kill yourself but tell your parents first, then lock the Bykers up."

Jon Langford also had a hand in what has arguably become one of the Bykers' most anthemic songs, Shoulders, beloved by the band and fans alike; the Bykers' self-proclaimed fan club, The Daye Trippers, adopted it as their signature tune. Whenever the Bykers played it live it was the cue for the Daye Trippers to clamber on each other's shoulders for the duration. Mary says, "It's probably one of the best songs we wrote, and again it has this Langford influence... do you remember The Mekons' song Where Were You?... There's a line about yellow

Story in The Sun newspaper mentioning Gaye Bykers On Acid. Source: Tony Byker's scrapbook.

hair." Yellow hair is a refrain throughout Shoulders. He recalls, with more than a little affection, "Yeah, it's about the Daye Trippers, and also, in some respects looking back, when I used to follow bands like The Cult around and stuff. It's not a particularly hard rocking song, but it's a part of that time. So, it's like 'Where were you that night I'll never forget'... It's a love song!"

The pun-titled Fairway To Heaven makes an analogy between life and a round of golf. Few can forget the immortal line, 'I feel just like Marc Bolan 'cos I've just driven into a tree,' accompanied by the riff from Children Of The Revolution. The Bykers, and Mary in particular, cultivated an interest in golf early in their career. Golf Trek is possibly the earliest manifestation of this interest. But other than its title the song has no overt connection to golf. Mary says that this fascination with golf came about because "it was the antithesis of where we were coming from at the time, it being an aspirational rich man's sport and all. However, in our eyes it did have one good thing going for it which was the clothing. It was obviously often very flamboyant, so golf gear was an attractive look for us — especially the trousers." The Bykers weren't the only rockers with an unlikely predilection for the sedentary sport. Mary continues, "We'd heard that Alice Cooper and my personal hero Iggy Pop were golfers, and it seemed so un-rock'n'roll. Fairway

"Golf gear was an attractive look for us — especially the trousers!" — Tony Byker backstage at the Town & Country Club, London.

To Heaven was us responding in some way to Iggy playing golf... and playing on the fact that the Butthole Surfers' album *Hairway to Steven* had recently been released." A quixotic Mary adds, "I have to admit I did have a fascination at that time for watching the golf on the telly. It was probably something to do with what I was smoking!"

The title Floydrix speaks for itself. Mary explains how the song was a case of the band trying to "do a song that sounds like Pink Floyd and a bit like Jimi Hendrix. Thinking about it, that's how the process used to be you know, 'oh let's do this mixed with that.' I guess we were so lazy by that point we couldn't even come up with a title, and we just literally put the influence there on the sleeve."

The overarching theme of the album was the future of the planet, but tellingly it echoed concerns relating more closely to the Bykers' own immediate future. In an interview with Edwin Pouncey of the *NME*, it was becoming apparent, if not overtly obvious, that all was not well between the band and their record label, Virgin. Replying to a question about whether the Bykers saw themselves as "budding surrealists" (following a not entirely serious discussion about the artwork on the sleeve of their new single), Kev retorted, "Naaaw! We're just a tax loss with a lobster on it." Pouncey learnt that the album had cost £33,000 to record in its entirety. *Stewed To The Gills* was therefore the cheapest album to have been recorded for Virgin in four years.

On its release, *Sounds* gave the album a glowing four stars out of five. Keith Cameron exclaimed the Bykers had "come up trumps. *Stewed To The Gills* is very good indeed." He noted how the band had moved on from the ignominious fate of its predecessor *Drill Your Own Hole*, by becoming not only adept musicians but decent songwriters too. He concluded his review: "*Stewed* is a knowing snog around rock's nether regions. Witty and impassioned, it might actually earn Gaye Bykers On Acid a little respect. Nothing less is deserved."

Tim Nicholson in *Record Mirror* commented: "Be prepared to irreparably damage your relationship with your neighbours, because however low you turn down the volume, *Stewed To The Gills* is still the loudest record you're likely to play." He too awarded it four stars out of five. *Metal Hammer*'s Liz Evans was unapologetically effusive. Awarding the album full marks, she wrote: "The Bykers are wizards of psychedelia spiked grungewarp metal... they're from a topsy turvy dream, only you're not sure if it's a nightmare." A little of her affection was directed at Mary, describing him as "deceptively pretty. He sings like an angel spawned in hell, and he instructs through his vocals." Of the single Hot Thing, Evans asked, "How can you resist such a proposition — *just cut the crap and take me to bed*—? A rare honesty indeed!"

The usually disparaging *NME* awarded *Stewed* seven out of 10. The author in this instance was Steven Wells, who seems to have had a bit of a soft spot for the band despite the jibes. Without a hint of sarcasm, Wells said that "Gaye Bykers On Acid is one of the all-time great band names" and that Rad Dude was "easily the best thing on the album". He was less sure about what he described as a tendency towards "B.A.D. type white boy rap doggerel" as evidenced on tracks like M.A.D. The band was at their "solid rocking best" on Ill and Harmonious Murder, with Wells admitting that while the new direction still wasn't the stuff his dreams were made of, at least it sounded as if the band been "listening to something other than Edgar Broughton on 78". His parting shot was glib: "In America they take this band very seriously. In the real world they are inches from a similar fate."

Paul Davies in Q awarded *Stewed* three out of five stars and likened it to being "faster than a speeding ball of sputum... GBOA continue to ram red hot pokers of post-punk energy up the rear end of metal guitar music. The resultant thrash is an unkempt roughneck beast which sometimes threatens to blur the boundaries between music and noise, but it is held back from the brink of hardcore headache by an abundance of genuine tunes".

Melody Maker was more reserved. Ian Gittins admitted that "*Stewed To The Gills* is not a total pile of doggy-doo. This comes as a shock. You *expect* a mess, somehow, from the Bykers, with their all-pervasive air of hopelessness. But this one rattles the nuts and bolts with no little verve. The band that never *were* up to their scams may now have some purpose to them... They seem, wisely, to have abandoned the jokes for this fuzzthrash assault." He remarked that *Stewed* was an improvement over the previous album, and that the band had "abandoned the limp humour of *Drill Your Own Hole* to launch a *weightier* (in all ways), sonic attack, cutting through the gristle to somewhere near the bone." Tempering his

Still from Night Network's Video View ITV show. From left to right, Roland Gift, presenter Paul Thompson and Mary Byker.

somewhat grudging praise, Gittins added, "We don't want to go over the top here. Some bits of *Stewed To The Gills* are still *dead*. Rad Dude is bad Zodiac [Mindwarp] and that *is* bad." He concluded on an optimistic note: "But just as we'd given them up, quite rightly, written off the whole sorry caper, Gaye Bykers skip back to show us they're *not*, in fact, totally useless."

At least two of the favourable reviews suggested that the band's return to form was down to Jon Langford. The Bykers themselves still hold Langford in high esteem. Mary says, "Working with him was so much fun, because the guy's really funny… he's got the most amazing sense of humour… and he was really helpful as far as production was concerned when it came to writing and changing things and making a little more sense. So, in that respect he was a big influence, you know? It worked so well with him from day one. He did well with Groovy, and it was a trust with him straightaway, we really had an enmity with him and respect. Langford was definitely part of the process."

Martin Elbourne stepped in to help the Bykers with a tour plan to promote the new album. Elbourne understood that the Bykers were not a stadium league act but would frequently sell out 400–500 capacity venues. On this basis, he approached Virgin, but was immediately struck by the danger signs. Says Elbourne, "It rapidly became obvious that the label was planning to drop them."

MARY AND SARAH'S WEDDING

Appearing on ITV's *Night Network's Video View* show, Mary and Roland Gift from the Fine Young Cannibals reviewed the latest single releases, including New Model Army, Gary Moore, Spagna, Andy Pawlak, King Swamp and Milli Vanilli. During some light hearted badinage between the host and his guests at the end of the programme the presenter announced that Mary was soon getting married to Sarah Corina.

The wedding of Mary and Sarah's wedding took place on 11th February at Leicester registrar's office on Pocklington's Walk. As well as close family, also in attendance were members of the Bykers and Crazyhead, as well as Sarah's bandmates from The Bomb Party. A reporter for *Leicester Mercury* was also there, Graham Danter, who noted in his article that "A groom called Mary and a witness named Jesus [Andy 'Jesus' Mosquera] were just two of the oddities at Leicester's rock society wedding of the year." Mary had swapped his "grebo garb" for the occasion, wrote Danter. Indeed, the bride and groom had dressed up: Mary wore a £900 Georgio Armani suit borrowed from a friend, with a slightly oversized Homburg hat, while Sarah was resplendent in a vintage white

Photo courtesy of Sally Jones.

"Leicester rock royalty wedding". Signing the register. Mary Byker and Sarah Corina's wedding, February 1989.

Mary Byker and Sarah Corina's wedding. "Anderson [the best man] was late and the last to arrive at the registry office". Anderson (wearing shades in doorway), Penny, Tony Byker and Thommo.

lace wedding dress offset by a white floral garland headband, with pearl earrings and necklace. Most of the bandmates and other friends had made concessions to smartness, but were clearly keen to retain their non-conformist identities, as evidenced by their alternative appearances.

It would have been too good to be true for the day to have passed without at least one hitch. Best man, Anderson, holds his hands up. "The plan was for me to stay in the night before and practice my speech. I ended up going out pubbing and clubbing getting rat-arsed 'til 2am, then getting off with a girl and going back to hers. I woke with a hangover, late for the wedding, and in a student house miles from town." Anderson was late and the last to arrive at the registry office, after the wedding service had begun. Mary was forced to make his brother an emergency stand-in. While the bride and groom didn't really mind, not everyone was so accepting. Jon Langford recalls another gaffe with some hilarity: "Anderson fluffed the toast, saying 'Raise your glasses to Mary and Sarah', and when everybody started shouting Mary's real name, Anderson confused the family further with 'Raise your glasses to Mary and Ian'." Anderson admits, "I ballsed-up the speech, had nothing to say, and was given a right slagging off — and fair enough — by Sarah's mother! I drank heavily all day to compensate."

After the reception, the wedding party moved on to the Magazine whereupon the finer points of the day recede into the mists of time. "I have very vague

Mary and Sarah's wedding caricatured in Sounds, 1989. Cartoon by A. Pen, Kev F. & Alan Seaman.

recollections of my wedding," says the groom. "I remember the crazy mix of my straight family and all the crazy crew being there. We were all pretty out of it to be honest, it was a pretty mad party. Sarah and I spent our wedding night in the bridal suite at the Holiday Inn."

Among the cynics were Robber. "I think they did it just to get in the press to be honest," he says. "I thought it was a bit of a farce at the time, which I think most people did." Either way, the newly-weds would forego a honeymoon due to band commitments, notably preparations for the Bykers' forthcoming *Stewed To The Gills* tour. The marriage ended in the early 1990s, although Mary and Sarah remain friends.

STEWED TOUR

After the initial media buzz surrounding the band, getting through the Lafront debacle, and the disappointment over the *Drill Your Own Hole* album and movie, Virgin had begun to lose patience with the Bykers. They were unhappy with the results of the session with Vic Maile, the punk fuelled demos for *Stewed*, and also unhappy with the album itself. It was telling that promotion for the new album and imminent *Stewed To The Gills* tour was nowhere near as conspicuous as it had been for *Drill*. Mary says, "I think once they realised we weren't a band that was going to bend over backwards to their will, that was the end. I mean, you've got four blokes who are into the anarchy thing, into 'smash the system', and the only reason we'd signed with them in the first place was 'cos they'd put out a few decent records in the seventies!" Virgin had, in all likelihood, made up its mind to drop the band by this point.

The *Stewed To The Gills* tour kicked off at the Riverside in Newcastle on 22nd February 1989, a favourite venue for both the Bykers and Crazyhead. In reviewing the gig for Newcastle University student newspaper *Courier*, Jem Axford was unrestrained in his praise: "Visually brilliant and musically excellent — this was a damn fine evening. The Bykers are more of a threat to our retinas than they are to our moral integrity but that's a risk well worth taking. Get up — get on down!!"

The following night's gig at Edinburgh University was reviewed for *Sounds* by Andrew Tully. His review started favourably enough, lamenting how the band had too long been "scorned as a joke without a punchline" and that "tonight the Bykers proved — for half an hour at least — that they are the last, great rock'n'roll band." For 30 minutes it seemed to Tully that nothing else existed, "as if *this* was the apotheosis of rock'n'roll." Then, "the engine dropped out of the set. The energy and life dribbled away to an inconclusive end. And there was a sadness in Mary's eyes, as if he knew the monster he'd unleashed was about to turn on him."

A little over a week after the tour began, it was reported in the music press that Kev had fallen off the stage at Warwick University and broken his arm. One report claimed he would be temporarily replaced by a drum machine, operated by "throwing a pint of beer into it". Like the fishy tale about the piscine intestinal infection, this was another publicity stunt according to Tony Byker. The band was playing some of the tightest live shows of their career. It even seemed as if the media backlash that had proved so costly to their reputation a year earlier was finally subsiding.

Stewed suffered a setback of sorts by the time it reached Brighton, for Thee

Photo courtesy of David Arnoff

Thee Hypnotics.

Hypnotics at least, the main support on the tour. Thee Hypnotics were a hot Stooges-style outfit from High Wycombe, whose frontman, James 'Jim' Jones, would later lead the Jim Jones Revue. According to the *NME*, their van was broken into, their equipment was stolen and the band had to spend the day "scouring secondhand shops… for replacement stuff." They were fortunate enough to find one of their own guitars for sale but weren't able to retrieve the rest of their gear — or the bag of dirty laundry that was also taken!

Heading up north for gigs in Liverpool and Manchester, the tour then crossed into Wales for two back-to-back shows in Cardiff on Saturday 4th and Sunday 5th March. This wasn't as straight forward as it might sound. While in Cardiff, the Bykers headed to London for a memorial gig for Robert Calvert at Brixton Academy, before returning to Cardiff for their show later that evening. The former Hawkwind lyricist, singer and poet had died unexpectedly from a heart attack the previous August, and a cast of old and new underground bands played in tribute to Calvert and as a benefit for his widow. Hawkwind were headliners, Doctor and the Medics were second on the bill, with Gaye Bykers On Acid originally billed third. Elsewhere were The Pink Fairies Psychedelic Rock Revue, Man, Here & Now, Nik Turner's Fantastic All-Stars, Amon Düül II, Starfighters, and Atom Gods. The Bykers, billed as Lesbian Dopeheads On Mopeds, went on first and played to a largely empty Brixton Academy before

shooting off for the second of their two gigs in Cardiff.

Meanwhile, not a million miles away, Crazyhead were touring to promote the relaunched *Desert Orchid* album and the release of a new EP featuring Have Love, Will Travel.

HAVE LOVE, WILL TRAVEL (TO IRELAND)

At the beginning of 1989 Crazyhead received crushing news that a stadium gig they'd been booked onto with Bon Jovi and Guns N' Roses in Japan had been pulled. The date of the gig happened to coincide with a period of national mourning for Emperor Hirohito. Vom considers that failing to make it to L.A. for gigs at the Whiskey A Go Go is one of his greatest regrets, and he views the festival cancellation a close disappointment to that. Bon Jovi were, arguably, at the height of their ascendancy and Guns N' Roses were about to blast off "into their own stratosphere" — the significance of which is not lost on Vom. He muses, "Maybe nothing would've come of it… I don't want to look back with too much bitterness, it's pointless really, but it's interesting to imagine what would've happened if we'd done those two shows [at the Whiskey A Go Go] and I wonder what've would've happened if we'd made it to Tokyo."

In February 1989, Crazyhead followed up their single Rags with an EP to coincide with the relaunch of *Desert Orchid*. The lead track was Have Love, Will Travel, a cover of a garage classic often mistakenly credited to The Sonics, but written and originally recorded by Richard Berry, he of Louie Louie fame. However, The Sonics version almost certainly influenced Crazyhead's own revamp. In *Melody Maker* that February, Ian Gittins related how Have Love, Will Travel developed one Christmas, "with assorted Gaye Bykers, pissed after the pub in Leicester." Reverb remembers it differently. "Have Love was suggested as a cover by Cally, who used to send us cassettes of great music," says Reverb. "On a Sonics tape he had put an asterisk next to Have Love with a note saying we ought to do it. The recording was done in an evening at the studio when we were meant to be recording B-sides for singles. It was one of the quickest recordings we did at the Music Station."

1960s retro cover for Crazyhead EP, 'Have Love, Will Travel'. Photo by Phil Smee with Donato Cinicolo III.

The EP was released on 7- and 12-inch vinyl, and as a CD single. All formats featured Have Love, Will Travel, and blistering live versions of Baby Turpentine and Snake Eyes. A fourth track on the 12-inch and CD was (Here Comes) Johnny, replaced on the 7-inch by Out On A Limb. Writing for *Sounds*, Ralph Traitor called Have Love, Will Travel a "tasteful choice of cover… the ability to interpret it with a surprising freshness enables one to overlook their own meagre material… Keep those covers coming boys!" It was a weighted complement, favouring as it did cover material over Crazyhead's own compositions. But it could have been worse. The EP sleeve featured sixties inspired artwork, which Traitor rather liked. The ever-acerbic Stud Brothers in *Melody Maker*, however, saw the retro design as emblematic:

In March 1989, Desert Orchid was relaunched with "a completely new cover designed by Phil Smee from Waldo's Emporium".

This pale, spirit-sinking thing might perhaps be treated as symptomatic of a culture so obsessed with

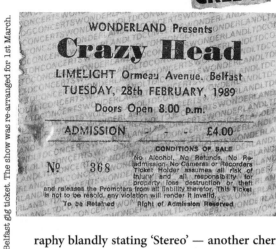

WONDERLAND Presents

Crazy Head

LIMELIGHT Ormeau Avenue, Belfast

TUESDAY, 28th FEBRUARY, 1989

Doors Open 8.00 p.m.

ADMISSION — £4.00

CONDITIONS OF SALE

Nº 368

No Alcohol, No Refunds, No Re-admission. No Cameras or Recorders Ticket Holder assumes all risk of injury and all responsibility for property loss destruction or theft and releases the Promoters from all liability therefor. This Ticket is not to be resold, any violation will render it invalid.

To be Retained   Right of Admission Reserved

the past it barely cares to think of how its future's being tampered with. Crazyhead appear on the sleeve as pieces of static memorabilia, not even parodying, but replicating the Stones circa '64. The sleeve even comes complete with the superannuated Parlophone logo and a jaded capital-less typography blandly stating 'Stereo' — another cherished artefact in the absurd sixties iconography. The songs obviously can only borrow from the past and this they do with all the panache of a Zodiac aping Wayne County aping The Stooges. Parody upon parody, and not a hint of irony in sight. Tch.

NME's Len Brown pretended he was reviewing two different bands when he reviewed Have Love, Will Travel back-to-back with a 12-inch Radio 1 session recorded two years earlier. Describing the Crazyhead of 1987 as "a post-grebe grunge outfit whose baby gurgles turpentine", he went on to liken the Crazyhead of 1989 as "a surprising[ly] likeable, rather crisp rock combo, with a nose for hooklines and a wallet hungry penchant for those buttock-clenching charts." Although his comments might have been construed as a compliment, Brown seemed to imply that Crazyhead had cleaned their act up for the sake of commercial gain.

Coinciding with the EP, *Desert Orchid* was re-released — although repackaged would be a better description. Putting a positive spin on things, Anderson told the *NME*'s Stuart Maconie that the decision behind the release was to better promote the album on the back of the recent European support with Iggy Pop. The truth of the matter is that the band didn't much like Dave Balfe's original sleeve design. Visually the re-released album was given a complete makeover. The original Balfe endorsed design was scrapped in favour of a new cover by Phil Smee from Waldo's Emporium. Reverb elaborates, "The first sleeve was a David Balfe concoction — some sort of early day pixelated distortion of an orchid? He didn't think the rooftop photos we had done for the first release were strong enough. Phil Smee did the second cover at the same time as the Have Love EP

cover — much better!"

The 21-date promotional tour for the new EP and repackaged album kicked off at the Pink Toothbrush in Rayleigh, progressing to Wales, before heading back to England. Adrian Goldberg caught the band at Junction 10 in Walsall, a venue he described as a "rock'n'roll sanctuary" amid a landscape of warehouses and council houses. "To the denizens of Nowheresville, Crazyhead are king," wrote Goldberg. "The epitome of heads down, good time, no nonsense Saturday nights out, their hyper-charged rock-a-boogie is chock-full of stomping, punch-air choruses and fiercely jousting guitars." Goldberg reserved his highest praise for "a sledgehammer version" of Have Love, Will Travel, but was impressed by the band's own material, referring to "a bumper bag of originals". Perhaps in reference to *Desert Orchid*'s polished production, he considered the gig a "multi-vitamined onslaught" and a revelation.

A few days later, Crazyhead crossed the Irish Sea to play a couple of gigs in Ireland — one in the Irish Republic, and the other in the then still war-torn province of Northern Ireland. They had been scheduled to play at the Limelight in Belfast on 28th February and the Dublin Baggot Inn on 1st March (as reflected in various live ads and promotional t-shirts). But down the line the dates were swapped round, as it was deemed better to travel to Edinburgh from Belfast rather than having to dash back from Dublin to catch the ferry. Reverb has good memories of the Irish gigs, Dublin in particular: "We travelled the night before from Fishguard to Dublin. The next day we did an interview at our hotel but the chap doing the interview baulked at the quality and price of the beer at the hotel bar and suggested we went to his favourite place, the International Bar — we stayed there the rest of the day. Fantastic place. Met loads of poets, fellow racing punters, fellow drunkards etc... half the bar was at the gig that night!"

Reverb recalls that the Belfast gig was well attended, but that this was because few outside bands played there, rather than Crazyhead being particularly popular in the Province. However, Porkbeast is of the opinion that Belfast was a "stormer... rammed and rocking" due, in no small part, to Crazyhead's recent appearance on *The Chart Show* on television. He also remembers the Limelight's security staff were quite violent and that Reverb admonished them, much to the approval of the audience. Naturally the bully-boy bouncers didn't take kindly to being humiliated by a rock musician — an English one at that — and according to Porkbeast, Reverb got quite seriously "menaced" by them, with thinly veiled threats like: "This is fucking Belfast mate, people die here!" The Northern Ireland conflict, or "The Troubles" as it was more commonly known, was at its height, and the presence of British army troops on the streets was resented, particularly by the Catholic population who regarded them as an English occupying force.

It wasn't the first time Reverb had put his mouth into gear before thinking of the consequences. It might not be a coincidence that after the set, taking a respite before the encore, the band were met on the street by an armoured patrol car with guns trained on them, driving past. Unnerved, Crazyhead returned to the stage and managed to survive any recriminations the bouncers might have had in mind for them. Some of the entourage had already had a close encounter with an armed patrol when crossing the border earlier that day, and Vom was more than ready for a drink to help wind down. He'd downed a bottle of Bushmills Irish whiskey by the time they arrived back at the hotel and continued to drink through the night at the hotel bar. Understandably he was feeling the worse for wear the following day.

"We got to the ferry and I'm feeling like shit, like really shit, and they cancelled the ferry crossing because the weather was so bad," recalls Vom. It was an hour's wait for the next ferry, but a three-and-a-half-hour crossing to Scotland. Things went from bad to worse for the drummer, who soon lived up to his nickname. The ferry was rolling and pitching in the rough sea. "I'm just immediately in the toilet, and I spent three-and-a-half hours just throwing up all this whiskey, all this Guinness," says Vom. "It was the worst journey I've ever had in my life, and by the time we got there I was like just gone, I was just dead. That was my experience of it. I don't know what everybody else did, they probably ate breakfast and just relaxed."

Vom didn't have the luxury of a day off from the tour. No sooner had the ferry arrived in Scotland, the band was met by a driver to take them to their gig in Edinburgh that evening. Bushmills and Guinness were not on the menu that night; all that passed Vom's lips was bland soup from a Chinese takeaway.

The promotional tours for both the Bykers and Crazyhead finished within a day of each other, the 17th and 18th March. But unlike Crazyhead, the Bykers were soon back on the road. The *Stewed* tour concluded with gigs at the Electric Ballroom in London and Holloway College in Egham, after which it was announced that the band had lined up another set of shows through April, which they would headline and also — as Lesbian Dopeheads On Mopeds — support too. According to Mary it was Elbourne who encouraged them to capitalise on the Lesbian Dopeheads On Mopeds pseudonym. He had realised the potential mileage in a ruse whereby the band played twice on the same bill, ostensibly as two different bands and get paid twice. Lesbian Dopeheads On Mopeds were from New Zealand, promotors were told. The Bykers would perform in full drag and reappear later as themselves for another set. Whether or not many promoters were fooled is anybody's guess, but it provided light relief at a time when matters were becoming tumultuous with Virgin. It also gave the Bykers the opportunity to get in touch with their feminine sides, and camp it up outrageously.

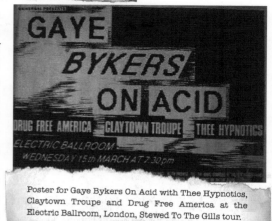

Poster for Gaye Bykers On Acid with Thee Hypnotics, Claytown Troupe and Drug Free America at the Electric Ballroom, London, Stewed To The Gills tour.

Crazyhead, on the other hand, had been invited to play at a music festival in the Soviet Union on behalf of the British Council.

13TH FLOOR INEBRIATORS — MOSCOW 1989

The British Council is an organisation that promotes cultural relations and educational opportunities worldwide. In the late 1980s, they were behind a drive that saw several UK bands playing an important series of gigs that coincided with and arguably exacerbated political and cultural shifts in the host countries. These included Moscow before the collapse of the Soviet Union, Romania after the fall of Nicolae Ceauşescu, and Namibia's independence celebrations. Among the bands on this historic tour was Crazyhead.

Reverb believes the band's involvement came about through Fizle Sagar, who worked at the band's agency, Station. According to Reverb, Fizle was also an interpreter for the British Council and made suggestions for suitable bands to represent the UK at overseas events. "She liked us," says Reverb, "and put our name forward." Anderson is more pragmatic about how Crazyhead came to be involved with the British Council. "They really wanted someone more famous on EMI, like Tanita Tikaram, but all the famous acts were busy, so Fizle kept selling them this new band — Crazyhead!" Anderson had been reticent about whether the band should play Moscow, given the Soviet Union's poor human rights reputation and voiced his concern to Reverb, citing Mark E. Smith of The

Photo courtesy of Kev Reverb.

On the steps of Hotel Ukraina with members of Crazyhead (front four), Skin Games (back four) and Crazyhead's roadie, Spike (far right).

Fall as an example of someone else who had boycotted Russia. Reverb allegedly responded by saying it was up to Anderson, but the rest of the band were going, whether he liked it or not. Anderson's bleeding-heart liberal conscience dissipated upon realising, as he puts it, "an all-expenses paid trip to gig and see behind the — soon to be crumbling — iron curtain was not to be missed!"

It was spring and Anderson had expected Moscow to be gloomy and snowbound. Nothing could be further from this misconception though, and the band spent five gloriously sunny days in Moscow. They were still there for the traditional May Day parade, when the Soviet Union displayed its military hardware in a show of force, pomp and ceremony in Red Square. Descriptions of the band's accommodation vary slightly. Porkbeast says they were "billeted in a huge Stalinist building", which Anderson believes was actually a top Moscow hotel. Reverb confirms it was the Hotel Ukraina. They even had a coach at their disposal to ostensibly take them wherever they wanted, but realistically only to the places they were allowed to go. In return Crazyhead were expected to play one 20-minute set at a festival that included bands from all over the Soviet Union, as well as a number of other western bands, including The Scramblers (from Canada) and It Bites (also from the UK). Not a bad deal for an all-expenses paid five-day trip.

Although *Perestroika* and *Glasnost* had yet to fully come to fruition, early

Crazyhead enjoying some R 'n' R — rest and recreation...
"By day they'd explore the city and enjoy the sights."

east-meets-west music festivals such as this one indicate just how much relations between Russia and the west had thawed. However, the Soviet Union was still something of an unknown entity, not least as far as rock music was concerned. Talking to Bataille Fidol in *Sniffin' Rock* magazine later that year, Reverb described how the Soviet audiences really din't know how to react, and nearly all the other bands they saw were "mainline and derivative, hitting all the poses from cabaret rock to heavy metal". Many of the bands simply mimed to backing tapes. Unsurprisingly, the equipment was the worst the band had ever used, and Vom's safety was somewhat compromised when he had to play his drums barely three inches from the edge of a 20-foot drop. No matter though, the band played "a stormer", according to Anderson, after which they were left with several days R&R to enjoy the rest of their stay. By day they'd explore the city and enjoy the sights, such as the huge park where spaceships from the Russian space programme were on public display. Anderson recalls that everywhere they went they were followed by two men in suits and raincoats, which they figured were KGB. Porkbeast describes "uniformed Russians with those old video cameras the size of a small suitcase, videoing everything we did".

To highlight the contrary nature of Moscow, Anderson recalls the band one night getting drunk with the Chief of Police for that area of Moscow, who was a big Elvis fan. Yet, on another night, a Russian rockabilly band they had befriended

Photo courtesy of Crazyhead.

Crazyhead's Fast Dick and Anderson with the Moscow music festival promoter (centre). Moscow, 1989.

called Mister Twister fell foul of the laws about alcohol. Crazyhead had gone to see Mister Twister in an old 1960s style Soviet cinema and were backstage with the band when police burst into the dressing room and a heated discussion in Russian took place. The cops stormed off, sour faced. Mister Twister told Crazyhead that they had been accused of drinking alcohol, which was against the law unless the premises had a restaurant. It was a lucky escape: contravention of the law could result in arrest and a night in the drunk tank.

Invariably, all of Crazyhead's evenings involved copious quantities of alcohol. According to Anderson, "Every night was a drunken vodka party in the hotel, with musicians from east and west hanging out and partying." The Ukrainian "champagne" was dirt-cheap and plentiful, as was the vodka, and both flowed freely. Some of these booze-fuelled shenanigans have become the stuff of legend. One notorious incident involved the ledge on the 13th floor of the hotel. For no particular reason, other than the consumption of alcohol, Spike and Fast Dick clambered out of the window onto a two-foot-wide ledge and edged their way around the hotel before entering through the window of a stranger's room. In doing so they "scared the living daylights out of a poor old Russian lady," recalls Anderson. The incident was immortalised by Reverb in song, 13th Floor, for a later line-up of Crazyhead in the late-1990s.

According to Anderson, the other UK band on the trip, It Bites, were somewhat

Photo courtesy of Crazyhead.

"Russian music fans, Crazyhead members, and member of great Russian rockabilly band Mister Twister on his scooter". Moscow, 1989.

aloof, constantly moaning about how Moscow wasn't as good as Las Vegas. The two bands didn't bond on the visit, despite one drunken chat on the flight home. But this was after the managers of both Crazyhead and It Bites ended up in a fist fight. It is perhaps ironic that the two English bands sent by the British Council to foster harmonious relationships between east and west found it difficult to get along, never mind helping to build bridges between the Soviet Union and the so-called Free World! ☠

VIRGIN ON THE RIDICULOUS

T THE END OF APRIL, THE BYKERS FOLLOWED THEIR SHORT run of dates as Lesbian Dopeheads On Mopeds by headlining an all-day indie benefit festival. This was in aid of the National Anti-Vivisection Society and was held in Birmingham. Adrian Goldberg for *Sounds* clearly had an axe to grind. Although the bill included Mega City 4, Snuff, The Senseless Things, Anhrefn and World Domination Enterprises among others, a diatribe levelled at the Bykers took up half of his review. Goldberg stated in his opening paragraph that the Bykers were a "clod-hopping rock'n'roll grotesque" that had "long outstayed its welcome." It didn't get better. Referring to "shoestring talents", he thought it was funny that the band had managed to dupe Virgin into "giving them mega-tracked studio access, when even their mastery of six-stringed technology is so patently limited." The Bykers, Goldberg hoped, were

Music press ad for 'All-Day Anti-Vivisection "Indie" Festival'. 30th April 1989. Source: Tony Byker's scrapbook.

"a moth-eaten panto horse ready to be wheeled off for the last time." Of the three other bands mentioned in the review, only World Domination Enterprises came out with their dignity intact.

If live reviews like this were somewhat symptomatic, it was not typical for *Sounds* to be so scathing. Now even the Bykers' own label was turning against them. Having invested a significant amount of time and expenditure on promoting the band for little reward, Virgin seemed unwilling to do likewise with *Stewed To The Gills*. After a lacklustre promotion campaign for both the album and accompanying tour, it was not entirely surprising that *Stewed To The Gills* didn't yield the returns it deserved, this in spite of its comparatively low production cost and some favourable reviews. Had Virgin put the same energy into the new album as they did *Drill Your Own Hole*, then, says Mary, "maybe we'd have broken through and maybe reached more people again. But they just released the record, and we were just another album."

Sacking their manager the previous year had not helped the Bykers, nor had the problem of trying to find a replacement for Stacey Lafront. "Major labels," says Robber, "like to have a formula whereby they deal with the manager and won't deal with the artist, and because we couldn't get a new manager… that was the reason we got dropped." At this point, Virgin were biding their time and fulfilling contractual obligations, which meant they were only required to release two of the 10 albums the Bykers had initially signed up for. That spring, Virgin finally let the band go.

Mary recalls the moment. "Virgin showed us the door — literally. We were in the office with Simon Draper,

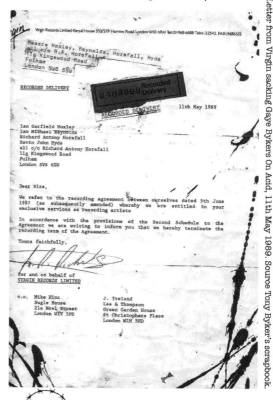

Letter from Virgin sacking Gaye Bykers On Acid, 11th May 1989. Source Tony Byker's scrapbook.

Photo courtesy of Phil Nicholls.

Crazyhead, Melody Maker photo shoot. Leicester, 4th February 1989.

who was the head of Virgin at the time, and I think we were asking for money, or for them to do something else for us, and they weren't happy with sales. Something else then happened. I don't know what. All I remember was that Simon Draper got up from behind his desk, went to the door and opened it, and said, 'Right, that's it, that's enough, you're out of this building!' He literally showed us the door!"

Even if Draper's actions in the Virgin office had taken the Bykers by surprise, the band wasn't entirely shocked. Tony says, "We knew that *Stewed* would be the last album. Virgin only did it because they had to in the contract. The third album they could drop us."

Formal notice of the sacking came in the form of a recorded delivery letter from Virgin Records, dated 11th May 1989, addressed to 'Messrs Hoxley, Reynolds, Horsfall and Hyde all c/o R.A. Horsfall [AKA Tony]' at Tony's Fulham, London address. Mary considered being dropped by Virgin something of a relief. In typically upbeat fashion, he told one music paper, "It's not a problem at all. We were just banging our heads against a brick wall there. It's the best thing that could have happened to us, and we've had offers from three record companies already."

Despite the brave face, there was a general feeling of trepidation. Robber says, "I felt right pissed off, really. I thought we were just going through the motions for the next couple of years. It's like when you've signed to a label like Virgin you've got a career going, you've got a job going…" Pausing for reflection, he adds, "but in retrospect a lot of bands only last a couple of years on a label anyway, so thinking about it, it is probably about right ain't it?"

Without Virgin, the Bykers now had greater creative freedom, if not

necessarily the financial clout. Virgin wrote off all the dues the band owed them. As Mary points out, "They didn't come after it, 'cos that's their bet at the end of the day." Unfortunately the same could not be said for Crazyhead a little over a year later.

SHUTTING THE STABLE DOOR AFTER THE HORSE HAS BOLTED

Things didn't start well. Having completed the promotional tour for the relaunch of *Desert Orchid*, Crazyhead were now focused on producing new demos for a follow-up album. Rick Willson was their first choice of producer, but he proved to be unavailable because of commitments with his own band, Diesel Park West. They approached EMI and were landed with an A&R man, to see if he could help. Vom describes "a public schoolboy [who had] been given a nice little cushy job at EMI… he became our A&R man. He was just so wet behind the ears it was incredible! We didn't want to record in London, 'cos we were just sick of it, and we said can't you find us a studio somewhere else, maybe somewhere out in the country — on the East Coast, Norfolk way?"

The A&R man booked the band into a studio in Lincolnshire, called GEMS, for three days. Crazyhead weren't prepared for the greeting they received on their arrival. A farmer and his family welcomed them with plates of haslet sandwiches and steaming hot cups of tea. Apparently, the farmer had decided to diversify and had built a recording studio, probably at the behest of his son. According to Vom, the son was called Graham and the dad Eddie, ergo GEMS — an anacronym of Graham and Eddie's Music Studio.

The equipment itself was good, but it seems Graham and Eddie had little clue about how to use it. Another spanner in the works was the ban on smoking. It also became evident that Crazyhead weren't going to be able to make themselves at home the way they would at Rick Willson's Barkby Road studio. There was a no smoking rule in place that extended to the studio and the control room. According to Reverb, this "was not the norm at the time. As a result, none of us spent much time listening to what was going on, and trusted that the engineer knew what he was doing. It was only towards the end of the first day that we all went in to hear the results."

Vom concurs. "It just sounded awful. They obviously had no idea how to record a band, or how to mike anything up." Ultimately nothing came out of

GEMS. Says Reverb, "We left and went back to the B&B we were staying at and decided there was no point in going back the next day. Spike went back on his own in the morning and got them to wipe the tapes. It was that bad!"

TIL THINGS ARE BRIGHTER

In May 1989, a cast of mostly indie musicians, many of whom had contributed to a Johnny Cash tribute album the previous year called *Til Things Are Brighter*, reconvened to perform a live concert at the Powerhaus in Islington, also in honour of the Man In Black. The album project was initially mooted in late 1987, when Marc Riley told *Sounds* how he came up with the idea: "I just thought that it would be really good to do an LP of Johnny Cash songs. And then I got together with Jon [Langford] and we decided that it would be even better if we could get lots of other artists involved and then donate the profits to [Jello Biafra's] No More Censorship Defence Fund."

It must be remembered that this was before Cash's final collaboration and rehabilitation with Rick Rubin, and the critically acclaimed series of albums that emerged in the 1990s. Things weren't so rosy for Cash a few years earlier: at the end of the eighties, Cash had been dropped by Columbia, his label of over 30 years, and Langford has said Cash's main audiences by then consisted of the "purple rinse brigade". But Riley and Langford's love of Cash was sincere, and at the time Riley stressed, "We're *not* doing it to take the piss out of Johnny Cash... He's one of the best."

Somewhere along the way, both the album and the live concert became fundraisers for the Terrence Higgins Trust, a charity in support of AIDS research.

Cover of Til Things Are Brighter, the Johnny Cash tribute album on which Mary Byker contributed 'A Boy Named Sue'.

Mary Byker performing a "show stealing" version of 'A Boy Named Sue' at an AIDS benefit and Johnny Cash tribute show at Islington Powerhaus, May 1989.

Photo courtesy Mary Scanlon. Originally printed in Sounds, 27th May 1989.

Langford recalls, "It was Marc Riley's idea to make an album of Johnny Cash songs, but probably my idea to give all the money away to the Terrence Higgins Trust — I think it was originally going to be just me and Marc singing, but we were uncomfortable about that and got a bunch of chums on board." Mary Byker, Stephen Mallinder from Cabaret Voltaire, Marc Almond, The Mekons' Sally Timms, Cathal Coughlan of Fatima Mansions, former Buzzcock Pete Shelley, and Michelle Shocked, contributed tracks. *Til Things Are Brighter* was released on In-Tape in 1988.

The project received an endorsement from Cash himself. Riley and Langford met him backstage at one of his gigs at the Manchester Apollo in May 1988. Given that AIDS was still largely associated with the gay community at this time, Langford and Riley were unsure of how Cash would react when they told him that an AIDS charity would benefit from the project. They need not have worried. "Cash really liked this idea," Langford recalls, "The surgeon who performed his and Waylon Jennings' heart operations was an AIDS victim. There was also a story in a Nashville paper which asked whether Johnny Cash knew the proceeds from the album were going to homosexuals! Cash was quick to say he was very pleased the money was going to Terrence Higgins."

Cash was also touched that a largely British collection of young indie musicians were inspired to pay homage. It certainly boosted his morale at a time when it seemed that hardly anyone wanted to touch him with a bargepole. It was also, arguably, the first step towards Cash's critical rehabilitation.

The benefit gig itself took place a few days after Cash had played at the Royal Albert Hall. Cash is reported to have been disappointed he had not known about the event sooner, as he would have postponed his scheduled return to the States to attend. Keith Cameron reviewed the gig in *Sounds* and was disappointed at Frank Sidebottom as compere for the evening. Although considered something of a cult figure in the British indie scene, with his distinctive oversize papier-mâché head, Sidebottom simply got on Cameron's nerves. However, he was impressed with the other acts and considered Mary Byker's performance of A Boy Named Sue to be the show stealer. The song was a perfect choice for a boy named Mary — who couldn't resist the temptation to replace the "son of a bitch who named me Sue" line with "motherfucker".

When asked what he considered the Bykers' most enduring legacy was, Jon Langford said in 2011, "My favourite moment was after Mary sang A Boy Named Sue… Cash went on BBC2 saying how great the album was and naming his favourite tracks, which included 'Mary Mary of the Gaye Bykers On Acid…' I think getting Cash to say those words on the BBC is perhaps their most enduring legacy — The Bykers wouldn't have wanted a legacy though — they wanted it all right then!"

CRAZYHEAD RADIO TOUR OF USA

Meanwhile, Crazyhead were still trying to demo material for a follow-up album. After the debacle of what has come to be known as The Haslett Sessions at the farm-cum-studio in Lincolnshire back in the spring, another producer was suggested. Zeus B. Held was best known for his electronica-oriented productions and remixes, and had been enjoying success in the charts as Transvision Vamp's producer. In June, Crazyhead decamped once again to Townhouse Studio in London, to record what was ostensibly meant to be their next single. It was a new song called Night Train and was a Reverb and Anderson composition. Anderson's lyrics were about a brand of cheap but potent citrus flavoured fortified wine of the same name, favoured by winos and anyone else seeking a cheap booze buzz.

Eric Clapton also happened to be at Townhouse, in another studio recording what would become the multi-platinum-selling *Journeyman* album. Clapton was

by now not only a reformed heroin addict but had not long knocked alcohol on the head too, found God, and was a staunch advocate of the Alcoholics Anonymous 12-Step programme. Vom recalls an amusing incident concerning 'Slowhand': "Eric was OK, but there was this shared lounge and kitchen and one day we were just having a little break from recording, and me and Kev walked into this lounge area. The cricket's on the telly, and Eric's sitting in his armchair, and he's fallen asleep, right? He's kind of dozed off like an old man, and he's got his mouth open, and me and Kev just look at each other, and Kev puts his finger to his lips and goes, 'shhh, shhhh, shhh' like that, and he's got a camera, and he passes me the camera, and he goes, 'quick, quick, quick!' And he goes and starts to crouch over Eric Clapton, and literally — this is a true story — starts to undo his zip, right? And I could see what he was doing, he was going to be standing over Eric with his cock near his mouth, and I'd then take a photograph of it really quickly. He's getting nearer and I'm getting ready, and then all of a sudden Eric just goes (makes snoring noises) and wakes up, and Kev just immediately springs back and goes 'Alright Eric, how you doing mate? What's happening with the cricket?' So, we were that close!"

Vom says "Eric was OK". But had his and Reverb's jape come to fruition, or if Clapton had got wind of it, then it's highly likely things would not have been so "OK". In any case, certain members of Slowhand's entourage were not so accommodating towards Crazyhead. The next day, one of Clapton's assistants approached the band and told them that Eric didn't like them using his room. Vom picks up the story: "We were like, 'What do you mean?' and he says 'Well, that lounge is Eric's room', and I said, 'No it's not, it's a lounge for anybody who's using the studio', and then [Fast] Dick made this gold star and put Eric Clapton's name on it and stuck it on the lounge door!"

At the behest of the record label, Anderson and Reverb were flown to the US that summer to stir up pre-release publicity for the album. If it had been up to Dave Balfe, Food and EMI, Porkbeast would have accompanied Anderson and not Reverb, the argument being that Porkbeast "was good for the US market". But Anderson put his foot down and insisted that Reverb accompany him. "It seemed insane not to have the band's songwriter, leader and founder on a radio tour to promote all the songs he'd bloody written!" says Anderson. "I can be a bit quiet. So, it was always good to have motormouths like ol' Rev to bounce off."

Departing Heathrow on 2nd July 1989, singer and guitarist had the good fortune to be upgraded for the flight. Naturally, they didn't waste the opportunity to take advantage of the perks of this upgrade and downed several bottles of champagne during the 13-hour flight. Anderson still recalls the thrill of travelling

Reverb and Anderson in Los Angeles — "the Sunset Marquis — not far from Sunset Strip — ... would be their home for the next week".

to America, "hovering over L.A. in all that smog and sunshine, thinking we're finally in the USA , birth of rock'n'roll and the blues and country."

They arrived at Los Angeles airport early in the afternoon and were met by Kim White for EMI. According to Reverb, Kim was to be their "tour guide and nurse maid for the next three weeks." She drove them around Hollywood to give them a taste of the area and, after a couple of drinks at Barney's Beanery, asked if they would like to meet her folks. Reverb recalls how hospitable Kim's parents were. Her father had been a stills photographer in the film industry and had drawers full of photos he'd taken over the years. Many would never see the light of day, because they featured Hollywood stars who were clearly inebriated; their careers would be compromised if were the photos were made public.

Reverb and Anderson were booked into the Sunset Marquis, a hotel not far from Sunset Strip, which would be their home for the week. Severely jetlagged, they only managed two hours sleep before they had to get up for an early morning flight to San Diego, where Kim had booked a hire car to take them over the border to Mexico. Here they had been booked for an interview with one of the high wattage radio stations that transmitted out of Mexico across California. Queuing at the border crossing, they noticed an ominous sign reminding drivers that hire cars were not insured in Mexico. Kim assured the pair that everything was OK, and on they went. With time to kill before the interview, Kim drove

them past Tijuana City to a place on the coast, where they rode some "near death horses", as Reverb now puts it, and had a few beers. Not realising there was a law against "open containers" they took a few bottles back to the car with them and Kim headed off for the radio station in Tijuana. For some reason they couldn't shake the distant air of paranoia that had niggled them since they saw the signs about uninsured cars at the border crossing. Maybe it was the jetlag, or maybe it was partying late the night before, or maybe it was a combination of both, but what happened next more than justified their anxieties.

While Kim was trying to find the rendezvous point with her contact from the radio station, she alerted her guests that they were being followed by the police. The cops then pulled them over. Reverb describes what followed: "Two cops get out and walk either side of the car and tell us to wind the windows down. I'm in the front with Kim, and Ian's in the back. They tell us that we're in big trouble, the hire car is not insured, we're going to prison, the car will be confiscated etc… Then one of the cops sees a beer bottle near Ian and his eyes light up, 'Ah! Opened container!' He leaned through the window, moved his finger in a cutthroat motion across his neck and said, 'you could die here and no one would know'. Ian tried to talk to the cop and started to wave his arms about. The cop didn't like that, so pulls his gun and orders Ian to get into the police car."

The second cop offered to make a deal: Either the car got confiscated and they would then owe the hire company and go to prison, or they paid the cops off. Asked how much money they had, Kim said $100. Having been given their entire per diem, Reverb and Anderson had considerably more than that. But Reverb bluffed that he too had $100. As he fumbled for his wallet, the cop freaked out, pulled his gun and ordered Kim to drive round the corner where no one could see the money change hands. Anderson was finally released and pushed back into the car. The gun toting officers proceeded to remind everyone how lucky they were, before ordering Kim to drive to the border and leave Mexico right away.

Following this eye-opening introduction to Mexico, Reverb and Anderson were more than happy to leave. But Kim had other ideas. Shortly after leaving the cops they came to a fork in the road. Straight on and out of Mexico, or turn right and head back to Tijuana for the interview? Kim bemoaned the fact they would miss the radio interview if they left Mexico now and so put her foot down on the accelerator — "Starsky and Hutch style", as Reverb puts it — and headed back to Tijuana. Reverb and Anderson were speechless. They could still hear the police siren in the distance, and although the cops hadn't seen them turn off for Tijuana, they still consider it was a close call. To be on the safe side, Kim pulled off the road into a shopping mall car park, where they left the car and

Photo courtesy of Crazyhead.

On the Radio Tour of the USA. Anderson on the coast, San Francisco, April 1989.

arranged for their radio station contact to pick them up. The interview itself went according to plan. After it was over, the three of them were given VIP passes by the station manager, concerned for their safety, which helped them through the queue at the border.

Another stop on the radio tour was San Francisco, which Anderson says was "a different vibe" and loved it even more than L.A. In San Francisco, they bumped into an old friend of theirs from Leicester called Skip, who was working at Jello Biafra's Alternative Tentacles record label. Skip was well connected in the Bay Area and knew many interesting people, including some local gang members. "He really showed us a good time," Anderson recalls. Late one night, Skip decided to go "roof-hopping", whereby, "You go up on the roof and jump from block to block, as they're so close… bloody stupid! I was steaming drunk, as per usual."

On another night in San Francisco, they were taken to see an Elvis impersonator called El Vez at the Full Moon Saloon. As the name suggests, El Vez was a Mexican American Elvis impersonator, but far from being just a novelty act he was quite a serious satirist. He was dressed in a white jumpsuit, Vegas-era Elvis, with his female backing band the Elvettes dressed resplendently in polka dot dresses, huge beehive hairdos, and oversized earrings. He parodied songs like In The Ghetto, renaming it En El Barrio. The English entourage met

El Vez backstage (talk of trying to get El Vez to support Crazyhead in England came to nothing) and Anderson, drunk as usual, tried to flirt with the Elvettes, but the language barrier proved an obstacle — or so Anderson was led to believe.

The next morning, hungover and the worse for wear, Anderson and Reverb visited the apartment of an EMI rep, where they proceeded to get righteously stoned on some particularly strong weed. This was something of an exception for Anderson, who had effectively given up dope and acid sometime in 1987 because, in his own words, "I just couldn't handle the trippy stuff anymore". Anderson recalls the trio suddenly became bathed in bright sunlight as if they were being touched by a celestial visitation, before he realised it was the sun reflecting off a window on the building opposite. Stoned, Reverb and Anderson decided to do their washing and headed to a Chinese laundry. In Anderson's paranoid state of mind the place was full of Chinese gangsters, some dressed in sharp 1940s style suits and looking mean. He recalls, "There were about six of them, they walked out the laundry either side of us, but Reverb and I avoided eye contact by staring at the washing or the floor. They reminded me of the Wongs in the *Wanderers* — 'no one fucks with the Wongs!'"

Reverb concurs. "The six guys that walked past us — three each side — were clicking their fingers in unison, like something from *West Side Story*." Who should then pull up in an open-top black Cadillac with flames painted down

Photo courtesy of Crazyhead

Reverb (left) and Anderson (right) with The Elvettes, the backing band of a Mexican Elvis Presley impersonator. San Francisco, 1989.

the side, but El Vez. On the backseat were the Elvettes, screaming "Crazyhead! Crazyhead!" El Vez looked much the same as the previous night, but the Elvettes had removed their bouffant wigs to reveal dyed punky hairstyles, and they wore leather jackets as opposed to vintage dresses. It transpired they actually spoke perfect English and had only pretended otherwise the night before to deter Anderson from hitting on them! "I chatted to them," says Reverb, "but Ian wouldn't talk to them and insisted on sitting some distance away as he still couldn't handle that it was the same people." If Anderson was feeling foolish for having fallen hook, line and sinker for the backstage patter the previous night, he was in no condition to show it. Even when the Elvettes pulled out a video camera, he couldn't react or ham it up.

Anderson and Reverb hadn't fully recovered as things moved on to the next scheduled stop of the promo tour. "The journey on the plane was a nightmare as well," says Anderson. "Everyone else had suits on, so we stood out like sore thumbs in our newly purchased bright retro fifties' jackets. Normally I wouldn't care, but I had the horrors!" Reverb interjects: "I was wearing a fifties' retro jacket, but Anderson was wearing a NYC cops leather jacket. He got it into his head that he would be nicked for impersonating a cop and ripped the badges off of it."

Anderson says they were always being asked if they were in a band, or being mistaken for someone else: "We were in a truck stop in the Deep South and the gum chewing waitress was convinced that we were Gene Loves Jezebel... The fact that those guys wore full make-up and looked nothing like us wouldn't deter her!" On another occasion, when going through airport security, a security guard insisted that Anderson was Tom Petty. "I was wearing blue Lennon shades, a top hat, and a blue drape coat, but looked nothing like Tom Petty," says Anderson, "who was at least 10 or 15 years older. I was only 23! It was a heavy tour!"

Tour guide and EMI liaison, Kim White, had security issues of her own. Having triggered the metal detector at the airport, her luggage was duly searched and a steel dildo was found, about 15 inches long and encrusted with skulls. Red-faced she insisted that it had been a promo given to her by a death metal band.

In Chicago they visited the renowned Cabaret Metro, a venue Crazyhead were booked to play on their tour in the autumn. The club owner gave them "huge amounts of beer tokens", which they quickly cashed-in at The Smart Bar upstairs, and introduced Anderson to Guns N' Roses drummer, Steven Adler. Guns N' Roses had been holed up in the Windy City since June, writing songs and rehearsing for their follow-up to *Appetite For Destruction*. Adler was at the bar with his two huge minders, getting stoned. Says Anderson, "They were dressed identically — the trio in bleached blonde, long spiky hair, denims and

Red Hot Chili Peppers' Flea (centre), with Anderson and Reverb in New York at a joint launch for Mothers Milk and Desert Orchid.

Photo by the late Adie Johnson, courtesy of Kev Reverb.

leather trousers. He was a nice friendly chap and offered us a joint and said, 'I don't think I've heard of you guys'." A drunk and immodest Anderson replied, "Don't worry you will!" The riposte would haunt Anderson on his return to the Metro in October.

In New York they hooked up with Adie Johnson, a renegade from the Leicester rockabilly scene, now a drum technician for Icelandic indie rock band The Sugarcubes, who were supporting PiL and New Order on a US tour. Anderson, Reverb and Kim were invited to the gig and aftershow party, held in a luxury high-rise apartment overlooking the city. Booze was flowing freely, and the Leicester contingent were convivially chatting and admiring the New York skyline when, according to Anderson, Reverb started "taking the piss out of a member of The Sugarcubes". The target of Reverb's abuse — "a HUGE man" — picked Reverb up and dangled him over the balcony to shut him up. Silent and shaken, Reverb was returned to the balcony. Soon enough it was as if the incident hadn't happened and the party continued into the night at the hotel in which The Sugarcubes were staying. Anderson recalls "a party room and various Sugarcubes, friends and crew dancing madly around a beat box blasting out rave music". Adie confided that this is what it was like most nights. Says Anderson, "The Sugarcubes were some of the maddest, strangest people — but in a jolly, friendly way — I have ever met in my life. I suspect E was involved, or maybe they were naturally loved up and mad? Something in the Icelandic water maybe?"

Also in New York, the Crazyhead duo attended the launch party for the Red Hot Chili Peppers' *Mothers Milk* album which also doubled as a promo opportunity for *Desert Orchid* too, according to Reverb. The radio tour was an experience the pair would never forget, and Anderson recalls that all the staff at EMI USA were hospitable and helpful. "Every person there was really cool," he says, "from the record company boss all the way down. Everyone seemed sure we were about to become a huge rock band and I believed it was really going to happen 100%." Anderson and Reverb reserve particular praise for Kim White, whom they nicknamed "Big Sister". During those few weeks, Kim drove them hundreds of miles, and with her love of indie rock — she had a collection of well over 100 different band t-shirts of which she was enormously proud —taught Anderson and Reverb

much about alternative USA. She would eventually be immortalised in song, Big Sister, on Crazyhead's second album. (The Chinese laundry is also mentioned.) Anderson feels rightly justified in having put his foot down in his choice of travelling companion. Without any disrespect to Porkbeast, he considers Reverb ideal and that he "turned out to be Reverb all the way, witty and charming, plus zany and sick. He reminded me of a sleazier Harpo Marx, dressed in his leather waistcoat, goatee beard and trademark cowboy hat. It was a good job someone without a permanently booze-sozzled brain was on that radio tour."

OUT OF THEIR
TREWORGEY TREE FAYRES

Over the summer of 1989, the Bykers played several festivals. One of these in July was the renowned Roskilde Festival in Denmark on a weekend bill that included My Bloody Valentine, Nick Cave and the Bad Seeds, Georgia Satellites, Camper Van Beethoven, and Dinosaur Jr, as well as more mainstream acts like Suzanne Vega, and Katrina and the Waves.

Although it has gone down in Bykers lore that many promoters fell for the ruse that the Gaye Bykers on Acid and Lesbian Dopeheads On Mopeds were two different bands and booked them accordingly, the reality of the situation is that most promoters probably weren't that blinkered. Martin Elbourne says, "We did about three or four festivals like that. The bookers and promoters just went along with the thing that it was a separate band. I don't think anyone was duped, apart from the audience maybe, and I don't think they cared either!" Elbourne remembers Roskilde being a win-win situation for the band. "In those

days, Roskilde was surprisingly drug free… even getting hold of cannabis. So every band on site turned up to see Lesbian Dopeheads, assuming with a name like that that they'd have some drugs on them, and obviously some of them did. So, it was a double winner basically. They got double the money, got a big dressing room, and all the headline acts turned up to see them — yeah!"

The rest of July was relatively quiet, apart from a couple of gigs at The Cresset in Peterborough, heralded by the local newspaper as something akin to visiting dignitaries. They also played one of their favourite venues, the

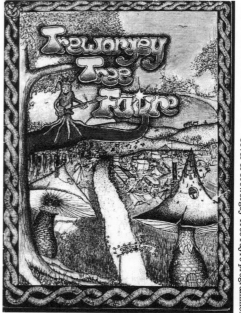

Cover of Treworgey Tree Fayre programme.

Powerhaus in Islington, London, before heading to the wilds of the West Country in darkest Cornwall, where they rounded off the month with an appearance at the Treworgey Tree Fayre.

Treworgey Tree Fayre is remembered for more the wrong reasons than music or recreational fun. Although it started out as a paying festival Robber says it soon became a "Wild West free festival". One fan who attended the event, Martin, recalls that Treworgey was "the most disorganised, anarchic, scary, exciting and absolutely brilliant festival ever." In a retrospective article, the Cornwall Live website described it as "the most terrifying, ramshackle, crime-ridden yet bizarrely fun festival that has ever taken place in Cornwall." Accounts vary, but all sorts of horror stories have been related about Treworgey over the years. It appears that scores of people succumbed to a mystery illness that is often attributed to a dead sheep contaminating the water supply, or to some airborne virus spawned by dust and the dry weather. Poor sanitation is always a festival bugbear and Treworgey was no different, a toddler reputedly drowned after falling into a fenced-off pond, travellers' dogs lay dying because of a rampant canine disease, and there were violent clashes between security guards — fearing they would not be paid — and festival organisers. Apocryphal or not, these are just a few of the tales to emerge from the legend that is the Treworgey Festival.

The Bykers played the main stage on Saturday, to a crowd of crusties, punks, hippies, ravers, goths and bikers — a hearty cross-section of most UK subcultures of the time. In an army surplus GI helmet, and a mishmash of Hawaiian shirts, shorts and hippy beads, Robber looked like he'd just stepped off the pages of a sci-fi comic such as *2000AD* or *Crisis*. He came across like a psychedelicized 'Nam vet crossed with a less sartorial Hunter S. Thompson. Centre-stage was Mary, wearing a black leotard and tie-dyed Janitors and Bomb Party purple t-shirt ensemble, with his white underpants worn on the outside. His straggly blonde hair was piled back on his head as he led the band through a set that included some favourites (Everythang's Groovy, Nosedive, TV Cabbage), a significant number of new songs (Welcome Cancer Planet Mission, Bleed, Advertise, Face At The Window, Catalytic Converter), and material from *Stewed*, including a rousing version of Shoulders that was dedicated to the band's loyal followers, the Daye Trippers. Joined onstage by The Janitors for their encore, they ripped through various covers, including Cinnamon Girl, Rock & Roll Part 2, Five Years Ahead Of My Time and Bar-B-Q Pope. It was a rousing and solid set by a band recently unshackled from major record label constraint.

Also performing on the main stage that weekend were The Seers, Carter The Unstoppable Sex Machine, Loop, Here & Now, Misty In Roots, Nik Turner's

Fantastic All-Stars, and Thee Hypnotics. Treworgey was not a free festival, but it certainly carried a new age traveller-oriented vibe, as evidenced by the bands playing the two other stages, which included The Oroonies, Magic Mushroom Band, Ozric Tentacles, 2000 D.S., Screech Rock, Hippy Slags, Doctor and The Crippens, Chaos UK and a relatively unknown Levellers. Headlining the second stage on Saturday night was Hawkwind. Also in evidence at Treworgey was a sense of cultural shift, in that the rave scene and free festival travelling culture were coming

Photo courtesy of July Taty AKA Julie Brown.

"Coming across like a psychedelicised Vietnam vet crossed with a less sartorial Hunter S Thompson in Fear And Loathing In Las Vegas" — Robber Byker at Treworgey Tree Fayre.

together to form an unholy union. Robber recalls spending much of his free time hanging out at an impromptu acid house rave that had sprung up on the site. The Bykers themselves would become immersed in the acid house scene over the coming months. But first they turned their attention to a more thrashy project.

READING BETWEEN THE LINES

In August 1989, Mary compered what he describes as an "Anti-Poll Tax benefit-cum-Nicaragua solidarity campaign" gig at the Boston Arms in Tufnell Park, featuring his fellow Leicester friends and mentors, The Bomb Party and The Janitors. Simon Price in *Melody Maker* was disparaging of "Grebo — that pathetic one-joke 'movement'", as well as the Leicester coterie of bands and friends. Likening Mary to "the nearest thing to a real celebrity" (in the absence of Voice of the Beehive, who didn't show up), Price lamented that The Bomb Party and The Janitors shied away from "any real disorder" and that the night in general was "an incestuous little do where everyone knows everyone else."

Also in August the Bykers appeared at the Waterpop Festival in the

Photo courtesy of Sally Jones.

Lesbian Dopeheads On Mopeds, Waterpop Festival, Netherlands, August 1988.

Netherlands. Now one of the oldest free music festivals in the country, Waterpop boasts a more alternative line-up than the more famous Dutch music festival, Pink Pop. In 1989, the Bykers appeared on a weekend that included Wreckless Eric, House Of Love, and a homegrown rap rock outfit from Utrecht called Urban Dance Squad. Once again, they reprised their female band alter ego, Lesbian Dopeheads On Mopeds, doing their first set in this guise, before reappearing later as Gaye Bykers On Acid.

Shortly after Waterpop, the Bykers and Crazyhead both appeared at the traditional August bank holiday rock festival in Reading. The Bykers played on Friday, and Crazyhead on Sunday. Chris Roberts, reviewing the festival for *Melody Maker,* missed the Bykers' because of traffic tailbacks. However, he described how, having met Mary at a Butthole Surfers gig in London the previous night, it appeared that the frontman was somewhat disillusioned with his own band's musical competence. The Bykers had given a lacklustre performance at Subterania a few days earlier with Tony on guitar clearly the worse for wear. Discussing the band's forthcoming appearance at Reading, Mary apparently told Roberts, "Don't bother about it, we're crap anyway. Well, we've been brilliant five times in 155 gigs."

Sounds was disparaging of the Bykers' Reading performance from the off, likening them to "a dum dum pub rock punk band in the tradition of Slaughter

Photo courtesy of Sally Jones.

Hyde's herbal clinic — backstage at Waterpop Festival. Kev Byker (left) and Mary Byker (right).

and the Dogs and Peter and the Test Tube Babies — significantly all bands with *dead funny* names". The review noted that while the Bykers gave the Reading crowd their all, they were "still a two-stroke running low on oil". The Bykers were the opening act at Reading. This lowly billing and the critical indifference that met them is an indicator of how far the Bykers had fallen in popularity in two years. Which is not to say that Mary would pass on any opportunity to liven up proceedings should the occasion warrant it. Will Carruthers, bass player for then up-and-coming psych band Spaceman 3, recounts in his autobiography his experience at Reading that year. It was the first time his band had played the festival and their set had followed the Bykers. Spaceman 3 expected to have occupancy of their backstage caravan for the rest of the night but were turfed out by festival organisers to make way for another band. Finding themselves at a loss, the band sought refuge from the increasingly wet weather — it was the English August bank holiday weekend after all — in the backstage bar. According to Carruthers, it was a particularly soulless affair. "The beer tent had been done out in ribbons and bows it looked like it was going to be the scene for a bad wedding reception. Given that this was the height of acid house, there wasn't much of a party going on." That was until "Mary Mary from Gaye Bykers On Acid walked into the tent looking like everyone's idea of a good trip. 'SKIN UP, YOU BORING BASTARDS,' he screamed, laughing through his psychedelic megaphone. 'This is

Gaye Bykers On Acid, Waterpop Festival, Netherlands, August 1988.

supposed to be a fucking party. What's wrong with you?'"

Mary recognised Spaceman 3 as kindred spirits, says Carruthers. He continues: "'THANK GOD!' [Mary] shouted through his megaphone, even though he was quite close to us. 'SOMEBODY HAS GOT SOME DRUGS.'" Mary then apparently offered the Spacemen some acid, which they politely refused before handing him the joint they'd just rolled. Whipping out the megaphone again, the Bykers' singer proceeded to emphasise how boring it was backstage, "BORING, BORING, BORING." Once he'd finished partaking of the proffered joint, Carruthers says Mary "then pranced off in his pink docs and his tutu with his psychedelic megaphone."

The backstage atmosphere appears to have changed by Sunday. Crazyhead's Anderson recalls a fine old time: "When we played Reading festival in 1989, I knocked out a camera man by accident with the stand, only finding out when the backstage crew told me. I blagged in Leicester mates to the backstage area. Gaye Bykers On Acid, ourselves and crew managed to keep reusing our passes to get loads of mates to the backstage bar area. There were more Leicester drunks and wreck-heads backstage that year than anybody else, including various Bomb Party members, Janitors, Abandoned Babies, and Welphead/Grumble Grinder — Leicester's answer to Hawkwind! It was such a buzz to see so many people from the Princess Charlotte and Magazine pubs at Reading festival!"

Photo courtesy of Gaz Birtles.

Crazyhead with the Space Bastards backstage at Reading Festival, August, 1989. (L-R) John Barrow, Tony Robinson, Reverb (in hat) Anderson (partially obscured by Reverb) with beer can, unknown, Porkbeast

Also on the Reading bill were Pop Will Eat Itself. Says Anderson, "I remember when we did Reading festival, one of the Poppies said to us, 'Aren't you nervous?' Vom replied, 'No mate, we're professionals!' As we hit the stage, I got a feeling of fear at the huge sea of faces, though we had a great gig once the band kicked in."

Neither the Bykers nor Crazyhead were mentioned in the *NME* write up of the festival, who reserved praise for the Poppies. Anderson jokingly attributes this oversight to his journalist ex, Barbara Ellen. "Every other band was reviewed," he says. "Maybe she was pissed in the bar!"

Crazyhead fared marginally better than the Bykers in the other music papers, although the best the *Melody Maker* could muster was that "Crazyhead *rock out* and on a day stillborn with mediocrity, they are as good as any." *Melody Maker* claimed that Porkbeast saved the band from the ignominy of being "yet another long-haired crew of failed car mechanics". Video footage of the day suggests that critics were unduly harsh in their summation of Crazyhead's performance. The alternative arrangement of Train is particularly impressive, and the band itself more energetic than a room full of jumping jacks. This was a band on fine form in readiness for their US tour, just over a month away.

While Crazyhead prepared for their Stateside jaunt, the Bykers played a handful of gigs in September, including the "grand reopening" of legendary

Photo courtesy of Gaz Birtles.

Crazyhead live at Reading, August 1989.

Sheffield venue The Leadmill. The Bykers were again routinely savaged by the music press. Dave James for *Sounds* criticised everything about the evening, not just the bands (support was God's Ultimate Noise), but also the audience, the lightshow, and even the newly refurbished venue itself. He referred to "an air of desperation and their lack of a creative spark", and considered of the new Byker material unveiled that night "to be lacklustre attempts to woo the new generation of skate thrashers". What James couldn't know was that some of this new material would constitute the band's next, and arguably, most audacious stunt yet.

THE REKTÜM SCAM

At the Treworgey Tree Festival, the Bykers had bumped into one of their old Mutant Skaties connections from Bristol, Shane Dabinett. Dabinett owned a record label, Manic Ears, specialising in thrash metal, and with the promise of studio time convinced the Bykers to record a thrash metal album for him. One good thing about being dropped by Virgin was that the Bykers no longer suffered the constraints often imposed on bands signed to major labels. Mary found this new freedom liberating. As evidenced on *Stewed To The Gills*, the Bykers had

returned to their punkier roots and with a collective interest in thrash metal, Dabinett's offer seemed too good an opportunity to turn down. However, it was decided that a radically different direction wouldn't sit too well with fans. So a plan was hatched. Mary came up with the idea of using yet another pseudonym under which to release the material. Along with Shane and the ever-reliable Martin Elbourne, the Bykers concocted a story that Manic Ears had taken under its wing an East German thrash metal band called Rektüm.

In October, the music press announced that Rektüm, hailing from Karl Marx Stadt, had managed to defect from East Berlin via Hungary. The band, it was claimed, had released several recordings on bootleg cassettes and played underground concerts in the East. They had also lost all their equipment and possessions during their escape, and Manic Ears were said to be organising a benefit gig for them on 21st October at Bristol Bierkeller, featuring Manic Ears stablemates Extreme Noise Terror, Sore Throat, and Doctor and The Crippens.

Employing the services of agency actors for publicity photos, the story found its way into the general press, notably the German weekly magazine, *Stern*. Says Dabinett, "We really scammed *Stern*. They wanted to interview the band, so we got an actor from Bristol, who was in the Rektüm press photo, as he could speak fluent German. I took him to London, where we did an interview with *Stern*, this actor answering questions in German! Mary was there and Martin. As we were leaving, Mary was whispering to us, 'Hook, line and sinker!' and suddenly the guy from *Stern* shouted back down the street. The actor just turned around and spoke German back. We thought we had blown it!"

DJ John Peel got wind of these supposed East German thrash metallers and the fact they were planning to record an album in the UK. Peel was already a champion of Dabinett's label and didn't hesitate to contact him about Rektüm. "John Peel had left a message on my answer machine saying he had heard about the band and was wondering if there was anything he could do, like a session," recalls Dabinett. "I spoke to Martin Elbourne about it. I was uncomfortable about scamming John Peel. Martin agreed. John Peel had done a lot of sessions for Manic Ears bands in the past. I certainly did not want to scam him. He was trying to be helpful." As a result Peel was notified of the subterfuge but apparently was not too pleased and pulled the offer of a session. This still rankles Robber, who considers Peel a poor sport for cancelling. "I think he should have given us the session anyway," says Robber, "because the music was quite good. I was a bit disappointed with John Peel for that."

The Bykers recorded and mixed the Rektüm material at Holy Ghost Studios in west London, in August and September 1989. Most of the songs were written

The Rektüm press photo featured actors as the fictional East German thrash metal band.

on the spot, according to Robber. "We just made it up as we went along. There were a few ideas there, but most of it was like, 'We'll do it like this and see if it happens,' so it was definitely punk-by-numbers, as you go along, out of your head, just record it!" Mary's version differs only slightly. He thinks the Bykers spent a few days in the rehearsal room, where they churned out "fifty-odd tracks" before committing anything to tape. "We thought fuck it, let's just do it!" he says. "It was our anti-record company stance, and that was the contrariness of the band."

On 13th October 1989, the *Independent* newspaper reported on the Rektüm story without a whiff of suspicion: "The last batches of refugees to slip loose over the Hungarian border before regulations tightened up again included an East German thrash metal band. They call themselves Rektüm, and all signs suggest they enjoyed what you might call a safe passage." Detailing how the band had lost everything in their bid for freedom, the report stated that "were it not for the warm-hearted generosity of the British thrash metal community" Rektüm "would now find themselves without so much as a guitar string to their name". Shane at Manic Ears was singled out for his kindness in housing the band in Bristol and for helping to reassemble their career with a benefit gig.

The first fruits of the Rektüm sessions were unleashed by Manic Ears later that autumn. The buying public by now was not entirely unsuspecting. The *Real Horrorshow* EP features the tracks Deth Soup, Sexy Salman/God Sold Me Bad Acid, Dead Heads In Red China and Cocaine Metallic Be-Bop. Sexy Salman was a somewhat inflammatory inclusion, given the furore surrounding British writer Salman Rushdie, and the fatwa declared on him by Iran's Ayatollah Khomeini following the publication of his 'blasphemous' novel *The Satanic Verses*. The notion of fundamental Islamic extremists listening to a death metal record by a group of fictitious East German dissidents is a bit of a headfuck anyway.

Despite being advertised to appear with other Manic Ears bands for the 'benefit' in October, it appears the Bykers only ever played one gig using the moniker Rektüm and this was the Manic Ears Christmas Party on 28th December. Billed as "East German Defektors", Rektüm topped a line-up that included Doctor and The Crippens, Hotalacio, Purgatory, and Prophecy Of Doom. Robber admits that Rektüm was never anything more than a side project and by the Christmas Party had effectively run its course, anyway with the band introduced to the stage as the "real Gaye Bykers On Acid". They then ripped through a set that included material that would feature on the forthcoming Rektüm album, as well as the next Bykers' album, *Cancer Planet Mission*.

Rektüm's 25-track album *Sakredanus* was released by PSI Records the following year. Mike Barnes of *Select* magazine said that having long given up the pretence of being "an authentic East German hardcore band", the Bykers were indulging in a little fun, and described *Sakredanus* as "A sort of What We Did On Our Holidays After We Emptied The Drug Cabinet". Barnes argued that it was difficult at times to discern any individual tracks "from the chaos" and conceded that the album "works best as relentless aural assault". Although he cited Rektüm as belonging to a canon of English bottom humour, whose lineage included Chaucer and *Carry On Up The Khyber,* Barnes still only awarded *Sakredanus* two out of five. 💀

CHAPTER TEN

... MEANWHILE BACK IN THE STATES

I N OCTOBER ANDERSON AND REVERB RETURNED TO THE States but now with the band for an extensive tour, taking in 22 cities in just over a month. Accompanying them was a crew headed by the indefatigable Spike. Initial dates started well for Crazyhead with two gigs in New York, and then dates in Washington D.C. Vom remembers, "The two gigs we do in New York are kind of like showcases… they were really good shows — packed out! We're here in America, it's all going good — we've made it, there's this sort of feeling that this is it — *America!*"

The first blip was Boston, a big venue with a very small crowd. It was the seventh date on the tour, 13 October. Reverb recalls, "It was an early evening show. I asked the promoter if early shows were a regular thing. He said 'No, the last time we tried it, it was a disaster.' It was a good thing that several people drove up from the previous night's gig in Providence to see us again."

Among the small Boston crowd were five truckers, who had been drinking in the venue all day. Anderson recalls them being "at the end of a long table drinking beer, sneering at the band — there were loads of empties". As often is the case with frontmen, Anderson was not immune to behaving like a prima donna when the occasion warranted. His mood exacerbated by his own heavy drinking and bruised ego, Anderson addressed the disrespectful element of the audience mid-set. In his own words, he leapt onto the truckers' table, "crawled along it singing, pushing glasses off the table, stopped at the end, sang a verse in their faces, turned round, crawled back and got on stage to finish the song. These guys were massive, so I thought 'Fuck, I am doomed'. They simply got up at the end of the song muttering, shaking their heads, and walked out looking disgusted."

Leaving the stage, Anderson proceeded to punch holes in the dressing room wall. "The others were really patient and calming during my drunken self-indulgent rages on tour," he recalls. Vom was the calming influence on this occasion. "Vom spoke sense to me re: professionalism and carrying on with the show and entertaining the five people who had come." Indeed, "the five" had travelled more than 100 miles to see the band and the band dutifully returned to the stage. Despite the damage to the dressing room wall, or perhaps ignorant

Photo courtesy of Crazyhead.

At Elvis's graveside, Crazyhead went through the 'Heartbreak Hotel' routine from Spinal Tap. Crazyhead at Graceland, Memphis. October 1989.

to it, the barman took pity. Vom remembers, "he brought us a massive tray of drinks, so we just kept playing."

The next night the band was back in New Jersey. Here they played at Maxwell's, Hoboken, before travelling through the night to Nashville, home of country music, where they stayed on the main Strip. Heading out for food they visited the legendary Tootsie's Orchid Lounge. Except for Reverb and Vom, the Crazyhead entourage didn't have their passports on them and couldn't get in. The Tootsie staff were of the opinion there was a conspiracy to get the place closed, so wouldn't risk admitting anyone without ID. Most of the next day was spent checking out Music Row and a visit to the Country Music Hall of Fame. Despite their relative anonymity it was obvious that the motley bunch of Englishmen was a band and consequently they were treated like royalty. "The cinema was showing programmes in rotation," recalls Reverb. "We noticed there was a film about Elvis on the list. Rather embarrassingly, the staff stopped the programme, made an apology, and put the Elvis film on. They hoped the rest of the audience would understand as 'our honoured guests from the UK, the band Crazyhead, would like to see the Elvis film.'"

It speaks volumes that Reverb can remember more about what they did in Nashville than of their gig forty miles down the road in Murfreesboro. Next, they travelled to Atlanta, Georgia, on 17th October. Things didn't bode well on arriving

PRAYERS ANSWERED: **The King Lives!**

Elvis' Sweat!

LIMITED OFFER
ONLY for the most devoted fan.

The IMPOSSIBLE has happened! Elvis poured out his soul for you, and NOW you can let his PER-SPIRATION be an INSPIRATION. Yes, dreams do come true. In loving memory, send this greeting and show the world you really care!

ALSO AVAILABLE contains a few genuine drops of Elvis' perspiration

SERIOUSLY

HE WAS A MAN ... NOW HE'S A LEGEND!

"The trip [to Graceland] was rounded off by the inevitable gift shop purchases — Reverb bought some Elvis sweat."

at the Cotton Club. Vom recalls incredulously, "The fucking promoter was outside the venue, and he was literally sticking up posters as we pulled up for the soundcheck, and we thought, 'Well this ain't going to be any fucking good is it?'"

Road weary and disheartened by the poor attendance in Atlanta, the band cancelled their next show in Hallendale, Florida. It would have entailed another gruelling drive and an equally tortuous journey back up to St Louis. A couple of days' break was welcome, which the band spent in Memphis with a pilgrimage to Graceland.

Graceland was fascinating and tacky in equal measure. Porkbeast marvelled at the Cadillacs installed with record players. Then there was Elvis's collection of guns and police department badges, and the gold-plated safety belt buckles from his private planes. At Elvis's graveside, Crazyhead went through the Heartbreak Hotel routine from *This is Spinal Tap*, attempting to harmonise on the 'Since my baby left me' line. Crazyhead would collect all manner of things on the road, often requesting Kinder Eggs as part of their rider, and they had a particular penchant for religious paraphernalia. The Graceland visit concluded with a visit to the gift shop where Reverb bought some Elvis sweat, a *Jailhouse Rock* clock, and a t-shirt with Elvis depicted as Jesus wearing a crown of thorns.

Following Memphis, the band headed to the Midwest and arrived in Milwaukee on 22nd October to a lukewarm reception. Eight people had turned up to see them play. What particularly galled the band was that in the bar adjacent to the venue a band played Foreigner covers to a packed audience. But if that wasn't enough, the diminutive Crazyhead audience was halved when, during their own set, Reverb remarked, "Whatever made Milwaukee famous is a fucking mystery to me!"

Things went from bad to worse. They played Minneapolis the following night and reached Chicago only to find the promoter had cancelled the gig because of poor ticket sales — just four tickets had been sold. Reverb and Anderson had

visited the Metro Club on their radio tour several months prior, where they had met Steven Adler, drummer for Guns N' Roses. Anderson couldn't help but remember the self-aggrandising comments he had made to Adler, which now seemed hollow. Muses Anderson, "Within a few years, I was back on the dole and Guns N' Roses were one of the biggest rock bands on the planet."

Despite the cancellation, the band enjoyed the hospitality of the club owner and partied for free. Anderson got extremely drunk with Spike, who had been given PCP and was dancing madly. Anderson eventually left the venue with a Revolting Cocks groupie and accompanied her back to her place. But after she produced a bag of smack, Anderson made his excuses and left. The groupie screamed at him, "This is Chicago man, you can't just walk around at this time!" But Anderson left and made it back to his hotel in one piece. "The hotel was huge and visible from her pad and, astoundingly, the man with no sense of direction got back there!"

In Detroit the next night, Crazyhead were mistaken for Johnny Cash's backing band. Spilling out of their tour bus, a group of middle-aged women spotted Crazyhead and were convinced that the Man In Black was in town. An earnest mistake, given that Crazyhead were in a bus with a roll-down that had Johnny Cash's name on it. Of the excited Cash fans, Anderson says, "they were very keen to meet JC himself, so we assured them his personal tour bus would roll in within the next hour or so." The gig that evening at St Andrew's Hall was great, despite the absence of the country legend. Mischief aside, what sticks with Crazyhead about Detroit is the poverty and destitution. With the tour bus parked a hundred yards from the venue, Reverb recalls having to walk a gauntlet of homeless people and the general air of unease that hung over the city. "Downtown Detroit was quite edgy after dark, I remember that me and Geoff [Perrin], the soundman, went for a walk. We ended up down by the river. We were just standing there looking over to Canada when a police helicopter appeared just over our heads with its searchlight on us and shouted something through a megaphone." He adds, sardonically, "we guessed it wasn't 'Welcome to Detroit', and did a runner."

Detroit was followed by Cleveland, Ohio. Again the audience wasn't as large as they had hoped, but Crazyhead played a good set and were well received. A couple of nights later they were back in New York, where they played a blinder at the Pyramid Club. However, there was a falling out among the crew at around this point of the tour. The parties involved were Jos Grain, Vom's drum roadie, and Geoffrey Perrin, sound engineer and inspiration for the Gaye Bykers On Acid's alter egos, Lesbian Dopeheads On Mopeds. Grain had previously worked for the likes of Siouxsie & The Banshees and Iggy Pop and was not a person to mess with. He didn't think twice about offering truckers out for a fight, as had

Photo courtesy of Ian Anderson.

Crazyhead on the road in the USA. Sound engineer, Geoffrey Perrin (left), Vom (right).

happened earlier on the tour. But the dispute between Grain and Perrin came about after Perrin decided to get 'experimental' with the band's sound. According to Anderson, Perrin did not consider sound experimentation a problem at empty gigs. But it pissed people off, among them Grain. Perrin is of the opinion that Grain took a dislike to him from the start, which marred the whole tour experience as far as he was concerned. Says Perrin, "I pretty much consigned the tour to the 'don't need to go there bin' in my head. Such is life."

The band relied on door takings to support the tour. They still had to get to Denver, and then on to the final leg on the West Coast in California, with gigs lined up in San Diego, San Francisco and Los Angeles. But in Detroit they had run out of money with no funds for airfares or petrol to continue coast-to-coast. Vom says they wired EMI in England to send more money. But the request was refused, with EMI claiming they'd already invested enough in the tour. No help was forthcoming from the American office either and the band was left with no alternative but to abandon the last dates of the tour. They had to borrow money from a roadie for the flight home.

What they didn't know was that at least two West Coast gigs — at the Whiskey A Go Go in Los Angeles, no less — had sold out. If the record company had had the foresight to check pre-sales, the band would undoubtedly have continued the journey to California. It was only later, when Vom visited L.A. with Zodiac

Mindwarp and the Love Reaction, that the sell-out dates became known, long after the fact. Crazyhead had been a hot ticket, bass player Tex Diablo informed Vom. There had even been a billboard announcing their imminent arrival.

LIKE PRINCES DO

Between the Zeus B. Held Night Train demo and American tour, Crazyhead contributed to *The Food Christmas EP*. It comprised of Food Records covers by Food Records artists. Crazyhead's contribution — a version of Diesel Park West's Like Princes Do — was recorded at Rick Willson's studio on Barkby Road. Anderson remembers the squalor of the session with undisguised affection. "We went back to Rick 'Kipper' Wilson's studio in the middle of an industrial estate in the corner of a big industrial car chopping garage — filthy oil everywhere! And a three-legged dog with an eyepatch was still there. We recorded the band live while I overdubbed vocals in the tiny toilet in Rick's studio. We liked the sound of the toilet flushing — 'when you grra go, you grra go!' — so we put it on the track. I guess the heavy dope smoke affected us all, even the non-tokers… which was just me I guess!"

The Food Christmas (which also featured Jesus Jones and Diesel Park West)

The Food Christmas EP. Crazyhead covered Diesel Park West's 'Like Princes Do'.

was released in December 1989. Apart from Have Love, Will Travel and the repackaged *Desert Orchid* it proved to be Crazyhead's only new release for the year — and a cover version at that. Reverb was under no illusion as to what was responsible for the slow-release rate. He told *Sniffin' Rock* magazine, "Things did slow down a lot for us because EMI has to work with so many major acts. The actual mechanics of the business are drawn out; they negate any idea of imagination and excitement because everything has to be worked out."

Reverb's patience with EMI was thinning, which suggests that his hitherto favourable remarks were begrudging ones rather than sincere; Crazyhead were still under contract and it wouldn't do at this stage to start biting the hand of the label that was supposedly feeding them. But things soon came to a head. For their follow-up album, Crazyhead had been having trouble finding a suitable producer. Eventually they enlisted an old muso mate from Leicester, Andy Povall, and produced a bunch of demos at his Slam Jam studio. The songs were Everything's Alright, Big Sister, Movie Theme, I Can Do Anything, and a cover of I Can Only Give You Everything, with brass provided by old chums The Space Bastards. Tony Robinson contributed keyboards. There was also an early version of what would become Some Kinda Fever, and an instrumental that would eventually become Death Ride To Osaka, which would find its way onto the B-side of Everything's Alright. In this early incarnation it had a title that echoed the band's disillusionment with EMI: Looking For A New Deal.

BLUE FLARES DON'T MAKE IT

Rektüm had been an amusing aside but now the Bykers turned to their own new album. For the task the band once again ensconced itself in Alaska Studios, where they remained through winter 1989/90. Martin Elbourne had proved indispensable in booking comparatively high-profile festival gigs over the past year, but the Bykers remained rudderless in respect of a long-term manager and a producer for their new album. Meetings with various producers had amounted to nothing and Elbourne suggested they approach John Leckie, a good friend of his, who also happened to be a top producer. Starting out as a tape-operator at Abbey Road in 1970, Leckie had worked with John Lennon, Syd Barrett, The Adverts and PiL, among others.

In the 1980s, Leckie was becoming increasingly involved with the controversial Rajneesh Movement, and sometimes went by the name, Swami Anand Agara

John Leckie, "Possibly one of the biggest producers in the country at the time."

(bestowed upon him by Bhagwan Shree Raj Neesh). His sannyasin non de plume appears on the credits for *25 O'Clock*, the mini album by the Dukes Of Stratosphear (XTC under a different name). It was his work on *25 O'Clock* that helped to generate interest from a Manchester band called The Stone Roses, and Leckie was hired to produce their eponymous debut album, released in 1989, which would become a platinum seller. At the time not many people wanted to employ Leckie, says Elbourne, "because they thought he'd just gone mad, so obviously after The Stone Roses he got fully employed again." Says Mary, "Leckie brought The Stone Roses around from being a Manchester psychedelic goth band into being the biggest thing since sliced bread!"

Leckie wanted to do something fun and thought the Bykers would be just that. However, it wasn't to be. A meeting was brokered, which sadly came to nothing. Leckie recalls how the Bykers "all seemed like nice chaps and had some great ideas, but I don't think we got as far as talking about making a record together."

Leckie was "really up for it", recalls Mary, and visited the band at Alaska several times before things fell through. By this point the other Bykers were already fostering ideas of their own. According to Mary there was a growing consensus that the band didn't need a producer, and that they could "do it ourselves". The clincher apparently was Kev taking exception to Leckie's trousers. Despite Leckie's exalted reputation in the business, Kev insisted he didn't want "anyone in

UFO contact from Planet **ITIBI-RA**

March 1967, 17130, Rungay, Peru, Sr. Augusto Arzando shot 4 color photos with a 40-year-old box camera.

CANCER PLANET MISSION

Ludwig F. Pallmann
and
Wendelle C. Stevens

"UFO contact from Planet Itibi-Ra" — cover of the book Cancer Planet Mission by Ludwig F. Pallmann, the inspiration for Gaye Bykers On Acid's third album.

pale blue flares producing an album of ours".

This still rankles with Mary, who believes the opportunity was there to go to the next level. "Leckie was somebody who could've taken the Bykers, moulded us, helped us grow as songwriters and make something really sonic and really good," he says. "But somehow, they [Kev, Robber and Tony] were so short-sighted they didn't see it. I was always trying to look at the bigger picture, and if you have good songs they're the things that people remember. And, if you have an idea for a song that somebody can help you make even better, then for me that's not a problem, but for the other guys it was like 'oh no, we can do it ourselves.'"

Mary was not of the opinion the band could do everything themselves and losing Leckie had far greater implications as far as he is concerned. He says, "That was my turning point with them: when I didn't really take them so seriously anymore. My opinion was we sounded OK, but I think we never really went into the studio with somebody who truly got the best out of us. Keep doing things your own way and it becomes a bit frustrating if you think you know everything." In Mary's opinion, Jon Langford had been a great help and had got the band to the point it was with *Stewed To The Gills* but adds that he "wasn't really a name producer. I mean that wasn't really his gig. He was a musician. Production was a thing he did as side-line, but John Leckie was at that time somebody record companies would pay a lot of money for, to take a fledgling band and help form them. That's a big bugbear with the other Bykers,

and it has been for years. I don't think they realise how much of an opportunity we missed there. Musically we would have grown, and I think we would have definitely been around for longer [had we gone with Leckie]. We shot ourselves in the foot."

Martin Elbourne agrees. "John Leckie's one of the world's best record producers," he says. "It would've been good for the band to move out of their little cupboard [Alaska Studios]. Had they done so they might just have gone on to create a legacy masterpiece. But we'll never know now."

Dress sense aside, it is worth considering another important factor that might have weighed against the employment of a top name producer, notably having to pay Leckie for his services. The Bykers were in the process of setting up their own record label, Naked Brain. They still had the vestiges of their Purple Fluid Exchange subsidiary of Virgin, using the moniker when it suited them. But they considered Naked Brain necessary in any case. Says Robber, "If you get kicked off a major label, no other label's going to touch you, and you can't get back on an indie label. I think that's why we had to start our own label really."

The fruit of the Bykers' winter recording sessions was *Cancer Planet Mission*, the band's second concept album of sorts. If *Stewed To The Gills* had been concerned with health care and environmental issues, *Cancer Planet Mission* took matters one step further. Mary explained in *Sounds* in March 1990 the inspiration for the album: "It's based on a book [of the same title] by Ludwig K Pullman [actually Ludwig F Pallmann], a German chappie who wrote it when he came into contact with the Itibi Ryan, who are aliens who observe our planet because it's a cancer planet — they've realised that the Earth shows all 14 symptoms of cancer." Asked about the veracity of the story, Mary replied, "Well if it's a hoax, it's a really elaborate one. But anyway, it seems to be true. The album's about loving your planet. God is nature, that sort of thing."

Mary says today, "Call us naïve, but *Cancer Planet Mission* was definitely the green thing… it was the way we were thinking and obviously we're hearing all these things, that was the beginning of the alarm." Acid rain was one of the major environmental issues at the time, and deforestation was becoming part of a wider consciousness. Mary considers the album a sort of clarion call. "Now the sea's just literally full of microbeads of plastic… *Cancer Planet*'s all about how wasteful we all are, and how we're just fucking everything up. That's what we were all about — that was our preoccupation… apart from going out and getting laid and pissed!"

The album opened with Welcome Cancer Planet Mission, which makes reference to a genie being let out of its bottle: 'Heaven only knows exercise your mind / Wake up to the things you know you should believe in / Heaven only knows green and tangerine aboard your yellow submarine / This is a genie, gotta heal it heal it so power kill above the cosmic glow.'

Taking the main guitar riff from Larks' Tongues In Aspic Part II by arch-progsters King Crimson, the track is a collision between punk and prog rock — two genres that did not sit comfortably together in the decade that followed punk. Indeed prog was considered archaic and uncool to many but the Bykers. Mary sees this attitude as typical of the UK. "In this country we always live with this thing about if you were a punk, you're not supposed to like Led Zeppelin, Pink Floyd — you're especially not supposed to like prog rock. But again, punk is meant to be about liking whatever you want to like... you know, being yourself, so musically bringing those things that were desperately unfashionable into it. We always thought some of that stuff was great music. Robin Trower and Caravan... we used to listen to, and obviously Hawkwind was massive, but then the American bands would have no compunction talking about Rush."

Another track on the album, Catalytic Converter, namechecks the Book of the Dead and makes a subtle reference to the book on which the album was based. It mentions the cosmophilosophy of the Amat Mayna, one of the central tenets of Pallmann's *Cancer Planet Mission*. More obvious to the layman is the device in the song's title. Increasingly, catalytic converters were a legal requirement for motor vehicles on Britain's roads, helping to filter out noxious pollutants. Says Mary of the track, "It's all about God is nature and nature is God." Another track that deals with the unwitting destruction of the planet is Bleed, in this instance the erosion of the ozone layer. Hope & Psyche and Satyr Naked are largely experimental tracks, with lyrics that draw on the cut-up techniques popularised by William Burroughs and David Bowie. A different version of Satyr Naked had been recorded for the unreleased Rektüm album and the track here exhibits the influence of the band's thrash metal alter ego. Lines such as 'subway brakes spit ozone, this is a no-go zone' lament the health of the planet, but are also a direct lift from Burroughs' *Naked Lunch*. "Yeah, it went through the David Bowie cut-up thing, and it's a lot of William Burroughs' words."

Advertise was a more poppy affair. It takes a swipe at the advertising industry from a vegetarian standpoint (the band being vegetarian). In a twist on an earlier refrain, the song concludes with the line, 'If you are what you eat then I must be an egg mayonnaise sandwich.' Mary admits this was his preferred sandwich from the sandwich shop near the studio. He holds Advertise in high esteem. "It's one of my favourite ever songs... I was trying to write an R.E.M. song. I really liked

them… they used to sing about the green thing… I loved It's The End of The World As We know It and stuff like that, that early stuff was great, and that was one of my influences." Not everyone in the band was similarly inclined. "It was very difficult sometimes to get Kev to like that… or The Pixies or Sonic Youth. He was quite difficult at times, you'd play him something and he'd look at you like, 'That's not heavy enough', whereas Robber was very openminded, and he'd like all sorts of music. R.E.M. was at the lighter end of the spectrum for Kev for sure, and it was quite difficult to get him interested in writing that kind of song."

Contrary to what one might initially think from the title, the track Demon Seed is not about the 1977 Donald Cammell sci-fi horror movie of the same name (but does sample dialogue from David Cronenberg's *Videodrome*). Mary explains how it came about. "That's Kev going into the studio, saying, 'I wanna write a really heavy song, it's gotta be the heaviest thing ever' and asking me to sing like I'm in a heavy metal band. He didn't write the lyrics, though. I did." Not far beneath the surface lies another environmental message. Says Mary, "It's about a car that kills people! It's sci-fi, *Mad Max*."

Among the other tracks are songs dealing with nationhood, the poll tax and insomnia, while Face At The Window makes reference to drug-taking and the attendant paranoia that can entail. Mr Muggeridge AKA What Happened To Malcolm? addresses the UK's waning sphere of influence on the global stage. The track opens to a sample of dialogue in which Malcolm Muggeridge, advocate of Christian morality, describes a field in which British Tommies in full battle dress are "having a quiet knock-up game of cricket" and that it makes him think of "Francis Drake and Plymouth Hoe!" Mary appears to be directing his opening salvo at the hagiographic Muggeridge: 'What happened to Malcolm, where did he go, please tell me frankly does anyone care or know?' But he also claims the song is directed at former Sex Pistols manager, Malcolm McLaren, and that its underlying message is whether the UK should bow down to America or embrace Europe.

The cacophony of the various samples throughout *Cancer Planet Mission* makes it a claustrophobic sounding album at times. There are some disposable tracks. The poll tax referencing song, Alive Oh?, and Candle come to mind, both replete with a slow-burning dub reggae skank vibe, popular with the crusty fraternity and traveller type bands. God Is The Kink is a direct lift from Death Of An Electric Citizen by one of the Bykers' most dominant influences, the Edgar Broughton Band. Insomnia adapts the lyric of a Gilbert and Sullivan song, written for the operetta, *Iolanthe*. A cheeky alteration implies that drug use is the source of sleeplessness. Mary admits that he still occasionally suffers from insomnia, notably when it's time to fill his in his tax return.

During the making of the album, Mary refuted the idea that the Bykers had set up their own label because they couldn't get a deal. He told *Sounds* that One Little Indian was interested in signing them but had taken too long. He revealed plans to sign other bands to Naked Brain but admitted that this wouldn't likely happen for another six months at least because the Bykers were "skint". There was plenty of Byker activity however, with mention of a new Rektüm record and a forthcoming dance EP, due to be recorded in March using the PFX moniker. Mary was also busy with a newly launched fortnightly club night, Megalomania Unlimited, at the Opera on the Green in Shepherd's Bush. The live act on the opening night featured the hotly tipped Keith Leblanc-produced Hotalacio, while DJ Mary Mary himself and guest DJ Pineapple Head spun "an eclectic mix of noise from Pixies to Public Enemy".

More intriguing was the news that Mary planned to record an album of Leonard Cohen songs. Mary had been supplementing his meagre income working at a vintage clothes shop with Bomb Party guitarist Steve Gerrard. Steve had fantastic music taste, recalls Mary, and "turned me onto the lyrical genius of Leonard Cohen. I listened to pretty much nothing else for a few months." *Sounds* got wind of the fact that Mary was a Cohen fan and announced a covers album. "Only I never got around to it. Lenny wasn't particularly fashionable then. He had the reputation of being music to slit your wrists to. I found his music to be quite the opposite of that — being very darkly funny and very uplifting!"

The Bykers may have been moving in a different musical direction, but it wasn't towards Leonard Cohen. On 8th March they played the London Astoria, as support for the Red Hot Chili Peppers on the last date of a sold out European tour. It is around this time they recruited an old friend, Ron Moreau. Rockit Ron, as he was commonly known, had first met the Bykers at a bill they shared with The Bomb Party and The Janitors in 1987. Born in the Northern Irish border town of Newry, growing up amid "the troubles", he was some years older than the Bykers. Ron recalls a strong hippie contingent in his hometown, and that he and his mates had been influenced by the records belonging to older siblings. Records by Ten Years After, Black Sabbath, Incredible String Band, Edgar Broughton Band, Pink Fairies and Hawkwind had been brought back from sojourns to London. His literary influences were suitably bohemian and included Jack Kerouac, Hunter S. Thompson and Tolkien. Ron got out of Newry as soon as he was able and spent a short time in the merchant navy — a decision influenced by Kerouac — before arriving in London. He was involved in the nascent acid house scene and even had a small home studio set-up, later selling the studio equipment to

"Mary [Byker] cites Rockit Ron Moreau as being the Bykers' 'conduit into the dance world'" — Kev and Rockit Ron (at back) soundchecking with Gaye Bykers On Acid, 1990.

the Bykers when he moved to America for a few years.

The Bykers had utilised sampling technology on *Drill Your Own Hole*, but not to their satisfaction. The album was still rock based and it made sense at the time to invest in equipment with a view to further experimentation. The Bykers had proved they could cut it with dance/rock crossovers: Their first song committed to vinyl (on the *Just Say Yeah* compilation, back in 1986) was After Suck There's Blow. A more dance-oriented version (The Blow-Back Mix) later appeared on the B-side of the Hot Thing 12-inch single. But an even earlier acid house remix of the track also exists, which, had it been released, would have preceded the acid house explosion in 1988 by almost a year. Mary recalls, "Some kid from Essex turned up, I can't remember his name, and did this proper acid mix… We met him when we were making the [*Drill Your Own Hole*] film, before acid house was big time, it was like bubbling underground, and people were talking about it. We all listened to this track, and even though we were pretty out there, we couldn't really fathom out what was going on at all… he did this remix which was just like a load of 808s and 707s bleeping around."

Robber recalls that he and Tony were both at the session and suggests they had a hand in the final mix. "The acid house remix was sorted out by our young hip A&R man at Virgin," says Robber. "He was already on the scene deejaying clubs. At the time he said 140 bpm was too fast — we invented acid techno before the London liberators!"

Regardless of how deep the Bykers were immersed in the acid house scene, its influence didn't permeate their own work to any great extent until 1990. Mary credits Rockit Ron Moreau as the Bykers' "conduit into the dance world". Prior to the Red Hot Chili Peppers show, Rockit Ron had been on hand in an advisory capacity in the recording studio. But on the night of the Chili Peppers gig, Mary insisted their newly acquired mixing desk was set up with the band on stage, almost as part of the line-up. Rockit Ron was behind the desk. Ron recalls being "cajoled with a little chemical inducement to enhance the band experience with some choice dance moves" and peppered the music with the band's "trademark zany samples from both their library and mine."

COACH ROCKIN' IN THE FREE WORLD — ROMANIA 1990

In a volatile era of political change, Crazyhead found themselves in Romania as unlikely musical ambassadors. The Soviet Union's sphere of influence over Communist Eastern Europe had diminished with the collapse of the Berlin Wall in November 1989 and Glasnost and Perestroika soon after. Uprisings brought an end to several dictatorships. Romania was one of the last Eastern Bloc communist countries and suffered one of the bloodiest revolutions. Although not strictly under Soviet control in the same way that Czechoslovakia or Hungary had been, Romania was still ruled by the iron fist of Nicolae Ceaușescu. Events that resulted in the overthrow of the Ceaușescu dictatorship moved swiftly throughout December 1989. A measure of the extent of this change was a request for British rock bands to play in the newly liberated country less than two months after Ceaușescu's removal. Andrei Partos and Darius Anastasescu of *Metronom*, a Romanian organisation concerned with the performing arts, appeared on British television and made the appeal.

Romania had enjoyed a small but flourishing "beat music" scene in the 1960s. But when Ceaușescu came to power in 1965, such liberties were taken away. The July Theses of 1971 heralded a nationalist cultural revolution, which in effect outlawed rock music, forcing it underground. Singing in English was banned, as indeed was singing in any language not of the Eastern Bloc (the exception being Italian and French). Ceaușescu was tireless in trying to prevent external influences reaching the people of Romania. Cut off from the rest of the world for

CHAPTER TEN

many years — socially, politically and culturally — the young people of Romania couldn't wait to throw open the doors once again.

'Rock For Romania' was a call to action with backing from the British Council. Veteran DJ Annie Nightingale implies in her autobiography, *Wicked Speed*, that she played a major role in galvanising the project. Nightingale claims she spoke to Fizle Sagar, a "rock-agent friend" of hers at the Station Agency, who in turn contacted Edward Craxton at the British Council. Sagar proposed three bands for the Romanian tour: Skin Games, Crazyhead and Jesus Jones. All were on Station's books, with Crazyhead and Jesus Jones even sharing the same label.

Time was of the essence. The British Council pulled strings to ensure that the bands, plus respective crews and equipment, were booked onto a chartered flight for Bucharest. The late addition of the Rock For Romania entourage delayed the flight by five hours, much to the chagrin of other passengers. These included a ski-party, whose ire was further compounded by a hitherto unscheduled stop at Timişoara, where the bands disembarked.

According to Nightingale, the initial five-hour delay had resulted in all three bands adjourning to the airport bar for a bonding session over much booze. The following morning however they got off to an early start and visited Timisoara's main square, Piata Operei. Hangovers soon dissipated on meeting some victims of Ceauşescu and on hearing witness accounts of those who had participated in the revolution. The horrors of the regime were still in evidence. They visited the spot where Ceauşescu's Securitate had opened fire on a demonstrating crowd just two months previously, massacring no less than 124 people. Now people lighted candles and replaced photographs of lost loved ones. Says Reverb, "The whole trip was pretty emotional. I think finding bullet holes in the hotel room windows in Timisoara put a bit of perspective on the whole affair. That was the first place we played. We arrived on the Saturday night, and most of us walked into town on Sunday morning. The central area was festooned with makeshift shrines to people, and there was a service of remembrance in the Cathedral. It felt a bit weird to be catapulted into someone else's grief, but everyone we met was really warm and welcoming."

Timisoara has long been regarded as the cultural capital of Romania (becoming, over 30 years later, the European Capital of Culture 2023). Home to artists, writers, musicians and other freethinkers, it is also widely considered to be the place where the revolution started. It is in Timisoara that the Rock For Romania tour opened with a showcase of primarily Romanian and Yugoslavian bands, who, for the first time in a decade, were permitted to sing in English. Terry Staunton of the *NME* described the line-up as "weak on technical expertise and inspiration but rich in enthusiasm". Belting out standards like Free's All Right Now and John Lennon's Power To The People, the audience "yelled along with a fervour to match Beatlemania". Watching from the wings the British bands were choked with emotion at the unbridled enthusiasm and sense of liberation.

The British contingent performed the following night. Still emotionally charged, they were further stoked by the packed 8,000-capacity sports arena. Not even the technical gremlins with Jesus Jones' sampler could detract from the effort and enthusiasm each band put into their set. Skin Games had "the honour of being the first western band to play in Timisoara since the revolution," noted Staunton. Next up was Jesus Jones. For an audience only familiar with western rock in the vein of Queen, Iron Maiden and Genesis, the use of samplers was akin to a revelation. According to Staunton, the Romanians were stunned into silence by Jesus Jones. Crazyhead, on the other hand, were much closer to what deprived music fans expected of a rock band. Indeed, the audience went into overdrive, and the resplendent Porkbeast became their champion, bedecked "in lime green shorts, Deadhead shirt, shades, cap and rusty handlebar moustache."

The tour was underway. After a short flight to Bucharest on Tuesday morning, the bands faced an unexplained hold-up exiting the airport. A hungover Anderson dealt with the tedium of the delay by crashing out on a bench and spilling his duty-free Jack Daniel's and two bottles of Romanian champagne on the airport floor. Nightingale notes how "Anderson woke, surveyed the scene, looked distractedly depressed, and went back to sleep". Shortly after arriving at the hotel, members of the entourage headed out to fulfil press commitments during which time Anderson swapped his Sony Walkman for a woolly army hat belonging to a Romanian soldier, complete with the insignia of the old regime. "We did the deal, then he insisted on having my tape as well," recalls Anderson.

Crazyhead's Anderson, Mike Edwards (Jesus Jones) and Wendy Page (Skin Games) in front of the Monument of The Heroes of The Fatherland, Bucharest, Romania, 1990.

CHAPTER TEN

Photo courtesy of Derek Ridgers. Originally printed in NME, 10th March 1990.

Crazyhead in front of former Romanian dictator Nicolae Ceausescu's Palace of the Parliament, Bucharest, Romania, 1990.

"Odd to think of that Romanian soldier getting down to my seventies rock tape, including Stones, Slade and Chicory Tip."

On Wednesday a party was held at the British embassy with the British bands as guests of honour. Ambassador Michael Atkinson was present, as was cultural attaché Ken Bamber, who produced his acoustic guitar for a singalong. Reverb and Porkbeast then regaled everyone with folk songs and standards, including Neil Young's Rockin' In The Free World. The lunchtime soiree evidently impacted on the show that night, held in an arena on the outskirts of the city. It was the turn of Jesus Jones to headline but all three bands returned to the Bucharest stage for the finale, a hastily rehearsed cover of Rockin' In The Free World. This became the closing standard for the shows on the tour, which Reverb admits to being a "good choice and was pretty current at the time. The plan was that the last band on — we alternated between the three UK bands — would lead the encore. I hadn't intended to sing it myself, but at the very last minute the tour manager came up and said that, as I was the only one who knew the words, I'd got the job. I don't normally sing lead vocals, and never in front of 8,000 people and the TV cameras. But I kind of got away with it."

Anderson agrees. "It was great to jam out with assorted members of Jesus Jones and Skin Games each night. It was Reverb's idea for all the bands to do Rockin' In The Free World. I didn't sing it because I didn't know the words. I

Photo courtesy of Crazyhead.

"Anderson swapped his Sony Walkman with a young Romanian soldier for his woolly army hat, replete with the insignia of the old regime" – Crazyhead with Romanian soldiers, Bucharest, 1990.

finally got to sing it about 20 years later with The Lazy Drunks, my rock/blues covers band in Cambodia."

The song had been written by Young soon after the inauguration of George H.W. Bush as US President. Allegedly it was intended as an indictment of western capitalism but in turn became a de facto anthem for the collapse of communism. Mike Edwards of Jesus Jones told the *Times*, 'It's a very ironic song… It's meant to be a condemnation of capitalism and the west, but here [in Romania] they imagine it is about liberty and a time for rejoicing. And who are we to tell them otherwise?"

Staunton reported that while the bands were all enthusiastically received, the combined finale was "solid gold mayhem [...] Boys no older than 12 are slam-dancing by the barriers and holding lighted matches at the same time." Bucharest in particular was nothing short of rapturous, with many members of the audience surging through the barriers and onto the stage. Security had no option but to let them through. Nightingale recounts how "artistes and the audience embraced and laughed in a confused emotional throng. Afterwards the bands were euphoric, buzzing off their heads, staring into space, reeling with adrenaline rush. The only way to come down was to party."

And party they did, although for Anderson it came with a price. "I remember getting really sick one night early on," he recalls, "vomiting and pissing blood with a high fever. I decided to have a wank to cheer myself up and ended up coming blood as well! I got taken to the doctors where I was told I had a dose of NSU [Non-Specific Urethritis, a type of sexually transmitted disease], and they were convinced I had been sleeping with some of the prostitutes that hung around the hotel. Not true, though some of our party had!" According to Anderson the infection was a malady from years ago, a "one in a thousand chance" as he puts it. "For the rest of the tour I was as sick as a dog, on prescription antibiotics and sober, while all the other musos were getting absolutely para every night on the oceans of free booze. No more Transylvanian lemon vodka for Anderson!"

Much of the next day was spent with Metronom, the collective that had instigated the tour. After this came the second performance at the Bucharest Arena. The British entourage invited local bands to perform and Rockin' In The Free World — concluding the show once more — met with even greater heights of emotion. Staunton called the audience "crazed" and added that "Porkbeast's reputation as the George Michael of the Eastern Bloc grows by the minute."

Despite the revelry, the bands never lost sight of the significance of the tour and their visit to Romania. There were some cynics. Correspondent for the *Times* Mike Nicholls suggested that the participating British bands were "marketing missionaries". Wendy Page of Skin Games countered, "We're not doing this for the money, we're doing it for the Romanian kids." She added that the bands were not in Romania selling records. "There's not even any record company

On the coach winding its way through the Transylvanian mountains into Brașov the band invented a new pastime — "coach surfing".

Photo courtesy of Fizzle Sagar.

"It took another rousing version of 'Rockin' In The Free World' before the audience entirely lost their inhibitions." Still from YouTube video, British Rock For Romania, Braşov, February 1990 — 'Rockin' in the Free World'.

involvement. No one from Epic or EMI is even here." Also on the side of the bands was Nightingale. She remarks that "it was obvious everyone was on this trip for the right reason. It was not about promotion or marketing or making money or getting a lot of good press. It was about three bands playing their hearts out to what turned to be the most appreciative audiences anyone had ever experienced."

No label or promotor had underwritten the tour, but rather the British Council. Edward Craxton offered his own rebuttal to allegations that the enterprise was a moneymaking promotional campaign: "Harvey Goldsmith reckoned any Romanian tour would cost at least £100,000. We've managed to do it for a quarter of that, and in the process spread enough goodwill to give British music a good name for years to come." In a final article about the tour, a more conciliatory Nicholls wrote in the *Times*, "Just a few months after December's bloody revolution, three British bands have toured Romania. The accepted wisdom of the music industry is that artists play abroad in order to sell records in other territories. In Bucharest, it seemed that this could not be further from the minds of the members of Skin Games, Crazyhead and Jesus Jones."

The final stop was Braşov, a three-hour coach ride that was tortuous and exhilarating in equal measure. Reverb had found a bottle of Southern Comfort in his bag, forgotten since departing Heathrow almost a week before. This

encouraged various hi-jinx, including bawdy country and western songs and a new pursuit: indoor coach surfing. All of this was to the backdrop of the Romanian countryside, with the coach winding its way through the Transylvanian mountains into Braşov. Support in Braşov was once again Romanian bands, Compact B and Holograf. But the atmosphere in Braşov was edgier, with soldiers and civilians fearing that members of Ceauşescu's Securitate and other supporters were hiding in the mountains, ready to regroup and perhaps take control of the country again. Or, at the very least, take the opportunity to kidnap these unlikely diplomats from the UK. Terry Staunton's description is dramatic. "Armed guards greet us and bundle us from the coach to the security of the building. Marksmen are in position on the roof, and inside the corridors and hall are patrolled by armed guards." Despite the tension, the show passed without incident. Staunton describes the Braşov audience as being as enthusiastic as any witnessed on the tour, whose noise "threatens to overcome the powerful western amplifier". He concludes that the bands "rip the hall apart, playing with a passion and commitment they're never likely to equal".

Sounds agreed. Journalist Mr Spencer noted how the crowd were at first reluctant to leave their seats — "old habits die hard here" — but that in the end "The Braşov show tops them all, as all five bands play the gigs of their lives". Another rousing version of Rockin' In The Free World loosened what remained of any inhibitions. Aided and abetted by Crazyhead, Jesus Jones and the two Romanian bands, it was the turn of Wendy Page and Skin Games to lead the encore. They had spent the coach journey to Braşov learning the words to the song. It proved a life-affirming moment for *NME* journalist Staunton, who describes "Charging into the crowd, who've now broken free at the front of the stage." By the end of the number, "I am crouched on the floor shaking frantically, tears pouring down my face having just experienced the greatest four minutes of my life."

The British entourage adjourned to the basement nightclub back at the hotel. Borrowing instruments from the club's resident musicians, Crazyhead knocked out versions of Heroin and I'm Waiting For The Man. Anderson recalls how Reverb had a penchant for this sort of thing, busking "in Leicester city centre in the early to mid-eighties, entertaining grannies with songs about smack addicts, often getting loads of cash around Christmastime." There was no time to sleep. The dash to catch the early flight out of Bucharest entailed an overnight coach ride through the Transylvanian mountains. Annie Nightingale describes how everyone was lucky to make it to the airport in one piece, given the drunken shenanigans of that journey. "Deafening sound systems appeared courtesy of

Jesus Jones, and upside-down bodies of half-clad men swung uncontrollably from one side of the bus to the other before crashing with a sickening thump to the floor, which was awash with spilt beer and littered with rolling empty champagne bottles."

As a postscript to the visit Nightingale relates that the flight back, as had been the case with the journey over, met with a five-hour delay. Crazyhead took the opportunity to decamp on the airport floor and, for no good reason, stripped off most of their clothes. Much like an episode in a predictable television sitcom, the skiing party that had been annoyed by the bands on the flight out, then rolled up and were annoyed all over again.

Despite the success and camaraderie shared in Romania, it stuck in Crazyhead's craw that their label sent Jesus Jones back on the road in March, no less as support to the Cramps on the European leg of a spring tour. This was followed with tours of Australia and Japan. Crazyhead were privileged to have supported Iggy Pop in Europe the previous autumn, but it was apparent that Balfe and EMI were beginning to favour Jesus Jones. Vom recalls how Andy Ross, the A&R man at Food, instrumental in signing Crazyhead, had soured toward the band by the time of the Romanian tour. "He just did not speak to us all week… he was just up Mike Edwards' arse — Jesus Jones — all fucking week! He thought, 'these are the boys, these are the boys!'"

This was perhaps inevitable given that Jesus Jones was achieving a greater degree of commercial success. The obverse effect was that Crazyhead were left by the wayside. To cap things off, soon after the Rock For Romania tour, Food signed a new band by the name of Blur.

MEGA IN NAMIBIA — 1990

Even if the band's own label was now less supportive, at least the British Council appreciated Crazyhead. Following Romania, the British Council offered the band another prestigious overseas gig. This time the location was Namibia in South Africa, where the Independence Day Festival was scheduled. It was a bill headlined by Ziggy Marley, son of legendary reggae artist and political activist, Bob Marley. Other artists included Thomas Mapfumo, Sipho Mabuse, Mango Groove, Brenda Fassie, and a Russian group called St Petersburg. Despite initial concerns that the audience wouldn't take to a band that was musically so different to the rest of the line-up, Crazyhead went down well with the 50,000 strong crowd.

Crazyhead's Vom mixes it up with the locals and Reverb nearly gets a mouthful at the Independence for Namibia Festival, March 1990.

The fledgling country of Namibia had only just received independence from South Africa, following a protracted guerrilla war that had raged since 1966. Crazyhead were happy to be part of this latest cultural attaché, organised again by Fizle Sagar. Restraint was not necessarily the order of the day in Namibia. Porkbeast holds his hands up to at least one incident. "I got us all thrown out of a United Nations party in Namibia for standing up to a local fascist Namibian mercenary who was itching for a fight and found me up for it. That did not go down well with the band though. I was always upsetting them with my wayward behaviour."

Anderson remembers the event differently. "Porkbeast did get in a row with a special forces mercenary guy, but the guy barked a lot louder! It became pretty obvious he was not to be messed with, hence Porkbeast had to leave for his own safety. He may have been asked to leave by the British Council too." It wasn't the first time that Porkbeast would bite off more than he could chew, and Anderson is put in mind of another encounter in which the wayward Porkbeast met the Northern Irish snooker maestro, Alex 'Hurricane' Higgins. "We were at an airport and the two of them collided. Porky bawled him out and Hurricane Higgins gave him a mega mouthful, telling him loudly to go fuck himself. Higgins may have been a small, wasted guy but he wasn't intimidated by the stocky, shades and leather-clad bassist. In fact, he looked ready to fight!"

Photo courtesy of Fizle Sagar.

Crazyhead made the most of the free Windhoek Namibian Independence Lager they were given on their visit to Namibia, March 1990.

The Independence Day Festival passed without incident and soon it was time to return home. The dilemma the band faced at this point was what to do with the bin-bag full of "killer African weed" that they had scored for nearly next to nothing on their arrival. The task of smoking it all before their departure proved too monumental, even for them, and so they left half for the hotel cleaners. There was a 12-hour stopover in Johannesburg, still in the grip of apartheid. The band decided it was preferable to sit up on the airport roof drinking, rather than join their soundman, who had gone for a stroll through the South African capital. "We settled there," says Anderson, "tucking into the crates of free Namibian Independence Beer the festival organisers had given us — 'cos they liked us so much! It was better up on the roof, as down on the ground it was full of apartheid-era Nazi security guards."

Anderson describes what happened next. "Reverb decided to drop his trousers and expose his large todger and gonads, and proceeded to do a rain dance in protest of South Africa's apartheid regime! We were shocked at the dare, but not as much as our poor soundman who [having returned to his hotel room, adjacent to the airport] picked that moment to wake from his slumber and peer out of his window." Anderson concludes, wryly, "The rain dance didn't bring rain, but a year later the apartheid regime started to crumble. And Reverb would never tire of reminding us of his bottomless, exposed rain dance, and his conviction that he had aided the fall of apartheid. Reverb, great songwriter and friend, but a twisted old fruit."

Crazyhead were also pencilled in for gigs in Lithuania that summer, courtesy of the British Council. But this showcase never materialised because of tensions between the recently self-proclaimed Lithuania and the Soviet Union. Political instability in the Baltics was probably not high on the band's agenda by this point; their own future looked to be in turmoil, courtesy of record label politics.

FOOD FAMINE

Less than a week before the flight to Namibia it was announced that Crazyhead had parted company with Food Records. The news broke with a cheeky fax sent to *Sounds* by the band's management. Thanks to the split, the fax stated, 'the band find themselves free to actually release a record in the near future'. Much like the Gaye Bykers when they parted with Virgin, it seemed a great weight had been lifted from Crazyhead. Talking to *Sounds'* Mr Spencer, Reverb reflected, "It changed a lot when EMI took over Food. There's all these people who tell you *this* is the way you should do things, and they're all totally obsessed with shifting a large amount of units, which is fair enough 'cos that's what record companies are there for. But the whole thing about a band like us is that the way we're going to shift units is by just being what we *are*, by being us, one hundred percent."

What Reverb had once considered "a great adventure" had turned into a "nightmare. We were finding we were having to argue and fight things out all the time." Anderson agrees: "Once the honeymoon period was over with Food/EMI, they were always trying to get us to soften, go more pop."

As to the softer approach that the band felt was being imposed on them, Reverb recalls Food's Dave Balfe's fleeting obsessions with certain bands. "Balfe had a thing about Aerosmith's Love In An Elevator and wanted us to be them that week." Even after the band was dropped by EMI, Balfe was willing to back Crazyhead should they decide to be more commercial. Reverb explains why the band was taken by the idea: "It would've been Food without EMI, if we agreed to work with some producers/songwriters Balfe had come across. It would've been studio-based writing with them and them acting as producers." In the end the band declined. "We'd already been pulled a long way from what was the essence of the band by the machinations of the EMI deal."

CANCER PLANET MISSION

The Bykers released *Cancer Planet Mission* on 2nd April 1990. This, their third studio album, marked the launch of their own Naked Brain label. To say the album was not a critical or commercial success would be something of an understatement. The reaction of the *NME* was entirely expected. Simon Williams

Front cover of Gaye Bykers On Acid's first self-released album on their own Naked Brain record label.

mauled it with a rating of two out of 10, going so far as to call it a "disgraceful" record. "GBOA administering GBH with disastrous consequences", he wrote. Williams concluded that the album was "a stunning load of bollocks.'"

Only marginally more favourable was Q magazine. Paul Davies dismissed the Bykers' lofty claim that they were throwing off the shackles of major label attitudes with their self-financed album, and saw it instead as them being dumped by Virgin. "On the evidence of [Cancer Planet Mission]," wrote Davies, "it's not difficult to see why." Conversely, one could easily have been moved to investigate the album following Davies' description of "a frazzled melange of hyperactive hardcore, grungey metal acid rock and caterwauling guitars loosely held together by sampled fragments of American B-Movies, grunting warthogs and scrambled dubwise experimentalism". He may not have liked the "tuneless dirge", but he made it sound exciting all the same.

Tim Peacock in Sounds mentioned the Bykers' problems with Virgin and described Cancer as a "typically idiosyncratic third album." While he praised some tracks — describing Face At The Window as "monstrously excellent, swamped in heavenly squeals from Tony's tortured axe and Mary's feverish, Antwan Keidis psycho blabber" — Peacock bemoaned the album's shortcomings, specifically a "distinct lack of bloody good tunes!" The suckerpunch he saved for last: The Bykers are "capable of a masterpiece but this inconsistent, burbling from the Tropic of Cancer falls woefully short."

The album is sprawling and at times disjointed, which to unsympathetic ears might make it a difficult listen. Many so-called "concept" albums have been misunderstood and Cancer Planet is no exception. Melody Maker's Push AKA Chris Dawes, was torn between criticism and praise. He described an album that had "no consideration for consistency", veering wildly from "rock slogs" to "pop kitsch", "Tex Avery cartoon themes", "meaty dub reggae", "undisguised

Hendrix rip-offs", "snatches of classical music", and "wailing bagpipes". Mary's vocals, he said, were fighting a losing battle against the multitude of "sampled voices." But Push is also conciliatory, saying that most of the songs "reveal not only a sense of the absurd but also a broad streak of originality". In conclusion, Push drew on the motto for the band's new label: "Beats for freaks? Absolutely."

Back cover of Gaye Bykers On Acid's first self-released album on their own Naked Brain record label.

Today, Robber stands by *Cancer Planet Mission* and considers it the Bykers' finest album: "I like that LP! It's raw and full of good, stolen Bad Brains and Peter Frampton riffs and ideas. It only cost us £3,000 to record!… You can tell by the production… which we co-produced a lot of, and we crammed in, Crass-style, as many tracks as we could onto it. I was also responsible for all those abstract tape loops, noises, and random samples in-between the songs which I had done on our four-track."

Two days after the release of *Cancer Planet Mission*, the Bykers embarked on a month-long UK tour, starting at the Windsor Old Trout and culminating at Manchester UMIST. If the album was met with a stony response in some quarters of the music press, the Bykers were still able to cut a dash as far as their live act was concerned, both visually and musically. Robber remembers that they'd bought a lot of white camouflage netting for the *Cancer* tour from Silverman's Army & Navy Store in East London. The flight cases that they'd bought with their Virgin advance were painted ultraviolet lime green. John Harris in *Sounds* had conceded that *Cancer Planet* was "something of a disaster", but he had nothing but praise for the band's performance at the Jericho Tavern in Oxford, citing it as "final proof that the Bykers are still today's definitive rock nutters". Face At The Window was a highlight amongst the new numbers, but it was old favourite Nosedive Karma that proved to be the pièce de résistance as far as Harris was concerned. He signed off: "Beautiful insane bliss — a live album must surely follow." It would be another 22 years before a semi-official

Photo courtesy of Andy & Julie Purple.

Gaye Bykers On Acid. Tony, Mary and Rockit Ron, on stage, 1990.

live album would see the light of day, *A Big Bad Beautiful Noise*.

Halfway through their promotional tour, the Bykers gave an interview to *Sounds*' John Robb. The album was barely touched on, suffice to say that Robber dismissed it as "crap" because "we were stoned when we produced it". Robb himself called *Cancer* "yet another unfocused rabble-rousing ramble through squelchy guitars, ridiculous lyrics and bad assed boogie". One of topics of conversation was the poll tax. Of the recent Anti-Poll Tax riots in Trafalgar Square, Robber described "total anarchy", likening the riots to recent events in Romania: "It was a case of people saying enough was enough." The Bykers bassist was surprised at how quickly the whole thing escalated: "The police just charged into the crowd with riot vans, they were taking people out, who were not doing anything, pushing people back till they were really panicking so, of course people thought, 'That's it', and went for them." The band's stance on the poll tax was clear, as Mary said: "The Gaye Bykers endorse non-payment." He was quoted in *City Limits*: "I'm not paying it, and I'd go to prison for it and so would most of my friends. These protests are great. People who have never demonstrated before are doing it."

It is surprising that so little of the interview was spent on promoting the new album. But perhaps the band's thoughts were already turning to their next project — a collection of dance-oriented numbers under the guise of PFX.

Gaye Bykers On Acid with new member and "dance consultant" Rockit Ron Moreau, 1990.

This was alluded to in the *Sounds* interview. Mary insisted the band wasn't simply jumping on a bandwagon with the mooted project. In the face of Robb's scepticism, Mary cited the fact he used to sell acid at the Haçienda and was a regular at acid house club Shoom. He also reminded Robb that he had released a version of The Temptations' Psychedelic Shack with the Big Zap side project back in 1987. There was some discussion about E culture, which revealed that Robber hadn't quite grasped the significance of MDMA yet, even if Mary had. Robber said, "Why not take some acid, some speed, a little coke and smoke some blow. I'm sure it has the same effect."

In an interview for Sheffield fanzine *Repeater*, the Bykers revealed more of their plans for a dance-oriented EP. Refuting the interviewer's suggestion that it was going to be an "acid house" EP, Mary and Rockit Ron, the band's new DJ and sample machine operator, conceded that it had a "dance sound". They agreed that the EP would be released under the PFX moniker, partly to circumvent the airplay restrictions the band suffered as Gaye Bykers On Acid. But a suggestion made by Rockit Ron that Andy Weatherall had been on board was apparently unfounded — as was the alleged altercation that unceremoniously nixed the supposed relationship. Ron claimed that Tony had beaten up and bound the DJ, songwriter, producer and key figure in the acid house movement. Band members are adamant that the story is a figment of Ron's overactive imagination. Says

Robber Byker at Dudley JBs, Cancer Planet Mission tour, 26th April 1990.

Photo courtesy of Andy & Julie Purple.

Mary, "Tony is, and was, a pacifist. I don't think he had it in him to beat up Andy Weatherall! Fighting is not something we got involved with!" Robber agrees, saying the story is bollocks. However, Mary believes that Gary Clail of the On-U Sound System was perhaps sounded-out to do a mix, being "more hardcore… more political… and more into… the crack better." If that partnership bore fruit it has yet to materialise.

The PFX dance EP and a similarly dance-oriented LP, *Pernicious Nonsense*, were released later that year. A dance track, Disinformation Rise And Shine, had been part of the Byker's set since they played the Reading festival, and they were now working on more material for what would become the dance rock crossover EP, S.P.A.C.E. The *Cancer Planet* tour began to reflect the new Bykers sound. Once the tour was over, and while preparing for the next one (another tour of North America), the band immersed themselves in their dance projects.

BLACK IS BLACK

Cut adrift from EMI, Crazyhead found salvation of sorts in a new deal with Black. Black, or more accurately its parent company FM Revolver, is perhaps best known for an altercation with The Stone Roses, when it re-released an early single to capitalise on the band's success. In January 1990, The Stone Roses vandalised property belonging to their former label manager, Paul Birch, throwing paint at him and his wife and a Mercedes, causing in excess of £15,000 worth of damage. The band was duly prosecuted.

Shortly after this incident, negotiations between FM Revolver and Crazyhead took place. Nick Raybould, in-house graphic designer for the label, reconsidered Crazyhead a step up for FM Revolver: "I was already very familiar with Crazyhead, having seen them live and splashed all over *Sounds* and the *NME*. I also owned a couple of singles. During one of our silly Monday briefing meetings, Dave Roberts, our A&R director, mentioned that we had a chance of signing them. I was rather startled by this, as they were a very cool band. Way cooler than most of the bands still on our books."

Raybould's enthusiasm resulted in a trip to a Crazyhead gig in Manchester the following week, accompanying Birch and Roberts (in a freshly resprayed Mercedes). Raybould remembers that when they arrived at the venue, Crazyhead "were already on and really going for it. I immediately pushed my way through to the front to get amongst it all, soaking up the raucous noise. I promptly got an elbow in the face. Their crowd were a lot wilder than I was familiar with. Black Country hairies, like Pop Will Eat Itself and The Wonder Stuff, seemed to attract a more gently boisterous crowd. I dunno, or maybe it was just a Manchester thing."

FM Revolver signed Crazyhead to Black soon after the Manchester gig. The demos previously rejected by EMI were approved by Birch and plans for a new single and album were quickly set in motion. The band approached former Vibrators bassist Pat Collier to produce their second album. Collier was a renowned producer in his own right and had established Alaska Studios as a rehearsal space for his new band, The Boyfriends. Alaska, of course, was where the Bykers had made their second home for much of the last two years. Collier had since set up Greenhouse Studios on Old Street, which is where Crazyhead went to record their forthcoming album.

Tasked with designing a sleeve for the new single, Raybould remembers being thrilled at the opportunity to do "something groovy... Up until now, my sleeves for Revolver had consisted of a band photo sent to me by a bossy and deluded manager and a rubbish logo to be superimposed over, either that or some awful, airbrushed art that was either skulls or babes, or both!" He familiarised himself with the Crazyhead demos, which he considered "very good... Mostly rough and ready garage guitar rock that reminded me of The Stooges, punctuated by twangy guitar solos, and held together by a kicking rhythm section."

Raybould worked on the sleeve with Reverb (who kept calling Raybould "chap" in typical idiosyncratic Leicester fashion) and decided on a style that owed more than a passing nod to The Wonder Stuff. According to Raybould, Crazyhead were all in favour of introducing a new logo or dropping their logo altogether. He talked them out of it. "I liked it and thought it best to keep it for

Photo courtesy of Fizle Sagar.

Fizle Sagar with Vom and Reverb in Graceland, an Elvis Presley themed restaurant on Old Kent Road, summer 1990.

now," he recalls. "They'd not released anything for a while and a bit of familiarity might be useful for a while."

Says Reverb, "Pat Collier had a good track record. We recorded Everything's Alright over a weekend, then went back to record the album a short while later. It was done a lot quicker than *Desert Orchid* and was a lot less painful." Anderson recalls cajoling Collier to regale them with tales of the early punk scene and The Vibrators, especially the making of Baby, Baby, which was a favourite with the band.

Crazyhead alternated their time at Greenhouse between recording the album and watching England's progress in the Italia 90 World Cup. Something more serious began to cast a shadow over events, however, notably the looming Gulf War, a US coalition in a war against Iraq. The song Some Kinda Fever was rewritten in response to the conflict, the last song they recorded in these sessions. The song opens with the lyrics, 'Let's go to war then watch it on TV / Too much mirth at the end of the money for me / And sometimes when there's no one else around it's like some kind of fever shines down.' The song's ominous bridge features a slow, pounding, death-beat drum and the howling of air raid sirens.

Once recording on the album was completed, Collier, Reverb, and Vom began

Vom, Reverb and Fast Dick in Graceland, an Elvis Presley themed restaurant on Old Kent Road, summer 1990.

Photo courtesy of Fizle Sagar.

work on production and mixing, leaving the rest of the band free to enjoy some downtime. Porkbeast, ever the keen antiquarian, went to look at some standing stones and irked an angry famer who chased him off his land with a shotgun. The tale found its way into Julian Cope's superlative guide to Britain's megalithic sites, *The Modern Antiquarian*. Referring to Porkbeast as 'my sensitive friend Alex Peach', Cope mused, 'What energies did Alex contribute to the stones as he ran screaming into the night? It must surely be difficult to measure ancient subtle energies when such modern technological/human paranoiac energies are bouncing around.'

Collier remembers another incident in which he and the band piled into a Chinese restaurant on Old Kent Road called Graceland. "Its unique appeal was the proprietor who came on as Elvis around 11pm and sang with a heavy Chinese accent," says Collier. "He apparently had another restaurant somewhere where he did an early set, so when he got to us, he wasn't entirely sober, which probably aided, rather than hindered, the overall effect. The performance was remarkably well received, with much dancing on tables and Kev kissing Elvis full on the lips — which didn't go down so well."

It seemed things were beginning to look up for Crazyhead.

IT'S A TRIP! IT'S GOT A FUNKY BEAT AND I CAN BUG OUT TO IT!

Having drafted Jon Langford and Ian Caple to help with some of the production and engineering, the Bykers' excursion into dance territory continued with what would become the S.P.A.C.E. EP and the *Pernicious Nonsense* album. The rigours of touring, drinking, and drugging had taken a toll on Robber and he returned to Leicester for a break. For the most part the band booked studio time and pressed on without him, rehearsing and recording new material. When Robber did turn up at sessions, he was told that, rather than learn bass parts for the songs written in his absence, it would be quicker for the band to lay down the basslines on his behalf. Robber walked out and left the band to it and for a while took a job as a courier.

Robber says he hardly played a note on the album, with most of his parts filled by Tony. "I didn't have much to do with *Pernicious Nonsense* 'cos I kind of threw a wobbly. I walked out halfway through the recording of it. I played bass on a few bits and pieces, and I did a bit of the production work later on, but that

was mainly Kev, Mary, and Tony." His main contribution to the album, as he recalls, were a "Pink Floyd sounding groove" (presumably the snatch of Astronomy Domine at the end of Killer Teens In New Orleans), the bass line on Disinformation Rise And Shine, and the bass solo on John Wayne Was A Fag (Kev played the main fuzz bassline). Robber admits he was losing interest by this time: "the rock'n'roll dream was over for me by then and my full-time drug habit was consuming my time." He

Cover of dance orientated 12" EP S.P.A.C.E. released under the pseudonym Purple Fluid Exchange (PFX)

adds, "I don't like that LP, it sounds like half ideas, and there is not one stand-out song on it. …The others may disagree."

Of the sessions, Ian Caple says, "By then I had got my own studio — the Stone Room — just round the corner from the Townhouse in Shepherd's Bush. It was a smaller, much cheaper version of the Townhouse. I was again working with Jon on a Mekons album, and the Bykers had been dropped by Virgin. They only came into the studio for three or four days, I think. It was great to work with them again — the same band except they also had a DJ with them who was really good. I don't remember much about the sessions. I think they had some tracks already recorded and we did some wacky 12-inch mixes." Tellingly, he adds how the band "weren't the happy bunch that I knew from a few years before".

Jon Langford remembers the sessions with fondness. "The stuff at the Stone Room was fun, except for the microwaved asparagus we ate that made our pee turn brown and noxious! Tony did a talk-over through various guitar pedals for a Mekons track called Hashish In Marseilles during those sessions. But again, mostly good-humoured chaos — I loved being around the Bykers, but probably wasn't the best influence at the time."

Hashish In Marseilles takes its title from an essay written by twentieth-century German philosopher, Walter Benjamin. The Mekons track was included on their *F.U.N. 90* EP that, as Langford says, sees the Bykers guitarist reciting parts of the essay through a variety of effects pedals. The result is psychedelic in a queasy kind of way: the pedals sound like auditory hallucinations and Tony's distorted voice undulates as it pans back and forth from channel to channel. The track ends with a distant sample of Judy Garland singing Somewhere Over The Rainbow. The Mekons EP also includes a track called One Horse Town that incorporates by rant by gonzo American rock journalist Lester Bangs. The *Chicago Tribune* said of the track: 'House music is in vogue and the Mekons don't want to get left behind.'

If *F.U.N. 90* was the Mekons' reaction to house music, then S.P.A.C.E. was a wholehearted embrace from the Bykers. The lead song on the 12-inch single was laden with samples, an epic 11-minute dance crossover driven by Tony's funky guitar and Robber's motorik I Feel Love bassline, over which Mary rapped and sang. Embracing the burgeoning dance scene with the fervour of lysergic zealots and MDMA proselytisers, the song manages to capture the zeitgeist. It features Johnny Marr's shimmering guitar from The Smiths' How Soon Is Now? and snatches of contemporary acid house hits such as Technotronic's Get Up (Before The Night Is Over). It also included a sample of Brother J.C. Crawford's rabble-rousing testimonial to the MC5 from their 1969 album *Kick Out The Jams*. Admittedly, some of Mary's rapping appears dated today, but it holds its own against many indie rock contemporaries who ventured into similar territory. To quote a sample on S.P.A.C.E. from B-Boy Bouillabaisse by the Beastie Boys: "It's a trip! It's got a funky beat and I can bug out to it!" That about says it all. ☠

CHAPTER ELEVEN

I'M NOT AMERICAN YET, BUT WHAT A STATE I'M IN

FOLLOWING UK GIGS THAT SUMMER AT THE LINK ARTS Studio in Swindon and Tufnell Park Dome in London, the Bykers set off again in August to tour the United States and Canada. But all was not well in the Bykers camp, as Robber explains, "Officially, in my mind, I was no longer a part of Gaye Bykers On Acid, and was talked back into the band to tour the USA. Good job, as I had the only credit card at the time!"

The first gig of their second North American tour was at CBGB in the Bowery in Manhattan, where they were supported by an all-female trio from Minneapolis, Babes in Toyland. It was quite something to play the legendary Bleecker Street venue where many New York punk acts had cut their teeth. Rockit Ron says, "Tradition has it whenever a UK band is in town ex-pats congregate, and we met up with some proper hardcore Bykers fans."

One of these Brits was Robbie Lunnon, in New York with two friends. He recalls that the venue and audience were not what he'd imagined them to be. Tables extended almost up to the stage, and the audience mainly sat, watched, and politely applauded between songs. Lunnon confesses, "We were tanked up to the max and having none of that sitting down malarkey. We just went berserk from start to end." Naturally, the Bykers appreciated the boisterousness of their compatriots and invited the trio backstage. The

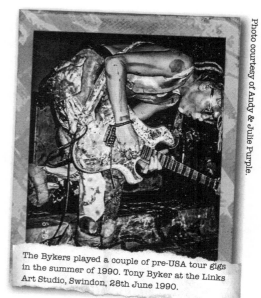

The Bykers played a couple of pre-USA tour gigs in the summer of 1990. Tony Byker at the Links Art Studio, Swindon, 28th June 1990.

The Gaye Bykers On Acid arrive at CBGB, New York, August 1990.

bar had closed by this time, but the Bykers had been given cartons of beer that they shared with their fellow Brits, who were more than happy to indulge.

The Bykers also had the pleasure of meeting the legendary Dennis and Lois, a couple who met at the club. Over the years they became regular fixtures at punk and indie gigs by visiting Brit bands. Dennis and Lois even had a song named after them by Happy Mondays on their *Pills 'N' Thrills And Bellyaches* album. The couple have also collected memorabilia over the years, and, on their apartment wall next to a leather jacket and ripped jeans worn by members of The Ramones, are framed socks worn by the Bykers at CBGB.

Commencing in New York, the tour went north and then west in and out of Canada, to the West Coast, through the south and back to the East Coast. Says Kev of the border hop into Canada, "Going from America into Canada was no problem at all. Border officials would invite us into the office — there were pictures of the Queen on the wall, it was all very nice — and they'd chat to us about what we were doing there. 'You guys, you're in a band?' The only problem was going back into America!" Kev thinks that one of the US border guards took exception to Ron because he'd "given them some lip" when leaving the States. Ron had the misfortune of encountering the same guard when re-entering the States, who claimed Ron's "attitude problem" was reason enough to have him deported. Ron was not deported but re-entry into the States was

Photo courtesy of Tony Byker.

Mary Byker and Hoppy with Lori Barbero from Babes In Toyland, New York, August 1990

refused. Ron's attitude may not have helped his case, but the real reason he was stopped, according to Ron, was a previous drugs conviction. He says, "Extensive research had come up with an LSD bust when I was returning from Stonehenge in 1974 — yes, I am that old — with a tab and a half of the finest purple blotter… It was enough for the US authorities to refuse me re-entry."

The band left Ron in Canada and pressed on with the tour without him. Kev says with some regret, "It was such a shame to lose Ronnie. You wouldn't have thought that would happen in a million years. It was just one of those things. It was sad to see him go but we had to continue, you know. We had contracts to fulfil."

The incident echoes that of Hawkwind many years earlier. During their 1975 North American tour, Hawkwind decided to leave bassist Lemmy in a Canadian jail while they continued without him. Lemmy's problems had been with the Canadian authorities, whereas Ron's were with the Americans. Furthermore, Hawkwind had been in a position to fly out an experienced replacement at the drop of a hat; the Bykers couldn't afford any such luxury and had to muddle on without Ron. Luckily, Penny had experience with samplers on the 1988 US tour and stepped up to the plate. Mary says, "We managed to function quite well without Ron… I wouldn't say he was like a Bez [Happy Mondays' dancer], because he actually used to play stuff, but once he'd gone, we figured out a way to

Mary and Kev in a hotel room somewhere in the USA or Canada, August/September 1990.

get by without him, although we desperately missed him, obviously."

The Bykers were to face another border incident, but this one due to an error with paperwork. After playing Minneapolis, the Bykers headed north to Winnipeg. Unfortunately, they forgot to get the carnet for their music equipment signed and were sent back to the US. Robber gave Hoppy a break and took over the drive for the reverse border crossing. Robber explains what happened next. "They jumped on us and took the van and U-Haul trailer to bits! The customs guards lined us all up in the office. The guards declared, 'You guys are in serious trouble, we have a zero tolerance of drugs,' before waving the van keys around demanding to know who the driver was. I sparked up 'Me', not knowing what they had found." Given their appearance, the Bykers were often a target for over-zealous authority figures and so tended to be diligent and had the foresight to remain clean for the border crossing. Nevertheless, a roach was discovered in the van's ashtray and two cannabis seeds in Mary's wallet. The drama wasn't over yet. Tony recalls, "I also remember them looking through our photos and finding one of us puffing away! They asked 'So, do you have anything in the U-Haul trailer? Shall we take that apart and search it?' At this point I completely confessed to the guy that we were indeed a 'crazy rock'n'roll pot-smoking band', but 'I must also tell you that we would not jeopardise our tour by bringing weed over the border' and told him that we actually cleaned out the van especially before we came to

The Bykers' hired U-Haul trailer outside the Satyricon Club in Portland Oregon, September 1990.

the border and were completely shocked we still had the two seeds. The customs guy seemed cool with that explanation and let us carry on!" The upshot was that Mary and Robber both received on the spot fines of $250 and were made to write letters of apology to the US government.

Touring was not without its temptations and the attendant pitfalls. Kev recalls some of the riders provided by promoters. "To be honest, the back of the U-Haul looked like fucking Oddbins! We were rattling around with all this booze — we can't drink all of this!" Wherever they went, the band was pursued by hangers-on and dealers with all manner of weed and other pharmaceuticals. Kev continues, "They would literally give you anything you wanted. Plus, if you go to America and you're in a band called Gaye Bykers On Acid — the people that were turning up to see you! They were just bringing stuff to you, stuff that I'd never even heard of, saying, 'God man you gotta try some of this, get some of this down you maaaaan!' And they were bringing us this mescaline stuff, and… Fucking 'ell have you ever tried that? It's nice!"

Kev recounts a mescaline experience that took place when one of the Canadian gigs was cancelled. The tour party was stuck in a hotel in Edmonton, the rain hammering down outside and with nothing to do. Kev had picked up a few pellets of the psychedelic cactus on their travels and shared them with Penny and Hoppy. Kev recalls that after taking the mescaline he decided to have a bath and while soaking in the tub, looked at his body turning into an orangutan with long orange hair. "I didn't give a shit," he says. "In fact, I was quite happy about the whole thing!" As his metamorphosis continued, he got out of the bath and opened the blinds. "I squinted my eyes and out in the car park Penny and Hoppy were in the rain and they were sort of holding hands and twirling round together in a sort of weird, fucking manic, dance together. And I just stood there looking at them dancing in the rain in the light of the car park, and I thought, 'Yeah, that's fine, that happens all the time doesn't it?'" Kev concludes, "I was a bit disappointed when I woke up the next morning and I wasn't an orangutan anymore."

EVERYTHING'S ALRIGHT

By the time the Bykers finished their second stint in Canada, heading down the West Coast back into the States, Crazyhead were about to embark on a major tour in the UK. It was to promote their latest single Everything's Alright and their forthcoming album *Some Kind of Fever*. The tour opened at the Tic Toc in Coventry, followed by gigs in Leeds and Manchester, before returning to the Midlands to play that bastion of Black Country music venues, JBs in Dudley. Reviewing the gig for *Sounds*, Frank Arroll likened the band to "pimply, hairy-arsed grunge with nary a sniff of a poncey ballad". He was moved to say that the new numbers were on par with those on *Desert Orchid* and may have had a point when he determined them "neither extreme enough for youthful death/thrash metallers, nor polished enough for your CD types into US-style stadium pap".

Nick Raybould's cover for Crazyhead's 'Everything's Alright' single was in stark contrast to all those earlier retro sixties style single covers.

The single was released

early in September, backed with two demos Crazyhead had recorded at Andy Povall's studio in Leicester: I Can Only Give You Everything and an instrumental, Death Ride To Osaka (formerly Looking For A New Deal). Reverb says the title comes "from a 1983 film about the white slave trade in Japan. I don't think I was crazy about the film but loved the title". Nick Raybould's artwork graced the sleeve, featuring the jagged Crazyhead logo and the two-tone faces of each band member against a black background, a stark contrast to the retro sixties-style sleeves of Food and Parlophone. There were similarities to Wonder Stuff artwork, and it could be construed as an attempt to redefine the band as a product of the nineties rather than sixties garage throwbacks.

The single received mixed reviews. John Harris of *Sounds* awarded it seven out of 10, saying that the Keith Richards guitar licks helped transform what could've been a mediocre effort into "something rather groovy". He suggested that Crazyhead would be worthy playing support for The Rolling Stones. *Melody Maker*'s Andrew Mueller was downright facetious. In a combined review with The Family Cat's Place With A Name, he said, 'This sort of anaemic guitar pop-by-numbers is the inevitable result of existing on a diet of overcooked mushy vegetables and the lust-crazed pursuit of badgers and weasels that won't come near you because you poms never wash. Right kids?'

The single's distinct psych-pop sensibility and Middle Eastern overtones had the potential for indie — if not mainstream — chart success. But without the clout of a major label it bombed. However, Reverb still ranks it as one of his best songs. "Even Balfe thought it should've been a hit," he says. "Like Rags, it was written using a different tuning. I wrote it while I was living in Saxby Street in Leicester. It was a crazy area at the time. It's about the life I was living and trying to keep your head up when so many people around me were losing theirs. I'm quite proud about this one, it's up there with So Amazing and Baby Turpentine as far as my compositions go."

Sadly, everything wasn't alright in the Crazyhead camp. Porkbeast was becoming disillusioned with Reverb's songwriting capabilities and dictatorial grip on the writing. There was also disagreement about the title of the forthcoming album. Porkbeast refused to put his name to the mooted *What 'Ave You Come As?*, preferring the more mystic-sounding *Magic Eye* (the title of one of the tracks on the album). *Some Kind of Fever* was the compromise, a variation on the track Some Kinda Fever. Porkbeast felt increasingly marginalised by the rest of the band, in particular Reverb. He says, "There was total lack of respect for me after that."

The Bykers' tour truck and U-Haul combo. They disconnected the mileometer and reconnected it again at the end of the trip.

Photo courtesy of Tony Byker.

GIBBY, GIBBY, GIBBY
A MAN AFTER MIDNIGHT

Back in North America the Bykers' truck and U-Haul combo rolled from state to state, greedily clocking up miles and burning up the tarmac. Tony recalls how they managed to negate much of the cost of long-distance travel as part of the hire agreement. "The Dodge van hire company charged for mileage, and that would have cost us a fortune, so we disconnected the milometer and reconnected it at the end, but also had to carefully time it with various service stops — that was quite something!"

The band's name raised the hackles of the redneck element in some places they visited. Kev recalls an incident at a little venue somewhere in Texas, where much of the audience had come for trouble. "It was a bit like that scene out of *The Blues Brothers* where the band puts chickenwire in front of the stage, so we had to get out of there pretty quick before they started dishing out whatever they do to the— 'Fucked Up Faggots On What?' That's what they said to us! This big bloke came up to me and he just leaned down on me with his beer-stinking breath and says (in redneck Southern drawl), 'You're the Fucked Up Faggots On What?', and

I said, 'Well, I'd love to stay and chat with you, sir, but I really have to run away — I can't deal with this!'" Although the Bykers were fans of *The Blues Brothers* (taking inspiration from the roadhouse scene for their own *Drill Your Own Hole*), they were not fond of its real-life counterpart: a mob of angry shit-kickers hurling abuse at them. Such situations were quite scary and not dissimilar to those witnessed on the Sex Pistols' final tour at venues like Randy's Rodeo.

Thankfully, not everyone in Texas was as intolerant and the Bykers found time to make a detour to the Butthole Surfers' ranch in Driftwood, 30 kilometres outside Austin, Texas. They'd long admired the Surfers, not just for their stance on anti-censorship issues, but for pushing boundaries in terms of musical direction. Arriving at the Cannibal Club in Austin for a soundcheck, the Bykers were greeted in the venue carpark by Buttholes' frontman Gibby Haynes and bass player Jeff Pinkus. "They both had these fuck-off muscle cars!" recalls Mary, who admits, "we worshipped the Butthole Surfers!" Driving to the Buttholes'

ranch in Gibby's hot rod was a career high. A meeting had been arranged to discuss the release of a Butthole Surfers offshoot album on the Bykers' Naked Brain label. "On reflection," says Mary, "it wasn't the greatest thing committed to vinyl, but it was worth it for hooking us up with the band."

At the ranch Gibby's Jack Russell, Mr Cigar, jumped onto Gibby's lap and pissed himself with excitement. Robber remembers with amusement, "The Butthole Surfers thought me and Mary were gay lovers when we stayed at the ranch in Texas and set aside a nice bed for us." Kev's recollection of the ranch is more narcotic in tone, in that Gibby "was

Gaye Bykers On Acid and Last Rites poster, Cannibal Club, Austin, Texas. September 1990.

"Cabin fever... after being cooped up in the tour van for miles upon miles." Gaye Bykers On Acid taking a break on the road somewhere in America.

smoking some serious tackle — I don't know what it was". But in any case it prompted a spiel about *Mary Poppins*. Says Kev, "Gibby goes, 'D'you ever see *Mary Poppins*? I love *Mary Poppins*, I love it! D'you see Dick Van Dyke? Yeah, Dick Van Dyke... Suck my Dick Van Dyke!' And we're all sitting there thinking, 'Well, we're in his house, so obviously we have to appreciate the young fellow', so we just sat there staring at him as he went off on one... He just went off on this fucking *Mary Poppins*/Dick Van Dyke thing, and just didn't shut up for hours!"

The combination of strong weed and Gibby's raving eventually took its toll on Kev who, in need of respite, sought an escape route by telling Gibby he was off to bed. The Butthole Surfers frontman rejected the idea, saying something along the lines of, "You don't go to bed now, you don't go to bed — you smoke this! You sit up maaan!" Recalls Kev, "We were all big Butthole Surfers fans and had been for a long time, and he was our hero, and there we are sitting in his ranch in Texas with him ranting at us. 'Yeah, you can rant at us as long as you like, mate, hahahaha, I'll sit here and take this, that's no problem at all!'... A nice man, though, a really nice man."

The psychedelic shenanigans continued after Texas when, in the Midwest, the band met someone claiming to be Timothy Leary's cousin. He gave Robber a sheet of LSD blotters that Robber secreted in the battery compartments of his effects pedals for the rest of the tour, tearing off tabs for the entourage as

and when required. An audio recording of a gig at The Outhouse in Lawrence, Kansas, would seem to affirm that certain members of the band had indulged prior to the performance. Experiencing technical issues, Robber stops to talk about the t-shirts for sale in a manner that suggests he is completely off his head. Tony and Kev improvise some funky psychedelia and Robber continues to hawk Bykers' merchandise to the audience, until Mary announces the problem is fixed and dedicates the next song, Cocaine Metallic Be-Bop, to former manager Stacey Lafront.

After Kansas, the Bykers proceeded south. Like Crazyhead, they often faced gruelling drives between destinations. Tony recalls how they adapted the truck as best they could into their home. "We lived in that van. It became really smelly after a while, especially by the time we reached Florida, and tempers were getting tight too! Because we had to sleep in the van the journeys were so long, we each had a row of seats, and we built a platform off the back seat so that someone could sleep on top, also creating 'Kev's Kennel' between the back seats and the back door. The only way he could get out was if we opened the back doors!"

Despite the cabin fever the band was still pulling together to kick out tight performances, as evidenced in Florida. Here the Bykers were supported by local band Psycho Tribe at Club Detroit, within the Jannus Landing venue in St. Petersburg. Reporting for local music magazine *Thrust*, journalist 'Stiff' said he fully expected the local heroes to blow the Bykers away, just as they usually did when opening for visiting headliners. He admitted he had underestimated the Bykers and conceded that he had witnessed one of the best shows he'd seen in a long time. After two more dates in Florida, the band headed back to New Jersey via Raleigh, North Carolina, to the 9:30 Club in Washington, D.C., before ending up back on the Eastern seaboard in New Jersey at The Fast Lane, Asbury Park.

TIMOTHY LEARY'S COUSIN SOLD ME BAD ACID

The last night of the US tour didn't pass without incident. "We all dropped the last of the LSD I scored from Timothy Leary's cousin," recalls Robber. "Kev dropped quite a few tabs, I think, and freaked out. He ran off the stage halfway through and hid in the dressing room and wouldn't come out. Penny played drums, Mary tried to get my cock out and suck me off, but I, rolling around on the floor, fought back for two whole songs! It ended when I smacked him over the head with my bass guitar. The locals loved it and thought it was all part of the show — they loved us!"

Because they couldn't get anything to smoke, Kev, Robber, and Mary decided to take acid before they went on stage. Kev remembers that the effects of the LSD were deceptive; nothing seemed to be happening as far as Kev was concerned, and he shrugged it off as one of those things. Then suddenly the acid took hold. "I remember about halfway through the first song it sort of kicked in, and every time I hit the drum it was so loud it was freaking me out. And then I looked out to the crowd and thought 'Uh oh, everyone's looking at me'... It was coming up really strong, it was very, very strong acid." Kev's paranoia intensified as he imagined the music becoming louder and the audience all staring at him. Robber had already stripped naked, joined soon after by Mary, which only compounded Kev's anxiety. Says Kev, "Mary jumped on Robber's back, but both were totally bollock naked. He's riding around on his back, and by this point I'm fucking freaking out!" It was too much for the tripped-out drummer, who leapt off his stool, ran backstage, flung the fire doors open, and ran into the street — where he was greeted by the sight of three police cars, lights flashing and sirens wailing. In his irrational state of mind, he thought they'd come for him, so ran back inside. Tony, who hadn't taken anything, was standing on the stage in disbelief. "You've got Mary on Robber's back, naked," laughs Kev. "Tony saw me run across the stage with fear on my face because I thought the police had come for me! I ran past, pushed Tony out the way and locked myself in the changing room!"

The bewildered Tony didn't know what to do at this juncture. The band was barely halfway through the set, the drummer had gone AWOL, and the singer and bassist were naked and riding each other bareback around the stage. Meanwhile, Penny had gone backstage to try to coax Kev out of the changing room, but to no avail. As Penny re-emerged, the audience was applauding, believing the madness was all part of the act. He managed to bring some order to the proceedings as he took to the drums, and the rest of the band composed themselves enough to continue the set. Kev concludes, "I can't remember what happened after that. I was a gibbering wreck... I was probably in need of therapy to be honest! I don't know how they got me out of the changing room, but after that it seems a blank."

What a way to end their North American tour! After two months of intensive touring, the mayhem in Florida seemed a perfectly logical finale and now the Bykers were headed home.

SOME KIND OF FEVER

Some Kind of Fever, Crazyhead's long awaited second album, was released on 19th November 1990, in a sleeve that featured artwork by Nick Raybould. He'd been "sketching out ideas" on the assumption that the album would be called *Magic Eye*. Raybould says, "It was an awesome anthem when they played it live, and had a very infectious Hot Love-like singalong outro, that some nights went on and on and on, building and building... I liked the inner centrespread of Alice Cooper's *Love It To Death* sleeve and was thinking of doing something along those lines." Raybould toyed with the idea of shooting the band through a fisheye lens, but when informed by the label boss the art for the album needed to be less labour-intensive than the single, he scaled things back. He decided to take photographs of the band on the road promoting Everything's Alright and went to see them play at JBs in Dudley. Despite the lively audience, and the photos being rough and ready and authentic — "Ramones-like, almost," says Raybould — in the end they were rejected. Says Raybould, "owing to the slow shutter speed required for the low lighting, they were often blurred. Let's face it, Crazyhead don't stand still much onstage at the best of times!" Returning to Leicester, Raybould took what appeared to be a live photo of the band, but one that was actually staged in their rehearsal studio. "They'd set the room up like a stage. All the backline and drum kit — and Anderson's mic stand at the front. We had a brief discussion where I showed them the sketches I'd prepared, and they assumed their positions and threw a few shapes, as I snapped away giving out a few directions. I knew I'd got my shots pretty much straightaway."

The design followed the cover for Everything's Alright. The band's logo is emblazoned in white across the top half, contrasting with the black background, while bright colours pick out the band members. The rear sleeve features a collage of the band's friends and fans over the years, including Jesus Jones, Voice of the Beehive, Diesel Park West, Annie Nightingale, and the now disgraced Rolf Harris, whose photo had been taken with one of their friends during childhood. It's strikingly effective despite its simplicity, but Raybould is less then enamoured today. "While I was happy I'd brought all these disparate elements together and it all looked bright and lively, I don't think it had the clout of the single sleeve. Looking at it now, I think it's a bit flat, sadly. I didn't have the benefit of seeing it up on a screen like these days."

Songwriters are informed by life experiences, and for Reverb travel had

Front cover of Crazyhead's long awaited second album Some Kind Of Fever. Art by Nick Raybould.

begun to figure prominently in his lyrics. The album's opening track, Big Sister, is a paean to their chaperone on the US radio tour, and also references the Chinese laundry incident. But it also has a bitter-sweet edge: while the song was about living the high life on tour, Reverb's domestic situation in the UK was falling apart. Similarly is another track on the album, Rome. In an interview with Bataille Fidol in *Sniffin' Rock* in 1989, Reverb said that Rome was actually a song about Scotland. Pressed by Fidol as to whether his lyrics would expand from hometown-centric themes to "larger impressions", Reverb conceded that the travel opportunities afforded by being in a band gave him more material, but quipped, "I don't think we're going to be writing songs about driving down the highway with our groovy chicks for a while." Today, Reverb says, "Rome was meant to have a sort of 'country' flavour, it's about not feeling like you belong in one place. Which I guess is how I thought at the time. I've lived in Leicester for 45 years now, so what was all that about?" Another song influenced by Reverb's deteriorating domestic situation and personal life was Talk About You, "a feeling sorry for myself ditty," as he describes it. For the track Magic Eye, Reverb claims to have discovered a different chord shape, and now refers to the song as "a dark, sleazy one… On reflection, a lot of the songs on this album are quite bleak."

The lyrics to Above Those Things are self-explanatory and were written before Crazyhead were formed. Two of the 10 songs on the album were co-written with Anderson, who provided the lyrics to Train — as noted, his ode to a brand of cheap, fortified wine — and Movie Theme. Reverb recalls that he tweaked Anderson's lyrics for Movie Theme, adding a few lines of his own. As for the musical arrangement, "When we did the demo, I had the idea of spinning in a bit of Gram Parsons from the pseudo live take of Cash On The Barrelhead/Hickory Wind into the middle bit, I don't know why. It worked perfectly on the demo version —

this was the pre-digital era — but it took a bit more juggling on the album version, as the tempo must have been different."

Mary Anne Hobbs at the *NME* was savage, describing *Some Kind of Fever* as "an appallingly weak and extremely disappointing second album from a band who were considered, in their 'What Gives...' daze, the potential UK equivalent of Guns N' Roses." With reference to stablemates Zodiac Mindwarp, Hobbs resigned Crazyhead to the same fate; in other words they were a flash in the pan.

Art and design by Nick Raybould.

Among the faces on the rear sleeve of Some Kind Of Fever is "now disgraced Rolf Harris, whose photo had been taken with one of their friends during childhood".

Paul Mardles for *Sounds* also put the boot in. He lamented how "there's almost nothing worthy of applause", that the band were "finally loosening their grip on reality and disappearing down the chute of oblivion", and that "inspiration is conspicuous by its absence". He singled out Big Sister as the album's saving grace before concluding, "To call this fever 'serious' is an understatement. The patient's virtually dead."

Caren Myer's review of *Fever* for *Melody Maker* was more effusive. She asked rhetorically why the band was on a "tiny little label where they will probably sell 2,000 copies, while Quireboys are filling stadia?" Preferring it to *Desert Orchid*, she said *Fever* was "a great little record... with a decent proportion of absolute crackers". Myers' only real criticism was the artwork, which she likened to an eight-year-old's drawing. She also expressed concern that the band were "not goal-oriented" or "ruthless enough" to succeed and lamented that "nice guys finish last, and Crazyhead are, if nothing else, diamond geezers. It's just not fair."

Even if Crazyhead themselves didn't want to admit it, there was a sense that the race was run with *Some Kind of Fever*. Vom considers it "a great album, and we're all really proud of it. But we knew it was all over by then. We kind of knew it was a swansong when we were doing the album — unless something amazing happened, unless the BBC cottoned on to it all of a sudden, which was never

going to happen. We knew it was just going to be sort of warmly received by fans, but the press wasn't really interested."

Some Kind of Fever wasn't a critical or commercial success, which is perhaps unsurprising: it wasn't raw or heavy enough for fans of thrash metal, grunge, or punk, and not commercial enough for fans of more mainstream pop/rock. Had it been released a few years later, it would have fitted into what came to be termed Britpop and might have been better received. Certainly the landscape was changing: The Stone Roses were rollercoasting through the UK indie charts and Blur, briefly Crazyhead's labelmates, were about to embark on their own path to superstardom. It's easy to see how Crazyhead might have fitted in with the 're-invention of the guitar' that came with Britpop. Of course hindsight is a wonderful thing…

Matters were coming to a head between Crazyhead and record label Black, which had fulfilled the terms of the original contract: one single and one album. The band had discussions with label boss Paul Birch about the possibility of future releases. Birch put them in touch with a potential new manager when they raised concerns about Andrew Cheeseman, but nothing came of it. The band was desperately cash-strapped after being cut adrift from Parlophone and in addition to an outstanding debt they owed to EMI, other financial irregularities were coming to light that would soon strain relationships within the band.

PERNICIOUS NONSENSE

The Bykers had barely been back in the UK a month when they started gigs to promote *Pernicious Nonsense*, their fourth studio album, and second on the Naked Brain label. It was different from its sprawling predecessor, *Cancer Planet Mission*. Gone were the thrashier elements, and experimental aspects, that at times sounded awkward, had been finely tuned on the new album to create a more fully formed and satisfying whole. The samples also slot in more coherently than those on *Cancer Planet Mission*. Mary has already stressed how Rockit Ron was the Bykers' "conduit into the dance world" but intimates that things didn't really gel until the band — Kev in particular —fully grasped the technology. "I think towards the end, once Kev got into the programming thing, it was like 'Oh, we can do this in a different way, we can play all these funky loops.' That's when we actually got the dance phenomena. It's like sometimes you have to embrace the culture, really go deep into it and live it to make that kind of music. So I think, in-between *Cancer Planet Mission* and the last album, that is what happened… Even though we always listened to hip hop and stuff, I think Kev probably went off his Black Sabbath and the darker sort of stuff and got more into the hip hop and the rap, definitely Public Enemy and stuff like that!"

Nobody realised at the time, but *Pernicious Nonsense* would prove to be the Bykers' last official studio album. Given Robber's increasing disillusionment, it's perhaps not so surprising. S.O.S., the album's opening track, is a scathing indictment of politicians and world leaders, as well as a comment about humankind's self-destruct mentality. Musically, it's a storming techno-rock beast propelled by a relentless bassline lifted from The Osmonds' unlikely environmental warning Crazy Horses. Elsewhere, it utilises a then seemingly obligatory sample from James Brown's Funky Drummer, as well as one from The KLF's What Time Is Love? Continuing in a similar vein, Disinformation Rise & Shine is concerned with the destruction of the planet. The song contains some of Mary's most memorable lyrics, interweaving them with the chorus of Sister Sledge's Lost In Music and the guitar solo from Jimi Hendrix's 1983… (A Merman I Should Turn To Be) to great effect. The opening lines are as resonant now as they were in 1990: 'Wisdom it brings humility in this tortured 20th century / Which began as a golden age and now stumbles to suicide / As men see no purpose in their lives / They eat they drink they make merry / For tomorrow they will die and wonder why.' Despite its apparent pessimism, the song ends on a positive note: 'You gotta take the time / You gotta be more positive / Use your intellect.' Mary says, "I think… it's always trying to find something positive in all this madness that seems to be going on."

Another track, Flowered Up, borrows its title from the name of a band, baggy-trousered scenesters that were London's answer to Madchester and had a couple of minor hits. However, the lyrics owe more to King

Front cover of Pernicious Nonsense. "Although the name Gaye Bykers On Acid was present, it was secondary to the larger PFX logo that it encircled" Cover art and design by Tony Byker.

Crimson, its opening verses cribbed almost wholesale from Formentera Lady and later Ladies Of The Road ('A flower lady's daughter / As sweet as holy water'), then harks back to the Bykers' original incarnation, 'pulled apart she sends me into a petal frenzy.' Mary's lyrics are a stream of consciousness, melding contemporary and retrospective reference points — De La Soul's D.A.I.S.Y. Age and The Rolling Stones' She's A Rainbow ('The sun's coming up from the daisy age / She comes in colours centre-stage'). Mary says, "We were listening to a lot of De La Soul, so it's that whole sort of dancey psychedelic thing. It's almost like coming out of the angry other stuff and actually being a bit more up, and sort of getting out of it and more cerebral."

It's a sentiment Mary extends to another track on the album, Falling Fruit. "This is also a bit more about E and getting out of it… Basically we were into that dance thing, the punky edge had come off and it was more like we were getting into the zeitgeist. Do you know what I mean? That was what was going on!" Within the first 35 seconds Falling Fruit samples Captain Beefheart, The Doors, Bad Brains, and the riff from Led Zeppelin's Kashmir. It later includes snippets from The Power, which had been a hit for German techno duo Snap! earlier in the year. Then there's another Hendrix sample, the distinctive guitar refrain from Highway Chile. Listening to Falling Fruit today Mary jokes, "We've got a sampler and we're going to use it! Man! We'd have got sued to fuck with this record if we'd got a hit!"

Although the name Gaye Bykers On Acid was present on the cover of *Pernicious Nonsense*, it was dwarfed by the PFX logo. Nonetheless, it wasn't enough to fool anyone and the album was reviewed as a Bykers' album by the press. Paul Davies, reviewing the album in Q magazine, noted how the Bykers had been influenced by dance music, "dropping cluster bombs of hip hop drumbeats into their gargling thrashed-up psychedelic soup, the end product conjuring up visions of a bloody studio fist fight between the Beastie Boys and Hawkwind." Killer Teens In New Orleans certainly brings to mind the Beastie Boys and Public Enemy. Kev provides lead vocals. Mary says Kev was "falling out of love with drumming" by this point and recounts an instance on their US tour when they were supported by local band, Loud Sounding Dream, whose drummer was a young Jimi Hendrix lookalike. For a while they were all up for getting him to drum for them, and even on returning to the UK there were still mutterings about doing this. But circumstances conspired against them. Having become involved in singing and using drum machines and sequencers on the album, and having contributed the fuzz bass on Radiation/John Wayne Was A Fag, Kev was quite taken by the idea of relinquishing his drum stool.

In his review, Davies bemoaned the Bykers' "pet obsessions with ecological desolation and world destruction" residing within "the sonic static of sampled movie dialogue, Led Zeppelin riffs and psychotic barroom banter". Many of the dialogue samples on the album were taken from Alex Cox's cult movie, *Repo Man*. Indeed, the album took its name from a line in the film. Radiation/John Wayne Was A Fag sampled dialogue from both *Repo Man* and *Taxi Driver*. The music is an electronic onslaught on the senses, not far removed from Hawkwind, lending credence to Davies' comparison to the uber-space rockers. Unfortunately, Davies thought the song titles promised more than they could deliver, and mean-spiritedly concluded his review by awarding the album just two out of five stars.

Mary Anne Hobbs was equally critical in her four out of 10 review for *NME*, and was particularly cynical about the dance-oriented path the Bykers were now tripping down. She related how Mary had told her the Bykers had been "stiffed because they'd got their drugs wrong. Should've been Gaye Bykers On E, not LSD", and that they had "found renewed stimulation through rave culture". Citing the new album as the result of this acid house epiphany, Hobbs described "familiar phlegm-sodden mutant Byker spasms, flooded with torrents of fragmented sampling and beginner-rapping all set against a house beat", and likened it to early Pop Will Eat Itself. As with Davies' comparison to Beastie Boys and Hawkwind, there was truth in the PWEI comparison. Mary wouldn't disagree: "This album is the culmination of like, 'We've got a sampler — we can do this', it's basically what happened with Pop Will Eat Itself in a way, once they'd made that decision… we could have easily done that early on, but we didn't. The Poppies did and they carried on that route and became a sort of dance/sample-based band… Our thing was that we couldn't decide one way or another, we were just too busy sort of wanting to be one thing or another." In summing up *Pernicious Nonsense*, Hobbs described it as "the obligatory crap GBOA LP. The Bykers are, meanwhile, like a car wreck on the hard shoulder. You know it's going to be a horrible mess, but you'll never be able to resist having a little look."

It was down to George Berger for *Sounds* to put in a good word, describing the album as "an expertly welded mutation of grunge, psychopathic raps and… dance beats". For Berger, this was "off the head music for cadets who like a bit of a prank… chillum house for natty heads. It might be asking a touch too much for ravers to get into it, but only a touch." With reference to the chorus the Bykers had lifted from Sister Sledge, he declared a band "Lost in space, lost in music and, theoretically at least, on the right side of the barricades in the information war, Gaye Bykers are either up a blind alley to hell or part of the next great evolutionary jump. *Pernicious Nonsense*, laced with madness and happiness, sounds like the

Gaye Bykers On Acid in Old Time Wild West photograph taken on the US tour, 1990.

latter." Berger signed off: "These scumbags, ever tripping the light fantastic, still deserve to dominate the world — if it ever becomes ready for them." Alas, the world never did, and *Pernicious Nonsense* remains the great unsung Bykers' album. Eclectic in scope, it contains some of their finest and most interesting material. Mary blames the fickleness of the music press for its disappointing reception. "They really did get behind us initially, you know we had all of them on our side," Mary says. "We got written about, and I think what happens is if you don't make it big time it's almost as if they feel like you've cheated them in a way, and they look a bit stupid after they've backed you so much. It's quite swift, the retribution, it's like they build you up and knock you down."

As noted, *Melody Maker* and *NME* were often quick to put the boot in, but Mary has only praise for *Sounds*: "They were always great with us, very supportive and never really slagged us off. If we got a bad review it would be written in such a way that you could take [it], whereas some of the other papers were just downright nasty." Of the other papers, Mary adds ruefully, "We could've put out the best thing ever and they still wouldn't have liked it."

LAST STAND AT NEW CROSS

As well as their own material, the Bykers made the decision to diversify and use their label Naked Brain as a springboard for albums by other artists. This would ultimately be one of the contributing factors to the band's own demise, although the Bykers couldn't know it yet. The first guest artist release was *Digital Dump* by The Jackofficers, a side project of Butthole Surfers' Gibby Haynes and Jeff Pinkus. The deal was struck when the Bykers were touring the US and met the Butthole Surfers, with the album being released shortly afterwards, in 1990. Charlie En-

dell in his review for *Sounds* failed to touch on the unusual experimental electronica of *Digital Dump* but noted in a roundabout way that it may never have seen the light of day had it not been for the Bykers. The album, said Endell, was recorded "over the last two years at the Butthole Surfers' ranch in Austin, Texas" where it "lay unloved and unreleased in one of the outhouses — due to various contractual wrangles and obligations — until the timely arrival of the Bykers on their

Cover of Jack Officers' Digital Dump album. Gaye Bykers On Acid licensed and released it on their Naked Brain record label.

GAYE BYKERS ON ACID/PURPLE FLUID EXCHANGE 'PERNICIOUS NONSENSE' > on LP, Cass, CD <

BEATS FOR FREAKS

NAKED BRAIN

INTERNATURAL

OUT NOW

JACK OFFICERS 'DIGITAL DUMP' featuring Geoff & Gibby from the Butthole Surfers

annual trawl through the States."

Robber says someone that Mary knew, called Charlie (*not* Charlie Endell), who worked for a distribution company, had helped broker the licensing deal. "I don't know how much they handed over to pay for licensing the Jackofficers," says Robber, not without cynicism. "I didn't have anything to do with it... To be honest, I thought it was a *bad* idea... handing over loads of money to the Buttholes to put that out. I thought I'd rather have the money myself. But at that point I'd totally removed myself from it all, and I was like, 'sod this!', just plodding along." If Mary felt a sense of liberation after being sacked by Virgin, Robber admits to being "right pissed off really. I thought we were just going through the motions for the next couple of years."

Naked Brain released another album before the year was out — *Bombolini Hey!* by Ultima Thule. It sounds like the bastard offspring of eccentric jazzy post-punkers The Cravats, with some of the theatricalism of The Cardiacs. Today, none of the Bykers have any recollection of Ultima Thule or *Bombolini Hey!* — which isn't necessarily a reflection on how forgettable they were, as the album certainly has its moments. After this, there would be just two more releases on Naked Brain, a 12-inch single and album by Bugblot, *Improve Your Petrol*. Bugblot featured Karl Leiker on bass, who would later form Hyperhead with Mary in 1992. All in all, it was possibly the worst time to have chosen to start their independent record label, as would soon become apparent.

The Bykers began their *Pernicious Nonsense* promo tour in hometown Leicester and then revisited venues they had played six months earlier, including Newcastle Riverside, Coventry Tic Toc, Leeds Duchess of York, Manchester

SATURDAY 1st DECEMBER

GAYE BYKERS ON ACID

SCAT OPERA

WORKING WITH TOMATOES

VENUE

THE VENUE
2A CLIFTON RISE
NEW CROSS, LONDON SE14
081 692 4077
NEW CROSS/NEW CROSS GATE TUBE & BR

£3.50 Before 9.30pm £5.00 After. BANDS FINISH 11 pm
CLUB TILL 2 am COACH AFTER CLUB TO TRAFALGAR SQUARE

Music press ad for Gaye Bykers On Acid and Scat Opera at The Venue, New Cross, 1st December 1990. It turned out to be the last Gaye Bykers on Acid gig ever before they reunited in 2016.

UMIST, and The Jug in Doncaster, culminating at The Venue in New Cross, London, on 1st December 1990. Little did they know it would be their last gig. Consequently, in terms of a last hurrah, it was a somewhat understated affair.

The band's performance was solid, opening with a very dance-oriented version of Everythang's Groovy before powering through fan favourites from *Stewed To The Gills* and *Cancer Planet Mission*. New material came in the shape of the S.P.A.C.E. single, while *Pernicious Nonsense* was represented with Disinformation Rise & Shine, Flowered Up, and S.O.S. There was no indication that this would be the final gig for the band, no fanfare or announcement (other than it was Tony's 25th birthday: Mary encouraged the audience to join in a rousing version of Happy Birthday). But beneath the surface it was clear that all was not well. The rigours of the tour treadmill combined with recording and the ubiquitous drinking and drugging had taken their toll, particularly with Robber, still frazzled after the punishing two-month tour of the States. The final straw came after the evening's performance.

Robber had one of his prized bass guitars stolen. Mary exclaims, with undisguised outrage, "Some cunt actually got backstage and nicked it… Robber's bass actually got stolen!" Robber is still unable to hide his bitterness: "That's

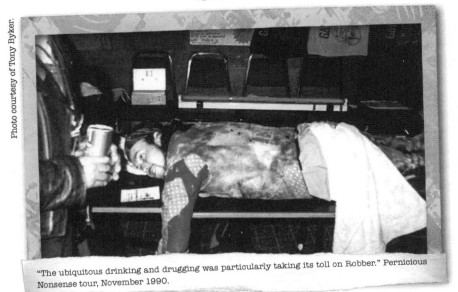

"The ubiquitous drinking and drugging was particularly taking its toll on Robber." Pernicious Nonsense tour, November 1990.

where it all ended for me. The band was over, it was the sign that I was finally going to quit. If a so-called fan can rob your prized painted unique Fender Jazz Bass instrument off the stage and walk out the front door with it, well, what's the point…? I had no music gear insurance to cover it, and no money or car to chase him up. That was the catalyst that ended the band for me, and everyone else. He [the thief] hammered the final nails in the magic carpet ride. I vowed that night never to play any Gaye Bykers On Acid songs ever again."

Robber stood by his promise for 25 years.

Mary attributes the band's demise to exhaustion, exacerbated by alcohol and drug use, and if Robber was burnt out, then the rest of the band wasn't far behind. "I think the general thing was tiredness — fatigue," he says. "I think it was called amphetamine sulphate 'burnout', that and smoking chillums and hot knives — that was the main thing!" In Mary's view the excess was never, well, *excessive.* "Nobody was really doing more than each other… We smoked a bit of pot, we all did a bit of opium, but we were never *really* into coke, like most bands I know." Despite a band name that might suggest otherwise, Gaye Bykers On Acid weren't tripping on acid every day. Mary says, "The acid was more of a recreational thing for us, because we couldn't really function on the road on that to be honest. Occasionally we did it at a festival, but to be touring on it you just couldn't do it, it wasn't conceivable, but speed? Obviously yes!" In hindsight, their US tour,

although an amazing experience, played its part. "Everybody was a bit tired… It's not like we really argued. We didn't have really bad blazing arguments, but it was a combination of that and the amount of time we'd spent together in each other's company."

THE NUMBER OF THE PORKBEAST

The Bykers' sudden demise coincided with the end of Crazyhead in their first incarnation. Following the critical mauling of *Some Kind of Fever*, Crazyhead supported The Ramones at the Brixton Academy on 8th December 1990. Like the Bykers, all of Crazyhead were big fans of the New York punk band and thrilled by the gig. Reverb even went as far as to write a song about them (N.Y.C.) for a later incarnation of Crazyhead in the late 1990s.

It could have been disastrous for Crazyhead, though, as there was a mix-up with the travel arrangements. On the day of the gig Anderson was waiting in his Leicester home for the tour van to pick him up when his telephone rang. It was Vom, asking where he was. Believing Anderson was already in London, staying with his London based girlfriend, the rest of the band had already set off and were halfway to the capital. They only realised he wasn't in London when they made a call to Carol during a pitstop. It was too late for the tour van to turn back and collect Anderson. There was only one thing for it: Anderson would have to catch a train to London. Normally this wouldn't have been a problem, but it was December, freezing cold, and had started snowing. Anderson recalls, "It was chaos due to the weather, trains were being cancelled or running late, there was snow everywhere. I took three trains in all, the second I was thrown off by the conductor. It was some private line that my ticket wasn't valid on, all the time the clock was ticking towards gig time! I was going mental along with crowds of other people. I finally got on the third train. It was packed — nowhere to sit! Then I spotted Lisa — a girl I knew from Leicester — with a spare seat. I was ranting, effing and blinding on a crowded family train about my travel problems. She talked me down, handed me her Walkman with laidback bossa nova tunes on, and that chilled me out. A very calming woman…"

It's hardly any wonder, then, that in her review of the gig for *Sounds* Cathi Unsworth reported that Anderson was in a fractious mood, which she considered a "Good thing too, because spitting out bile to an audience of scuzzy punkers is where this band work best". Unsworth was more positive toward

Crazyhead supporting The Ramones "was a major tick on Porkbeast's bucket list".

Crazyhead than she was The Ramones, unlike some other reviews. According to Anderson, Crazyhead "played a stormer to a very loud and appreciative crowd of nearly 4,000 Ramones fans. Before the last song I said, 'Not bad for a support band?' to huge cheers." Porkbeast remembers The Ramones gig being "a monster! We played a blinder and the crowd loved us." The icing on the cake for Porkbeast was blagging his way backstage and chatting to Ramones' bass player C.J., who signed a paper plate for him. He also managed to speak to Marky, Johnny, and Joey, who gave the starstruck bass player a drink. Along with Iggy Pop, The Ramones were Porkbeast's favourite band. Having supported both was a major tick on his bucket list.

A week later Crazyhead were back in Leicester to play two homecoming gigs at the Princess Charlotte. There should have been more to celebrate after several years of hard work honing their musical skills, building up their reputation, and releasing their second album, but internal divisions, as well as dissatisfaction with management, had come to a head. Something had to give — and that something was Porkbeast.

Despite still being on the Station Agency's books, Reverb laments that gigs were getting smaller. "We were also searching for our own gigs to keep a few quid coming in as our 'wages' had ended," he recalls. "We played a gig at a pub in Earl Shilton outside Leicester, it was all a bit tawdry and everything was getting a bit fractious between us. Little niggles became major." Porkbeast's relationship with Reverb worsened after the band played a charity gig for one of Reverb's friends. Reverb apparently had spent the evening telling Porkbeast there was no room for him to have a lift in his wife's car, only to inform him at the last minute there was. If his intention was to wind the bass player up then he certainly succeeded, and the next day Porkbeast called Vom to inform him they needed a new bass player.

Vom says Porkbeast's departure "was a shame. Looking back, I never wanted Porky to leave the band, nobody did! But at the time, relationships within the band were so bad… I remember when he rang me up, and said, 'I'm leaving the band, I quit, it's over', I went 'Well, don't expect me to fucking beg you back!' and he goes, 'I won't!', and we just slammed the phones down and that was that."

Manager Andrew Cheeseman was the next to go. Reverb recalls, "Our deal with Black/Revolver had fizzled out, so we were going to have to look for a new deal. We were only doing odd gigs, so there wasn't any money coming in. Cheeseman wasn't managing us because he loved the band, it was a purely business thing with him, and so that was that really. He rang me and said that with Alex leaving, and things not exactly going too well, it was probably a good time to part company… He did make sure that he got his wedge from the next gig, though!"

To compound their woes, Anderson remembers that the band owed a huge debt to EMI which eventually was written off after Reverb negotiated a deal, but only after "the big boss made him sweat". Reverb confirms the amount owed to EMI was in the region of £127,000 but emphasises that the band weren't personally liable for it as it was recoupable against record sales. Nevertheless, it was a huge sum of money to have hanging over them. More worryingly, Anderson says that thousands of pounds were owed to various companies from deals ostensibly made in the band's name via their management. Thankfully, Anderson seems to think they were let off the hook to some extent when many of these creditors went bankrupt during the financial crash of the early 1990s. The band were not so lucky when it came to HM Revenue and Customs, as the taxman was not so forgiving. Anderson says, "that was one that had to be paid by us out of our dole money etc. for years, to avoid going to prison!"

INDEPENDENCE DAZED & CONFUSED

Another major factor in the Bykers' demise was the collapse of indie distribution network The Cartel. As with many bands and small labels, The Bykers' relied on The Cartel to get their material into stores. When it folded in July 1990 the regional distribution companies that constituted The Cartel came under the control of Rough Trade Distribution in London. This centralisation ultimately proved to be the undoing of Rough Trade Distribution, so too the Rough Trade record label. In the wake of managerial changes and bad business acumen, the tatters of the old Cartel soon began to fragment as regional distribution outposts — such as Revolver, who handled Naked Brain — were subject to statutory redundancies or split from the distribution network altogether.

Less than a year later, Rough Trade had folded, and the distribution network was left in disarray. While some of the larger independent labels, like Mute and 4AD, were in a better position to deal with the bankruptcy, many smaller ones weren't so lucky. Richard King sums up the devastation in his book, *How Soon Is Now?* He writes,

> the remaining smaller labels, the kind that had thrived and been created under Rough Trade's off-the-street production and manufacture deals, were forced into closure along with Rough Trade. Many of them were bedroom operations with few overheads and several hundred copies of their singles piled up on the shelves in the overspill warehouse in Camley Street, but the dream of starting a label for no other reason than releasing some music that might turn the heads of John Peel and his audience was over.

Naked Brain's product was primarily dealt with by Revolver in Bristol, but centralisation meant that the Bykers' label suffered the repercussions of Rough Trade's collapse. Even if Revolver managed to weather the storm, the damage was done, exacerbated by the mysterious broker, Charlie, and alleged mismanagement of the label's affairs. Mary suggests as much: "We had so much invested in it at that point, it was our only means of income... Obviously, had we not had this guy Charlie run away with all the money and sort of rip us off, and if Rough Trade hadn't gone bankrupt or whatever, things might have been different 'cos we might have then thought 'OK, this is worthwhile. We're doing

alright out of this', but it was just a part of that whole sort of thing as to why things disintegrated really."

Tony still winces when thinking about this period. "That particular time was a bit embarrassing. We got *Cancer Planet* and Jackofficers and Bugblot CDs, vinyl and cassettes all made and ready for distribution when Rough Trade went bankrupt. It was a disaster! We had bedrooms full of all these items and we couldn't do anything with them! I feel bad thinking about the friendship we made with the Buttholes and how we didn't pull off our end of the deal."

Robber reflects on the Rough Trade collapse: "Yeah, well they had all the sales money for the records, and they also had all the records in their warehouse and stuff like that, so I knew the [majority of] records never got distributed... All those *Cancer Planet Mission*, *Pernicious Nonsense* and S.P.A.C.E. records, they never got distributed out to the record shops. There were thousands of records just sat there, and that messed up the whole release and distribution, as well as us not getting any money off them."

Despite the thousands of records languishing in warehouses and bedrooms, the Bykers' distribution conduit no longer existed, and it would be impossible to realise even half of their stock's potential value. Tony sums up the whole sorry situation thus: "Robber sold handfuls to record shops for pennies over the years, I gave all my copies to him. I kept one of each, I think my dad has them in Huddersfield." The Naked Brain back catalogue was still being sold by Robber on eBay and Facebook over 20 years later.

The Bykers were by no means the only band, nor Naked Brain the only label, to be affected by the collapse of Rough Trade. But few other bands had invested everything as had the Bykers. It was an unfortunate end to a brave venture, and it destroyed the Bykers in one fell swoop. Come the end of 1990 the party was well and truly over for Gaye Bykers On Acid.

THE FINAL CURTAIN

In their end of year round-up for *NME* in 1990, Stuart Maconie and Andrew Collins wrote about the 'Madchester' scene. While somewhat dismissive of it, they believed it to be the better of two evils and that it might at least sound the death knell for 'grebo': "The initial sartorial, musical and attitudinal impact of 'Madchester' was somewhat diluted by legions of knob-heads-cum-lately and mooching Minnies — but Joe Bloggs wasn't complaining, and anyway at its best, the

music wiped away the last vestiges of Gaye Bykers On Acid and their grubby ilk."

Maconie, who had never really liked the Bykers and was an unlikely champion of Crazyhead for a while, is entitled to his opinion like anyone else. Nevertheless, at the risk of portraying the music papers as manipulative puppet masters, ever-changing editorial stances undoubtedly had some bearing on the success of a scene or style or music. Grebo was no different. For a while it had been the flavour of the month with the British press; now they wouldn't touch it with a bargepole.

Vom is still ambivalent about the 'grebo' tag all these years later. "We never really felt like a 'grebo' band, and OK, to begin with that kind of helped us in getting some press coverage… but that soon wears off after a while, and then the Nirvana/Seattle thing happened, and because they were from Seattle that was cool… If you're from Leicester that ain't cool!" Vom has a point: West Coast America has always had hip credentials in rock history, from the surf sounds of sixties California, typified by the Beach Boys and Jan and Dean, to the psychedelic era. Seattle was no different; the locus of attention simply shifted further north. But it wasn't just grunge from Seattle that was beginning to overshadow 'grebo'; arguably its UK counterparts, Madchester and Britpop, loomed on the horizon. Happy Mondays openly embraced getting wasted and were staunch advocates of the drug Ecstasy. Although the Bykers' last album, *Pernicious Nonsense*, was by far their most dance-oriented, Robber says the Bykers were late converts to MDMA, and he himself didn't really get into it until after the band had imploded. Although the release of *Pernicious Nonsense* coincided with what is argued to be the Happy Mondays' career pinnacle, *Pills 'N' Thrills And Bellyaches*, by then the Bykers were old news. The more commercial dance rock fusion of the Happy Mondays had captured the zeitgeist, and ultimately proved to be more enduring.

Another Manchester indie rock band with dance vibes and psychedelic undertones was The Stone Roses. They also helped to define a generation when they played Spike Island, the now legendary music festival held on a reclaimed toxic waste dump in the Mersey estuary in the summer of 1990. But by the end of the year the Madchester scene had arguably reached its apogee and something more quintessentially British was developing in tandem with the American grunge phenomenon. The significance of Britpop, if not realised at the time, has not gone unnoticed by Vom. He sees it as a contributing factor to the demise of bands like Crazyhead and the Gaye Bykers. The greatest exponents of Britpop would eventually be Oasis and Blur, with record companies and the press exploiting the north/south rivalry between the two bands to help fuel record sales. Says Vom, "Manchester, London — we didn't really fit into either, so we always fell between these schools."

Mary is of the opinion that the Bykers, Crazyhead, and 'grebo' in general were overshadowed by Madchester and then grunge. However, he suggests that the likes of Gaye Bykers On Acid and Pop Will Eat Itself were ahead of their time and should not be understated, having experimented with sounds that industrial bands only started to do later with programmed beats and guitars. "We were also making it acceptable to like heavy rock again, which until grunge was not particularly fashionable," says Mary. "When you think about it, we were an

Photo courtesy of Christina Wigmore.

Christina Wigmore was a veteran of the Leicester music scene and had been in rockabilly band Return Of The Seven.

amalgamation of the grunge and Manchester thing because we were using dance beats and heavy rock riffs." When pressed on the legacy of 'grebo', Mary is self-deprecating enough to recognise the Bykers' own shortcomings: "In the end, the main legacy any band can leave behind are the songs, and in all honesty, I think that's where the Bykers came up short. We were more about the attitude, and after we signed to Virgin, we lost it, we got a bit lazy. The thing is, we had a lot of fun and didn't take ourselves too seriously. When it stopped being fun, we split up, which I think was the proper thing to do."

If the road had run out for the Bykers, Crazyhead reached a crossroads and careered into the signpost. But they picked themselves up and dusted down their battered leather jackets; following Porkbeast's departure they recruited a new bassist. Vom remembers that Porkbeast had only been gone a day or two when, "Dick rings me up saying 'I've got Christina in', it was like that." Christina Wigmore was a veteran of the local music scene and had been in Leicester rockabilly band Return Of The Seven some years previously with Fast Dick. Christina had deputised for Porkbeast when he was unable to fulfil a gig commitment due to a "home crisis", as she puts it. In truth, he failed to turn up for the mini-bus on which Crazyhead (along with Diesel Park West) were travelling to London. Christina, as a friend and follower of the band, happened to be travelling down with them and had already had a few strong vodkas when the band put her on the spot, deciding she should stand in for Porkbeast. It was too late for Christina to learn the whole set, but after a couple more strong vodkas she took to the stage for a very stripped down Crazyhead set that consisted of Have Love, Will Travel and a cover of The Stooges' TV Eye, which she just about had time to learn in the dressing room.

A few weeks later, Fast Dick called Christina to say Porkbeast had left the band and would she like to join, kicking off with a gig at The Mean Fiddler in Harlesden the following week. Seven days of full-on rehearsals ensued. Christina says, "It was a big scary challenge for me as I'd only really played in bands where we wrote our own stuff, so never really needed to learn other peoples' songs apart from the odd cover version. On the other hand I felt really honoured to be asked to play in one of my favourite bands, so of course I said yes."

Before the Mean Fiddler gig Vom warned Christina that she might be spat at by some fans disgruntled that Porkbeast had been replaced by another bassist — and a female one at that. As it happened Christina wasn't spat on, although she may have been subject to some verbal abuse. She was too busy concentrating on playing the songs and getting through the set to let it bother her. "It was a great feeling afterwards", she recalls. 💀

CHAPTER TWELVE

LONG DARK DAZE

N ITS FIRST ISSUE OF 1991, *SOUNDS* ALLUDED TO A NEW record deal. "Crazyhead are making up for their lack of activity in recent years with a frenzied output this year. Expect a new single in April followed by an LP entitled 'Goose' in May, plus as many gigs as they can lay their hands on. Apart from that, according to guitarist Kev, 'we'll wait for the world to grow feathers.' What a cackle." Neither a single nor an album materialised that spring, but the gigs continued.

Christina Wigmore believed the Mean Fiddler gig would be a one-off, and that Porkbeast and the others would soon sort out their differences. It became apparent this was not going to be the case. Porkbeast did, however, graciously return one more time for a gig at Camden Underworld. Christina had officially replaced Porkbeast by this point, and had quickly learned the songs, but there hadn't been

enough time to prepare her for a whole set. Reverb says, "It wouldn't have been fair on her, so we asked Porky if he would step in for one last gig — which he kindly did. The gig was obviously a bit weird and it didn't help that the support band for the gig was Urge Overkill, who were flavour of the month, and we certainly were not! I think half the audience turned up to see them. It was a bit of a *Spinal Tap* 'they were still booing them when we came on' moment."

Christina got to grips with the material and settled in.

Crazyhead's Christina Wigmore, Abbey Park Festival, 1991. Photo by Jenny Carruthers.

Photo courtesy of Christina Wigmore.

Crazyhead MKII featuring Christina X AKA Wigmore.

She recalls an article in the *Leicester Mercury* publicising the new lineup. Much to her chagrin, the band had elected to call her Christina X, and admits, "I thought that was a bit naff, but I went along with it."

The gigs continued throughout 1991. Although the band was still selling out decent-sized venues, in general they were becoming even more low-key than before. Christina says they still had a loyal following, but "having no record deal back in the nineties meant that the band didn't get press, so it was hard to pick up new followers and gigs started to dwindle." It was becoming apparent that the glory days were well and truly over. Vom admits that, given their circumstances, it was going to be difficult to "re-fly" the band. They would never achieve the stature they had between 1986 and 1990.

The lack of steady income impacted on the road crew too. Spike continued to work for Crazyhead, but it wasn't as regular or lucrative a job as it had been a few years earlier. Tragedy struck in February 1992 when Spike was killed in a road traffic accident. He happened to be working in Germany for a band called Dream Grinder at the time. Spike's best friend Steve Ashton recalls when he first heard the news: "I had a day off in the week and decided to call in early on Reverb for a cuppa and a smoke. He lived close by. Rev opened the door, saw me into the living room and went to make tea. He returned, handed me the tea and a joint and said, straight out, very sternly and bravely, 'Spike was killed last night, in Germany'. Those words hit me like a hammer. I went home, bought a bottle of Jack on the way, and sat on my own sobbing all day, until I passed out."

Crazyhead arranged a gig in Spike's memory at Leicester University the following month, joined by The Wonder Stuff and the Milltown Brothers. Spike is still held in high esteem by the band members. Vom, in a Facebook tribute in 2013, wrote, "He was a tough bastard and a real gent, sadly missed." Says Reverb, "The live footage used in the Have Love, Will Travel video has a bit where Spike hands me a guitar. It always chokes me up a bit when I see it. Spike was a great

character, a dedicated roadie and a bit psychotic at times — but I remember him most as a lovely warm human being who could be incredibly kind and thoughtful."

RATTENKELLER BLUES

In April, Crazyhead returned to Germany as part of a three-week tour organised by a London promoter and fan. The impetus for the tour appears to have been a conversation that followed an event associated with sci-fi comic *2000AD*. With the band at a loose end, Crazyhead contacted the Westworld agency at the suggestion of the drummer for Doctor and the Medics (another Vom). Despite a mercurial itinerary during the planning stages, Rudiger, their Westworld contact, eventually came up with a list of dates that began in Prague and crossed over into Germany, with one date in Switzerland. Things didn't bode well when, a week before the tour, much of the band's equipment was stolen from a van purchased especially for the tour by Big Tony AKA Tony Brookes, former singer of Return Of The Seven, who was just starting out as a tour manager.

Hastily borrowing equipment, the band embarked on a two-day drive across Europe. Travelling with them was former Gaye Bykers On Acid roadie Keith Penny. First stop was the passport office in Peterborough as Big Tony, at that time, only had a visitor's passport. Although this was generally valid in western Europe, including Berlin since the collapse of the wall, a full passport would be required for former Eastern Bloc countries. Things went from bad to worse when they got to the Czech border and Big Tony was refused entry into the country. Christina recalls: "We had to put him on the train back to Berlin, and I carried on driving as none of the others could, or would, drive!" At least that evening's show at the Rock Club was well received, as Christina remembers, "the turnout and reaction was amazing as it was not long after the fall of communism there."

The band's elation was short-lived. The promoter offered to drive them back to their hotel and ended up inadvertently ripping the bumper off another vehicle. The police were called and demanded to see their insurance papers. Naturally, they didn't have any, but Christina eventually managed to fob them off with her UK AA breakdown cover. They spent the rest of the night getting hideously drunk. They woke up with monstrous hangovers, and discovered that the tour itinerary's estimated drive time to Berlin was grossly inaccurate. Arriving late, they found the promoter had cancelled the gig — but at least they were reunited

"We were all going a bit insane, and... decided to play in underwear." Members of Crazyhead in Braunschweig, German tour 1992.

with Big Tony! After spending a free day in Berlin, the band headed up to the Line Club in Braunschweig.

It was only day five of the tour, but according to Reverb, "we were all going a bit insane". To alleviate the boredom, the male members of the band played the gig dressed only in their underwear. The following night's gig at Bielefeld Zak Club was sparsely attended, despite the band's best efforts to promote it, leafleting before the show. Matters didn't improve when Crazyhead discovered that their accommodation, sorted by the local promoter, was a hut they shared with the out-of-town support band and their large entourage. All Crazyhead wanted to do was sleep, but everyone else in the hut insisted on getting drunk and partying hard throughout the night. It "nearly ended up in World War III", according to Reverb.

Wandering round Bielefeld on their day off, the band shuddered at the thought of another night in the hut and decided to use what little money they had on a hotel. However, the respite from dodgy digs was short-lived and continued in Hamburg, their next stop. Although they had only played twice at the Marquee Club in the Reeperbahn, the club's owner let them stay in the cellar for four nights, quickly christened by the band as the "rat cellar".

Hamburg was not without further incident. As in Bielefeld, Crazyhead resorted to printing up their own flyers. Reverb recalls bumping into Sisters Of

Mercy frontman Andrew Eldritch while handing out flyers on the streets of the Reeperbahn (who turned up that night for the gig). On his return to the club after leafleting he was told Vom had been rushed to hospital. He had experienced an anaphylactic reaction after eating peanuts. The medication Vom was given made him extremely drowsy and he fell asleep at his drumkit during the band's set. Says Reverb, "He was in a right state. He shouldn't have played, but we were desperate for the money, so we waited until way past midnight before we went on and had given Rob [Vom] a bit more time to recover."

The next few gigs were well received and passed without too much incident: Penny found a revolver in a drawer in Bonn and proceeded to freak out the rest of the entourage with it, and there was the luxury of a decent hotel when they played in Bern, Switzerland. But the journey between venues continued to take its toll, and not just on the van — Reverb says only half-joking that it was costing them more in oil than they were earning. Reverb recalls an incident at the Jazzhaus music festival in Freiburg, where Crazyhead were due to play an hour before Californian punk band Legal Weapon (former Gun Club and Sisters Of Mercy bassist Patricia Morrison was a founder member). Legal Weapon's singer, Kat Arthur, had apparently picked up a German groupie. Reverb elaborates: "He [the roadie] was an asshole, we had a shared dressing room, and he was acting like he owned it." Penny, who at the best of times was not a person to be wound up, grunted something about the prima donna groupie. Things reached boiling point with Reverb and the promoter outside the venue: "He was getting a bit worried as we were all a bit wired by this time. I was trying to convince him we were all nice guys and wouldn't cause any trouble at the hotel he'd booked for us, when behind him Penny CS gassed the German groupie and [Big] Tony knocked him out!"

Reverb has little recollection of the following night's gig in Voerde. But he does recall things becoming a little more relaxed in Düsseldorf and Darmstadt, where they were meant to have a couple of free days. They ended up playing a local rock venue, The Golden Krone, arranged at the last minute by a friend of Reverb who lived locally.

It was all downhill for the last few dates. In Nuremburg, Crazyhead made their way to The Slash Club. The club owner and bar staff were nice enough, but the venue was in the cellar. Reverb shudders at the memory: "It was just that, a proper dank, small dark cellar that smelt of damp with a couple of bulbs hanging down. It was all too much for us, we decided not to play but borrowed a couple of acoustic guitars and busked for beers in the bar. I can remember me and Tony had an emotional breakdown outside the bar."

They next day was spent travelling in a van that was clearly on its way out, but somehow managed to make it to Uelzen. According to Reverb the gig itself was okay, but the journey was punishing. The thought of an even longer drive south to Backnang filled the band with dread. They were late, despite setting off from Uelzen at 8:00am and travelling for 10 hours. "This was pre-mobile phones, and we couldn't contact the promoter," says Reverb. "When we arrived, they'd pulled the gig." This proved to be the final straw, even for a tour-hardened band like Crazyhead. "Next day, we were meant to drive to Düsseldorf to meet Rudiger and pay him any money we owed. He'd taken some from previous gigs, and we had just about enough to get back to the ferry, so at the hotel we had a meeting and decided to head straight back to the ferry in the morning."

It was a somewhat ignoble end to an ill-planned tour. But even if Big Tony Brookes' first real foray into road management was a disaster, it didn't deter him. He is now a hugely successful tour manager for the likes of The Kooks, Beverley Knight, Soulwax, Michael Kiwanuka, and Kaiser Chiefs, among others.

FUCKED BY ROCK

On returning to Leicester, Crazyhead continued to knock out demos. Reverb set himself up in a corner of Stayfree Music rehearsal studios, recording bands to make a living. As 'Memphis Studios' he recorded among others Cornershop, Zodiac Mindwarp, Scum Pups, and Kev Byker and Thommo's industrial techno outfit G.R.O.W.T.H. This also meant that Crazyhead now had access to free recording and rehearsal space. One of their demos attracted the attention of CBS, but nothing came of it because, says Anderson, CBS didn't like his voice. In 1993, the band planned to release the results of some of these sessions on the Stayfree label run by studio boss and former Hunters Club vocalist, Ian Redhead. The initial idea was for Stayfree to release a four-track EP of cover versions, followed by an LP of original Crazyhead material. "I can't remember which tracks we chose to do first," Reverb says, "but I think we wanted to do another version of Have Love as we had never recorded it with the brass section. I think once we started, we just kept going until we had a whole LP's worth."

The potentially misleading title of the LP was *Live In Memphis*, a reference to Reverb's studio set-up and in turn a homage to Elvis Presley. It was where they recorded the album, which consisted of covers of artists like Michael Jackson, The Beatles, Captain Beefheart, Jim Reeves, and Roxy Music. Review

Randy Loverod & The Health & Happiness Show — Reverb (L) and Anderson (R) AKA the Very Reverend Rooster Reverb and Jefferson T Dogwinkle.

copies were circulated to the press. Peter Kane in Q magazine was unforgiving in his appraisal. Following a disparaging reference to the band's 'grebo' past, he said that Crazyhead were now "operating as a cover band dishing out some unspeakably heavy handed torment" while "[r]arely bothering to rise above the threshold of garage band competence." Kane also believed there was "something pleasingly incongruous about the exercise" and that Crazyhead's version of The Shirelles' Baby It's You was the album's high point. Nevertheless, he still awarded it a measly two out of five stars. Unfortunately the album never saw an official release. The company with which Redhead had negotiated a distribution and manufacturing deal went bust before it ever saw the light of day.

As a distraction from Crazyhead's travails, Reverb and Anderson started a side project called Randy Loverod & The Health & Happiness Show — self-described as "country & western with a tongue in both cheeks"! In 1994, Randy Loverod performed at Leicester's annual Abbey Park Festival and continued to appear at Leicester venues sporadically throughout the nineties. They could sometimes be found cavorting on stage with Reverb as a cross-dressing American Bible-belt preacher and Anderson as a TV evangelist in little more than a 10-gallon hat, Raybans and a gold-lame posing pouch. Needless to say they didn't take themselves too seriously.

By1994 Vom had also drummed for Zodiac Mindwarp & The Love Reaction a

Pete Creed had previously been in the band Bomb Everything, formerly known as Bomb Disneyland.

number of times, and recorded two albums with the group. In the same year he also became a father. His son was born three months premature, resulting in a long period of hospitalisation and a range of health issues throughout childhood. As a result of the experience, Vom and his wife Fiona were moved to set up a charity, Adapt, which "aids babies born prematurely, and takes a load off parents enduring sleepless nights of worry". It was a tough time for Vom, what he now refers to as his "'my son's dying, let's start a charity' period of my life'". He moved out of his comfort zone to train as a massage and soft tissue therapist, which led to a working relationship with Leicester Tigers Rugby Club that continues to this day. In 1996, he and his wife also had a daughter, but this didn't conclude his rock'n'roll days. "I was ready to settle down," says Vom, "but not hang up my sticks." Inspired by Adapt, Vom and Fiona later established another beneficent organisation, Rhythms. Vom explains: "Rhythms' mission was bringing music to those lacking it. Myself and Fiona taught beats, chords, and scales to adults in prisons and mental health units, children tackling learning difficulties, and everyone in-between. The mantra that music's there for everyone guided us. Kev [Reverb] even joined us for a few years."

There was a hiatus of sorts in 1997, when Fast Dick departed the band. Christina says, "I made the stupid mistake of getting involved with Dick during my time in the band and he left me and the band… and disappeared to Derby. He hadn't been very enthusiastic about the band for quite a while and was more interested in being a sound engineer, talking about speakers, amps and knobs… and soon turned into one!" Crazyhead spent some months looking for a replacement guitarist and vetting various applicants. In the end Fast Dick's replacement followed an encounter at Leicester's legendary Tube Bar night. Christina again: "We chanced upon Pete Creed. Ian knew him and asked him." Pete had been in the band Bomb Everything. They had previously been known as Bomb Disneyland, but due to threats of legal action from the Walt Disney corporation, their record label made them hastily change their name.

Creed proved to be a more than adequate replacement for Fast Dick. They changed the band's name to Zipperfish and recorded a self-produced EP of cover versions, *Dirty 4 Tracker*, and one more CD. Zipperfish's activity coincided with the release of a Crazyhead retrospective, *Fucked By Rock*. The title was attributed to Zodiac Mindwarp, who, according to Anderson, had used the phrase "to describe a drug,

Crazyhead's Fucked By Rock comprised of various demos and live recordings.

drink, and music business-addled rocker". The compilation was comprised of various demos and live recordings dating from the first song the band recorded at Rick Willson's studio in Barkby Road, to studio outtakes such as Time Has Taken Its Toll On You, the Vic Maile version of Dragon City, I Can Do Anything, a cover of Gram Parsons' Baltimore, and a little-known number called Fish recorded at the London Matrix sessions. It also included a live version of Bang Bang and an alternate version of Out On A Limb. There were several recordings made at Memphis Studios in Leicester with the line-up of Anderson, Reverb, Christina, Vom, and Fast Dick. Some of the newer songs — Every Mother's Monkey, Sweet Sweet Life, Pretty Sick, Dragster Girl, and Long Dark Daze — had a heavier and rawer garage sound. Crazyhead might have fallen off the radar, but they proved they could still cut it. It was a shame hardly anyone was taking notice anymore.

Dirty 4 Tracker was re-released as the *Chemical Lunch* EP when the band changed its name back to Crazyhead. It was a self-produced CD-R made available at live gigs. Like the unreleased *Live In Memphis* album, it consisted of cover versions but here a drug theme ran through the songs. The opening track was a rambunctious version of The Fugs' I Couldn't Get High. Reverb had recently been reading about the New York countercultural avant-rock outfit and decided to check out their first album. He says, "I thought most of it was a load of hippy

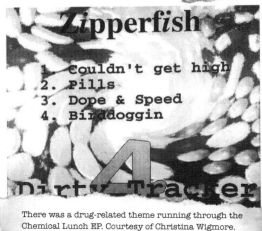

Zipperfish

1. Couldn't get high
2. Pills
3. Dope & Speed
4. Birddoggin

A Dirty Tracker

There was a drug-related theme running through the
Chemical Lunch EP. Courtesy of Christina Wigmore.

tosh, but I liked I Couldn't Get High, and we thought we could do a good version of it." This was followed by an equally sleazy, rough and ready version of Pills that owed as much to Bo Diddley's original version as it did to the New York Dolls' update of 1973. As Reverb says, "Everyone does a version of Pills, so why not us?" Next up was a more contemporary cover: Out Of My Mind On Dope And Speed was originally by Julian Cope, released on Cope's semi-official bootleg *Skellington* in 1989. The last song on the EP bucked the drug theme: Bird-Doggin', from a Gene Vincent compilation that Reverb owned. Justifying its inclusion on *Chemical Lunch*, he says: "It was one of his later, little-known tunes, but was still great." If ever proof were needed that the band had returned to a heavier, rootsier garage rock sound, then this was it.

In 1999, *13th Floor* was released, a mini album on Snatch Records that featured previously unheard songs. (The one exception, Pretty Sick, had appeared in early demo format on *Fucked by Rock*). The album's eponymous opening track, 13th Floor, relates the incident in a Moscow hotel when Spike climbed out of a window and made his way around the outside of the building. It was as much a homage to their greatly missed friend and roadie as it was a recollection of the trip itself. The rest of the songs are a combination of contemporary-sounding rock tunes that could be categorised at the heavier end of the Britpop spectrum, and punkier garage-style numbers. The album closes with

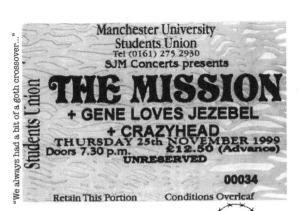

"We always had a bit of a goth crossover..."

Manchester University
Students Union
Tel (0161) 275 2930
SJM Concerts presents

THE MISSION
+ GENE LOVES JEZEBEL
+ CRAZYHEAD

THURSDAY 25th NOVEMBER 1999
Doors 7.30 p.m.   £12.50 (Advance)
UNRESERVED

00034

Retain This Portion   Conditions Overleaf

a fast and furious tribute to The Ramones, N.Y.C., which in typical 'brudders Ramone' style clocks in at just 58 seconds. Lacking management and label backing, *13th Floor* didn't receive significant coverage. A series of gigs towards the end of the year proved to be a mixed blessing: the band secured support dates with goth behemoths, The Mission, All About Eve, and Gene Loves Jezebel. Reverb says, "We always had a bit of a goth crossover, so some of the audience were into it but some we were obviously too

Named after an infamous hotel window ledge incident when Crazyhead were in Moscow in 1989, 13th Floor was Crazyhead's last record and released in 1999.

'rock' for." And therein lay the perennial problem with Crazyhead — caught between a rock and a hard place; too rock for some but not heavy enough for others.

Fast Dick's replacement, Pete Creed, admits that in 2000 he had developed a drug habit. He is now clean but is certain that he likely contributed to the band's demise. "I can't have been too much fun to be around," he says. Creed aside, audiences were dwindling and individual band members were turning their attention to personal ambitions. For instance, Anderson had completed a TEFL (Teaching English as a Foreign Language) course. Just before Christmas 2000, the band finally bowed out in front of a hometown crowd at the Princess Charlotte. Christina says wistfully, "It was a fantastic gig — a great turnout and a stomping last set to say farewell." It was an emotional end to an odyssey that had started out some 15 years earlier at Leicester venue, The Fan Club, with five young friends kicking out raucous, rock'n'roll garage punk jams, not knowing what the future held for them. Now, conversely, they faced the future without the bonds forged by a band together for so long.

... NEVER SEE A BROTHER GO SOLO

The members of Gaye Bykers On Acid had largely gone their separate ways. Fragmenting at the end of 1990, after completing the UK dates to promote *Pernicious Nonsense*, the original plan had been to take a break. Mary says, "a couple of weeks I'd imagine and then just plough on and make another record from what I remember". On Robber's decision to leave, Mary says, "Robber was always extreme and, I think I've said this before, he was always very contrary as well... So that whole thing as well, 'I'm not playing anymore, I don't want to be in it anymore!', and Kev's reaction to that was, 'I don't wanna be in a band without Robber, it's not the Bykers without Robber."

As noted, Robber's disillusionment boiled over with the theft of his bass guitar in New Cross. "I sold all my bass backline after that and spent all the money on drugs, getting totally wasted and partying at free festivals and raves in London for a year." He became a techno DJ with Zero Gravity Sound System, former bandmate Rockit Ron, and various old and new friends from the London scene. He admits that, "It was life changing stuff and I took lots of Es... In retrospect

Rockit Ron remained immersed in the hardcore techno scene.

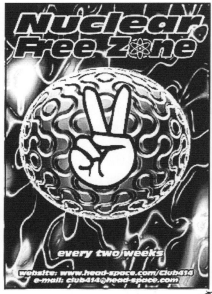

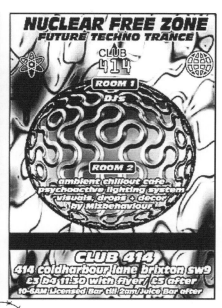

I was suffering from my bipolar disorder." Rockit Ron remained immersed in the hardcore techno scene, involved not only with Zero Gravity, but also the legendary Stay Up Forever Collective, with whom he set up Nuclear Free Zone nights at the Brainbox on Wardour Street before it became Club 414 in the nineties.

As time marched on, the chances of the Bykers picking up where they had left off became more remote. When it was apparent that Robber was sticking to his guns,

Front cover of Tony Byker and Kev Byker's industrial project, Jism Harvester. Cover art and design by Tony Byker.

Mary and Tony tried getting something together with another bass player from Leicester, Brad Lee, who would earn some minor notoriety in the early 2000s with Discordinated. They also tried out Angus Duprey, the brother of Fuzz from Silverfish, on drums. Mary believes the band may have done one rehearsal with Lee and Brad, but "it didn't really work out. And then it was like… It just wasn't going anywhere."

In 1993, Tony hooked up with Kev again and briefly collaborated on an industrial hardcore techno project called Steroid, releasing one album on Clay Records called *Jism Harvester*. After a collaboration with Brad Lee in a band called Camp Collision, which soon dissolved, Tony got back into his artwork and did a few exhibitions. He also started growing hydroponic bud to supplement his income, and learned to scuba dive in Stoney Cove, an inland dive centre in Leicestershire. Earning his PADI Divemaster certification, he decided to close the grow room (becoming too paranoid), before leaving for Mexico and, as he puts it, "the prospect of life on the beach, diving, and siestas in a hammock." He spent some years in the Caribbean, eventually relocating to Tokyo, where he now resides. Kev stayed in Hackney, where he took various jobs and released another industrial techno album, *For Lack Of Horses They Saddle Dogs*, as G.R.O.W.T.H., which comprised of Bomb Party's Thommo and Jeff Murray from The Janitors. After these projects, Kev and Tony dropped off the music radar.

G.R.O.W.T.H., Abbey Park Festival, Leicester, 1994. Photo by Jenny Carruthers.

It was Mary Byker who maintained the highest profile of all the Bykers. After several aborted attempts to start new bands, Mary received an unexpected leg-up when he went to an all-dayer at Finsbury Park in June 1991. On the bill were Bleach, The Rollins Band, Killing Joke, New Model Army, and The Mission. A backstage encounter with his friend Paul Raven, bassist for Killing Joke, resulted in him joining industrial supergroup, Pigface. Initially Mary didn't take the offer seriously. He recalls, "Raven gave me £200 and said, 'Get yourself a ticket to Chicago... Come and join Pigface', and

Front cover of For Lack Of Horses They Saddle Dogs. This was a collaboration between former Gaye Bykers On Acid (Kev), Bomb Party (Thommo) and Janitors (Tony Murray).

Raven and Mary outside the Astoria, London. 1988.

he introduced me to Martin Atkins who was playing drums with Killing Joke. Martin was like, 'Yeah, come over, come and play with Pigface!'" Mary pocketed the money and forgot all about the invitation until he received a couple of phone calls assuring him that both Raven and Atkins were deadly serious. Mary jetted over to the States and joined Pigface, appearing on the albums *Fook*, *Washingmachine Mouth* and *6*.

Later, Mary formed a new band, Hyperhead, with Martin Atkins, William Tucker (formerly of My Life With The Thrill Kill Kult and Revolting Cocks),

IT'S THE INDUSTRIAL SHOW FROM
THE BLACKEST PIT OF HELL ...

pigface

PIGFACE HAS
MORE FANS THAN
SPINAL TAP!!

PIGFACE *IS* (This Time Around):

MARTIN ATKINS *(PIL, Ministry, Murder Inc.)* ★ OGRE *(Skinny Puppy)*
EN ESCH *(KMFDM)* ★ WILLIAM TUCKER *(My Life With The Thrill Kill Kult)*
MARY BYKER *(Gaye Bykers On Acid)* ★ HOPE NICHOLS *(Fetchin Bones)*
GENESIS P-ORRIDGE *(Psychic TV)* ★ ANDREW WEISS *(Rollins Band)*
PAUL RAVEN *(Killing Joke)* ★ FLOUR

SAT.•JAN.23•BLIND PIG

Advance tickets: $9.50. Available at all [TICKETMASTER] outlets. Charge by phone: 645-6666. For 24 hr. concert & club info, dial 99-MUSIC. To join the Concertgoers Mailing List, dial 665-4755. A Prism Production.

Stop The Rock was one of several Top 10 hits Mary enjoyed with Apollo 440.

DONNERSTAG, 21. FEBRUAR 2002, 21.00 UHR

MAXIMUM ROACH

MAXIMUM ROACH sind ein wilder Haufen, spielen Jungle Surf mit viel Bass und ein wenig Rock, welchen sie mit fettem Hip Hop und Funky Grooves mixen. Zusammen kamen sie, als Teile der bekannten Live Band und co-writer von Apollo 440...
Auf der U2 Worldtour, wo Apollo 440 das Vorprogramm spielte, hängten sie eines Tages in einem türkischen Hotelzimmer und waren frustriert immer nur für andere Leute Musik zu schreiben und zu spielen. Soviel zur Gründung der Band.
MAXIMUM ROACH haben seit dem so bekannte Bands wie „Bloodhound Gang" und „Asian Dub Foundation" geremixt, waren unterwegs in England und haben an vielen europäischen Festivals gespielt. Ihre erste Single, die sie aufgenommen haben „Wanna Be A DJ" / „Feel It" wurde von ihnen und Chris Brown / Radiohead, produziert.
Die Single kommt pünktlich zur Europa-Tour, die im Februar 2002 stattfindet. Mit dabei sind Freunde wie Manchild und FJ Flightcrank (Leeroy, ex Prodigy), und ihr eigener DJ Harry K.
Mit MAXIMUM ROACH gibt es eine Perle der englischen Musikszene zu entdecken.

"A wild bunch... jungle surf with a lot of bass and a little rock... fat hip hop and funky grooves." German press release for Maximum Roach.

Karl Leiker, and Paul Dalloway. Hyperhead built a respectable following but split after a couple of EPs and one album, *Metaphasia*. Towards the end of the 1990s, Mary would achieve greater commercial success than he ever did with the Bykers, as a member of Apollo 440 (later Apollo Four Forty), an electronic outfit that racked up a string of top 10 UK chart hits. It is not possible to cover Mary's post-Bykers activity in detail, as it is worthy of a book in its own right; suffice it to say that while he wasn't so active through the noughties, he has remained the most proactive and prolific member of Gaye Bykers On Acid. After Apollo 440 took a hiatus of sorts, he formed Maximum Roach with former Apollo 440 bandmate, Noko. Also in the line-up was Paul Kodish, Mary's ex-wife Sarah Corina, and Felix Howard. Son of English folk musician Roy Harper, Howard had been a celebrated child model before achieving success as a songwriter and A&R man. Maximum Roach's surf/rockabilly drum and bass sound was a live pull, especially in Germany, Switzerland, the US, and even Turkey. "People loved us live," says Mary, "but record labels wouldn't touch us with a shitty stick… Too old and ugly maybe?"

Maximum Roach courted interest from Trent Reznor's Nothing label, but this came to nothing when the label was consumed as part of a corporate merger. Mary no longer felt Maximum Roach was sustainable and relocated to Rio de Janeiro. In 2007, he married his Brazilian partner, and they had a son. The couple established a restaurant and bar, where Mary frequently DJ'd along with other regular spots at clubs and bars in Rio. He also hooked up with some Brazilian musicians to work on soundtracks for an underground film production company. In 2011, Mary received a call from Graham Crabb who offered him an interesting proposition. The two of them announced in July 2011 that they would front a rejuvenated Pop Will Eat Itself. (Poppies frontman, Clint Mansell, had participated in a one-off PWEI reunion in 2005, but these days had other commitments, scoring Hollywood movie soundtracks such as *The Wrestler* and *Black Swan*.)

The latest incarnation of Pop Will Eat Itself was more than simply a band trading on past glories. It was an ongoing concern. Over time, former members Richard Marsh and Adam Mole would also rejoin. To date, the Mary and Crabb-fronted line-up has released two albums, an EP, and toured the US and Australia.

(L-R) Mary Byker and Graham Crabb fronted version of Pop Will Eat Itself. Bristol, December 2013.

Photo by Rich Deakin.

SWAMP THINGS

While Mary was busy jetting between the UK and Brazil to tour with Pop Will Eat Itself, Robber had reached a crossroads. For a while he had been living on a converted bus with his partner, Zoe Charles, and their two sons. Having previously recorded material together as Surfin' Bernard, the couple then briefly formed a 1960s soul and R&B covers band called The Nutters. When Robber split up with Zoe in 2013, he returned to Leicester where he wasted little time seeking out old friends and associates. He hooked up with Porkbeast, who, in the intervening years, had become of all things a professor!

Porkbeast confesses that for some time following his departure from the band, rock'n'roll was far from his mind. He had had his fill of it, in fact. With expectations now elevated above that of a life in a factory, however, Porkbeast decided to go back to school. He won an Arts and Humanities prize at college, and earned a first-class degree in English, History, and Politics. He received a scholarship, completed an MA, and then a PhD in Social History. An expert on the history of immigration, race, and ethnicity, Dr Alex 'Porkbeast' Peach then became a secondary school teacher. One might expect, given this change in vocation, that his musical days were well and truly behind him, but he kept his hand in with a band called Stressbitch, who played at one of Hawkwind's Easter weekend extravaganzas. However, a new band was the last thing on his mind when Robber got back in touch.

Robber's thoughts had already turned to new musical projects. It was over a drunken homebrew session around a bonfire in Porkbeast's garden that the idea for the band took shape. Porkbeast says, "We were lamenting that Crazyhead and Gaye Bykers On Acid might never get back together again." The obvious solution was to "form our own band, draw on our back catalogues, but do something new too". Calling it Swamp Delta, this is exactly what they did. Anderson might not have been the obvious choice for a frontman, given that he'd been teaching English in the Far East for most of the new millennium, but he'd kept his hand in musically and had performed in various cover bands, including Lazy Drunks and Stiff Little Punx, while in Thailand and Cambodia. Anderson picked up the gauntlet almost immediately. "I had to come back [to Leicester]," he says. "I'd got quite ill and then the chaps got in touch and they were doing some music and I had

some ideas for a song. I suggested doing a Stranglers-y Doors-y type of thing and that eventually became the track, Heavy Water."

A mooted Crazyhead reunion had already fallen through. Gaz Birtles, part of Crazyhead's Space Bastards brass section, had asked Reverb if he would be interested in getting the band back together to play Simon Says, a festival in Leicester. "That was the start of it really," recalls Vom. "I tracked down Alex [Porkbeast] through a friend, called him up, and we went out for a beer and a chat. Funnily enough, it wasn't too dissimilar to our very first get togethers when we discussed the band. Alex then managed to track Dick down, and with Kev in agreement we met for coffee, at — of all places — Fosse Park shopping centre. Ian couldn't make the meeting, but that was cool because we knew he was on board. It was great to meet up again." Unfortunately plans fell through when it became apparent there were issues between Reverb and Fast Dick that couldn't be resolved. Porkbeast refers to the rift as "a bit political".

Disappointed they were, but Porkbeast and Anderson didn't give up hope. Instead they concentrated on Swamp Delta, which would fittingly become something of an amalgamation of both Crazyhead and Gaye Bykers On Acid. It soon became obvious that things weren't working out with the original drummer of Swamp Delta, and Vom stepped up to the plate.

After Crazyhead called it a day in 2000, Vom and his wife Fiona began to concentrate on the company they had set up in 1997, Rhythms. They were later joined by Reverb, and for the next decade taught music in secure mental health units, special need schools and prisons. Their first Category A prison was Woodhill, where they were given access to its Close Supervision Centre. It was here Vom taught the so-called "most violent prisoner in Britain", Charles Bronson, "a great guy whose rendition of My Way will remain with us forever. He passed his Grade 3 Rockschool vocal exam with distinction," says Vom, and notorious serial killer, Levi Bellfield AKA 'The Bus Stop Stalker', who was in the Vulnerable Prisoners' Unit. Of Bellfield. Vom says, "sometimes you come across people who should remain in prison. He was one of them."

KLF founder Bill Drummond also joined Rhythms for one of their prison sessions. Among the participating inmates in this instance was a rabid Echo and the Bunnymen fan, a band who Drummond had once managed. Awestruck by Drummond's presence the fan became intensely fixated on him and gradually sidled up to within an inch of his face — much to the disconcertment of the usually unflappable Scotsman. Vom recounts another occasion when Zodiac Mindwarp expressed an interest in accompanying them on one of the prison sessions, too. Despite initial reservations, he acceded to Zodiac's request, pondering to

"Swamp Delta — the bastard son of Gaye Bykers On Acid and Crazyhead," live at The Donkey, Leicester, 6th December 2014. Photo by Rich Deakin.

himself, "what could possibly go wrong?" He says, "Prisons tend to have two-hour lunch breaks and during this time we went out for a pub lunch, without giving this proper thought. Five pints later, Z was far too refreshed, and the afternoon was spent following him and apologising to anyone who suspected he had been drinking, explaining he wasn't feeling well. We hammered out a version of Prime Mover with the Love Commander himself, me on drums, Reverb on guitar, Fiona on bass and some unsuspecting prisoners on percussion. You can imagine what it sounded like!" Once the session was over, they dropped "an agitated and slightly aggressive Zodiac" at the train station. "Later that night Z rang, drunk and angry, accusing us of

Poster for early Swamp Delta gig.

Swamp Delta — festive frolics at Karns, Hinckley, 27th December 2014.

traumatising him, blaming us for not only taking him into prison, but also for making him sleep with a prostitute when he jumped off the train at Kings Cross!"

Vom had also reunited with Zodiac Mindwarp & The Love Reaction in the early 2000s, and recorded several more albums with the group, played two American tours plus several more shows in Europe and Russia: "We were the first band to play New York, one week after 9/11." Vom then joined his old friends and erstwhile mentors, Diesel Park West, in 2007. Since then, he's performed on several albums and an EP with them, including *There's A Grace*, *Do Come In Excuse The Mess*, and *You, You, You & You*. During 2008 he formed his own band, Scaley Fuego, with Reverb and singer Kev Blackley, from another Leicestershire band, Black Carrot. They later changed their name to The Marinuccis. Vom soon found himself juggling drumming duties with Swamp Delta, who then enlisted Anthony 'Blink Cyclone' Smith on rhythm guitar to augment their sound. Blink, an old friend of theirs, was a veteran of the Leicester music scene, and at the time a member of another Leicester band, Gestalt. Anderson says, "We were all from the same roots. We're all old punks! All of us have played in Leicester bands."

Their old friend Greg Semple at this point plays a significant role, as it is he who helped to get Swamp Delta off the ground. Semple ran his own "social enterprise", Excluded, which assisted homeless people and recovering drug addicts to reintegrate into society through music. Robber, still living on a converted bus,

Anderson and Robber Byker's old childhood friend Greg Semple (AKA Bud Longtooth) helped the fledgling Swamp Delta get off the ground with his mini-mobile recording studio.

Leicester's oldest punk, Johnno, was in the video for Swamp Delta's Cut Loose single.

was effectively homeless and also unemployed. Semple carried a mini mobile recording studio in the back of his car as part of his rehabilitation scheme, and was happy to offer this, and the services of Excluded, to the fledgling Swamp Delta.

Robber and Porkbeast wasted no time in getting a set together and began gigging soon after. They had a wealth of songs from their time in the Bykers and Crazyhead, and it made sense to incorporate a few songs from each of their respective back catalogues to get things moving. They also included a few Stressbitch tracks and set about writing new songs, a necessity if they weren't going to be regarded as just another covers band. Their first song was Hanging Man. The fact that Anderson lived on the other side of the world wasn't insurmountable in the digital age. But he was due to visit the UK in any case, and Greg Semple drove to the hostel where Anderson was staying to record his vocals.

They made videos for The Hanging Man and Heavy Water and another new one, Cut Loose, which featured a star appearance from Johnno AKA John Goddard, miming the lyrics. A tattoo-covered septuagenarian, Johnno is a familiar face around Leicester and a legend in the national punk scene, reputedly having seen The Damned more than 550 times!

Swamp Delta turned their attention to recording an album. Even when Anderson returned to the Far East, he was able to contribute vocals, "thanks to the wonders of modern technology". The album itself was recorded at Bob Bryars' Quad Studios in Leicester, and the first three video singles were made available as downloadable MP3s. One of these, the video for title track Sick Liver Blues, featured uber fan and Las Vegas porn star Caroline Pierce. In April 2016, the Swamp Delta debut album *Sick Liver Blues* was released. It

Robber and Mary Byker at Gaye Bykers On Acid roadie Keith Penny's funeral. Leicester, July 2014.

came in the wake of other news: Gaye Bykers On Acid were reforming to play a mini tour that would culminate at the Indie Daze festival in London.

Sadly, around this time, Keith Penny's health took a turn for the worse. Penny had worked as a roadie for both the Bykers and Crazyhead at various points and remained firm friends until his untimely death from kidney-related complications in July 2014. At Penny's funeral, Robber read a eulogy for their stalwart roadie, and both he and Mary praised him in a *Leicester Mercury* tribute. Mary described Penny as "the fifth member of the band... He was always such a positive and good-humoured part of our crew, a good drummer in his own right and was our rock. He always had a smile on his face and was always prepared to help those in need. It was a privilege to have such a well-loved person by our side. He'll be sadly missed." ☠

CHAPTER THIRTEEN

THE ELECTRIC BANANA
BLOWS YOUR MIND

INDIE DAZE, AS ITS NAME SUGGESTS, IS A FESTIVAL THAT promotes reformed, or even still going, indie bands — primarily from the glory days of the 1980s and 1990s. Held annually each October, Graham Crabb DJ'd at the first event in 2014 and Pop Will Eat Itself played the second Indie Daze at The Kentish Town Forum in London the following year. Mary was already acquainted with promoter, Grant Holby, of Mute Elephant Music, and so it was somewhat inevitable that Holby would approach him to see if he'd like to reunite the Bykers for the next Indie Daze all-dayer, in October 2016.

Mary says it was Robber who had been "hassling" him for the last few years about getting the Bykers back together. Initially Mary resisted the idea, not least because of the logistics involved — Mary lived in Brazil, Tony was in Japan, and Kev was now in Brighton. Mary had vowed he'd never resurrect the Bykers, and when Holby approached him he might easily have kept quiet and that would have been an end to it. But the more Mary thought about it, the more he came around to the idea. His decision wasn't so much financially motivated, as much as it was based on a sense of closure, for himself, the band and the fans. That's not to say Holby's offer wasn't generous enough to make the reunion possible — what with the logistics of getting everyone in the same place together, and ensuring the band made something out of it too. Rockit Ron was unfortunately not able to partake in the reunion. Nevertheless, says Tony, "Getting the four of us together was quite an effort, and myself putting all the samples together, and Mary playing them seemed the easier way." Another face who played a significant part in the reunion was Jonny Milton AKA Jonny Reggae. Jonny had been the Byker's soundman and accompanied them again this time around.

The idea was to play just one or two gigs, which would serve as warm-up shows for Indie Daze. But as plans for the reunion unfolded more dates were added, making nine in total. Being well versed in performing live with Pop Will Eat Itself over the last few years, Mary had a handle on current promoters and the types of venues that would be suitable, and immersed himself in making arrangements for the tour. The internet obviously made matters easier. Things had come a long way since the early days of the Bykers, when he used to arrange gigs for the band with the help of Nick Toczek's photocopied loose-leaf bound *Independence File,* with its list of venues and other information useful to an aspiring indie band.

Mary acquainted himself with the Bykers' back catalogue. "I listened to everything and what I thought were the best pieces of music," he says. "The strange thing is we all pretty much agreed on the same things." Rehearsing together wasn't a viable option

Cover of Tony Byker's debut solo album Liquid Guru. Cover art by Simon Tripcony.

until closer to the tour, so the Bykers prepared for the reunion the best way they could, given their respective geographical differences.

Apart from playing his acoustic guitar, Tony had largely eschewed making music. But in 2012 he had begun working on new material and in March 2013 released his debut solo album, *Liquid Guru.* Thanks to the wonders of modern technology, the album included a collaboration with Mary Byker on a track called Dem King. Tony describes himself on his Facebook musician page as "Re-emerged, re-charged, re-vitalized, ready to mutate and create new Electro-Vybes, sending out new contradictions and collecting the old, in the crazy metropolis of Tokyo". By the time the Bykers' reunion was announced, he had another two albums under his belt, *The Apostles Of Absurdity* and *Orphic Hymns & Chronic Whims.* Like Mary, Tony and Kev had had no reason or compunction to revisit the old Bykers' songs in over 26 years. Tony explains his mindset, shortly after the second night of the reunion tour in Birmingham, "Lots of emails and Facebooking… I was sitting at home with my headphones on just jamming along. I had to analyse everything, because I haven't obviously for the last 20 years really got into it."

Kev, in the intervening years, had built a home studio in his back garden where he and guitarist friend, Tom Stanley, recorded mainly as a hobby. Despite having become more interested in drum machines, sequencers and digital

Kev Byker and Tom Stanley collaborate musically as Shed.

technology towards the end of the original Bykers, Kev kept his hand in with a real drumkit, so wasn't entirely rusty when preparations for the reunion tour began. He stands by the fact that a physical drum kit is also a good way to stay in shape, using it as part of a daily training regime. Says Kev, "playing drums is a lot better than jogging I can tell you... especially in the middle of winter! I'd try to recreate gig conditions because it was summer. I'd shut the doors on the shed, get it up to about 100 degrees [laughs] and sit there with a bright red head, sweating away — and it was good, I enjoyed it. I liked the discipline of it to be honest."

While preparations for the reunion came naturally for Kev, this wasn't necessarily the case for the other members. Tony admits he found it difficult to try to remember the songs, given the passage of time. Robber and Kev were the only two band members based in the UK at the time, so at least were able to rehearse together. Kev's musical collaborator in Brighton, Tom Stanley, had a playing style similar to Tony's and so stood in during Tony's absence. But it wasn't quite the same as all the band members being in the same room at the same time, like the old days.

During the last couple of years, Robber had had the opportunity to familiarise himself with some Bykers' songs, courtesy of Swamp Delta, and was regularly playing with local bands, including eighties Leicester punk outfit Rabid, and so was relatively match-fit. Rabid had been one of Keith Penny's early bands and now also included Colin Bennett on guitar, who knew most of the Bykers and Crazyhead, and over the years had played in numerous local bands. Bennett had roadied for Crazyhead in the late 1990s, more recently driving and roadie-ing for Swamp Delta. It made sense for the Bykers to employ him as their head roadie and technician. Initially Bennett was just going to help with the backline but ended up driving for the whole tour as well.

Having spent the summer preparing themselves individually, the moment of

Photo courtesy of Dokta Tinkle.

Colin Bennett (R) "knew most of the Bykers and Crazyhead from the Leicester post-punk/ alternative scene of the early eighties". Robber Byker (L) and Rob 'Vom' Morris (centre).

truth finally arrived. The Bykers descended on Quad Studios in Leicester for a week of intensive rehearsals prior to the tour. It was the first time in 25 years that all of them had been in the same room together. Any feelings of trepidation soon disappeared though, and the intervening years melted away. Mary recounts, "It was amazing! We walked into that room and I think someone said, 'Let's get the band back together', and everybody just started laughing. About five minutes later we all looked at each other and we went 'fucking hell!' It really was like we hadn't been apart."

The tour was named the Electric Banana, the pseudonym adopted by the Pretty Things for their appearance in *What's Good for the Goose*, a 1969 British film that starred comedian Norman Wisdom. (The Bykers had sampled a snatch of dialogue from the movie at the beginning of their 1989 song, Shoulders.) There hadn't been time to write or rehearse new material, so the set was a career spanning dive into the existing Bykers catalogue. It spanned their career evenly, although *Pernicious Nonsense* was perhaps under-represented with Disinformation Rise & Shine, but the set did include the PFX dance crossover song S.P.A.C.E.

The tour kicked off at The Doghouse in Nottingham on Friday 23rd September, with support from Evil Blizzard and The Go-Go Cult. Apart from the aforementioned PFX numbers, the set included, from *Drill Your Own Hole*,

Photo courtesy of Alex Peach.

Gaye Bykers On Acid at rehearsals, Quad Studios, Leicester, September 2016, "It was the first time in 25 years that all of them had been in the same room together."

TV Cabbage, Git Down, All Hung Up, After Suck There's Blow (something of a surprise inclusion, as it was very rarely played live first time around), *Stewed To The Gills* was represented by It Is Are You?, Better Off Dedd, M.A.D., Hot Thing, Rad Dude and Shoulders, the paean to their original travelling band of followers, The Daye Trippers. Mr Muggeridge was one of three cuts to make it from *Cancer Planet Mission* — the other two being Hope & Psyche and Face At The Window. Delerium from the *Nosedive* EP was another surprise addition to the set, in that it hadn't been played live since the Bykers supported The Cult at the Felt Forum in New York's Madison Square Gardens in July 1987. Despite Mary having admitted in a contemporary interview that Everything Groovy was one song he didn't like doing, it obviously couldn't be ignored — in many ways it was where it all began for the Bykers — and was the penultimate song throughout the tour. Invariably the finale was a rousing version of an all-time Bykers' favourite, Nosedive Karma. This set formed the template for the rest of the tour, give or take a few changes along the way.

Aside from a technical issue with Mary's microphone, all went smoothly, and considering it was the first time the band had played together in front of an audience in almost three decades, they were remarkably tight. The Bykers were well received in Nottingham and went down even better the next night at The Wagon & Horses in Birmingham, despite some difficulty finding the venue. The

CHAPTER THIRTEEN

band believed they had got lost because they were driving around what was an industrial wasteland on the edge of Digbeth and Deritend. Kev recalls his surprise on spotting the venue, one of the few habitable buildings still standing in the area. It looked rough and had no dressing rooms for the bands. But any misgivings soon dissipated as good old Brummie hospitality made up for the lack of creature comforts. As dusk settled, the venue area outside the back of the pub was transformed into what

Poster for Gaye Bykers On Acid, Electric Banana reunion tour, 2016.

Kev describes as "a little mini-festival". Support was from Kidderminster band Socio Suki and a prog/psych/punk outfit, Poisoned Electrick Head, who were popular on the festival circuit in the late 1980s and early 1990s. Shortly after 11:30pm the Bykers' took to the stage against a backdrop of synapse snapping psychedelic fractal videos and stunning light show. It was obvious from the get-go that the passage of time hadn't dulled the Bykers' passion or stolen their thunder. If anything, they were tighter than they'd ever been and performed with an urgency and maturity they could only have wished for the first time around, given the recreational excesses of their former selves.

The general consensus from the outset was that everyone wanted the reunion to be good. Getting wasted before going on stage wouldn't necessarily be conducive to achieving that goal. After the gig in Birmingham, Mary said that while in the past the band had "always gone on stage after drinking a load of beer and taking a load of speed, this time it was like 'let's all stay pretty sober.'" Not entirely sober as it turned

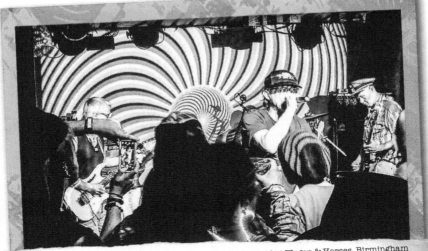

Second night of the Electric Banana tour. Gaye Bykers On Acid at Wagon & Horses, Birmingham 24th September 2016.

out. "We start drinking just before we go on to give ourselves a buzz and an edge… and I think it's great, because honestly it's shown a bit more respect for the fans — it's not cheap! People have paid to get in, so the last thing I wanna do is fucking leave them short-changed by a bunch of people off their heads!"

Kev takes a similar view. "We decided not to get fucked up before we played. Because very, very, very rarely did we all used to be on key, some of us would be tripping, or pissed, or… It didn't help, but at the time we didn't care. But this time we thought it would be a bit fairer to the people that were going to come and see us if we were actually a bit more coherent." In conclusion, says Kev, "it worked really well, we played a lot better."

It's unlikely the Bykers could have done anything wrong in the eyes of those watching at The Wagon & Horses. Kev was particularly touched by the enthusiasm of the audience that night, and considers it a favourite gig. "You got that real sort of raw anarchic feel to it where everyone was really up for it!" Leaving the Midlands on a high, the Bykers headed to the south coast for another couple of gigs. Southampton was not so well attended and then by the time they reached Brighton for a fourth gig on Monday 26th September, they were experiencing issues with the van. With five more dates to fulfil they had no choice but to replace it. Roadie Colin Bennett considers that Brighton was a turning point and, unlike the van, the Bykers were firing on all four cylinders

Photo courtesy of Mary Byker.

Gaye Bykers On Acid in front of the tour van outside Quad Studios, Leicester, with Colin Bennett (right).

by this point. Says Bennett, "Brighton was great. The gigs before it were good. However, I think the band had settled into it by the Brighton gig." Here they were supported by Deadcuts, fronted by former Senseless Things singer and guitarist Mark Keds.

The gig in Cardiff was more sparsely attended. Support was again Deadcuts, as it was for the following night at Fibbers in York. Bennett says that even the less well attended gigs were still worth it, and the audiences were brilliant everywhere, especially by the time they reached Trillians in Newcastle. The Bykers had always gone down well in the Tyneside city and tonight was no different. Several of the hardcore Daye Trippers hooked up here for the last few dates of the tour.

The Daye Trippers' trademark had been to clamber up on one another's shoulders for the song Shoulders, but Trillians didn't lend itself to such activities, due to its relatively small size and low ceiling. Nevertheless, one of the Daye Trippers, Tania Powell, got onto the stage during the song and Mary obligingly hoisted her up on his own shoulders. Also like the old days, some of the Daye Trippers, including Amy Freeman, helped on the merchandise stand. Another original Daye Tripper, Fifi Faiza Ariech, was serenading by a rousing rendition of Happy Birthday led by Mary. Another birthday girl was Las Vegas porn star and Bykers superfan Caroline Pierce. She flew from Vegas to follow the tour, and Mary bestowed upon her the accolade of "honorary Daye Tripper".

Photo courtesy of Glenn Sparrow.

Mary Byker, Indie Daze, October 2016.

"THIS IS ROBBER BYKER'S WORLD, AND YOU'RE ALL LIVING IN IT"

Throughout the tour Mary could at times be heard saying, "This is Robber Byker's world, and we're all living in it!" Taken in isolation, at just one gig, it may have appeared to be regular between-song banter, just another off-the-cuff comment typical of the singer. However, the remark in this instance had some cache. Mary suggests it came about during rehearsals, when it was observed that Robber was the only Byker still living in Leicester, and the rest of the band were merely "rehearsing in his manor". Robber is inclined to think it was more about Mary "taking the piss" out of him as anything else, "I think it's because I *am* living in my own world. I have issues with mental illness and drug addiction." The extent to which Mary agrees with Robber's issues is a matter of conjecture, what is not is the fact that the phrase became something of a Bykers in-joke.

The penultimate night of the tour was in Leicester. If the Bykers were sometimes met with indifference at hometown gigs back in the day, their sold out appearance at The Donkey had been hotly anticipated, especially as it was initially the only gig of the reunion apart from Indie Daze. The band was greeted

Daye Trippers "on shoulders" at Indie Daze, October 2016.

Photo courtesy of Glenn Sparrow.

by a partisan audience, consisting of the reunited Daye Trippers, friends, old punk scenesters and other travelling fans from far flung corners of the globe — some people had journeyed from as far as South Africa and Hong Kong. Colin Bennett says that if he had to pick a favourite gig from the tour, it was this one, "the homecoming gig." There were many old faces from back in the day, notes Bennett, but sadly one that was conspicuous in its absence — Keith Penny. Mary dedicated the night to Penny and later praised Bennett for having filled the boots left by the former roadie. High accolade indeed.

The Bykers headed to London the next morning for Indie Daze. Also on the bill were Jim Bob Carter, Pop Will Eat Itself, Echobelly and EMF. The Bykers' relatively lowly billing — coming on third, after Thousand Yard Stare and Bentley Rhythm Ace — was belied by the audience reception. If the number of Bykers t-shirts on display was anything to go by, many in the audience were there primarily for the Bykers. By the time the band took to the stage at 4pm, the crowd in the venue had swelled considerably. The pit at the front of the stage, energised by the Bykers, gathered momentum through a set that was shorter than the other dates of the tour — this was due to the day's schedule and running order times. The wider expanse of the Forum gave the Daye Trippers free rein to clamber onto each other's shoulders for their titular song. The set closed with Nosedive Karma once again, after which the Bykers took to the front of the stage

Photo by Rich Deakin.

A triumphant and emotional end to the Bykers' Electric Banana tour, Indie Daze, October 2016.

for a jubilant farewell bow. It was a triumphant and somewhat emotional end to the tour, ostensibly billed as the Bykers' last ever gig. But Mary's duties that evening were far from over: He returned with Pop Will Eat Itself to raise the energy levels once again, playing a set that included a mix of newer songs and Poppies' favourites. If two appearances would have been enough for most people, Mary later joined headliners EMF, along with an assortment of other Poppies and Jim Bob Carter, for the band's signature tune, Unbelievable. It provided a suitably boisterous finale to the evening.

Each of the Bykers enjoyed the reunion more than they would have imagined. Twenty-five years had passed since they last played together and yet, according to Mary, "when we got back together it was as if we'd never been apart. I forgot how much we all used to laugh, which, towards the end before the split, was rare as we'd lost our *joie de vivre*, it all became a bit of a chore. The reunion was a lot of fun!" With the exception of Southampton and Cardiff, the gigs were full, and the audiences were enthusiastic. The "hardcore" fans had the opportunity to see the Bykers play again, and those who had not managed to see them live suddenly had the chance to so. Some original fans even brought their children along! "We all wallowed briefly in nostalgia!" says Mary. "The support we got from the fans was amazing, it was great to see everyone ageing disgracefully!"

The financial outcome wasn't too bad, either. Says Tony, "It was cool to have

Robber Byker with Daye Trippers. Indie Daze, O2 Forum, Kentish Town, London. 1st October 2016.

fun, and actually make some dosh… unlike earlier Bykers tours." Mary concurs, "It was pretty good considering we promoted some of the shows ourselves, we all made a bit of pocket money." Grant Holby's role in the success of the tour is not to be underestimated. "The fact is we got offered decent money for the Indie Daze show," notes Mary. "Without that I doubt we'd have been able to afford to bring Tony over from Japan and me from Brazil." The money after all the overheads happened to be a rather pleasant bonus. The Bykers could also return to their respective lives safe in the knowledge they had achieved what Mary described as one of the primary motives for the reunion, and that was to have closure, particularly for the fans.

GONNA MAKE YOU AN OFFER YOU CAN'T REFUSE — CRAZYHEAD REUNION

Although an attempt to reunite the original line-up of Crazyhead had failed a few years earlier, the possibility had never entirely been ruled out. In any case, Swamp Delta featured three original members of the band, and also played a number of their old songs too. They'd also been prolific in writing new material,

30TH ANNIVERSARY
THE ELECTRIC BANANA TOUR

GAYE BYKERS ON ACID

2016

SEPTEMBER
23 NOTTINGHAM - THE DOGHOUSE
24 BIRMINGHAM - WAGON AND HORSES
25 SOUTHAMPTON - THE BROOK
26 BRIGHTON - THE KRUM?
27 CARDIFF - THE GLOBE
28 YORK - FIBBERS
29 NEWCASTLE - TRILLIONS
30 LEICESTER - THE DONKEY
OCTOBER
1 INDIE DAZE - LONDON FORUM

"A picture of a banana and a pair of oranges designed to leave little to the imagination." Reverse design for Electric Banana reunion tour t-shirt. Design by Tony Byker.

the fruits of which were borne out on their debut album, *Sick Liver Blues*, in April 2016. Indeed most of the former Crazyhead had projects to occupy themselves. Vom and Reverb were busy with The Marinuccis, and in August 2015, they released an eponymously titled debut album. Anderson was also establishing his other band, Brighton-based punkabilly quartet The Scavengers.

Given their current musical endeavours, a Crazyhead reunion was on the backburner. All this changed when Porkbeast went to see Gaye Bykers On Acid at Indie Daze in October 2016.

Once again, Grant Holby played a significant part in instigating the reunion. Porkbeast was backstage at the event and encountered Holby, who apparently made an offer on the spot for Crazyhead to play at the following year's event. Porkbeast couldn't answer for the others, but armed with the prospect of Holby's deal, they didn't take much persuading. The exception was Fast Dick, with whom matters still hadn't been resolved. In his place, the band approached Pete Creed, who readily accepted lead guitar duties. For Reverb the all-dayer was instrumental in pulling the band back together. "Indie Daze was a great target to aim for," he says, "I'm not sure if it would've happened without it." However, Anderson and Vom argue that the groundwork for the reunion had already been laid (at Fosse Park a couple of years previously, no less) and suggest it would have only been a matter of time before they got back together anyway. They acknowledge that Holby's intervention certainly hastened things along, and Vom makes no bones about the fact that the cash was a significant accelerant. "Grant offered us good money to play Indie Daze," says Vom, "which really made it feel worthwhile to do again. I feel no shame in saying that. It was our turn to cash in."

Given Porkbeast's return to the fold, there was no room for Christina Wigmore. The reunion line-up was one that had never played together before, being a hybrid of the original band that first played together in 1986, and the

Mark II line-up that bowed out in December 2000, minus the bridges between: Fast Dick and Christina. News of the reunion was kept under wraps for several months until Holby officially announced the bill for Indie Daze 4 in January 2017. The participating members of Crazyhead began preparations for the gig and fulfilled any outstanding commitments, such as Swamp Delta bookings. Conversely, the Bykers, fresh from their successful reunion, returned to their various day jobs and respective musical activities.

CHRONICLES OF THE ELECTRIC BANANA

The Bykers have always been a band that liked to keep things in-house, or within a coterie of friends and associates, and embrace the DIY ethos where possible. Their own Naked Brain record label comes foremost to mind, but on top of this the band has handled much of its own publicity and merchandising, designing and producing t-shirts. For example, the Electric Banana tour t-shirt design re-cycled Mark Wagstaff's original PFX logo for the front, and on the back was a picture of a banana and a pair of oranges designed to leave nothing to the imagination. It was in the same spirit of some of the Bykers' t-shirt designs from the late 1980s, even if not quite as anatomically explicit as the 'Strewth it's the Lesbian Dopeheads On Mopeds' design, or another memorable Bykers t-shirt, popularly known as 'The Surf Bastard'. As then, Bykers' merchandise, particularly t-shirts, proved to be a modest income supplement to the band's coffers.

The Bykers have never been shy of video experimentation either, as per their first attempts at music videos with their old pal Dave Bartram, and their over-ambitious foray into feature length film-making, the *Drill Your Own Hole* movie. Naïve they might have been, but they had been enthusiastic and eager to learn. Fast forward to the mid-2010s, which finds Tony on a roll with his recent prolific musical output. Tony had gained experience in digital video technology, producing promotional videos for several of his solo songs, and it was this immersive attitude that Tony applied to the Bykers Electric Banana reunion, specifically a multimedia project that would document the tour. He mobilised the Electric Banana video project largely via social media and mobile phone technology. Love it or loathe it, it's a simple fact of gig going today, and Tony exploited the notion that a fair percentage of the audience would be pointing their smartphones towards the stage. Whereas many bands baulk at the idea of

Photo courtesy of Tony Byker. Source: Gaye Bykers On Acid Bandcamp page.

Six DVD Electric Banana Tour 2016 box-set.

hordes of fans waving iPhones, the Bykers embraced the opportunity it offered and used it to their own advantage. The Beastie Boys had done something similar in 2005, when they handed out 50 Hi-8 video cameras to pre-selected fans before a gig at Madison Square Gardens in New York. The Bykers took it several steps further to its logical conclusion.

Tony utilised photographs, audio and video footage taken by fans and the band's entourage on their own devices throughout the tour, in return for a credit should the material be used. The task of sifting through the results was Herculean, the quality varied widely, but in the end, Tony painstakingly pieced the material together to recreate five full shows and two half shows out of the original nine dates. *The Electric Banana Tour DVD Box Set* is the result, a lavish package comprising six DVDs and bonus material composed from fan sourced snippets, photos and sound files. Simon Tripcony provided the boxset artwork, a graphic designer and fan who has since reimagined Bykers' covers for various live bootlegs and other rarities. *Electric Banana* is the culmination of six months' hard work by Tony, and represents a career defining showcase for the band and fans alike. ☠

IT'S THE...
LESBIAN DOPEHEADS ON MOPEDS!!

The monster phallus wielding transvestite "Strewth it's the Lesbian Dopeheads On Mopeds" [t-shirt] design adapted from Sally Jones' original photograph.

CHAPTER FOURTEEN

EMERGING FROM THE SWAMP

IT WAS INEVITABLE THAT SWAMP DELTA WOULD DISBAND once commitments had been fulfilled. Three members would be turning their attentions to the Crazyhead reunion, and it appears some of the fun had gone out of the whole thing. Rehearsals had become irregular, with members not always turning up. Travel expenses were not always forthcoming and, to cap it off, the fact that it had taken three years to record the Swamp Delta album had raised some eyebrows. Porkbeast, the driving force behind the band, had wanted the album to sound just right. Anderson says the process became tiresome.

Like the Bykers, Indie Daze became the focus for the Crazyhead reunion, with several gigs arranged around it. Although rehearsals weren't as logistically challenging for Crazyhead as they had been for Gaye Bykers On Acid, geographical differences were still prohibitive. Porkbeast, Vom, and Reverb all lived in the Leicester area, so getting together for rehearsals wasn't too much of

Poster for first gig of the Crazyhead reunion, 15th September 2017.

Photo by Rich Deakin

Anderson at The Donkey, Crazyhead's first gig in 27 years. The Donkey, Leicester, 15th September 2017.

an issue. However, for Anderson on the south coast and Pete Creed in Devon, it wasn't so easy. They did the best they could. Despite some differences of opinion in the past, and recent issues within Swamp Delta, rehearsals went smoothly. Reverb says, "It all came together really easy, I think everyone accepted that if it was gonna work then old rifts would have to be forgotten and we'd have to start with a clean slate. We could tell from the first rehearsal that the playing was not going to be a problem and we've all got on really well."

The day of reckoning arrived on 15th September 2017, at The Donkey in Leicester. It was the favoured local venue for Swamp Delta, Gaye Bykers, and now Crazyhead. Not only did members of the band have ties with the venue, but it was also frequented by many friends and contemporaries. Support came from Mystery Action. This was the band of Swamp Delta guitarist Anthony 'Blink Cyclone' Smith's — a psychobilly combo with a penchant for voodoo-style garb and make-up. Their Cramps-influenced set helped to warm-up a swelling crowd and the venue was full to capacity by the time Crazyhead took the stage. Launching their set with In The Sun, it was the first time in almost 17 years that a full Crazyhead line-up had played together, since the now defunct Princess Charlotte, also in Leicester. Jack The Scissor Man and Time Has Taken Its Toll On You followed, just as they do on *Desert Orchid*. Although the gig was billed as a 30th anniversary reunion — being almost three decades years since *Desert Orchid*

Photo by Rich Deakin.

Comeback kids! Crazyhead's first gig in 27 years. The Donkey, Leicester, 15th September 2017.

was released — the night was very much about their debut album. With the exception of Rags, all the early singles on Food and Parlophone were included, as were choice B-side tracks like Rub The Buddah and (Here Comes) Johnny.

If Pete Creed had only been familiar with about a third of this set previously, a crash course weekend staying with Reverb had paid off, and he handled the lead parts expertly. Anderson, resplendent in his trademark shades, a classic Vive Le Rock t-shirt, and with flowing locks, prowled the stage with the assured confidence of the frontman he always was. Porkbeast, wearing a replica German military helmet and novelty sunglasses, was certainly narrower of girth and less hirsute these days, but he still struck an imposing figure in his signature stance, leaning back, legs akimbo, thrusting his bass guitar skywards. Vom was spritely as ever, a veritable powerhouse as he mercilessly thrashed his kit. Reverb added a sense of gravitas to the occasion, attired in black-rimmed specs, smart cowboy shirt, and lariat tie. His hair may have disappeared, but his guitar skills were missing nothing. Several of the closing songs in the set were covers. These enveloped what is Crazyhead's defining track, What Gives You The Idea That You're So Amazing?, and included Bang Bang, Have Love, Will Travel, followed by TV Eye. A rowdy and appreciative hometown crowd lapped it up. If proof was needed that Crazyhead could replicate the incendiary live performances of their heyday, then this had been it.

With two more gigs in Nottingham and Derby, Crazyhead were more than ready for Indie Daze on 7th October 2017. The line-up for this year's annual all-dayer included Bis, Salad, Thousand Yard Stare, Miles Hunt & Erica Nockalls, Apollo 440 (with an appearance from Mary Byker), old friends and former Food labelmates Voice of the Beehive, and, topping the bill, House Of Love. Crazyhead were over halfway up the bill, and other acts paled next to their brand of grungy garage rock. If Leicester and the other two East Midlands gigs had been for the home fans as much as themselves, then Indie Daze was all-out for the fans. A group of these, the notorious Bug Eyed Monsters, grew in number come Indie Daze. Crazyhead's appearance also fulfilled the dream of other fans, not least a couple who had married after meeting at a previous Indie Daze. According to Anderson, the couple had said that "their perfect wedding gift would be for Crazyhead to reform and play the festival, so it would have been churlish not to".

More dates were added to the schedule and the band rounded off the year on a high with two gigs in December, one at The Lending Room in Leeds and the other at The Claptrap in Stourbridge, where they were supported by local band Flying Ant Day and Midlands garage combo, D.C. Spectres. Given the success of the reunion, thoughts turned to the possibility of more dates in the new year. But, as Reverb notes, "We all agreed that we didn't want to flog it into the

Poster for Crazyhead at the 100 Club, 4th May 2018.

ground." Crazyhead stuck by the idea of playing only five or six times a year. For a start they had day jobs to consider. Work commitments would be a barrier to an ongoing reunion, and so where possible the band would only play on weekends. Logistics and finance were also factors but, as Anderson points out, the reunion was never simply about money. "Some band members get highly paid for session playing and teaching work," he says, adding that the band could have played "hundreds of gigs" as opposed to the 20 or so they opted to do. The motivation behind the reunion was to do something "special" and the next gig they announced was certainly that. The 100 Club on London's Oxford Street in May 2018 was their first headline gig in the capital in 27 years.

Promoted by Mute Elephant, support was provided by Guttfull, self-described "Queercore sax punx", and The Hip Priests, manic, garage punkers who looked every inch like members of an outlaw motorcycle gang. Their boisterous high-octane rock'n'roll antics were always going to be a hard act to follow, and they might have upstaged a lesser headliner, but Crazyhead came on to huge applause and the launched into a powerhouse set. Anderson was less mobile than usual because of a leg injury, and consequently was on the receiving end of light-hearted jibes from his bandmates which he took in his stride — albeit a limp one. In the absence of new material, the set comprised material from *Desert Orchid* and a smattering of singles A- and B-sides. Cardinal Phink had been added to the set, as had Rags, albeit without horns. Everything's Alright was the only song played from the band's second album. The Bug Eyed Monsters made their presence felt throughout the set, but the greatest enthusiasm was reserved for the old fast and furious garage punk favourites, Baby Turpentine and What Gives You The Idea

Crazyhead, 100 Club, 4th May 2018.

Photo by Rich Deakin

That You're So Amazing Baby. They may not have played for months, but the band was tighter and more assured than they had been at the start of the reunion in September.

Crazyhead appeared at a handful of festivals through spring and summer. The first was the somewhat incongruous Uprising III, a heavy metal festival held at De Montfort Hall, one of Leicester's largest and most established venues. Despite hailing from the city, Crazyhead had only played De Montfort Hall once before, over 31 years ago when they were starting to make a name for themselves, supporting The Cult. Then in May they appeared at Bearded Theory's Spring Gathering, a respected annual event on the festival circuit. Other artists included Idles, Jimmy Cliff, Robert Plant, Sleaford Mods, The Coral, and The Jesus and Mary Chain. Pete Creed took the opportunity to resurrect Reverb's old white and tartan Bay City Rollers trousers, giving them an airing on the main stage.

It was obvious the Crazyhead reunion was shaping up to be a different beast than the Gaye Bykers Electric Banana tour. Whereas the Gaye Bykers reunion had been like a stealthy search and destroy mission, with nine live dates in just over a week, Crazyhead's was spread over a longer timeframe, with further gigs being added as an ongoing concern. Several more gigs ensued through the remainder of 2018 and early 2019. Festival dates were particularly popular, and in May 2019 they were booked to play Mute Elephant's Gigantic Festival. It was similar to Indie Daze

Pete Creed in Reverb's old Bay City Rollers trousers. Bearded Theory's Spring Gathering, May 2018.

in terms of the type of bands booked but was held in Manchester instead of London.

Crazyhead's next booking was a different proposition altogether. Established in 2011, Kozfest is held in the rural idyll of north Devon. A small paying festival limited to no more than 500 people, it has the feel of the free festivals of the 1970s and 1980s — very different to most contemporary summer music festivals. Kozfest puts on a smorgasbord of psychedelia and space rock, mainly featuring bands unknown beyond their own alternative circles. Bands such as Deviant Amps, Paradise 9, and Hoffman's Bicycle have all made appearances over the years, while some of the more established psych rock and acid punk acts like Gong, System 7, Vibravoid, Litmus, Pre-Med, and Bristol's cult stoner rock band The Heads, have played too.

Taking place on a late-July weekend in 2019, the organisers had secured veteran free festival acid punks Here & Now as Friday night's headliners, and German space rockers Electric Moon on Sunday, with Crazyhead topping the main stage bill on Saturday night. After the Gigantic festival, it was being advertised as Crazyhead's "last gig for some time" and other posts promoted it as their "last gig of the year" — it didn't take much to figure that a hiatus of some sort was in the offing. Two days later, and just two weeks before Kozfest, Reverb intimated that he had taken early retirement from his day job and was planning to relocate to the property he owned in Turkey. This suggested Crazyhead's activities would be curtailed in the near future, although it soon became apparent that Reverb intended to come back to the UK for a few weeks each summer and would be up for playing live dates if the rest of the band were. In the meantime, though, they had Kozfest to attend to.

Coincidentally, Nick Raybould, Crazyhead's graphic designer when they were on Black/FM Revolver in 1990, was also performing at Kozfest with his band

Delphini. He met the band again for what was probably the first time in nearly 30 years. Crazyhead weren't the usual fare on the Kozfest bill, and Raybould says he wasn't entirely sure how they might be received by the audience. "Sure there was that grimy Stooges reference in common, but Crazyhead were never actually what I'd consider a psychedelic band, despite creating such lush and swirly whirlers like Magic Eye. To my knowledge, they had never played any similar events to Kozfest either. I was a bit concerned that their period of inactivity through the nineties and beyond had meant they'd missed the space rock/psych/punk boat a bit."

Poster for Kozfest July 2019.

Any misgivings Raybould had soon melted away. Crazyhead took to the stage to blast through a 90-minute set. Raybould was pleasantly surprised to hear the band's repertoire still included Everything's Alright — a song he'd been very close to. In fact, he couldn't fault the set: "the mix was fantastic... The sound was appropriately brutal and the lighting and projected visuals were also on the money... This lovely vibe was clearly picked up on by the audience, many of whom were less familiar with what Crazyhead were all about but were all swiftly won over."

Anderson says he was surprised how many of the audience knew the Crazyhead songs and sang along to them, although "the [Crazyhead] virgins also loved it". Still imbued with the cosmic spirit of the occasion, he says, "There was a real livewire connection between the band and the audience, merging into a gestalt of messed up rockin', everyone was dancing and smiling like mad dervishes for the hour and a half set... We all agreed it was the best one [of the reunion] yet!"

Crazyhead's performance proved to be one of the highlights of a particularly

Kozfest 2019, Crazyhead clearly enjoyed themselves with "plenty of brotherly banter" between songs.

musical summer for Nick Raybould: "That's the lovely thing about being around this little musical scene, the lovely surprise reunions with folk. And in the case of Crazyhead… time actually had *not* taken its toll."

As much as Anderson enjoyed the festival vibes, he was unable to stay for the rest of the weekend as he was booked to play at Camp Bestival the following day with his other band, The Scavengers. Pete Creed dropped him off at Barnstaple train station on Sunday morning. Little did Anderson realise how long the journey would take. After nearly seven hours, he finally made it with five minutes to spare before The Scavengers went on stage. This was a more family-oriented festival than Kozfest, and one of The Scavengers' wives helped organise the Caravanserai stage. The band had played Bestival for free the year before, too, although they did get free camping and weekend passes. This was little consolation to Anderson who was somewhat exhausted, not to mention dispirited to find himself playing to a crowd of around only 30 people, compared to the nearly 500 at Kozfest the night before.

Although Kozfest was publicised as Crazyhead's last gig of the year, the band announced another date at short notice, scheduled for 30th August at The Donkey, their "spiritual rock'n'roll home". This was part of a series of weekend events in honour of departing landlords, Zoe Keightley and Warren McDonald. With Reverb's leaving date for Turkey now established, it would be Crazyhead's last gig for the "foreseeable future". An unfortunate clash of events meant that Swamp Delta guitarist Anthony 'Blink Cyclone' Smith was unable to attend. His own band, Mystery Action, were playing at another Leicester venue. Support at the Donkey was one of Colin Bennett's bands, The Rong'uns. Formed in 1997, the Leicester punk band underwent a few line-up changes before disbanding in 1999. In 2017, Bennett resurrected The Rong'uns on the 20th anniversary of their original formation, with a line-up that now included Robber Byker on bass. They played several gigs, including a benefit for homeless people in Leicester, and recorded an EP in time for their support slot with Crazyhead. Titled *No. 1*, the EP included three original compositions, Johnny Boy, Social Control, and Growing Old Disgracefully, plus a blistering version of the Slaughter and the Dogs speed freak classic, Cranked Up Really High. The former Swinging Laurels sax player, John Barrow, guested on the recording and joined the band on stage. Attending the Donkey gig was Leicester writer, poet, artist and long-time Crazyhead friend, Adrian Manning. He recalls that as the temperature rose during The Rong'uns' set, a couple of ska numbers helped slow things down, "but their cover of the Rocket From The Tombs/Dead Boys classic Sonic Reducer was just the prelude to the main act that was needed."

By the time Crazyhead took to the stage, another large hometown crowd had turned up to bid the band farewell. Manning recounts, "the love for them was evident from the off. The crowd were anticipating a great gig, the band themselves were in very good humour, and the air of celebration was evident." Many of the Bug Eyed Monsters were there to pay a heartfelt tribute. Manning continues, "It was a wonderful night, great crowd. There were a lot of people who used to follow us in the late eighties. They were very young then, hitchhiking from gig to gig, and sleeping wherever they could. They were lovely young people then and my heart swells to see what brilliant adults they've become."

Launching with In The Sun, Crazyhead then tore through a set that varied little from the ones they'd played throughout the reunion but didn't fail to entertain. The band was joined by Gaz Birtles and John Barrow to reprise their role as The Space Bastards on Rags. This was a highlight of the evening according to Manning, who recalls that The Space Bastards were "received with massive enthusiasm by the audience and played a blinder".

No Crazyhead set would be complete without Baby Turpentine or What Gives You The Idea That You're So Amazing Baby, which traditionally on the tour had been the set closer. Everyone knew there was more to come after this, though, and Crazyhead unleashed a barrage of encores, starting with a rough and ready version of The Ramones' Blitzkrieg Bop. It mattered little that Anderson

Crazyhead's last gig as of August 2019. Reverb moved to Turkey soon after. The Donkey, Leicester, 30th August 2019.

missed his cue and fluffed the words a couple of times; it was Crazyhead's party, or perhaps more appropriately Reverb's leaving party, and nothing was going to spoil it, not even cramp. Over the years, Reverb has had on-and-off issues with the index finger of his left hand in the form of cramp, with it sometimes locking completely. It usually surfaced towards the end of a long set, but here much sooner and he had to keep dipping the troublesome digit into cold water to try to alleviate the symptoms. Vom, with 22 years' experience as a professional masseur and soft tissue therapist at Leicester Tigers Rugby Club, was quite literally on hand to give Reverb "running repair" finger massages throughout the set.

It didn't detract from the performance. For the second encore, Have Love, Will Travel, Crazyhead were joined again by The Space Bastards. This being the first time in about 30 years that The Space Bastards had appeared on stage with Crazyhead, Reverb, ever the joker, took the opportunity to resurrect an old jape. "I used to have a wag where I'd stick my scaly tongue in John [Barrow]'s ear when he played a solo. I managed to repeat the trick." The band ran through two more songs, Sinking Feeling and TV Eye, then it was all over... for now at least.

Reverb, who had handled the sound at The Donkey many times over the years, says, "It was a great way to end this phase of Crazyhead." It had been an emotional farewell on more than one level. Soon after the gig, Reverb said with genuine affection that the venue was "unique... I'll be eternally grateful for

having the opportunity to be a small part of such an iconic moment in Leicester's diverse music and cultural history."

The whole reunion had been a success. The band could still pull a crowd when the occasion warranted it and had attracted new admirers — as Kozfest amply demonstrated. Like the Bykers reunion they proved that they had matured emotionally and professionally and were capable of putting old differences behind them, possibly playing better than they had in the past. Says Reverb, "we've really gelled as a band and as people." Performing 'straight' for the first time in years, Pete Creed was humbled by the reunion experience, particularly given his long-term drug problems. He'd only really managed to get his addiction under control 18 months before Crazyhead's first reunion gig and openly expressed his gratitude on social media for the band having given him the chance to play with them again, and among others extended thanks to Colin Bennett for "doing my dirty work and being a great pal".

A LOUD AND LOUSY BURST OF DIRTY THUNDER

Apart from forming at roughly the same time in the mid-1980s, various members of both bands are inextricably linked by childhood friendships, musical ties and geographical bonds. It's somewhat fitting then that Gaye Bykers On Acid and Crazyhead should both reunite within a year of each other over 30 years later, and then close another career chapter in a similar fashion. Some cynics regard such reunions as nothing more than jumping on the comeback bandwagon trail, on which bands canter through the most popular songs of their back catalogues, adding nothing to their respective legacies, but plenty of money to their bank accounts. There is possibly an element of truth to this, and members of both bands have admitted the initial financial package was an incentive, but this was because it actually made their reunions viable, rather than any illusions about becoming millionaires. That they ended up making a modest bit of moolah just happened to be a welcome bonus. Many fans welcome their favourite band's reunion, especially when the line-up contains nearly all the original members, as was the case with both the Bykers and Crazyhead. There is always going to be an element of nostalgia in these kinds of reunions, but both bands proved they could still cut the mustard and weren't just going through the motions — even if older, and in some cases a little balder.

With their glory days well and truly behind them, and the term 'grebo' long since confined to the footnotes of rock'n'roll history, both the Bykers and Crazyhead had largely been unfettered by the lack of media scrutiny and relative absence of any expectations to live up to, except those of themselves and their fans, and they achieved what they set out to do to, e.g. take care of unfinished business, at least as far as the Bykers were concerned anyway.

Although less encumbered by the negative connotations of the 'grebo' label, there can be no getting away from the fact that both bands will forever be linked to the genre, like it or not. Whether the term did them more harm than good in the long run is open to debate. What is not, however, is the role the media played. Who knows how differently things might have been had it not been for those self-proclaimed arbiters of cool, the British music press? Initially it was as much in the media's own interests to provide a ready-made platform for its self-constructed 'grebo' genre, as it was for the bands lumped under its umbrella. But it was a double-edged sword, and like smiling assassins the media munificently built the likes of the Bykers and Crazyhead up, only to ruthlessly cut them down again once it had turned its attention to the next big thing. Grebo became yesterday's news, and somewhat risible news at that, but in the process, for better (at least at first anyway) or worse, the Bykers and Crazyhead became forever guilty by association.

And what of its legacy? 'Grebo' might not have set the mainstream charts ablaze, but, if nothing else, for 18 months or so, it provided a welcome antidote to the pop charts. At one end of the spectrum you'd find manufactured pop-pap like Sinitta, Kylie Minogue and Rick Astley, straight off the Stock, Aitken & Waterman production line, and at the other end spandex-trousered, poodle-haired rockers such as Bon Jovi, Poison and Mötley Crüe. Even the indie charts, although not entirely the preserve of earnest, chin-scratching musos, were awash with fey, floppy-fringed, be-anoraked C86 indiepop bands. Unlike many of the po-faced indie and goth miserabilists doing the rounds, at least Gaye Bykers On Acid and Crazyhead didn't take themselves too seriously. Riding in on a loud and lousy burst of dirty thunder, they injected some much-needed anarchy and excitement back into the British alternative music scene at a time when it needed it most. ☒

EPILOGUE

2020 PARADIGM SHIFT

O N 3 DECEMBER 2019 IT WAS ANNOUNCED ON FACEBOOK that Gaye Bykers would be reuniting to play at the 100 Club the following May, and, just over two months later on 31st January 2020, released more tour dates. According to Tony Byker he suggested they call it the "2020 Paradigm Shift" tour, but, he says, "when the others asked what I meant, and I explained that this year [2020] was going to be a huge change in consciousness regarding New World Order takeover and general world madness they said it was a bit too serious. Hence '2020 Vision.'" News also broke of the first all new Gaye Bykers On Acid material in 30 years. Then, in February, Crazyhead confirmed several live dates for August 2020 with the possibility of recording new songs, the intention being that Reverb would tap into his inner muse now he had more time on his hands living in Turkey.

At around the time that the Bykers announced their tour, news of a flu-like virus — typified by pneumonia-like symptoms, and first recorded in the Chinese city of Wuhan in December 2019 — was identified by the World Health Organisation as Novel coronavirus (2019 nCov). It became better known simply as coronavirus or COVID-19. As the contagion took hold and the world went into a state of lockdown, inevitably both the Bykers and Crazyhead tours were postponed,

Mute Elephant poster for Gaye Bykers On Acid 2020 Vision tour. Artwork and design by Tony Byker/layout by Simon Tripcony.

MUTE ELEPHANT AND FRIENDS PRESENT

GAYE · BYKERS · ON · ACID

PFX

MAY	2020 VISION
22ND	SHEFFIELD THE FOUNDRY
23RD	LIVERPOOL ARTS CLUB
24TH	NEWCASTLE O2 ACADEMY
25TH	NOTTINGHAM BILLY BOOTLEGGERS
26TH	LEICESTER O2 ACADEMY
27TH	NEWPORT LE PUB
28TH	BIRMINGHAM HARE & HOUNDS
29TH	LONDON 100 CLUB SOLD OUT
30TH	BRIGHTON HOPE & RUIN

TICKETS// WE GOT TICKETS / SEE TICKETS & USUAL OUTLETS
MUTE-ELEPHANT-MUSIC.CO.UK

although the new Gaye Bykers On Acid EP was released as planned in April 2020.

Accompanied by a Tony Byker produced video that featured vintage footage of the band, the EP is representative of past glories — the lyrics even crib the opening line from Nosedive Karma! Picking up from where the Bykers left off 30 years previously, the title track, Sodium Sun, also appears to be a warning about

mankind's continued destruction of the planet. It also seems to be making a comment about the danger of supposed populist politics, and divisive events like Brexit. With its environmental message, and Mary's plaintive vocals juxtaposed with the screaming urgency of Tony Byker's sublime guitar, Sodium Sun is a dramatic exercise in 'exuberant melancholy', displaying a maturity and discipline that was perhaps not quite as evident back in the day. But, Back On Track is clearly as much a boisterous celebration of the band's last reunion tour. Rather than being just a pensive stroll down memory lane, Back On Track is as defiant as it is wistful. A heavy, funky slap bassline provides a Red Hot Chili

Poster for Sodium Sun E.P. Artwork & design by Tony Byker. Layout by Simon Tripcony.

Peppers vibe, but there's also a hint of Leicester descendants Kasabian too. The EP owes as much to the Bykers' legacy as it does other influences, and with industrial techno, acoustic and electro dub remixes, they've clearly brought elements of their own current musical endeavours to the table too. It may have taken 30 years to fully realise the potential of the technology they began to embrace years ago, but the Bykers really were on track with this EP. It's just a shame the '2020 Vision' tour wasn't able to complement its release. Originally postponed until February 2021, as of writing it has been rescheduled again for November 2021, while Crazyhead have tentatively pencilled in July 2021 for their three revised shows in Nottingham, Stourbridge and Leicester.

POST-APOCALYPTIC POSTSCRIPT
LIVING FOR TODAY, NO LOOKING BACK

Since the start of their respective reunion activities, various members of both the Bykers and Crazyhead have continued to pursue side-projects or solo endeavours

Rescheduled for a second time due to COVID-19. November 2021 tour dates. Artwork and design by Tony Byker/layout by Simon Tripcony.

MUTE ELEPHANT AND FRIENDS PRESENT:

GAYE BYKERS ON ACID

NOVEMBER 2021 RESCHEDULED DATES ALL ORIGINAL TICKETS VALID

11TH LEICESTER O2 ACADEMY 12TH LIVERPOOL ARTS CLUB 14TH GLASGOW BROADCAST
15TH NEWCASTLE THINK TANK 16TH NOTTINGHAM THE SQUARE CENTRE 17TH NEWPORT LE PUB
18TH BIRMINGHAM HARE & HOUNDS 19TH LOND *SOLD OUT* CLUB 20TH BRIGHT *SOLD OUT* E & RUIN

TICKETS: WE GOT TICKETS / SEE TICKETS & USUAL OUTLETS   MUTE-ELEPHANT-MUSIC.CO.UK to varying degrees (all impeded to some extent by the coronavirus pandemic).

Mary Byker: In early 2019, he was working on a new dance project called Magnetic Empire. Mary reunited with his former Apollo 440 and Maximum Roach bandmate Noko and crowdfunded a new project *Am I Dead Yet?* to favourable reviews. Sounding at times like a cross between an Ennio Morricone score and a film-noir soundtrack, this writer likens it to "a mid-life meditation on love, loss, longing and facing up to one's own impending mortality. There are also echoes of Scott Walker and David Bowie in that respect then." Mary hooked up again with Apollo 440 for the Shiine On Weekender in November 2019 and soon after toured the States with Pigface. Mary continues to co-front Pop Will Eat Itself with Graham Crabb and live-streamed a gig limited attendance performance at the Islington Assembly Hall, London, in December 2020.

Robber Byker: In 2018, Robber adopted the pseudonym Sebastian T. Palmer and co-established Ubertroll Recordings. The label has released several volumes of original Ubertroll albums that feature a variety of guests, including Anderson and musicians from the Leicester scene from bands such as Mystery Action, Tri Subversion, Swinging Laurels and The Rong'uns. Of the 2020 lockdowns, Robber says, "I'm on a three-day working week, which means a four-day weekend… so I've been in the studio and on the Xbox a lot." The fruits of the recording studio are manifest on Ubertroll Recordings under the pseudonyms Billy Bob Thorton the 3rd and The Walton Clan. He has also been working on a band idea

Am I Dead Yet? promo shot. Photo courtesy of Simon Cusick.

Photograph courtesy of Ila Desai, I Was There Photography.

Mary Byker with Pop Will Eat itself, Islington Assembly Hall, 12th December 2020.

Robber AKA Sebastian T. Palmer AKA Billy Bob Thorton. Photo courtesy of Billy Bob Thorton.

with Crazyhead's Vom and Cobalt Stargazer from Zodiac Mindwarp & The Love Reaction.

Kev Byker: Kev has continued to work with Tom Stanley as Shed and they have collaborated with Robber Byker on two volumes of *Shed v Robber*. In 2018, Kev and Tony Byker reprised their early nineties industrial techno hardcore outfit Steroid, and, with additional assistance on guitar from Tom Stanley, released two albums, *Scrotox Ulcer* and *Baptising The Alien*. Kev has also released albums of cover versions using the name Kev Byker's All Stars. He has interpreted songs by artists as diverse as Evil Blizzard, David Bowie, ABBA, Dead Kennedys,

Hawkwind and Gary Numan.

Tony Byker: Tony has taken on the role of preserving the Bykers legacy by maintaining a digital archive of their official releases, numerous live recordings, and other extras and videos. Since the Bykers reunited in 2016, he has also released six more solo albums, the last three of which might justifiably be described as his conspiracy theorising New World Order trilogy. On the release of the first of these, *IXXI*, in December 2019, Tony was

Cover of the third album in Tony Byker's 'Great Reset' trilogy. Released 2020. Artwork and design by Tony Byker/layout by Simon Tripcony.

warning of impending seismic events on a global scale: "2020 is Japan Olympics, and, for me, if you are into that shit, a huge consciousness shift of humanity. This push to a brave New World Order is in full effect. So many people don't see it… Bykers fans included!" In the space of three months during the global coronavirus lockdown, Tony released two more albums in his trilogy, *The New Normal* and *COVID-19: The Great Reset — Crispr Gnomes & Hybrid Clones*. The titles are self-explanatory, and the subject matter of some songs perhaps contentious, but the extent of Tony's conviction in these beliefs isn't… and neither is his prodigious musical output.

Since Crazyhead's last gig in August 2019, music related activities from band members have largely been down to Anderson and Vom.

Ian 'Delta' Anderson: Following *Picked From The Bone* in 2018, Anderson's band The Scavengers released their second album, *Rights Of Salvage,* in October 2020. With superior production to their debut, the addition of keyboards on some songs adds a degree of sophistication to a melange of rockabilly, garage and punk. With more songs in progress there are plans for a third album. Anderson also refers to a mooted collaboration with Mary Byker, Tom Stanley and Kev Byker on which they plan to record a cover version of Echo and the Bunnymen's Rescue for Kev's next album of covers.

Rob 'Vom' Morris: Vom continues to work at Leicester Tigers Rugby Union

THE SCAVENGERS

RIGHTS OF SALVAGE

Cover of Anderson's other band, The Scavengers' 2nd album Rights Of Salvage, released 2020.

Club as sports masseur, and also facilitates "alternative provision for students struggling with mainstream education teaching music, British Horse Society qualifications, and first aid, amongst many other things." He still drums for Diesel Park West and the band released their ninth official album, *Let It Melt*, in September 2019. Vom was due to visit Texas in 2020 to record their next album, but for reasons now clear it never happened. At the end of 2020, he provided Robber Byker AKA Sebastian T. Palmer with drum tracks for his Ubertroll project, Billy Bob Thorton the 3rd and The Walton Clan. He's also been demoing songs with Robber Byker and Cobalt Stargazer, as previously mentioned, while considering singers for an as-yet unnamed project together.

Alex 'Porkbeast' Peach: Soon after Crazyhead's last gig in August 2019, Porkbeast admitted that the future of Crazyhead was unknown following Reverb's departure to Turkey, but he still held out for the possibility that the band might come up with some new songs: "I would love to do more material, but logistics will be difficult." He also expressed an interest in resurrecting Swamp Delta for a number of songs that were originally earmarked for their

DIESEL PARK WEST LET IT MELT

Rob 'Vom' Morris played drums on Diesel Park West's 9th album. Released September 2019.

second album, but has since said, "it's not on the cards at the moment. I have no plans." As for projects post pandemic, he says, "If, and when, we get back to normal it will be Crazyhead first."

Pete Creed: After their gig in August 2019, Pete has said he has no plans to join another band during Crazyhead's hiatus. Although he continues to write songs and participate at open mic events in Plymouth, the lockdown has curtailed any live musical activities, as it has all musicians. He is currently involved with an arts project called Co-Creating Change: "I am working with people like myself who have, or are suffering with homelessness and drug addiction... This year we are hoping to do two 10-week sessions with the possibility of a performance, a musical, a play or an album at the end of it all."

Kev 'Reverb' Bayliss: Before departing for Turkey, Reverb discovered "a lot of unreleased [Crazyhead] stuff" from the 1990s on some of his old DATs. He says, "I sent it round to the other guys. I think some of it had merit, I don't have a copy of it myself at the moment as it's on my computer in Leicester. I'd hoped to get back in the summer to bring it over but obviously COVID prevented that. Whether anyone outside the band would wanna hear it I don't know." As for new material, Reverb has always been Crazyhead's main songwriter, and has confirmed, "I have been working at revamping some unfinished ideas and writing new stuff as potential Crazyhead songs. Hopefully I'll get something to record on soon and see what the other guys think. A recording session would be cool." As for revised Crazyhead dates, he says, "As far as I know the plan is still to play some gigs in the UK when things get back to some sort of normality. I'm up for it." In Turkey, Reverb continues to keep his hand in on the guitar, "playing garage rock covers with some fellow economic refugees, but there's no venues locally open at the moment of course."

With both Crazyhead and Gaye Bykers On Acid in an enforced period of stasis, and until such time that they are able to reunite again, their stylistically diverse extramural activities will continue to be the primary concern for many of the individual members. To quote a line from one of Gaye Bykers On Acid's Nosedive Karma: "We're living for today, there's no looking back..." 💀

Photo courtesy of Colin Bennett.

Curtain Call — Gaye Bykers On Acid, Indie Daze, October 2016.

Curtain Call — Crazyhead, Indie Daze, October 2017.

Photo courtesy of Colin Bennett.

ACKNOWLEDGEMENTS

FIRST, I WOULD LIKE TO THANK EUGENE BUTCHER, EDITOR of *Vive Le Rock!*, for commissioning me to write an article for the magazine in 2011 called 'Everythang's Groovy! 1987: The Year Grebo Broke'. It proved to be the genesis of this book. Thanks also to Jon 'Mojo' Mills for giving me the opportunity to flex my writing muscles for *Shindig!* magazine back in 2008. I am also indebted to my publisher David Kerekes for his enduring patience, and for persevering with me until I finally finished this book — when I started writing it in 2012, I didn't quite anticipate taking so long to complete it. Several factors conspired against me, not least some personal matters that proved to be inevitable but unwelcome distractions. In addition to this, as my research progressed, the sheer wealth of available material on both Gaye Bykers On Acid and Crazyhead soon became apparent, overwhelmingly so in fact. Combined with this was the fact that, by and large, nearly all the members proved to be very accommodating participants, partaking in numerous interviews, in person, by email and social media. I am particularly grateful to Mary Byker and Ian Anderson for not only their excellent forewords, but for going above and beyond the call of duty. My gratitude to all the other band members is inestimable too. Not only for patiently continuing to answer my questions throughout the course of writing this book, but also for not giving up on me, which they so easily could have done when progress began to falter. Cheers then, Kev 'Reverb' Bayliss, Kev Byker, Robber Byker, Tony Byker, Rob 'Vom' Morris, and Dr Alex 'Porkbeast' Peach — it must have seemed like a never-ending task at times! I am eternally grateful to you all.

A huge thank you also goes out to all the following, either for their friendship over the years, or for their encouragement, inspiration and co-operation, and without whose contributions, be they interviews or photographs etc., this book wouldn't have been what it is…

Rob Agg, Justine Alexander, cousin Andy Allen (R.I.P.), Carole and Steve Allsup, Peter Anderson, David Arnoff, Fifi Faiza Ariech, Steve 'Stevie Steve' Ashton, Ken 'Dokta Tinkle' Bailey, Dave Balfe, Iain Banks, John Barrow, Dazz Bartholomew, Dave Bartram, Richard 'Fast Dick' Bell, Richard Bellia, Colin Bennett, Trudi Moloney formerly Bennett, Melanie Berman, Gaz Birtles, James

Brown, Julie Brown AKA July Tafy, Jerusalem Brownsword, Nuala Bugeye, George Butler (R.I.P.), John Butler, Keith Cameron, Ian Caple, Kev Cardall, Russ Carvell AKA A. Pen, Donato Cinicolo III, Baz Clark, Su Clement, Norbert Cockhead Esq., Pat Collier, Andy and Helga Colquhoun, Sarah Corina, Ade Cox (R.I.P.), Graham Crabb, Pete Creed, Simon Cusick, Shane Dabinett, Jack Daniels, Andy 'Dice 67' Davies, Paul B. Davies, Phil Davis, Mike 'Dawkeye' Dawkins, DC3, my mum and dad, Dennis and Rosalind Deakin, who sadly both passed during the course of writing this book, Andrew 'Dentover' Denton, Jon Dubb, Martin Elbourne, Cris Elver, Liz Evans, Mick Farren (R.I.P.), Rebecca 'Beki' Field, Amy Freeman, Greg Freeman, Bean Gibson, Marco 'Frenchy' Gloder, Boss Goodman (R.I.P.), Steve Gowen (R.I.P.), Paul Griffiths, Ian Grant, Barry Grogan, Sue Grogan, Michael 'Spike' Hall (R.I.P.), Nick Hamer, James Hawkes, Richard 'Cornflake' Heathfield, Jozsef Hefter, Mike 'Banjo' Hemmings, John 'Huggy' Hughes, Russell Hunter, David Johnson (R.I.P.), Adie Jones (R.I.P.), Phil Jones, Sally Jones, Nish Joshi, Michael 'Ked' Kedward, Linda Knight, Hans Peter Kuenzler, Grant Langdon, Jon Langford, Wayne 'Spike' Large, John Leckie, Mia Lee, John Lovett, Mike 'Gris' Lunnon, Robbie Lunnon, Adrian Manning, David McGregor AKA McStonner, Mick Mercer, Ron Moreau AKA Rockit Ron, Rick Mullard, Phil Nicholls, Christian Paris, Hilary Patton, Sparky Pearson, Keith Penny (R.I.P.), Geoffrey Perrin, Caroline Pierce, Steve Potz-Rayner, Tania Powell, Troy Pulley, Andy Purple, Julie Purple, Brian Ralph, Nick Raybould, Steve Redman (R.I.P.), Justine Reynolds, Peter Reynolds, Derek Ridgers, Ian Roche, Andy Ross AKA Andy Hurt, Jamie Rudd, Tim Rundall, Fizle Sagar, Duncan 'Sandy' Sanderson (R.I.P.), Mary Scanlon, Mark 'Scotty' Scott, Alan Seaman, Greg 'Bud Longtooth' Semple, Gina Shortt, Anthony 'Blink Cyclone' Smith, Bobby 'Slime' Smith, Mark Smith, Clem Snide, Carrie Spacey, Glenn Sparrow, Pete Stanley, Kev Sutherland AKA Kev F., Tone Sutterud, Paul 'Taggy' Tartaglia, Simon Thorp, Nick Toczek, Simon Tripcony, Suzanne, Mike and India Trisic, Tom Vague, Derek Von Essen, Mark 'Wag' Wagstaff, Paul Watts, John 'Welshy' Welsh, Harriet West, Danielle Wheatley, Kim White, Christina Wigmore, Dave Williams, Dave Wink, Trudi Woodhouse, Colin Woodland, Tom Worthington. Apologies to anyone who I might have inadvertently left off this list, all contributions however great or small have been greatly appreciated even if not ultimately used.

Finally, massive respect to Mark Critchell, the Headpress graphic artist and layout designer for his sterling work and great cover.

SELECTED BIBLIOGRAPHY & REFERENCES

BOOKS, NEWSPAPERS & MAGAZINES

Copies of Tony Byker's and Robber Byker's scrapbooks of Gaye Bykers On Acid clippings proved to be an invaluable source of articles, reviews, interviews, photographs and other ephemera. Unfortunately, not all the relevant details survived the scissor treatment. This is partly why some references to magazine and newspaper sources are incomplete, despite all best efforts to trace them.

Arroll, Frank, [Crazyhead — live review, JBs, Dudley, 14/9/90] *Sounds*, 13 October 1990, p.31
Author unknown, [Gaye Bykers On Acid — Nosedive EP cover, news item] 'And Bykers Censored... Naughty Bits Removed From Sleeve', *Sounds*, 2 May 1987
——, [Gaye Bykers On Acid — live review Glastonbury Festival, 21/6/87] 'Sunday Muddy Sunday', *Sounds*, 27 June 1987, p.19
——, [Gaye Bykers On Acid — Mary Byker] 'This Guy Mary's Big Ambition: He Wants to be a Gameshow Compere', (Scottish) *Sunday Mail*, 20 October 1987
——, [Gaye Bykers On Acid — *Drill Your Own Hole* album review] *Billboard*, 26 December 1987
——, [Gaye Bykers On Acid — *Drill Your Own Hole* album review] *The Independent*, 3 November 1987
——, [Grebo: the year in review] ''87 Review: Born To Be Wild', *Melody Maker*, 19–26 December 1987, p.34
——, [Gaye Bykers On Acid — *Drill Your Own Hole* video news item] *Record Mirror*, 30 January 1988, p.2

——, [Gaye Bykers On Acid — news item] *Philadelphia Inquirer*, 1 April 1988, p.95
——, [Gaye Bykers On Acid — news item about *Station KRAP* album] *Sounds*, 14 January 1989, p.41
——, [Letter of termination of contract] Virgin Records, 11 May 1989, Source: Tony Byker's scrapbook
——, [Rektüm — news item] 'Passage to Britain — Sleeve Notes on Exiled Thrash', *The Independent*, 13 October 1989
——, [Gaye Bykers On Acid news item — Mary Byker on Naked Brian label and *Cancer Planet Mission*] 'New Label Project and Album in the Pipeline: Bykers Ride Again', *Sounds*, 3 March 1990, p.9
——, [Mary Byker on the Poll-Tax] *City Limits*, 22–29 March 1990
——, [Crazyhead news item] 'Crazyhead Leave Food', *Sounds*, 24 March 1990, p.2
——, [Gaye Bykers On Acid feature] *Repeater* (Sheffield fanzine), No. 1, winter 1990
——, [Crazyhead — news item] '1991 — What's Going On?', *Sounds*, 5 January 1991, p.13
Axford, Jem, 'Gunge Core, Surf Nazis, Gaye Bykers' [Gaye Bykers On Acid & Thee Hypnotics — Live review, Newcastle Riverside 22/2/89] *Courier* (Newcastle University Student Newspaper), Thursday 2 March 1989, p.6
Bailie, Stuart, [Gaye Bykers On Acid feature] *Record Mirror*, 20 December 1986, p.4
——, [Gaye Bykers On Acid — Everythang's Groovy single review] *Record Mirror*, 20 December, 1986
Barnes, Mike, [Rektüm — *Sakredanus* album review] *Select*, No.5, November 1990, p.114
Barron, Jack, [Gaye Bykers On Acid live review, Croydon Underground, London, 7/8/86] *Sounds*, 16 August 1986, p.27
——, [Gaye Bykers On Acid's non-appearance at

Futurama Festival] *NME*, 21/11/87, p.51

——, [Grebo: The year in review] 'What the ****?: Grot 'n' Snot', *Sounds*, 19–26 December 1987, p.36

——, [Gaye Bykers On Acid — live review, Les Trans Musicales Festival, Rennes, France, 9/12/87] 'Trans-Europe Success', *NME*, 3 January 1988

Barrow, John, *How Not To Make It In The Music World (Diary of an Almost Has-Been)*, (Victoria, Canada: Trafford Publishing, 2003), p.200–214 & p.249–258

Beard, Tony, [Crazyhead, *Desert Orchid* album review] *Record Mirror*, 8 October 1988, p.29

Beauvallet, Jean-Daniel, [Gaye Bykers On Acid — Les Trans Musicales festival showcase] 'Les Fous Du Volant', *Les Inrockuptibles: Interviews & Chroniques*, No.9, Novembre–Decembre 1987, pp.23–24

Berger, George, [Gaye Bykers On Acid / PFX — *Pernicious Nonsense* album review] 'Scumbags Of The Universe', *Sounds*, 8 December 1990, p.44

Blade, Andy, *The Secret Life of a Teenage Punk Rocker*, (Cherry Red Books, 2005), p.150

Blake, John [On Gaye Bykers On Acid's name] 'White Hot Club' column, *Daily Mirror*, [exact date unknown] November 1986

Brown, James, [Pop Will Eat Itself cover artists, 'Bedtime Stories Your Mother Wouldn't Tell You' and feature] 'Pop Will Choke Itself', *Sounds*, 25 April 1987, pp.20–21, 34

——, [Gaye Bykers On Acid cover artists, 'Picking Up The Tab' and feature] 'Beer and Loathing On The Grebo Trail', *Sounds*, 2 May 1987 pp1, 22–23

——, [Gaye Bykers On Acid — Nosedive E.P. review] *Sounds*, 2nd May 1987, p.27

——, [Crazyhead review of Time Has Taken Its Toll On You single] *NME*, 2 July 1988

——, [Grebo phenomenon feature] 'Q; Are We Not men? A; We Are Grebo!', *NME*, 25 July 1987, pp.26–27

——, [Grebo feature],'Pop Will Eat itself's Guide To Grebo', *NME*, 25 July 1987, p.29

——, [Junior Manson Slags — live review, 100 Club, London, ??/7/87] 'Carry On Grebo', *NME*, 25 July 1987, p.39

——, [Ramones feature, referencing Gaye Bykers On Acid] 'Gorilla Thriller', *NME*, 31 October 1987, p.14

——, [Gaye Bykers On Acid feature] 'Greasy Rider', *NME*, 7 November 1987, p.14 & 40

Brown, Len, [Gaye Bykers On Acid supporting Siouxsie & The Banshees, live review, Finsbury Park Supertent, 25/7/87] *NME*, 1 August 1987, p.37

——, [Crazyhead — Have Love, Will Travel & Radio 1 Sessions / The Evening Show review] *NME*. 18 February 1989, p.12

Buchanan, Elie, [Gaye Bykers On Acid — live review, Govan Town Hall, Glasgow, 18/5/88] 'Acid Gig Leaves Taste', [Scottish newspaper? Exact publication unknown] May 1988? [exact date unknown]

Cameron, Keith, [Gaye Bykers On Acid — Stewed To The Gills album review] 'The Last Gill And Testament', *Sounds*, 18 February 1989, p.27

——, 'Pennies From Heaven', [Mary Byker — live review of Johnny Cash, Til Things Are Brighter Benefit Concert, Islington Powerhaus, ?/5/89 (exact date unknown)] *Sounds*, 27 May 1989, p.35

——, Robb, John & Wilkinson, Roy, edited by Phillips, Shaun, [Gaye Bykers On Acid & Crazyhead — live reviews, Reading Festival, 25 & 27/8/89] *Sounds*, 9 September 1989, p.50

Carruthers, Will, *Playing The Bass With Three Left Hands*, (Faber & Faber, 2016), pp.155–156

Cavanagh, David, [Crazyhead — *Desert Orchid* album review] 'Horses For Courses', *Sounds*, 8 October 1988, p.29

——, [Crazyhead feature] 'The Wacky Racers', *Sounds*, 25 February 1989, pp.20–21

Cheeseman, Phil, [Gaye Bykers On Acid — Hot Thing single review] *Record Mirror*, 4 February 1989, p. 29

Clerk, Carol, [Gaye Bykers On Acid cover artists, 'Ryders On The Storm' and feature] 'Dopeheads On Mopeds', *Melody Maker*, 17 October 1987, pp.1, 34–36

——, Melody Maker, [Gaye Bykers On Acid — Git Down (Shake Your Thang) single review] 31 October 1987, p.32

——, [Gaye Bykers On Acid — *Drill Your Own Hole* movie news feature] 'Driller Killer', *Melody Maker*, 2 January 1988, p.9

Coleman, Nick, [Gaye Bykers On Acid — live

review, Town & Country Club, Kentish Town, London, 8/11/87] *Time Out*, [exact date unknown] November 1987

Cook, Richard, [Crazyhead — 'Single of the Week', review of Time Has Taken Its Toll On You single] *Sounds*, 2 July 1988, p.33

Cope, Julian, *The Modern Antiquarian: A Pre-Millennial Odyssey Through Megalithic Britain* (Thorson: London), 1998, p.239

Culp, Nancy, [Gaye Bykers On Acid — *Drill Your Own Hole* album review] *Record Mirror*, 7 November 1987, p.16

——, [Crazyhead — review of Time Has Taken Its Toll On You single] *Record Mirror*, 9 July 1988, p.29

Danter, Graham, 'Rockin' Mary Finds Time to Wed — Just!', *Leicester Mercury*, 17 February 1989

Darling, Andy, [Gaye Bykers On Acid feature] 'Quite Contrary', *City Limits*, 5–12 November 1987, pp.84–85

Davies, Paul, [Gaye Bykers On Acid — *Stewed To The Gills* album review] *Q*, No.30, March 1989, p.76

——, [Gaye Bykers On Acid — *Cancer Planet Mission*, album review] *Q*, No.45, June 1990, p.94

——(Gaye Bykers On Acid / PFX — *Pernicious Nonsense* album review), *Q*, No. 54, March 1991, p.66

Deakin, Rich, [Grebo! Feature] 'Everythang's Groovy — 1987: The Year Grebo Broke', *Vive Le Rock!* , No.7, 2012, pp.62–65

——, [Gaye Bykers On Acid — CD liner notes] *A Big Bad Beautiful Noise: Live On Tour 1986–1990*, Gaye Bykers On Acid, [CD] Major League Productions Ltd., 2012

——, [Gaye Bykers On Acid — live review, Wagon & Horses, Birmingham, 24/9/16] *Slap Mag*, October/November 2016, p.35

——, [Gaye Bykers On Acid — news item] 'The Knowledge: The Electric Banana Blows Your Mind... ', *Vive Le Rock!*, No.40, 2016, p.14

——, [Gaye Bykers On Acid — live review, Indie Daze, The Forum, Kentish Town, London, 1/10/16] *Louder Than War*, No.7, Nov–Dec 2016, p.104

——, [Crazyhead — live review, The Donkey, Leicester, 15/9/17] *Vive Le Rock!*, No.50, 2017, p.104

——, [Am I Dead Yet? — *Am I Dead Yet?* album review] *Vive Le Rock!*, No.63, 2019, p.88

——, [Crazyhead — live review, 100 Club, London, 4/5/18] *Vive Le Rock!*, No.56, 2018, p.105

Deevoy, Adrian, '"Censored" What Do You Expect With A Name Like Gaye Bykers On Acid?', *Q*, No.15, December 1987, p.12

——, [Gaye Bykers On Acid video review] 'Turn On... Tune In, And Promptly Return To The Video Shop. On Yer Byke Mates', *Q*, No.20, May 1988, p.119

DEH, [Gaye Bykers On Acid — Drill Your Own Hole video news item] *Music Week*, 30 January 1988

'Dict Nietzsche: Vom Off' column, [Grebo special] *NME*, 25 July 1987, p.51

Endell, Charlie [The Jackofficers — *Digital Dump* album review] 'The Raw & The Half-Baked', *Sounds*, 15 December 1990, p.38

Evans, Liz, [Gaye Bykers On Acid — *Stewed To The Gills* album review] *Metal Hammer*, 20 March 1989

Fidol, Bataille, [Crazyhead feature] *Sniffin' Rock*, No.10, September 1989, pp.18–19

Gibson, Robin, [Crazyhead review of Rags single] *Sounds* 10 September 1988, p.33

Giles, David, [Gaye Bykers On Acid — *Drill Your Own Hole* video news item] *Number One*, 30 January 1988, p.31

Gittins, Ian, [Crazyhead feature] 'Travel Writers', *Melody Maker*, 25 February 1989, pp.22–23

——, [Gaye Bykers On Acid — *Stewed To The Gills*, album review] *Melody Maker*, 25 February 1989, p.28

Goldberg, Adrian, [Crazyhead — live review, Junction 10, Walsall 25/3/89] *Sounds*, 4 March 1989, p.32

——, [Gaye Bykers On Acid — live review, Anti-Vivisection Benefit, Birmingham, 30/4/89] *Sounds*, 13 May 1989, p.28

'GREBO! "A BURST OF DIRTY THUNDER" GAYE BYKERS ON ACID', 'THE POPPIES' GUIDE TO GREASY GODS' and 'CRAZYHEAD GET LOUD AND LOUSY', [Gaye Bykers On Acid cover artists] *NME*, 25 July 1987, p.1

Harris, John, [Gaye Bykers On Acid — live review, Jericho Tavern, Oxford, 3/5/90] *Sounds*, 12 May 1990, p.35

——, [Crazyhead — Everything's Alright single

review] *Sounds*, 1 September 1990, p.23

Hobbs, Mary Anne, [Gaye Bykers On Acid cover artists,'Touching The Almighty Testicles: Gaye Bykers Make The Mud Stick' and feature] 'Cod's Law', *Sounds*, 4 February 1989, pp.1 & 24–25

——, [Crazyhead — *Some Kind Of Fever* album review] *NME*, 1 December 1990, p.36

——, [Gaye Bykers On Acid / PFX — *Pernicious Nonsense* album review] *NME*, 15 December 1990

Holland, Roger, [Gaye Bykers On Acid live review, Town & Country Club, Kentish Town, London, 8/11/87] *Sounds*, 21/11/1987, p.38

Hurt, Andy, [Gaye Bykers On Acid live review — Timebox, Bull & Gate, Kentish Town, London — 6/6/1986] *Sounds*, 21 June 1986, p.29

——, [Crazyhead live review — Croydon Underground, London, 28/8/86] Sounds, 13 September 1986, p.38

——, [Gaye Bykers On Acid feature] 'Full Mental Jacket', *Sounds*, 14 November 1987, pp.40–41

James, Dave, [Gaye Bykers On Acid — live review, Leadmill, Sheffield, 23/9/1989] *Sounds*, 7 October 1989, p.31

Jennings, Dave, [Gaye Bykers On Acid — live review, University of London (ULU), 20/5/88] *Melody Maker*, May or early June 1988 [exact date unknown]

Joy, Alison, [Gaye Bykers On Acid supporting Motörhead, live review, Hammersmith Odeon, London, 10&11/10/87] *Kerrang!*, no.159, October 24th, 1987, p.50

Kadis, Alex, [Gaye Bykers On Acid feature] 'Camera Lights', *Underground*, No.10, January 1988, pp.30–31

Kane, Peter, [Gaye Bykers On Acid — live review, Acid Daze, Finsbury Park Supertent, London, 23/8/87] 'Grievous Intent', *Sounds*, 29 August, 1987, p.35

——, [Crazyhead — *Live In Memphis*, album review), *Q*, No.43, February 1993, p.81

Kenzo, [Gaye Bykers On Acid feature] *Lively Arts*, summer/Fall 1988, pp.20–22)

Kiley, Penny, [Gaye Bykers On Acid — live review, Planet X, Liverpool, 10/6/87] *Melody Maker*, 20 June 1987

King, Sam, [Gaye Bykers On Acid — *Drill Your Own Hole* album review] *Sounds*, 19/26

December 1987, p.38

King, Sam, [Gaye Bykers On Acid — *Drill Your Own Hole* video review] *Sounds*, 19/26 December 1987, p.45

King, Sam, [Gaye Bykers On Acid — live review, Mean Fiddler, Harlesden, London, 8/3/88] 'Crisis Time for Grebo', *Sounds*, March 1988

King, Richard, *How Soon Is Now? The Madmen And Mavericks Who Made Independent Music 1975–2005*, (London: Faber & Faber, 2012) pp.417–418

Kuenzler, Hans Peter, [Transcript from interview with Crazyhead's Reverb and Vom] 3 November 1988

Lake, John Anthony, [Gaye Bykers On Acid — live review, Bradford University, 17/5/88] *Sounds*, 28 May 1988

Langford, Jon, 'My Strange And Terrible Days With The Outlaw Gaye Motorcycle Gang', *Record Mirror*, 18 February 1989, p.14

Lee, Craig, 'The Manic Gaye Bykers and Morose Swans at Work', *LA Times*, 26 April, 1988

Maconie, Stuart, [Gaye Bykers On Acid live review, King George's Hall, Blackburn, 25/10/87] *NME*, 14 November 1987

——, [Crazyhead, Rags single review] *NME*, 3 September 1988, p.15

——, [Crazyhead — live review, La Cigale, Paris, France, 29&30/11/88] *NME*, 17 December 1988, p.37

——, [Gaye Bykers On Acid — Hot Thing single review] *NME*, 4 February 1989, p.17

——, [Crazyhead feature] 'Leicester Pig-Out A Paris', *NME*, 25 February 1989, p.17 & p.49

—— & Collins, Andrew, ['Madchester' & 'Grebo' — end of year review] *NME*, 22–29 December 1990, p.51

——, *Cider With Roadies*, (Ebury Press: London), 2004, pp.202–203

Mack, Tom, [Gaye Bykers On Acid & Crazyhead roadie Keith Penny tribute] 'City Roadie Was One Of The Best', *Leicester Mercury*, 24 July 2014, p.10

Mardles, Paul [Crazyhead — *Some Kind Of Fever* album review] 'Touch Me I'm Sick', *Sounds*, 24 November 1990, p.43

Martin, Gavin, [Gaye Bykers On Acid feature] 'Invaders from the Planet Bleg', *NME*, 25 July 1987, p.41

Mathur, Paul, [Crazyhead review of Rags single] *Melody Maker*, 3 September 1988, p.28

McDonnell, Evelyn, 'Homosexual Motorcyclists On Hallucinogens', *The NewPaper*, April 1988 [exact date unknown]

Mengede, Peter, [Gaye Bykers On Acid feature] 'Pink Angels On Acid Clouds', *Rockpool*, No. 193, 1 June 1988

Mercer, Mick, [Crazyhead What Gives You The Idea That You're So Amazing Baby single review] *Melody Maker*, 7 March 1987, p.31

——, [Gaye Bykers On Acid & Crazyhead — "grebo summit" feature] 'Rock of Ages', *Melody Maker*, 30 May 1987, pp.38–39

——, [Gaye Bykers On Acid — Hot Thing single review] *Melody Maker*, 4 February 1989, p.32

Morgan, Piers & Smith, Martin, 'Three Die In Devil Pact', *The Sun*, 1988/1989? [exact date unknown]

Mr Spencer, [Gaye Bykers On Acid — Everythang's Groovy single review] *Sounds*, 6 December 1986, p.21

——, [Gaye Bykers On Acid feature] 'Gaye Maniacs', *Sounds*, 20–27 December 1986, p.25

——, [Crazyhead — Baby Turpentine single review] *Sounds*, 8 August 1987, p.29

——, [Motörhead's Lemmy on Gaye Bykers On Acid] 'Traitors at the Gates of Hell', *Sounds*, 29 August 1987, pp.10–11

——, [Gaye Bykers On Acid — *Drill Your On Hole* album review] 'Driller Thriller', *Sounds*, 7 November 1987, p.28

——, [Gaye Bykers On Acid — All Hung Up single review] *Sounds*, 12th December 1987, p.34

——, [Crazyhead feature] 'Between Times: 99 Nervous Breakdown', *Sounds*, 16 July 1988, pp.42–43

——, [Crazyhead — live review, Rooftops, Glasgow, 30/6/88] 'Tougher Than The Rest', *Sounds*, 9 July 1988, p.34

——, [Crazyhead — Rock In Romania feature] 'Romania Mania', *Sounds*, 10 March 1990, p.15

——, [Crazyhead feature] 'The Boys Are Alright', *Sounds*, 4 August, 1990, p.17

Mueller, Andrew, [Crazyhead — Everything's Alright single review] *Melody Maker*, 1 September 1990, p.35

Myers, Caren, [Crazyhead — *Some Kind Of Fever* album review] *Melody Maker*, 15/12/90, p.30

Narvaez, Paul & Zahn, Jackie, 'Gaye Bykers On Acid — Hail Mary!', B-Side 1988 [exact date unknown]

Nicholls, Mike, [Crazyhead — Rock In Romania feature] 'After The Revolution, Let's Rock', *The Times*, 2 March 1990

Nicholson, Tim, [Gaye Bykers On Acid — *Stewed To The Gills* album review] *Record Mirror*, 25 February 1989, p.27

Nightingale, Annie, *Wicked Speed*, Pan/Macmillan, 2000, pp.186–198

Ó'Gormain, Réamann, [Gaye Bykers On Acid — Git Down (Shake Your Thang) single review] *Record Mirror*, 24 October 1987, p.16

O'Hagan, Sean, [Gaye Bykers On Acid — Git Down (Shake Your Thang) single review] *NME*, 17 October 1987, p.18

Paisley, Pete, [Gaye Bykers On Acid supporting Motörhead, live review, Hammersmith Odeon, London, 10&11/10/87] *Record Mirror*, 31 October 1987, p.48

Pallmann, Ludwig F. & Stevens, Wendelle C., *UFO Contact from Itifi-Ra: The Cancer Planet Mission*, (UFO Photo Archives), 1986

Peacock, Tim, [Gaye Bykers On Acid — *Cancer Planet Mission* album review] 'Malignant Tumours', *Sounds*, 7 April 1990, p.42

Pegg, Simon, *Nerd Do Well*, (Century, London), 2010

Peel, John, [Gaye Bykers On Acid — live review The Garage, Nottingham, 28/5/87] 'Superscruffs', *The Observer*, 6 June 1987

Penner, John, 'Furor Ferments Under Gaye Bikers [sic] Farce', *Anaheim Times*, Friday 22 April 1988

Perry, Neil, [Crazyhead — live review, Great Unsigned, ICA, London] *Sounds*, 7 February 1987

——, [Crazyhead — 'Single of the Week', What Gives You The Idea That You're So Amazing Baby single review] *Sounds*, 21 February 1987, p.27

——, [Gaye Bykers On Acid cover artists, 'Drilling Holes In America' and feature] 'Hail Mary and Three How's Your Fathers', *Sounds*, 14 May, 1988, pp.1 & 25–26

——, 'Straight From The Horse's Mouth', *Sounds*, 1 October, 1988, pp.20–21 & 40

——, [Lesbian Dopeheads On Mopeds — live

review, Sir George Robey, Finsbury Park, London] 'Dykes On Bykes', *Sounds*, 12 November 1988

Phillips, Shaun, [Gaye Bykers On Acid — Git Down, single review] *Sounds*, 17 October 1987, p.31

Pouncey, Edwin, [Gaye Bykers On Acid feature] 'We're Just A Tax Loss With A Lobster On It!', *NME*, 18 February 1989, p.14

Price, Simon, [Bomb Party & Janitors — live review, Anti-Poll Tax / Nicaragua Benefit gig, Boston Arms, Tuffnell Park, London, ?8/89 (exact date unknown)] *Melody Maker*, 2 September 1989, p.25

Push, AKA Chris Dawes, [Crazyhead live review — Electric Ballroom, Camden, London, 8/7/88] *Melody Maker*, 16 July 1988, p.19

——, [Gaye Bykers On Acid — *Cancer Planet Mission* album review] *Melody Maker*, 7th April 1990

Quantick, David & Barbara Ellen, [Gaye Bykers On Acid — live review, Acid Daze, Finsbury Park Supertent, London, 23/8/87] 'Sports Day In Hell', *NME*, 5 September 1987, p.49

——, [Gaye Bykers On Acid — *Drill Your Own Hole* movie premiere review] 'Gaye Bykers On Acid Movie Lig', *NME*, 1987 [exact date unknown]

Rasputin, Jimmi, [Crazyhead — feature] 'Jimmi Rasputin Enters The Mad Mad Mad Mad Mad Mad Mad Mad World Of Crazyhead', *House Of Dolls*, No.18, June–July 1988, pp.6–7

Redhead, Ian, 'This Much I Know', More Mercury, *Leicester Mercury*, 20 October 2012, pp.22–23

Riley, Marc, (Mary Byker — *Til Things Are Brighter* album news item) *Sounds*, 14/11/1987 p.9

Robb, John, [Crazyhead — live review, Manchester Boardwalk, January / Feb '88? Exact date unknown] 'Loud But Not Proud', *Sounds*, 13 February 1988, p.37

——, [Crazyhead — live review, Manchester International, 29/9/88] 'The Heads Go Up', *Sounds*, 8 October 1988, p.34

——, [Gaye Bykers On Acid feature] 'Mission Impossible', *Sounds*, 21 April 1990, p.24

Roberts, Chris, [Gaye Bykers On Acid — live Klubfoot, Clarendon Hotel, Hammersmith, London, 10/3/88] 'Slag Heap', *Melody Mak-er*, March 1988 [exact date unknown]

——, [Crazyhead — Time Has Taken Its Toll On You, single review] *Melody Maker*, 2 July 1988, p.36

——, (Gaye Bykers on Acid non-review at Reading Festival, 25/8/89), *Melody Maker*, 9 September 1989, p.25

Rom, Ron, [Gaye Bykers On Acid — live review, Klub Foot, Clarendon Ballroom, Hammersmith, London, 11/4/87] 'Gold In The Gutter', *Sounds*, 25 April 1987, p.30

——, [Grebo: The year in review] '1987 — The Year Inside Out: March — Grebus Bodily Harm', *Sounds*, 19/26 December 1987, p.14

Russo, Laurie, [Gaye Bykers On Acid — feature] 'Bykers Supply The Acid, Laurie Russo Supplies The House', *House Of Dolls*, No.20, October–November 1988, pp.30–31

Sandall, Robert, [Gaye Bykers On Acid — *Drill Your Own Hole* album review] *Q*, No.15, 1987, p.108

Scanlon, Ann, [Crazyhead feature] 'Urban Bastard Blues', *Sounds*, 15 August 1987, pp.10–11

Shaw, Jeff, *No Time To Cry: Tales Of A Leicester Bouncer*, special edition, (Lulu Publishing, 2012) p.145

Smith, Andrew, [Crazyhead, *Desert Orchard* (sic) album review] *Melody Maker*, 15 October 1988, p.38

Smith, Mat, [Crazyhead feature] 'The Outlaws', Melody Maker, 1 August 1987, p.10

Snow, Mat, [Crazyhead cover artists & feature] 'So What Makes You Think You're So Amazing Crazyhead?', *Sounds*, 4 April 1987 pp.1, 12–13

Solanas, Jane, [Crazyhead feature] 'Do It Clean', *NME*, 22 August 1987, pp.18–19

Stanley, Bob, [Crazyhead — live review, Abbey Park Festival, Leicester, 15/8/87] *NME*, 29 August 1987, p.46

Stanley, Bob, [Gaye Bykers On Acid — *Drill Your Own Hole* album review] 'Wah is Hell', *NME*, 7 November 1987, p.32

Staunton, Terry, [Crazyhead — Rock In Romania feature] 'Rockin' In The Free World', *NME*, 10 March 1990, p.14–15, & p.54

Stiff, [Gaye Bykers On Acid — live review, Club Detroit, St Petersburg, USA, September 1990] 'The Great American Stiff' column,

Thrust, Vol.2, No.11, 1990, p.72

Stubbs, David, [Crazyhead — Baby Turpentine single review] *Melody Maker*, 8 August 1987

——, [Gaye Bykers On Acid — *Drill Your Own Hole* album review] *Melody Maker*, 7 November 1987, p.30

The Stud Brothers, [Gaye Bykers On Acid feature] 'Raging Bull', *Melody Maker*, 9 May 1987, p.9

——, [Crazyhead feature] 'Yesterday Once More', *Melody Maker*, 9 May 1987, pp.30–31

——, [Crazyhead — Have Love, Will Travel single review] *Melody Maker*, 4 March 1989, p.31

Takiff, Jonathan, [Gaye Bykers On Acid new item] *Philadelphia Daily News*, 1 April 1988, p.39

Terminally Blitzed, Leicester punk fanzine (1977–1978)

Thorp, Simon, [Crazyhead cartoon] 'Viz Pop: The Page That Makes NME & Sounds Like a Pile of Shite', *Viz*, No.31, August/September 1988, p.15

Tilston, Lisa, [Gaye Bykers On Acid feature] 'A Rocky Horror Picture Show', *Record Mirror*, November 1987, p.38

——, [Grebo Frenzy issue] 'Gaye Bykers On Acid — Leicester's Filthiest Speak Out', *Record Mirror*, 14 November 1987, p.38

——, [Gaye Bykers On Acid — All Hung Up single review] 'Top of The Tree', *Record Mirror*, 19 December 1987, p.14

Thompson, Hunter S., *Fear and Loathing In Las Vegas: A Savage Journey to the Heart of the American Dream* (Random House), 1971

Toczek, Nick, *The Independence File*, [self-published directory of venues, organisers, indie labels, indie distributors, studios, pressing plants and various advice articles for indie bands] 1986

Traitor, Ralph, [Crazyhead — Have Love, Will Travel single review] *Sounds*, 18 February 1989, p.29

Treworgey Tree Fayre official programme

Tully, Andrew, [Gaye Bykers On Acid & Thee Hypnotics live review, Edinburgh University 23/2/89] *Sounds*, 4 March 1989, p.32

Unsworth, Cathi, [Gaye Bykers On Acid supporting Motörhead, live review, Hammersmith Odeon, London, 10 &11/10/87] 'No Spare Tyre', *Sounds*, 24 October 1987, p.31

——, [Crazyhead supporting Ramones — live review, Brixton Academy, London 8/12/90] *Sounds*, December 1990, p.31

Walker, Peter, [Gaye Bykers On Acid graffiti — Goscote House article] 'We Live In Terror, say tenants of 'High-Rise Hell', *Leicester Mercury*, 14 April 1987

Wells, Steven, [Gaye Bykers On Acid feature] 'Who Wants To Be A Pillionaire?', *NME*, 31 January, 1987, p.8

——, [Sarah Corina — Big Zap! News item] 'Grebogate', *NME*, 25 July 1987, p.9

——, [Crazyhead feature] 'We Gotta Escape From New Pork', *NME*, 23 July 1988, pp.22–23

——, [Gaye Bykers On Acid — *Stewed To The Gills* album review] *NME*, 18th February 1989, p.29

Wilde, Jonh, [Gaye Bykers On Acid live review — Klubfoot, Clarendon Ballroom, Hammersmith, London, 7/11/86] *Sounds*, 15 November 1986

——, [Gaye Bykers On Acid supporting Motörhead, live review, Hammersmith Odeon, London, 10&11/10/87] *Melody Maker*, 17 October 1987, p.31

Wilkinson, Roy, [Gaye Bykers On Acid, Bogshed live review, Sir George Robey, Finsbury Park, London, 16/12/86] *Sounds*, 3 January 1987, p.32

——, [Crazyhead live review, Town & Country Club, Kentish Town, London, 15/3/87] 'Digging the Dirt', *Sounds*, 21 March 1987, p.30

——, [Gaye Bykers On Acid & Crazyhead — live reviews, Reading Festival, 25 & 27/8/89] *Sounds*, 9 September 1989, p.50

Williams, Henry, [Crazyhead — *Desert Orchid* album review] *Q*, 26, November 1988, p.113

Williams, Simon, [Gaye Bykers On Acid — *Cancer Planet Mission* album review] *NME*, 7 April 1990, p.34

WEBSITES

Abbey Park Festival Archive https://www.facebook.com/Abbey-Park-Festival-Archive-107708104254357

Armitage, 'Deptford' John. Source: https://www.bookogs.com/credit/499111-john-armitage

Astbury, Ian & Billy Diffy of The Cult, NME, 5 December 1987, in The Cult Music website, [no longer available] http://www.thecultmusic.com/forum/viewthread.php?tid=1386

Byker, Mary, commenting as Byker-Mary, Sunday [16 March, 2014] 'PWEI Communications' message board, *PWEI Nation* website http://pweination.com/forum/viewtopic.php?f=19&t=854

——& Noko, Am I Dead Yet?, Facebook page, https://www.facebook.com/aidyband

Byker, Tony, Tony Byker's Facebook page, https://www.facebook.com/pg/Tony-Byker-365184850228456/about/?ref=page_internal

Crazyhead, 'Crazyhead' Facebook page, https://www.facebook.com/crazyheaduk

Cynthia Plaster Caster Nardwuar vs. Cynthia Plaster Caster https://nardwuar.com/vs/cynthia_plaster_caster/cynthia3.htm

Davies, Paul B., *Slave Clowns Of The Third Reich* poster, V&A Museum Online, https://collections.vam.ac.uk/item/O1163440/poster-archer-simon/

Deakin, Rich, Grebo! The Loud & Lousy Story Of Gaye Bykers On Acid And Crazyhead, www.greboloudandlousy.com

——, Grebo! The Loud & Lousy Story Of Gaye Bykers On Acid And Crazyhead, Facebook group, https://www.facebook.com/groups/750652648916051

Diesel Park West, Diesel Park West Facebook page, https://www.facebook.com/DieselParkWest

——, The official website for seminal rock band Diesel Park West, https://www.dieselparkwest.com/

Desai, Ila, *I Was There Photography* https://www.iwasthere.photography/

Edinburgh Gig Archive, The, http://edinburghgigarchive.com/wp-content/uploads/2020/08/GayeBykersTheVenue1987.jpg.

Fergusson, Alex. Source: https://punkmusiccatalogue.wordpress.com/alternative-tv/

Gaye Bykers On Acid, 'Gaye Bykers On Acid Music', Facebook page, https://www.facebook.com/GayeBykersOnAcid

——, 'Gaye Bykers On Acid' Facebook group, https://www.facebook.com/groups/7956739851

——, Myspace, https://myspace.com/gaye.bykers.on.acid

——, website, https://gayebykersonacid.wixsite.com/gayebykersonacid

Gendron, Bob, 'The Mekons Are History…"One Horse Town" 1990', *Chicago Tribune*, 24 July 2009, https://www.chicagotribune.com/news/ct-xpm-2009-07-24-0907220300-story.html

Leckie, John, Radiohead Wikia, Radiohead Knowledge Base website, https://radiohead.fandom.com/wiki/John_Leckie

Martin, 'Recordings and Recollections: Treworgey Tree Fayre, Liskeard, Cornwall, July 28-30th 1989', *The Archive*, [Created May 2007. Updated April 2015] http://www.ukrockfestivals.com/Treworgey-Tree-Fayre-89-2.html

Peach, 'Porkbeast', Alex, Crazyhead, [Old Myspace platform blog material no longer available] MySpace, https://myspace.com/crazyheaduk/blog

Pop Will Eat Itself, Official website, http://www.popwilleatitself.net/pwei/

——, 'Newsflash: Pop Will Eat Itself (Postponed/TBA)', [posted 5th March] The Zoo [website] http://thezoo.com.au/pop-will-eat-itself/

Ross, Andy. *Safety In Numbers*, No.5, 1979, p.12, Kev [surname unknown] interviews Andy Ross of Disco Zombies. *Bored Teenagers* website, https://www.boredteenagers.co.uk/disco_zombies.htm

Scavengers, The, 'The Scavengers' Facebook page, https://www.facebook.com/thescavengersuk

Sigler, Tracy, *I'm Here To Help* Blog, 13 August 2007, http://tracysigler.com/tag/gaye-bykers-on-acid/ [no longer available]

Sisters Of Mercy Bio, Jango website, https://www.jango.com/music/The+-Sisters+of+Mercy

Swamp Delta, Swamp Delta Facebook page, https://www.facebook.com/SWAMPDELTA

The Tea Set Facebook page, https://www.facebook.com/left12/

Trewhala, Lee, [Treworgey Fayre retrospective report] 'The shocking reality of Cornwall's Treworgey Tree Fayre where people died and over 300 were arrested: A dustbowl of death, drugs, dysentery, dirt and depravity', Cornwall Live, [24th April 2018, updated: 27th May 2018] https://www.cornwalllive.com/whats-on/music-nightlife/remembering-treworgey-tree-festival-most-1495294

Worthington, Tom, Misterworthington Flickr page — No More Censorship Defense Fund A3 poster — https://www.flickr.com/photos/misterworthington/5107295325/

AUDIO VISUAL

As well as each band's respective official discographies there is a plethora of audio and video material available. The following is just a small selection referred to in this book.

CRAZYHEAD RELATED

☐ BANDCAMP

Crazyhead, [Selection of Crazyhead's audio back catalogue and video available as physical formats, downloads or streaming] [Audio and video] Crazyhead Bandcamp, https://crazyhead.bandcamp.com/

Swamp Delta, [features Crazyhead downloads too] [Audio] Swamp Delta Bandcamp, https://swampdelta.bandcamp.com/music

☐ YOUTUBE

Promo videos for singles Baby Turpentine, Time Has Taken Its Toll On You Rags, and live video footage at the Town & Country Club, 1989 and Reading Festival 1989 can be found on the band's YouTube video channel.

Crazyhead, [Video] Crazyhead UK — YouTube channel, https://www.youtube.com/channel/UC3Nj5n88PcHPpfDvuDKDCKg

Crazyhead, [Video] [Includes promo video for 'Have Love, Will Travel' and several live videos of Crazyhead at the Abbey Park Festival, Leicester, 1987], Crazyhead Official — YouTube channel, https://www.youtube.com/channel/UCGXOp48wZvfZkXmjr5GtA7g

Crazyhead, 'British Rock For Romania, Brașov, February 1990 — 'Rockin' in the Free World'', [video] YouTube, https://www.youtube.com/watch?v=BnmH8VuMErc&t=214s

Crazyhead, 'Crazyhead — Everything's Alright, promo video 1990', [video] YouTube, https://www.youtube.com/watch?v=k5Jm-m98NqC4

GAYE BYKERS ON ACID RELATED

☐ BANDCAMP

Byker, Kev & Stanley, Tom [featuring Kev Byker's All-Stars and Shed material] [audio] Kev Byker & Tom Stanley Bandcamp, https://kevbyker.bandcamp.com/

Byker, Robber [features music by Robber in various guises, Ubertroll, Billy Bob Thorton etc.] [audio] Ubertroll Recordings Bandcamp, https://ubertrollrecordings.bandcamp.com/

Byker, Tony, [featuring all of Tony's solo output on CD, download or streaming] [audio] Tony Byker Music Bandcamp, https://tonybyker.bandcamp.com/

Gaye Bykers On Acid, [The essential archive of the band's entire back catalogue, including many live audio recordings and videos available as physical formats, downloads or streaming] [Audio and video] Gaye Bykers On Acid Bandcamp, https://gayebykersonacid.bandcamp.com/

Steroid, [Downloads of all three albums] [Audio] Steroid Bandcamp, https://steroid1.bandcamp.com/

☐ YOUTUBE

Gaye Bykers On Acid, [Live outside the Corn Exchange, Leicester Market] 'Gaye Bykers On Acid — Acid Alert', (1986), [video] YouTube https://youtu.be/flKMc9mvpxg?t=1129

BIBLIOGRAPHY

Gaye Bykers On Acid, 'gaye bykers on acid everythings groovy', (1986), [video] YouTube https://youtu.be/co9eHP_Z9mk

Gaye Bykers On Acid, [With Clint Mansell of PWEI performing 'Call Me A Liar'] 'GAYE BYKERS ON ACID LIVE ACID DAZE',(1987), [video] YouTube, https://www.youtube.com/watch?v=q7n1i1kPL1E

Gaye Bykers On Acid, 'Gaye Bykers On Acid — Drill Your Own Hole', (1987), [video] YouTube, https://youtu.be/aVFRRnK7UUM

Gaye Bykers On Acid — 'Live @ Groningen Holland (1988)', [video] YouTube, https://www.youtube.com/watch?v=hV3pQ1jtN-wY&t=1179s

Gaye Bykers On Acid, 'Mary Byker and Roland Gift on Night Network', (1989), [video] YouTube, https://www.youtube.com/watch?v=bew_9_QRnb8

Gaye Bykers On Acid, 'Sodium Sun', (2020), [video] YouTube, https://www.youtube.com/watch?v=LpQslkiXpLE

PHOTOGRAPHS & OTHER IMAGES

Photos and images have been credited / acknowledged in the captions next to the relevant pictures in the main body of text, and all identified photographers have also been included in the Acknowledgements section of this book. A Note about Photographs and Other Images: Every effort has been made to identify photographers but in some instances this has not been possible. Any errors or omissions will be corrected in future editions. Due to the nature of social media, extensive resharing of images, sometimes multiple times, across various social media platforms, has made it difficult to ascertain where certain images originated from. Many live pictures of Gaye Bykers On Acid and Crazyhead have been sourced directly from their social media pages with the bands' permission, and as such, have been credited "Courtesy of Crazyhead" or "Courtesy of Gaye Bykers On Acid" etc.

INDEX

INDEX

INDEX

GREBO!

BAND INDEX
CRAZYHEAD, GAYE BYKERS ON ACID & RELATED MUSIC

DIESEL PARK WEST

GAYE BYKERS ON ACID